FROZEN MOMENTS

FROZEN MOMENTS
Writings on *Kabuki*
1966-2001

Samuel L. Leiter

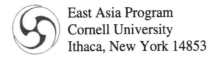

East Asia Program
Cornell University
Ithaca, New York 14853

The Cornell East Asia Series is published by the Cornell University East Asia Program (distinct from Cornell University Press). We publish reasonably priced books on a variety of scholarly topics relating to East Asia as a service to the academic community and the general public. Standing orders, which provide for automatic billing and shipping of each title in the series upon publication, are accepted.

If after review by internal and external readers a manuscript is accepted for publication, it is published on the basis of camera-ready copy provided by the volume author. Each author is thus responsible for any necessary copy-editing and for manuscript formatting. Submission inquiries should be addressed to CEAS Editorial Board, East Asia Program, Cornell University, Ithaca, New York 14853-7601.

Number 111 in the Cornell East Asia Series.
© 2002 Samuel L. Leiter. All rights reserved.
ISSN 1050-2955
ISBN 9781885445414

15 14 13 12 11 10 09 08 07 06 05 04 03 02   9 8 7 6 5 4 3 2 1

Cover design by Justin Leiter

To Jim and Len

For helping to build the bridge

Contents

Preface

I saw my first *kabuki* performance in July 1963, when I visited Japan on an East-West Center grant while a graduate student at the University of Hawaii. In those days, the chief Tokyo *kabuki* playhouses were the Kabuki-za, the Shinbashi Enbujō, and—remembered most fondly—a small theatre called Tōyoko Hall, located in Shibuya's Tōyoko Department Store (now Tōkyū Department Store), not far from where I was living (graduate students could still afford lodgings in Shibuya back then). Occasionally, *kabuki* could be seen at other venues, such as the Teikoku Gekijō (Imperial Theatre), and elsewhere. Since then, the cozy Tōyoko Hall has vanished and the grandiose Kokuritsu Gekijō (National Theatre) has opened; as before, *kabuki* continues to show up in one or two other locales, including a new theatre in the Asakusa section of town. In Kyoto, the Minami-za still devotes a couple of months to *kabuki*, and Nagoya's Misono-za occasionally houses *kabuki*, but Osaka's venerable Naka-za has given way to the new Shōchiku-za, where one passes through an imposing marble lobby to see local *kabuki* in which the artistry of the great Nakamura Ganjirō III is likely to be on display. In addition, touring versions of *kabuki* can be seen in otherwise nontraditional venues around Japan. More surprisingly, and most interestingly, a remarkable number of out-of-the-way towns maintain old-fashioned theatres—many of them out-of-doors—that preserve the essential features and spirit of Edo-period *kabuki*. In recent years, a small number of these have been visited by the great stars of Tokyo and Kamigata (the Osaka/Kyoto region, also called Kansai), who have found playing in them highly stimulating because they so ably capture the intimate spirit of yore. Most times, however, they host amateur *kabuki* enthusiasts for whom the old-time theatre remains a passion.

Many of the stars I worshiped in 1963 have passed away. Those who remain are known, for the most part, by other names, as per *kabuki's* custom whereby actors accept new names in recognition of their growing mastery. For example, Ganjirō III was Nakamura Senjaku II in 1963, and

Nakamura Tomijūrō V was Bandō Tsurunosuke IV (although he became
Ichimura Takenojō VI before I departed). Ganjirō and Tomijūrō, rising
young stars back then, are now among *kabuki's* doyens. Those theatrical giants of 1963 no longer with us include Onoe Shōroku II, Onoe Baikō VII,
Ichikawa Danjūrō XI, Matsumoto Kōshirō VIII, Nakamura Kanzaburō
XVII, Kataoka Nizaemon XIII, Nakamura Ganjirō II, Bandō Mitsugorō
VIII, and so on. The brilliant Nakamura Utaemon VI passed away in 2001
after a lingering illness that deprived the stage of his enormous talents.
Youths on the cusp of manhood in the early 1960s are now *kabuki's* rulers,
and their own children are burgeoning as the stars of the future. *Kabuki*
goes on, changing, adjusting to new audiences, finding new stars, even ex-
perimenting with radical staging notions called by such partially anglicized
names as "super *kabuki*," "rock *kabuki*," and "new" (or "neo") *kabuki*. It
was fascinating then and is fascinating now; however, what makes it so intriguing today may not be precisely what did so in the past. And this has
always been the case, century after century, generation after generation,
actor after actor. Within a core of tradition, there is always flux.

Since my first trip to Japan, *kabuki* has become what can easily be described as an international household word, even if those who use it don't
really understand what it means. An action-oriented comic book is called
Kabuki, even though it has nothing to do with classical theatre, and thousands of international bicyclers ride bikes bearing the word as a brand
name. Western theatre critics describe things as "*kabuki*-like" with amazing
regularity, whether they are commenting on some actor's exaggerated
speech or gestures, or the whitened makeup a character is likely to wear in
an avant-garde production.

In 1966, I published my first article about *kabuki*, a set of four interviews I had done in Tokyo with leading actors. Now, three and a half
decades afterwards, I have gathered a selected group of my *kabuki* writings,
including those interviews, in the hope that they will be of some interest to
the many lovers of Japanese theatre and culture wishing to pursue knowledge of *kabuki* in the twenty-first century.

One of these essays is titled, "The Frozen Moment." It discusses *kabuki's* iconic *mie* poses, during which the onstage action freezes,
although—like the creature embedded in ice in that 1950s horror film, *The
Thing*—a powerful stream of warm-blooded life continues within. In a
sense, the writings herein assembled are "frozen moments," essays written
at specific moments in time, capturing what most interested me then, and
hopefully still alive with whatever first inspired them. I have taken advantage of this opportunity to unfreeze most of them by introducing revisions,
some of them extensive, others only light. The texts have been corrected
(hopefully) and updated, and new material has been inserted where appro-

priate. All notes have been reformulated into the same parenthetical text reference system. Numerous illustrations that did not appear in the originals have been added. Three previously unpublished essays have been provided as well, one comparing the nineteenth-century actors Ichikawa Danjūrō IX and Henry Irving, another on the relative reality of female-role specialization, and the third on the rural theatres alluded to above. I accept responsibility, of course, for any mistakes that remain unthawed.

The book is organized into an introduction and four sections: "Actors," "Performance," "Theatres," and "History." The essays in these sections reflect my basic interest in *kabuki* as a performing art, and not as literature. They do not attempt to cover every aspect of performance, but only of those that drew my attention at the time they were written. They tend to be more descriptive than analytical, and do not pretend to make any great breakthroughs in insight or research, although they provide material that, for the most part, is not elsewhere available in English. Their strength, I think, is in clearly introducing those aspects of *kabuki* I believe will be of interest to Western readers who might otherwise not have access to the abundant Japanese literature in the field.

Japanese names are given in the standard Japanese way, family name first, except where it is of someone who has published in English.

I thank all those—including various granting agencies—who in one way or another aided me during the research and writing of the various essays in this book. For their help during my revision of "Four Interviews with *Kabuki* Actors" in identifying an actor misnamed in the original article, I offer my gratitude to Professors Mitsuya Mori and Kamiyama Akira. Professor Kei Hibino was his usual reliable self in responding to emergency questions, for which I cannot thank him enough. I also thank those publishers of journals in which these essays originally appeared for permission to reprint them, albeit in altered form. I am grateful to my son, Justin Leigh Leiter, for designing the cover. I thank my wife, Marcia, as I have on so many occasions in the past and hope to do on so many in the future.

List of Illustrations

Note: many of the following captions have been abbreviated from those in the text.

Cover: *Onnagata* Onoe Baikō VII dons his wig as a group of international theatre artists and scholars, crowded into his dressing room at the Kabuki-za, observes. The occasion is the first conference of the International Theatre Institute (ITI) to be held in Tokyo, November 1963. At the far left is famed scholar of Japanese theatre, Benito Ortolani; to his left and behind him are British director John Dexter and Romanian playwright Eugene Ionesco. The author is directly in front of Ionesco.

Introduction

In 1945, the American Occupation under Gen. Douglas MacArthur established a censorship system that threatened the survival of Japan's then three and a half century-old *kabuki* theatre. One of the chief censors, Earle Ernst, was gradually convinced to relax the censorship, which had been dismayed by *kabuki's* feudalistic tendencies, viewed as a threat to Japan's "democratization." The man most responsible for changing Ernst's mind was another American, Faubion Bowers, who had served as MacArthur's aide-de-camp. Bowers succeeded Ernst as chief theatre censor, eventually earning the label, "the man who saved *kabuki*" (see Okamoto 2001).[1] In the 1950s, when *kabuki* censorship was but a memory, both Bowers and Ernst wrote excellent books in which they introduced *kabuki* to the West. It is largely because of these men that Western studies of *kabuki*—which barely existed before the war—began to flourish.

Enthused by their writing, and by that of a small group of others, such as A.C. Scott, Donald Keene, and Donald Shively, as well as by several Japanese books translated into English in the late 1950s, a number of (mainly) American theatre scholars and artists of the 1960s began to see in *kabuki* an antidote to the uninspiring realism that then dominated Western stages. These Americans, among them James R. Brandon, Leonard Pronko, and myself, began regularly to write about *kabuki* with the hope of making it accessible to the West. As will be touched on below, we and others have even staged *kabuki* in English. Such efforts only made us that much more respectful of the enormous abilities of *kabuki's* actors, most of whom begin training from the time of childhood and never cease in the study of their art.

This collection, therefore, begins with a trio of essays under the heading of "Actors." If there was one thing that the censors learned during the Occupation it was that *kabuki* was not a theatre of ideas (although it is not devoid of them), but a theatre of actors, many of whom are indisputably among the best-trained and most talented and charismatic in the world. In "Four Interviews with *Kabuki* Actors,"[2] I discuss with four stars of the day—Nakamura Utaemon VI, Onoe Baikō VII, Bandō Mitsugorō VIII, and Tomijūrō V (his present name)—issues relevant to the training for and per-

1

formance of *kabuki*. In 1966, Stanislavski's methods were the goal of most Western-theatre training, so I was curious about the value of such ideas—associated with realistic acting—for actors in a form as highly conventionalized as *kabuki*. Whatever system they ascribe to, the best *kabuki* actors manage to behave honestly, with thorough motivation, and with deep feeling even when they are playing what seem exaggeratedly overblown or fantastical characters. Realism has no monopoly on artistic truth.

"Ichikawa Danjūrō XI: A Life in *Kabuki*" was written at a time when very few biographical accounts of *kabuki* actors' lives were available in English. Since then, there have been several others (see, for example, Kominz 1997). Danjūrō XI (1909-65)—whose remarkable gifts I was privileged to view in 1963-64—was the successor to a grand old line of *kabuki* actors dating back to the seventeenth century, and—although not a blood relative of the original family—had attained the name only several years before his premature death. The chapter provides an outline of what the life of this modern *kabuki* actor was like, and reflects the incredible devotion to their art exemplified by these men. It explains how—through adoption—an acting family can continue to provide stars over several hundred years, and also discusses the process by which leading actors achieve the names that mark their artistic attainments.

The final piece in this section looks at another actor in the Danjūrō line, one some say was the greatest of the greats, Danjūrō IX, who reigned in the late nineteenth century. But instead of focusing on his life alone, the essay examines the remarkable parallels between his life and that of his contemporary, the English star Sir Henry Irving. Such historical parallels between *kabuki* and Western theatre have always fascinated me, as another chapter, described below, demonstrates.

From these perspectives on specific actors, we move to what *kabuki* actors in general do, surveyed in the section on "Performance." *Kabuki* performance offers a multitude of conventions and practices to ponder. One of the most compelling is its reliance on theatrical posing, particularly by means of the *mie*. This device is the subject of the first chapter in this book's "Performance" section, "The Frozen Moment: A *Kabuki* Technique," in which the principal varieties of *mie* poses are described in detail.

Kabuki's status as a popular theatre used to be especially marked by its preoccupation with spectacular acting and scenic techniques designed to play wondrous tricks on spectators' perceptions. *Kabuki* revels in the art of transformation; it has created an abundance of "sleight of hand" methods generally classed under the term *keren*, the subject of the next chapter, "*Keren*: Spectacle and Trickery in *Kabuki* Acting." Quick changes of costume, makeup, and scenery, flying through the air, and other dazzling methods, sometimes decried as playing to the gallery, have made a comeback in the last four decades as certain actors attempted to restore *kabuki's* old-time flavor.

The historical antecedents to *keren's* present-day popularity were lovingly made public in a booklet called *Okyōgen Honsetsu no Gakuya*, published nearly a century and half ago. This booklet is discussed—and its chief illustrations reproduced—in "'What Really Happens Backstage': A Nineteenth-Century *Kabuki* Document." As this document reveals, much of *kabuki's* trickery involves devices for bringing horror to the stage. Just as violence is prevalent in today's films and television, so was it construed as a powerful lure for *kabuki* audiences of the past. In fact, so extensive is violent behavior in *kabuki* that a term—*zankoku no bi* (the aesthetic of cruelty)—arose to define it. This preoccupation with aestheticized acts of physical and psychological violence is summed up in the next chapter, "Beautiful Cruelty: Suicide, Murder, Torture, and Combat in *Kabuki*," an omnibus account that demonstrates this theatre's wide-ranging fascination with the darker side of human behavior.

By now the reader will have realized that *kabuki* cannot be easily classified as a purely formalistic theatre. Whereas some of its offerings are indeed essentially exercises in form and style, others—especially those of this theatre's later years—lean heavily on physical and psychological reality. At the heart of the debate about *kabuki's* essence as a hybrid of stylization and realism is the problem of the female-role specialist, the *onnagata*. In the next chapter, "*Kabuki's* Female-Role Specialists: How Real is Real?," I look at the *onnagata* from the point of view of this convention's place within the debate. When one recalls that the *onnagata* used to live their lives as women in order to play female roles more believably, one begins to see how theatrical reality as perceived by audiences and actors can shift to a rather complex level within a generally formalistic medium.

The theatrical conventions so far alluded to have been handed down as part of a powerful tradition of stagecraft and acting. The *kabuki* actor's art is among the world's most codified, so an often-asked question concerns just how much freedom the tradition allows for. One way to examine the nature of freedom within *kabuki* tradition is to look closely at a specific classical play and see just how much flexibility actors have. This is the subject of the next chapter, "*Kumagai Jinya*: Form and Tradition in *Kabuki* Acting," which describes the possible choices among the formalized acting patterns (*kata*) that have been transmitted by the leading actors through the years for one of *kabuki's* finest dramas.

Before introducing the next two chapters I would like to offer some general remarks on the topic of *kabuki's* relation to problems of interculturalism. *Kabuki* and other forms of classical Japanese theatre have made a strong impact on Western theatre practitioners, sometimes in obvious and sometimes in less acknowledged ways. Therefore, for many outside of Japan, *kabuki* is not something merely to be studied as an academic subject whose value is to enhance our historical, aesthetic, or intellectual appreciation. While not uninterested in academic questions, such persons also approach this theatre from a practical point of view in terms of what lessons it can provide for the staging of non-Japanese productions.

The process of intercultural or transcultural borrowing and adaptation, of course, is practically as old as theatre itself. Roman theatre, for instance, borrowed heavily from the Greeks, just as Molière took from the Italians. In such cases, the process led to a transcendence of the original and the creation of a completely new and organically unified mode of expression. Today, however, there is much debate about the ethics of such interculturalism, because the process too often involves an attempt at fusing disparate materials without a satisfactory comprehension of the borrowed materials. Many intercultural borrowings are superficial, used simply to give a gloss of exoticism to otherwise conventional fare. As Carl Weber (1989, 14) has noted, "a great number of transcultural projects, trying to combine, fuse, blend—or whatever you'd like to call it—features of the indigenous with those of an alien culture, arrive at performances which use the alien component as a spicy sauce to make some old familiar gruel palatable again. . . . More than a few among the transcultural performances mounted in recent years remind me of Chop Suey." The implications of this topic are too complex and digressive to go into here, but it might be worthwhile to look briefly at some of the traffic to which I have alluded. Perhaps some of the examples I cite will also be reminiscent of theatrical chop suey.

Apart from such obvious borrowings as the *hanamichi* and the revolving stage, we might look at how specific plays and productions have employed *kabuki* ideas. These can be organized into seven categories. First would be productions of Western classics, especially the Elizabethans, using *kabuki* conventions. Leonard Pronko, who used such Elizabethan texts as Marlowe's *Jew of Malta* and Tourneur's *The Revenger's Tragedy* for his experiments, has done several significant college productions in this manner. Other works in this provocative field have been Shozo Sato's productions at the University of Illinois and Chicago's Wisdom Bridge Theatre, such as those titled *Kabuki Macbeth* and *Kabuki Othello*. New York's Pan-Asian Repertory did a *kabuki*-influenced piece they called *Shogun Macbeth*. A recent production at New York's Queens College by Dallas McCurley dressed Wilde's symbolist drama *Salomé* with the trappings of *kabuki*, and I have done productions of Brecht's *Caucasian Chalk Circle* and Shakespeare's *The Tempest* with obvious borrowings from *kabuki*. Internationally known are the Shakespeare stagings of Ariane Mnouchkine's Théâtre du Soleil in France, especially her outstanding *Richard II*, which employed *kabuki* techniques alongside those taken from *nō*. Her production used four pathways suggestive of the *hanamichi*, each leading to the main acting area from cubicles placed at the corners of the square space. The actors wore elaborate costumes mingling elements of Elizabethan and *kabuki* dress, such as collar ruffs placed atop kimono-like garments. And, using a relatively common device when borrowing from *kabuki*, there were stage assistants dressed in black. Faces were decorated in a variety of ways, from *kabuki*-esque white makeup to *nō*-like masks. The acting employed highly formalistic means, with face-front projection, and sharply rhythmical movements accentuated by percussion.

From the Western play staged as if it were *kabuki* by non-Japanese theatres, we move to a second category, the Western play produced as *kabuki* by the Japanese. Although there have been many Japanese productions of Shakespeare starring major *kabuki* actors, including memorable performances of Lady Macbeth and Desdemona by the popular female-role specialist (*onnagata*) Bandō Tamasaburō V, none borrowed *kabuki* techniques for their staging. It was a *non-kabuki* director—Yukio Ninagawa— who decided to do his *Ninagawa Macbeth* using strong infusions of *kabuki* style. This production, which played in America, was especially notable in its use of *kabuki* makeup, movement, and vocalization for the three witches.[3]

A third such intercultural manifestation would be an actual *kabuki* play staged in translation but focusing on dramatic content, avoiding the classical conventions of the original form, and substituting for them contemporary Western methods. One example is David Greenspan's New York Public Theatre staging some years back of Chikamatsu's *Gonza the Lancer* (*Yari no Gonza*), where the characters—played by non-Asian actors—wore a mélange of Western clothes, performed in a practically bare space with a 1950s Formica kitchen set, and used only the sparest reminders of the Japanese origins of the play, such as samurai swords. Far more effective, I believe, was Jim Simpson's recent staging of *Benten Kozō* at Off-Off Broadway's Flea Theatre, in which a host of postmodern Western touches were mingled with Japanese elements in a wild free-for-all staging—using an ethnically mixed cast—that both spoofed the *kabuki* original and evoked much of the dynamic spirit that this play about a cross-dressing thief may once have inspired.

A fourth manifestation might be Western plays concerned with Japanese subject matter and intended to be staged in *kabuki*-influenced style, such as the Stephen Sondheim musical *Pacific Overtures*, about the opening of Japan to the West in the mid-nineteenth century. It actually built a *hanamichi* in Broadway's Winter Garden, used men to play women's roles, and employed black-garbed stage assistants, among other familiar *kabuki* conventions.

Number five are Western plays dealing with Japanese subject matter that allow for presentation in conventional Western terms or that may be staged in a manner approximating *kabuki*. An example would be *Rashomon*, by American writers based on a Japanese movie, and sometimes produced with *kabuki*-esque techniques, although—apart from a revolving stage—not in its original Broadway production.

A sixth category—and the one with which this book is mainly concerned—would be authentic stagings of *kabuki* plays in other languages, sometimes directed by actual *kabuki* performers, sometimes by foreign experts. This practice is most frequently found on American campuses, although there have been a couple of small-scale professional attempts directed by visiting *kabuki* actors. "Authentic *Kabuki*: American Style" recounts what happened at one of the latter when two famous actors, Matsumoto Kōshirō VII and Nakamura Matagorō II, came to New York in 1968 to stage *Kanjinchō* with a professional company at the Institute for Advanced Studies in the Theatre Arts.[4] My own solo attempt at staging a *kabuki* play with college students is described in "*Terakoya* at Brooklyn College."

More frequent practitioners of academic productions seeking authenticity of style include James R. Brandon, Leonard Pronko, Shozo Sato, Andrew T. Tsubaki, and Laurence R. Kominz. However, the first four of these have recently moved into semi- or full retirement. Apart from Julie A. Iezzi, who joined the University of Hawaii faculty in 1999, and whose first directorial assignment was to codirect (with Prof. Brandon) *Natsu Matsuri*, I am not sure who the new generation of American *kabuki* directors will be. A major problem is that, unlike most of the individuals just named, the *kabuki* specialists on today's campuses are—like Prof. Kominz—more likely to be found in departments of language and literature than in theatre programs.

Finally, there is the seventh category, which breaks down into two subgroups. One is the writing of actual *kabuki* plays in English, set in Tokugawa Japan, and using all the authentic conventions. Prof. Brandon has written two such plays, including *The Road to Tokyo*, which toured the West Coast. The other subcategory refers to plays—such as those staged and written or cowritten by Prof. Pronko—set in non-Japanese contexts but written and produced according to *kabuki* conventions. His *Revenge on Spider Mountain*, for example, took place in the Wild West and involved cowboys and Indians.

My point in mentioning these categories and examples is to demonstrate the rich diversity of possibilities inherent in the interchange of ideas, methods, and techniques between *kabuki* and the non-Japanese theatre, and even within certain Japanese contexts. Similar borrowings and cross-fertilizations are going on between other non-Western indigenous theatres and those of the West. The language of theatre is constantly expanding through this process, although there is a possibility that the effect may ultimately be harmful to native theatres or that the borrowed techniques are irrelevant or extraneous when removed from their original contexts and transposed where, some argue, they were never intended and do not belong.

In the book's subsequent section, "Theatres," I offer three chapters dealing more or less with the *kabuki* playhouse. One is my translation and adaptation of a brilliant exegesis by Prof. Haruo Suwa (Suwa Haruo in Japan) of Tokyo's Gakushuin University on "The Birth of the *Hanamichi*," *kabuki's* audience runway that has attracted so much attention outside of Japan. This essay sums up the various theories of the *hanamichi's* origins and puts forth a very strong argument for the theory Prof. Suwa proposes. It is followed by "The Kanamaru-za: Japan's Oldest *Kabuki* Theatre," an abundantly illustrated essay describing a recently renovated 1836 playhouse that replicates one of that period's no longer extant Osaka venues. This theatre teaches us what it might have been like to attend premodern *kabuki*, before the unfortunate influence of Westernization led to the overly large big-city theatres we have today. However, while the Kanamaru-za may be the oldest and best example of an Edo-period (1603-1868) theatre designed for professional use, Japan has a significant number of other still-active old-time theatres, a few originally intended for professionals but most built for and sustained by amateurs; the great majority are still in use, if only occasionally. The third essay in this section—"Gimme that Old-Time *Kabuki*: Japan's Rural Theatre Landscape"—introduces these theatres, spread throughout the country, most in out-of-the-way locales, some of them roofed and some out of doors, and all of them redolent of a *kabuki* that is usually thought gone for good. It also discusses the various unique features of rural *kabuki*, much of which is shrine-based and festival-oriented, and kept going by local preservation societies.

Closing out the book, under the "History" section, is "From the London Patents to the Edo *Sanza*: A Partial Comparison of the British Stage and *Kabuki*, ca. 1650-1800." This chapter describes the many striking similarities between late seventeenth- and eighteenth-century English and Japanese theatre and, hopefully, by holding these two periods up to one another, illuminates each.

Kabuki stands on its own as one of the world's theatrical gems, an internationally recognized—and enormously influential—art form that has survived and flourished for four centuries. It is impossible to predict if it will survive for yet four more, or even for one, as the rush of progress in Japan often makes it seem increasingly at odds with the modern temperament. But it is certainly here now and no trip to Japan should overlook it. Nor should theatre lovers outside of Japan pass by the opportunity to see it if it tours to their area. I hope this book and others like it make it seem not like something rare and exotic but—apart from the difficulties of its language—now commonly overcome through surtitles or earphone translations—more like a special friend one looks forward to seeing again and again.

NOTES

1. Actually, there is some controversy as to who—Ernst or Bowers—should properly be considered *kabuki's* savior.

2. Because I was just learning Japanese at the time, Dr. Benito Ortolani, then of Sophia University, later of Brooklyn College, CUNY, served as my interpreter. Two Japanese graduate students at the University of Hawaii helped me translate and transcribe the taped interviews.

3. See Brandon (1999) for an excellent survey of this issue.

4. A few years earlier, Onoe Baikō VII directed this company's actors in *Narukami*.

REFERENCES

Brandon, James R. 1999. "*Kabuki* and Shakespeare: Balancing Yin and Yang." *The Drama Review* (TDR) 43 (Summer).

Okamoto, Shiro. 2001. *The Man Who Saved* Kabuki: *Faubion Bowers and Theatre Censorship in Occupied Japan*, trans. and adap. Samuel L. Leiter. Honolulu: University of Hawaii Press.

Kominz, Laurence R. 1997. *The Stars Who Created* Kabuki: *Their Lives, Loves and Legacy*. Tokyo: Kodansha.

Weber, Carl. 1989. "AC/TC: Currents of Theatrical Exchange." *Performing Arts Journal (PAJ 33/34)* 11:3/12:1.

PART I

ACTORS

Four Interviews with *Kabuki* Actors

It is always a tempting idea, when working with some narrowly defined theatre style or form (such as *kabuki*), for the theatre practitioner and would-be theorist to attempt to sum up a universal approach to the art of acting within that form. Experience usually proves, however, that even within the limits of a conventional form, the participating actors are likely to be as divergent in their individual approaches to acting as are the myriad schools that teach the subject on the island of Manhattan. Nevertheless, generalities always lead the field in all discussions of acting and we are persuasively informed by them that most great British and French actors, for example, are purely cerebral in their acting methods, while such mummers as the Americans and Russians are praised (or damned) for the intensity with which they identify emotionally with the characters whom they portray. We thus have what may be boiled down into two philosophically opposed views on the actor's art: the classic idea of non-identification of the actor with his role, as exemplified in Diderot's *Paradox* (1957; 1970); and the reverse side of the coin, partial or complete role-identification.[1] The latter may be conveniently related to Stanislavski's theories, though, of course, it is as old as the art of acting itself.

Diderot's attitude is usually attributed today to actors in forms that are the polished receptacles of centuries of tradition, where the actor is assumed to merely place on his shoulders the mantle of technical virtuosity handed down to him in crystallized form by many preceding generations of role-polishers. The Comédie Française is—or was, in the early 1960s—the chief Western theatre laboring under this generality's assumptions. To Western viewers, a similar attitude prevails in regard to the acting of classical Asian theatre forms. In late 1963 and early 1964, I took the opportunity to question the actors themselves about their various acting approaches. The interviews that follow contain much notable comment on the art of acting as practiced by four of the most distinguished *kabuki* actors of their day.

One of the noteworthy conclusions afforded by the remarks of this quartet is that they all tend to agree with the ideas of the great nineteenth-century actor, Ichikawa Danjūrō IX (1838-1903), who, concerned with realistic accuracy of representation in *kabuki* acting, said, "When I am on the stage the true thing refuses to come forth unless I forget myself, forget the stage and become the thing I am playing"[2] (quoted in Toyotaka 1956, 350). Danjūrō referred to this inner realism as *haragei* ("stomach art" or "gut acting"). Another valuable word, commonly used by these actors in expressing their emotional mood, is *kimochi* ("feeling"). The actors usually use it to mean the opposite of external style, *kata*,[3] although, as noted below, *kata* often are based on *kimochi*. The actors frequently refer to these concepts in illustration of their approach.

It cannot, of course, be definitively set down in absolute terms what is the true and necessary way to act. *Kabuki* acting, an apparently formalized external art of beautiful and striking images, has achieved these images only through a basic interior need to express emotional contents visibly. The stylized and abstract movements are the external outgrowths of an inner emotion; else they would be empty or abstract gestures devoid of meaning. Since an initial emotion—and psychologically motivated rationale—was present to give birth to the outer form, it is conceivable that a performer can still have recourse to those feelings in his presentation of a traditional role. He may even, as Nakamura Utaemon VI points out, change the *kata* to suit his own physical and affective requirements. With the added element of belief, inspired by a creative imagination, the actor can—through the play of his own emotions—instill in the most conventional forms an inner intensification of truth. This "belief" is the understanding and acceptance of character and situation applied to imagination. No matter how stylized and symbolic the acting is, it will be more powerful if the actor allows his sensibilities to take part in performance. Naturally, there must be an intellectual control by the psyche over all such emoting, a control that acts as a balancing agent to keep the actor in complete command of himself. Danjūrō IX did not truly "forget" himself on stage; if he had, his sanity might have been questioned. Presumably, he was always aware that he was on stage *acting*, but his imaginative faculties, given full play, allowed for the intrusions of the audience and the stage in his fictions and imaginary play-world.

Earle Ernst (1956, 200) remarks that "the division between the personality of the [*kabuki*] actor and the role was not always as marked as it is today." In illustration he cites the old practice of female-role specialists (*onnagata*) living as women offstage as well as on. It is true that the *onnagata* of today do not follow the offstage behavior of their predecessors as closely as used to be the custom. Many, however, still believe in the principles involved in what some might deem abnormal behavior. The *Ayamegusa* (Dunn and Torigoe 1969; Scott 1999), an eighteenth-century manual of "secret commentary" for *onnagata*, stresses the value of female behavior offstage and on for true identification with the role; it seems still to be a valuable resource for today's *onnagata*.

Tsubouchi Shōyō (1859-1935), noted theatre scholar, playwright, novelist, and translator, pointed out that rather than the old *kabuki*, it was the *kabuki* of his own day that "inevitably tends toward a realistic, natural way of representation, stripping off the exaggeration, overemphasis of heaviness of the old way, thus resorting to psychic rather than sensual technicalities in accordance with the demands of the time" (Tsubouchi and Yamamoto 1960, 189-90). Actually, realistic acting dependent on an emotional and psychological concord between actor and role has been present in *kabuki* acting at least since the seventeenth century, when actors such as Sakata Tōjūrō I (1647-1709) enjoined their fellow players to participate emotionally in the performance of their parts. The Brechtian "showing" of emotions in *kabuki* does not necessarily mean that the actor must be psychologically alienated from his role for complete dramatic expression; it depends on the individual actor. The conclusion reached from the following talks is that he usually is not.

Interview with Nakamura Tomijūrō V (then Bandō Tsurunosuke IV; b. 1929): Tōyoko Hall, Tokyo, December 1964.

Tomijūrō, eldest son of Tomijūrō IV (1908-60) and the classical dancer Azuma Tokuho, plays both male and female roles. He debuted in Osaka in 1943, using the name Bandō Tsurunosuke IV, which he held at the time of this interview. His character was a dancing butterfly in Kagami Jishi, *starring his father. He spent much of his youth performing in classical dance (nihon buyō) concerts, rather than on the* kabuki *stage. His* kabuki career *began to blossom when he and Nakamura Senjaku II (b. 1934; the present Nakamura Ganjirō III) began to star in productions directed by the progressive director Takechi Tetsuji (1912-88). The young actors gained popularity as the so-called "Sen-Tsuru" combination. He also trained under masters of the* bunraku *and* kyōgen *theatres. The Takechi productions made him well known but* kabuki *began to decline in the Osaka-Kyoto region and he took to acting in films and dancing in concerts, even joining his mother's Azuma troupe for an American tour in 1955, and thereby being the first authentic* kabuki *actor to appear in mainstream American venues, although not in true* kabuki *performances. Afterwards, he resumed acting in Osaka, but in 1957 joined a Tokyo troupe, where he had to play supporting roles. In 1964, he became Ichimura Takenojō VI. He left the troupe for several years, returning in 1972 as Tomijūrō V, when he was widely recognized for his exceptional talent and versatility. The great Onoe Shōroku II (1913-89) saw in him a potential successor and gave him special training. This short, stocky, powerfully energetic actor is now one of the ac-knowledged masters of kabuki acting and dancing and has been designated a "Living National Treasure."*

Figure 1. Nakamura Tomijūrō V (then Ichimura Tsurunosuke) around the time of this interview. (Photo: *Engekikai* [1964].)

Q: When did you begin to learn *kabuki* acting, Tsurunosuke-san?

A: I was fourteen when I started my *kabuki* training, but I have been studying dance ever since I was four.

Q: Which do you consider to have been the most important elements in your training?

A: The most important training processes are involved with the dance. Above everything else, the actor must learn how to move his body. Second in importance comes voice training in *nagauta* [a narrative musical style], *utai* [*nō*-style singing], etc. Then comes training in the various forms such as *gidayū* [the chanting used as *bunraku* accompaniment], *shimai* [*nō*-style dance sequences performed without formal costuming], *kyōgen* acting, *kiyomoto* [a narrative musical style], and so on.

Q: Is there any fixed musical background that all *kabuki* actors must have?

A: No, there isn't any fixed background. It depends completely on the individual actor. A good deal of musical training is, of course, important for all actors.

Q: Are there any particular rules that the *onnagata* must follow in relation to the male parts?

A: First of all, the male character must always be in the forefront, the female behind. There is an imaginary line on the stage behind which the *onnagata* must stay. This is because of the feudalistic attitudes toward women in old Japan. The woman must do everything in a reserved manner, underplaying, never exerting her full external energies. The *onnagata* is more of a secondary role—a helper to the male role—to help the male role stand out. In the ballet it is the ballerina who has the main role and there the man is more or less her assistant. This is completely different in *ka-buki*—not always, but most of the time. The old concepts of women's inferiority combined with the samurai code brought this all about. There are a few plays that have a woman as the focal point, however. Regardless of the play, though, the *onnagata* normally refrains from facial expression and concentrates on the interior expression. The word "repression" is very important. There is a special beauty in this repression. In the West, women usually show every emotion that they feel.

Q: Is there still some value in the old practices of the *onnagata*, such as living their daily lives as women?

A. Yes, there is some value. There are two types of *onnagata*. Utaemon-san [Nakamura Utaemon VI, interviewed below], for example, follows the precepts set down by Yoshizawa Ayame I (1673-1729) in the *Ayamegusa*. Other actors do not. Both types are important to *kabuki*. There is something produced by an actor who practices the rules of Ayame, something that can't be explained in words. Out of living as a woman comes a certain mysterious mood in the actor's performance. This mood is very important. I couldn't give you examples of how these actors carry on their daily lives as I've never made a practice of observing their private habits.

Q: Have you ever studied Stanislavski or been influenced by his system?

A: No, I have never actually studied Stanislavski, but I have been influenced by him when playing under the direction of Takechi Tetsuji. When he was directing me he gave examples of Stanislavski's exercises, by way of illustration, for overcoming certain problems. Another important influence was Freud—this in relation to psychoanalysis of characters.

Q: Can the *kabuki* actor act in modern dramas (*shingeki*) without difficulty? Also, can the *shingeki* actor be trained to act in *kabuki*?

A. The *shingeki* actors can't play *kabuki* immediately, but should be able to do so after about a year's intensive training. On second thought, maybe it wouldn't work after all. It all depends— perhaps it's impossible. About thirty years ago Morita Kanya XIII (1885-1932) and Sawamura Sōnosuke (1886-1924)[4] played *shingeki* as well as *kabuki*. Sōnosuke also acted in English. He was a great genius but he died when he was only twenty-three or twenty-four. Normally, it is impossible for an actor to play well in both forms. Only the gifted ones are able to do it. *Shingeki* is an intellectual drama. Acting is a secondary thing in *shingeki* since the script is the essential element.[5]

Q: What, in your opinion, is the place of psychological motivation in *kabuki* acting?

A. There is a tradition in *kabuki* where the actor must act exactly as he has been taught by his father and master, minus any "psychological motivation," doing only what the previous generations has done. This is pure imitation. There is, as a phenomenon, the type of actor who doesn't think and tries to repeat on the stage exactly what was clone by others before him This is a danger. The Stanislavskian background of motivation is necessary for the actors of the future. In the case of highly exaggerated roles one needn't think too much of such motivational approaches, but the true thinking actor utilizes these approaches whether he tries to or not—as a natural thing.

Q: How free are you to interpret a traditional role for yourself?

A: The first month you perform it you are supposed to do it exactly as your teacher taught you. This is a matter of etiquette. Afterwards you are free to choose as you desire from those examples best suited to your interpretation. The performance that results must be good—justifying your interpretation.

Q: What do you consider to be the most important element in *kabuki* acting?

A: The most difficult element is the pause (*ma*)—filling up the empty space of time when the actor does not move. This same holds true for the *nō*. This is the most important element in *kabuki* acting.

Q: How important is it for *kabuki* actors to study the puppet theatre (*bunraku*)?

A: Very important, especially to learn the *gidayū* style of chanting. It is also of some importance to study the puppet's movements but this is nowhere near as important as the former.

Q: Which is the most difficult part you have ever acted?

A: I'm sorry. I can't really answer that question. I can say, though, that acting parts out of your type is extremely trying. Actually, just being an actor is difficult.

Q: What do you think about the *haragei* of Danjūrō IX?

A: Whether he knew it or not, Danjūrō was touching upon the ideas of Stanislavski. All famous actors, Chinese as well as Japanese, have always understood those things of which Stanislavski wrote.

Interview with Bandō Mitsugorō VIII (1906-75): Kabuki-za, Tokyo, January 1964.

Bandō Mitsugorō VIII was the adopted son of Mitsugorō VII (1882-1961), one of modern kabuki's greatest dancers. He debuted as Bandō Yasosuke II in 1913, and took the name Bandō Minosuke VI in 1928. He had a progressive theatre education, learning dramatic theory at a private school run by modern theatre pioneer Osanai Kaoru (1881-1928). During the 1930s he was one of several future stars to leave the major kabuki production company, Shōchiku, for the rival Tōhō troupe, but returned not long afterwards to Shōchiku and became active in the Osaka/Kyoto area where, after the war, he acted in the radical kabuki productions of Takechi Tetsuji. He returned to Tokyo kabuki in 1961 and inherited the name Mitsugorō VIII in 1962. He was an outstanding dancer and was especially good at villains (jitsuaku) and old men. Mitsugorō was one of the most knowledgeable ac-

tors of his day, wrote many theatre books, and was a connoisseur of various traditional arts. Unfortunately, his gourmet proclivities led to his death when he was poisoned by improperly prepared blowfish (fugu), an expensive delicacy known for its potential danger.

Q: Mitsugorō-san, could you describe briefly the most important elements of your early *kabuki* training?

Figure 2. Bandō Mitsugorō VIII and the author, January 1964, backstage at the Kabuki-za. (Photo: author's collection.)

A: Rather than any acting lessons per se, I, as many other *kabuki* actors, learned via the method of practical experience. I had to become used to the stage at an early age and thus gained my lessons in a natural manner. I, however, followed a somewhat different course from other actors between my sixteenth and twenty-first years. During this period I studied privately a good deal and the result of this study was one of confusion in my technique. Such study is a bit unique for a *kabuki* actor as most actors learn simply by performing. *Kabuki* acting is easier if the actor hasn't an intellectual side to his art. I studied the modern theatre from Ibsen on, including the theories of Stanislavski and others. This study only complicated matters for me. For instance, Stanislavski teaches that the actor must react naturally to the various stimuli in a dramatic performance. Such immediate participation is not permitted in the *kabuki* forms where the actor's reactions must wait.

Q: Do you know of any other actors who are familiar with Stanislavskian precepts?

A: No. Except maybe Onoe Kuroemon II (b. 1921).[6] We are about the only ones, I think. In connection with the problem of visible reactions, I recall a time when I was nineteen and acting with the great Nakamura Kichiemon I (1886-1954). I was playing as an *onnagata*. In the play the lover of the girl I was acting is killed and a strong reaction is necessary from the girl. Kichiemon said the line: "I have killed him." The girl is not supposed to react to this in *kabuki*, but, under Stanislavski's influence, I reacted immediately and the performance was a fiasco. This quick reaction made for bad *kabuki*. The entire atmosphere was confused.

Q: A theory exists that mastery of *kata* alone is sufficient for the good *kabuki* actor. Do you feel this to be true or do you believe feeling is needed to accompany *kata*?

A: I don't believe that an interiorization is absolutely essential to *kabuki* acting. The exterior is enough. However, the external form developed from an interior need and it is almost impossible to have this surface style unless the emotions are in communication. For me, identification with my roles is possible, though during my training only external acting was taught. Each actor makes his own approach to the psychology of a role. A true actor always finds identification with his role whether he says so or not and whether he looks for it or not.

Q: Do you have any difficulty in finding an emotional identification with your parts if you play several in one day?

A: No. I experience no difficulty in identifying regardless of the number of roles I must act.

Q: Do you prepare in any way for your emotional participation in a part?

A: Yes. I do. For example, I was once performing the part of the evil Moronao in *Chūshingura*. One morning during the run, I took my son to the zoo, before the performance was scheduled to go on. We took many pictures, and all in all had a really enjoyable and delightful time. I didn't realize my mistake until I was in my dressing room when I saw that the wonderful *kimochi* I felt was completely wrong for my portrayal of Moronao. I had to keep telling myself over and over, as Moronao, that I was a bad, bad, evil man. I worked very hard to approach the character through this and other imaginative techniques, an approach to character which I am sure is completely individual.

Q: Does the same emotional approach hold true for dance?

A: There is definitely a strong emotional approach to dancing. If the actor forgets to prepare psychologically for dance, the performance becomes as empty as a simple geisha dance. It is a great help to enter the psychological atmosphere once your external forms are perfected and clearly determined. You need only worry about interiorization while the externals take care of themselves. The *nō* concept of the flower (*hana*) cannot be attained without a complete mastery of *kata*. *Hana* is over and above these externals. It is an aesthetic quality emitted from the great artist. This quality exists in *kabuki* as well as in *nō*.

Q: Which roles have you found the most difficult to play?

A: All roles are equally difficult.

Q: To what extent do past actors influence the kata?

A: The *kata* is completely dictated by the styles of past performers.

Q: What have you, as an actor, learned from *bunraku*?

A: The most important lesson I learned from *bunraku* came from the delivery of the *gidayū* chanters. The acting of the puppets has exercised no influence on me.

Q: Would you like to act in any forms of theatre outside of *kabuki*?

A: I wanted to when I was young, but not now. I'm afraid I've come to think that it's better when the Englishmen give Shakespeare than when the Japanese do it.

[In further discussion Mitsugorō said that he felt the lack of sufficient rehearsal for *kabuki* actors to be a serious threat to the art. He called the existing practice of two or three days for rehearsal "suicide." At least ten days are needed, he said. Before he left the interviewers for his appearance on stage, Mitsugorō withdrew from a drawer beneath his makeup dresser an ancient piece of Japanese pottery. He explained that whenever he looks at this *objet d'art* he experiences an aesthetic satisfaction that so inspires him as to create the emotional mood helpful for various characterizations. He often sits and gazes at it before a performance in order to put himself into the proper state of mind for emotional creativity.]

Interview with Onoe Baikō VII (1915-95): Kabuki-za, Tokyo, January 1964.

This great onnagata *was the adopted son of the brilliant Onoe Kikugorō VI (1885-1949) and was intensively trained from childhood on. He debuted in 1921 as Onoe Ushinosuke IV, becoming Onoe Kikunosuke III in 1935. In 1947, after a year of studying business at Keio University, he returned to* kabuki *as Baikō VII, and in 1949, following his father's death, became a central part of the newly formed Onoe Kikugorō troupe. This "Living National Treasure" shared the limelight with Nakamura Utaemon VI as one of Japan's two matchless* onnagata. *He occasionally played gentle young men—more so than did Utaemon—but was nevertheless considered a pure* onnagata. *Known for his openhearted quality and grace, he was much more masculine offstage than most other* onnagata. *He appeared in America on several touring occasions and once directed the* kabuki *play* Narukami *for New York's IASTA company.*[7] *His son is the contemporary star Onoe Kikugorō VII (b. 1942).*

Q: What do you consider the most important elements of your training to have been?

A: The beauty of *kabuki* is said to be the beauty of form (*yoshikibi*). Exterior form, however, is not everything. In acting there must be a certain spirit that comes from the heart. To reach this spirit you must understand the psychological aspects of your character. Feeling (*kimochi*) comes first; then comes form (*kata*). Through *kimochi* you reach the appropriate exterior forms. There are, in *kabuki*, different ways of moving the finger for every situation, and these ways are fixed by tradition. If an actor plays only according to fixed forms, however, he will be no better than a puppet. If you are playing a young woman you must approach the role through the *kimochi* of a young woman. The same is true for all roles: that is, you enter the role according to the *kimochi* proper to the particular part you are playing.

Figure 3. The author with Onoe Baikō VII, backstage at the Kabuki-za, January 1964. (Photo: author's collection.)

Q: Is there any special formula for ap-proaching this *kimochi?* Do you study it by your-self or do others teach you?

A: Actually, you have to study by yourself. Of course, I teach it to young actors to a certain extent. I try to explain what the proper *kimochi* is for different roles, but beyond a certain point the teacher must stop, and the individual must progress for himself.

Q: Have you always wanted to be an *onnagata?*

A: No. When you are a boy it is not yet fixed as to what type of body and voice you will have when you are older. I started my *onnagata* training when I was eighteen. Most actors decide which type of role they will play when they are about fifteen or sixteen, after puberty, when their voices have changed. Before that most actors play both male and female roles. Even Utaemon-san played many boys' roles when he was young.

Q: How old were you when you first began your training in basic *kabuki* techniques?

A: When I was five I began taking lessons. Dance was the most important of the techniques I had to learn. Shamisen and *gidayū* training were also very important. *Gidayū* helps the actor to understand the emotions of a part. It also helps the actor learn proper breath control. The actor must be careful, when studying *gidayū*, not to fall into an exact copying of the real *gidayū* style. He must learn it as it is meant to be spoken for *kabuki*. The influence of *bunraku* is not as great in the acting as it is in the use of the voice. I wasn't as fat when I was eighteen as I am now, you know. If I had been fat then, I would have had to become a player of male roles.

Q: Most Western books on *kabuki* tend to emphasize the external forms in discussing *kabuki* acting. Do you take a different approach to the art, a psychological, and emotional approach to characterization, or do you depend on traditional external forms for your portrayal?

A: The inner approach comes first, then the outer. Both of them should be coordinated. It's a mistake to say that exterior forms are enough in themselves. Of course, certain forms are fixed in *kabuki* acting down to the smallest detail. These forms are condensed and highly polished: they are considered unimpeachable. [Baikō illustrated his point by giving examples from the role of Chidori, the island diving girl in *Shunkan*, in which he was then appearing.]

Q: Where, then, does the difference come from when two actors do the same thing in the same fixed form? What makes one better than the other? It must be that something else is expressed through these forms, something beyond a definition. Something, for instance, such as Zeami's[8] concept of the flower (*hana*) in *nō*. Do you agree?

A: [Laughs in approval.] Yes. What you say is true. The difference comes from the fact that there is a deepness, which comes from a spiritual background in the great actor. There is none of this spirituality in the poor actor whose acting is, therefore, only superficial. A good actor creates with the help of his personality something more than form, something that can best be called *hana*.

Q: Do you have any special way of preparing for a role?

A: I read the script and analyze the character I am going to play. I begin to study the character. The interpretation of a character is different from one actor to another. A part means something different to each actor.

Q: Suppose, for instance, the part that you are to play is that of a jealous woman. Is there a set *kabuki* way for expressing jealousy, or does the actor find his own way for expressing the emotion?

A: Both. If I can use a traditional form to portray an emotion I do so. If the traditional form in a certain scene does not suit my style, I think it over and proceed to perform as I see fit, even if it means a change from the conventional manner.

Q: Then would you say that the actor in *kabuki* begins by learning basic externals, while the good, experienced actor must give new life to the old forms or find new forms for himself?

A: I would say so. Young and inexperienced actors depend too much on outward technique and not enough on feeling. When I teach I try to approach the art of acting through the emotions, after which I concentrate on form. The forms, you know, have come into existence only because of an interior psychological need to express something. The forms therefore have meanings. Even the *mie* poses have such a meaning. The "stone throwing" *mie* was developed because in a certain play at a certain point, a stone had to be thrown.

Q: You teach like this, but were you yourself taught in this manner?

A: Yes.

Q: Have you ever studied acting techniques outside of those traditionally used in the *kabuki* theatre?

A: Yes. I was influenced when I saw a movie, *Wuthering Heights,* with Orson Welles [*sic*] and Merle Oberon. There was one scene in which there was an open window next to the bed in which Merle Oberon lay dying, and she was looking at the beautiful scenery outside of the window as she lay there. I used this scene when playing a part in which a princess has to return to the moon, from which she had come to earth. The fundamentals of Occidental and Oriental acting are the same—it's the externals that differ. Marcel Marceau, for example, expresses something one way while the *kabuki* actor expresses the same thing differently. The *kimochi*, however, is the same. Unless the actor has an interior approach he will never be great. There must have been just such an approach in the acting of men such as Sakata Tōjūrō I, Yoshizawa Ayame, and Danjūrō IX. Without an inner justification, they would not have been remembered for so many years. The same can be said for performers in the *nō* and *bunraku.*

Q: Did the *Ayamegusa* have much influence over you?

A: The *Ayamegusa* was very instructive. Some parts of the book are antiquated and are therefore not suitable for modern actors. Its fundamentals are still very useful though.

Q: Modern theories of acting state that the actor must identify himself with the character he plays. In your case, do you think such identification is possible?

A: Yes. I do. Unless I forget myself on stage, I can't act.

Q: Do you feel any distance between yourself as a man, and the women you play in *kabuki*? Does being an *onnagata* present any difficulty in obtaining the proper unity of interior and exterior?

A: I don't feel that they are so very far away from me. The psychological attitude of women hasn't changed much from the old days to today. Japanese life is changed when seen from the outside, but what is essential to the Japanese woman (qualities of modesty, discretion, restraint) still holds true. The spirit of woman's dedication to man is still present, I think. No, I don't feel any distance between myself and the women I play.

Q: Do you try to forget yourself even in those roles far away from yourself, the very exaggerated *kabuki* roles?

A: I try to. Though the world of *kabuki* plays is far away from the present day, the actor should try to enter the heart of the character. An emotional approach is also necessary to all dance. In *Musume Dōjōji* there is a constant interior psychological relation between Hanako and the bell. It must be felt by the dancer or the dance will fail.

Q: When do you begin your preparation for the emotional part of your portrayal?

A: As soon as I first read the script. When I read a novel, I try to identify myself with the hero, and I imagine the situation and the settings, costumes and designs, exactly as if it were a play. This is true for most of us, I believe.

Q: Is there any communication between actors in a *kabuki* performance?

A: Without communication between actors, there can be no unity to the performance—the play will be empty. To act individually is bad.

Q: Is it possible that discussions during the rehearsal period of a play may result in a performance style different from the play's conventional style? Does the play undergo an adaptation according to who is playing it?

A: There is rarely a change in the style of acting a piece from the classical repertoire. The *kata* there are too fixed. However, I may occasionally want to act in a new form in these plays, and when I do, there is a noticeable change. A reciprocal influence then becomes apparent in the acting. The actors, of course, will have agreed on the new forms beforehand.

Q: When you play a couple of different roles in two or three plays on the same program, is it easy for you to enter the emotions of the different characters?

A: If the first role is a big one, or if the second role comes right after the first, I find it pretty difficult to enter the character's emotions. There is no trouble when a short break intervenes, though.

Q: How many musical instruments does the well-versed *kabuki* actor have to master?

A: The *tsuzumi* (a hand drum) is very important, because its rhythm is closely associated with the concept of pause or timing (*ma*). The shamisen is also very important in developing a sense of rhythm. Knowledge of the shamisen is essential to the *kabuki* dancer. Most beginners learn *nagauta* and *gidayū* chanting. Others, according to their taste, learn *kiyomoto* and *tokiwazu* [a kind of musical narrative] singing. These are excellent aids for the training of the voice.

Q: What do you think of the future of the *kabuki* theatre? Do you think the *kabuki* should remain the way it is today?

A: Yes, it should.

Q: What do you think of the possibility of the *kabuki* remaining a vital force among the modern theatre movements of Japan and the world?

A: I look at *kabuki* as a kind of musical play. In this mechanized civilization, people are tempted to look at the world as if it were a dream. The *kabuki* leads people to a faraway world—to a world of dreams. Much of this dream world atmosphere is aided by *kabuki's* colorfulness. Even if the world of *kabuki* plays is old and feudalistic, the spirit of *kabuki* still lives in the Japanese mind and blood. I think it is our duty to maintain this art.

Q: Do you think it is possible for the modern theatre to use the dramatic elements that are characteristic of *kabuki* plays?

A: I don't see much difference between what we are today and what we have been in the past. I believe there must be a point where both the modern and the ancient mind can meet. There are many things the modern theatre can learn from *kabuki*.

Q: What method do you use in teaching the *onnagata* to speak in falsetto?

A: The basic lessons are learned from *gidayū* chanting. After the *gidayū* essentials are mastered, the actor studies with his masters.

Q: Do all actors have to learn to use their voices in this falsetto manner?

A: Actors of male roles don't usually learn the falsetto but rather spend their time practicing the use of a big voice.

Q: Have you ever read Stanislavski?

A: Yes, I have. What he says in his books is the same as I learned from my seniors. He describes what actors have always done, and therefore his writings were of no particular value to me. We learn by using our physical instruments, not by reading books. What Stanislavski says is basically what we already know.

Interview with Nakamura Utaemon VI (1917-2001): Kabuki-za, Tokyo, January 1964.

This actor, perhaps the most celebrated onnagata *of the postwar era, was the son of Utaemon V (1865-1940). He made his debut as Nakamura Kotarō III in 1922, and became Nakamura Fukusuke VI in 1933. In 1940, following his father's death, he was taken into the house of Nakamura Kichiemon I, and often played opposite this king of the* kabuki *stage. In 1941, he became Nakamura Shikan VI, and in 1951, Utaemon VI. Unlike the somewhat corpulent Baikō VII, Utaemon always retained his slender, sylph-like appearance, and his unusual beauty was present even in his old age. He held traditional attitudes toward the lifestyle of an* onnagata*, behaving in womanly ways offstage as well as on, and he only rarely played young men's parts. He was also among the greatest dancers of his age, and was an accomplished musician on various instruments. Some of his productions were known for their experimental qualities, and he was often fond of exploring new work. Among his many honors was being named a "Living National Treasure." After a long illness, Nakamura Utaemon VI passed away in the spring of 2001.*

Figure 4. The author
with Nakamura
Utaemon, backstage
at the Kabuki-za,
January 1964. (Photo:
author's collection.)

Q: Utaemon-
san, having been
educated in all the
facets of *kabuki*,
could you describe
what the most im-
portant aspects of your training were?

A: A *kabuki* actor is required to learn many things, such as the shamisen, koto, tea ceremony, flower arrangement, singing—everything. In
addition, of course, I had to specialize in playing women's roles. Above all,
however, the actor must master the art of dance since dance is the most important part of *kabuki* acting. The dance technique must be dominant in
forms such as *sawari* [a richly emotional *gidayū* passage], *kudoki* [another
emotional passage, expressing "lamentation"], and *gidayū* since without
dance the acting would lack beauty, taste, and depth. This is why everybody
begins to learn dance as a child before learning anything else. Child actors
must become apprenticed to a master in order to gain lessons. If—when a
teacher asks a child who has come for lessons whether he has had any dance
lessons or not—he answers no, the teacher will tell him to return in a year
or two, after he has learned something of the fundamentals of dancing. Actually, this type of occurrence was more usual in the old days. The situation
is somewhat different today.

Q: How did *bunraku* influence you in your acting? For instance, as regards the voice.

A: I had to learn *gidayū* chanting to train my voice. *Gidayū* is a highly
essential component that must be mastered. But if you learn something directly from the *gidayū* and reproduce it in *kabuki* in its original puppet
theatre form, it will be too much like pure *gidayū* for *kabuki* purposes. It
must be modified for *kabuki* acting. Naturally, the process of adaptation is a
difficult one. In the older *kabuki* plays the Tokyo actors read their lines in
Edo [Tokyo] dialect and it was essential that they change their accent patterns to read the *gidayū* lines, originated in the Kamigata [or Kansai] area
[Osaka/Kyoto]. *Gidayū*, read by actors in the pure form, robs the lines of
their emotional content since too much attention to techniques of delivery
hampers the actor's feelings. Human beings do not speak in so highly tech-

nical a manner. Thus the actors had to master the techniques as they might be applied to *kabuki*.

Q: At what age were you first aware, Utaemon-san, that you would definitely become an *onnagata*, as opposed to a player of male roles?

A: I first appeared on stage when I was five years old. From that time on until I reached fifteen I specialized in male roles, only occasionally playing the part of a female. When I was fifteen there was a special production of *kabuki* by young actors. We called it Junior *Kabuki* (*seinen kabuki*). That was the first time Junior *Kabuki* was ever held. I played the major role in the dance *Musume Dōjōji* and ever since then I have taken the roles of women.

Q: The training of *kabuki* acting has been described as first a mastering of the externals of style (*kata*), and then bringing an emotional approach to the enactment of the role. In the case of one actor I have interviewed, I received a different reply to the effect that the initial approach must come from the emotions, after which the externals are applied. I would like to know your opinion on this matter. Do you think *kata* alone is enough, or must there be an emotional approach over and above this?

A: I have been asked this question many times. My father, Utaemon V, used to teach me and other apprentices to learn the interiorization of characters before anything else. He used to ask us: "What is this part about? What emotions are proper to it?" That was the first thing. After that came the approach through *kata*. There is a difficulty in this sort of teaching since the *kata* differ from family to family. Even though the same role is played, interpretations and performances differ because of different *kata*. There is another method of teaching *kata*, and that is by paying special attention to the perfection of external details, through repetition, while at the same time giving clues to the emotional meaning behind the externals. My father taught me differently. He taught me the interior conception of the role before anything else. After that, he had me learn the *serifu* [speech/dialogue], *kata*, and movement. There are two types of teachers. One is the type of teacher who pays attention to the exact imitation of details and the other one is the type who teaches style in vague outlines. My father was the second type. He taught me vague conceptions. The reason why he taught that way is this: when he himself played a character his every movement was alive on the stage because of his own physical characteristics; there was always the possibility that if someone imitated him exactly as he acted that imitative acting would lack the same life my father had. That's why my father didn't teach anybody in detail and only taught the main stream or outline of the style. My father said that if he taught anyone what he did that person couldn't exceed the teacher's performance. Once the apprentice had the outline of the character it would be all right if he made a mistake in the external movement. What was important was that he had the interior conception correctly. The first thing is internal characterization. After it comes the external.

Q: When you take a part, then, you have to understand the psychological makeup of the character? You must forget yourself?

A: Yes.

Q: That's why *kata* alone is no good, I gather.

A: Yes.

Q: Practically speaking, when you are called upon to portray, say, a girl's jealousy, or the emotions aroused by self-sacrifice, do you prepare specially for these parts? If so, could you cite a specific example?

A: I do prepare, but it's very difficult to give an example. I think this preparation is something that can be acquired only after years and years of acting experience. If I try to approach a role with specific intentions the result is never satisfactory. That is why a great deal of experience is necessary. My best performance is when I arrive at a characterization unintentionally—when it happens naturally.

Q: Then you actually do not make any special preparation for a role?

A: That's right. I myself don't realize that I have something in my mind for a part, so that when I get to the stage I will do such and such at a specific moment. It is very hard to describe. I make preparations for certain roles, depending on the part. I simply cannot interpret any specific examples for you. If an actor tries to reach a specific emotion intentionally, let us say one of grief, and he keeps telling himself that at a certain point he must cry, the result will not be genuine.

Q: Besides having learned everything concerning *kabuki* techniques, have you had any similar experiences with the other theatre forms, say, *nō* or *shingeki*?

A: Most *kabuki* actors don't try to learn anything from *shingeki*, but they do attend *shingeki* as spectators. *Kabuki* actors have trained in *nō*. Some of us have also studied *kyōgen*, *nō* dance, and *nō* chanting (*utai*). It is quite important for me to go often to other *kabuki* plays and even to *shinpa*[9] and *shingeki*. Before I can criticize I must first see. There is a Japanese saying: "One must see others before one can correct oneself." That is why you have to see someone else's performance, especially if it is an excellent one—then you will know your own faults.

Q: I would like to ask you if you think the famous old actors, Sakata Tōjūrō, Yoshizawa Ayame, Danjūrō IX, etc., who were reputedly realistic performers, used an emotional approach as well as an external one?

A: I think so. *Kata*, *kimochi*, and personality made those actors great. That is why their performances could not be imitated. I believe that actors should have under control at least one thing that no other actor can imitate. Some actors are good at everything but are not masters at any one thing while other actors are extremely skilled in one aspect of acting that cannot be duplicated by anyone else, but are more or less limited to their specialty. This latter type of actor I feel to be the better of the two. I want to be the type of actor who can do something so well that I can have no superior at it.

Q: I would like to know if works on the *onnagata*, such as the *Ayamegusa*, influenced you.

A: Yes, I believe so. When you look into the *Ayamegusa*, for example, it describes how you should act such and such a role, what you should do and feel at certain moments, etc. I agree with it and am often impressed by what it has to say.

Q: It is often said that the old-fashioned Japanese woman, especially as she is represented in *kabuki*, is completely different from the modern woman. In terms of your internal concord with the character, does this fact in any way present obstacles to your interpretation of women?

A: Not really. I can see that the initial difficulty might arise from the fact that *kabuki* women are feudalistic and their way of thinking different from that of modern women. It is very difficult for young actors to bridge the gap that arises between the old and the new, and thus young *onnagata*-to-be experience trouble in creating the proper *kimochi* for these "old-fashioned" women. This is a threat to future *kabuki*, or rather to future *onnagata,* and I am deeply concerned about it. I myself don't feel any difficulty in creating the *kimochi* for these characters.

Q: In other words, you have found a universality in all women that allows you to achieve the proper *kimochi* for feudalistic women characters. Am I correct?

A: I think so. You see, no matter how much the world and its customs change, the innate gentleness of women and other such qualities never change. At least, I don't think so. But the number of actors who understand this is decreasing in the *kabuki* world. It is impossible to play *kabuki* unless this assumption is comprehended.

Q: That's extremely interesting. As regards dance, do you have to have *kimochi* in that realm as well?

A: Of course you do, but it depends to an extent on the kind of dance. There are dances you can do with little *kimochi* and there are dances that absolutely depend on *kimochi,* as for example *Musume Dōjōji.* Each dance decides the degree of *kimochi.*

Q: May I ask if, when given a new part, you try at rehearsal to find psychological nuances in it?

A: Yes. You have to understand the script and that means not only your part but the work as a whole. An actor can get nowhere if all he studies is his own part.

Q: Do you rehearse in your own way, as Utaemon, or are you apt to receive advice and instruction from some other party?

A: I rehearse in my own manner in traditional *kabuki* but I listen to a director in the case of a new script. I then carry on the rehearsal adding my own ideas and interpretation. This is strictly for new plays, though. As you know, the actor must especially take care to consider what the other characters are saying in a new play.

Q: What about traditional plays?

A: Well, sometimes it is the same procedure as just outlined. Another actor in a major role may have a different idea of the acting for the play, and you may have to adjust your performance. But when you play the main part, the other actors must adjust to you. You can tell them what you want them to do so there is usually a resulting coloration to the performance that stems from the main player's acting.

Q: Do you always play a role with the same *kata* or do you sometimes have to find a new style?

A: Sometimes I have to find a new style.

Q: Could you give me one example of a new interpretation through *kata* that you have brought to one of your roles?

A: This is another difficult question to answer. I used to perform in exactly the same manner as my father taught me, but after many performances in the same part I gradually realized that my *kata* was only truly good for my father and not for me because of differences in our physical characteristics. In that sense, I have changed the *kata* quite often to suit my own physical requirements. But it is impossible to give a concrete example right now.

Q: Do you experience equal ease or difficulty in finding an inner communion with all the roles you play, or do you find some roles more difficult than others?

A: There are certain roles that the actor doesn't feel right for because the nature of the role doesn't fit his physical qualifications. In other words, you have your strong points and your weak points and you are fully aware of them. Thus you experience difficulty in obtaining the right *kimochi* for all types of characters. I have been often asked what my favorite part is. There are those parts with which I can easily achieve a physical and emotional union and there are at the same time many parts that, try as I may, I can never completely master. Could you accept that as my answer?

Q: When you act in several parts in one day do you feel any difficulty in changing *kimochi* from one part to another?

A: No, not at all.

Q: Have you ever read Stanislavski?

A: No, I haven't.

Q: I believe it is very difficult for most actors to perform in exactly the same way, every day during a run. Is this true of *kabuki* actors as well? Is each performance the same during a twenty-five day run?

A: Although I try my best to perform at the same level every day it seems to me that I only give about seven or less satisfactory performances out of the twenty-five. I have often felt difficulty in achieving *kimochi* because of some physical condition or for any one of a number of reasons. The greater the difficulty I feel in grasping *kimochi,* the greater the effort I make to do my best in order to maintain a certain level of good acting. I only consider about two or three performances truly satisfactory myself, if you want to define the meaning of good acting strictly, with all its implications. In spite of this, one must try to give his best performance at each showing for the entire run. The difficulty is obvious.

Q: How long do you rehearse for a program?

A: At one time we rehearsed for fifteen days. There was no matinee then and we could rehearse all day, especially for new plays. Now, however, we are on stage from morn to midnight. Hard work, don't you agree? I believe this situation exists only in Japan. We actors really want to improve the situation since we are each and every one of us overworked. We rehearse three days, or at the most a week.

NOTES

This is a revision of an article that appeared in *Educational Theatre Journal* 18 (December 1966).

1. Complete role-identification is mentioned only as an ideal toward which the actor may work, the attainment of the ideal being almost impossible outside of insanity.

2. For more on Danjūrō IX, see the following chapter, "Parallel Lives: Sir Henry Irving IX and Ichikawa Danjūrō IX."

3. Simply put, *kata* are the numerous conventionalized moments of stage business, but it can refer to any actor's choice, from props to makeup to costumes. *Kata* may be traditional or new.

4. More than a revision, this represents a correction from the original interview, where, because of an apparent error in transcription, this actor's name was mistakenly given as Sawamura Tsurunosuke. Sawamura Sōnosuke was actually thirty-six when he passed away and he had been dead more than thirty years when the future Tomijūrō made these remarks. He was the second son of Sawamura Tosshi VII and was a member of the Teikoku Gekijō troupe when that famous playhouse opened in 1911. Sōnosuke was considered above the ordinary in traditional history and domestic plays, and also in newly written works. His acting in English-language plays was very unusual at the time.

5. *Kabuki* actors have appeared in modern drama since such plays were pioneered in Japan by the *kabuki* star Ichikawa Sadanji II (1880-1940) early in the twentieth century. *Kabuki* actors often appear in television dramas and films

(usually in period roles), and a number of them have starred as Shakespeare's heroes and heroines.

6. Kuroemon is one of the few *kabuki* actors to speak English well. After suffering a stroke in early middle age, he spent most of his life teaching about *kabuki* in American colleges and universities.

7. See the chapter "Authentic *Kabuki:* American Style" for more on IASTA and its *kabuki* work.

8. A reference to Zeami Motokiyo (1363?-1443?), the great actor-playwright-theorist who helped develop the *nō* theatre in its earliest days. His many influential secret writings, made public in the twentieth century, are filled with metaphorical terms like *hana* to which contemporary actors—even non-*nō* actors—often refer.

9. *Shinpa* is a form that arose in the late nineteenth century as an attempt to blend *kabuki* with modern (and, at the time, political) influences.

REFERENCES

Diderot, Denis, and William Archer. 1957. *The Paradox of Acting* and *Masks or Faces*. New York: Hill and Wang.

Diderot, Denis. 1970. "The Paradox of Acting." In *Actors on Acting*, eds. Toby Cole and Helen Krich Chinoy. New York: Crown.

Dunn, Charles J., and Bunzo Torigoe, eds. and trans. 1969. *The Actors' Analects*. New York: University of Tokyo Press.

Ernst, Earle. 1974. *The Kabuki Theatre*. 2d ed. rev. Honolulu: University of Hawaii Press; originally published 1956.

Komiya, Toyotaka, comp. and ed.. 1956. *Japanese Music and Drama in the Meiji Era*, trans. and adap. Donald Keene and Edward Seidensticker. Tokyo: Ōbunsha.

Scott, A.C. 1999. *The Kabuki Theatre of Japan*. Mineola, N.Y.: Dover. Originally published 1955.

Tsubouchi, Shōyō, and Jirō Yamamoto. 1960. *History and Characteristics of Kabuki*, ed. and trans. Ryōzō Matsumoto. Yokohama: Heiji Yamagata.

Ichikawa Danjūrō XI:
A Life in *Kabuki*

When the eleventh *kabuki* actor to bear the name of Ichikawa Danjūrō died of emphysema in November 1965, many critics felt that his passing signaled the end of the *kabuki* theatre. Such pronouncements following the death of great actors have been relatively frequent in *kabuki's* modern history and show clearly how dependent this Japanese theatre form is on the talents of its leading stars. Few persons will dispute that the actor is at the center of the *kabuki* art, all other theatre workers being subservient to his needs. Since the number of top quality *kabuki* actors has dwindled markedly in the twentieth century, Danjūrō XI's death at the age of fifty-six can certainly be viewed as one of the more crushing blows to fall on *kabuki* during the postwar period. When Danjūrō died the number of major stars was quite small; these men were getting old, most being close to sixty or past it. It was impossible to accurately assess the future by viewing the work of their young sons, since most of these fledgling actors were still artistically immature. By now it is clear, of course, that these budding performers have developed into actors worthy of carrying on the traditions of their fathers.

Despite the importance to *kabuki* of the actor's art, little has been written in English of the individual performers who have made *kabuki* the world-famed theatre form it is. From the Tokugawa era on, Japanese audiences have idolized their leading theatrical artists no less (and perhaps more) than have Westerners despite the low place on the social scale traditionally held by the actor in Japan. There is much biographical literature available in Japanese concerning Japan's most famed performers. The present essay presents a sketch of one of the most famous modern *kabuki* actors, Ichikawa Danjūrō XI, heir to the most prestigious *kabuki* name for actors who specialize in leading male roles (*tachiyaku*). Although it was atypical in certain respects, an examination of Danjūrō's career should provide a greater understanding of the world in which *kabuki* actors must grow and develop. I was fortunate enough to observe many performances by Danjūrō between 1963-64, and some of what follows is supported by my recollections.

Kabuki actors are usually the actual or adopted sons of other *kabuki* actors and all stage names are traditional and are handed down to worthy successors within the various actor families. Each new actor granted a certain name is known by the numerical position he holds among actors who have held the same name. Thus Danjūrō was the eleventh in his line, the first Ichikawa Danjūrō having lived from 1660-1704. As will be seen below, *kabuki* actors' names represent, to a degree, levels of attainment in the art of acting, and accession to a new name is often a way of awarding the actor with public acknowledgment of his developing skills. If no actor worthy of a name left vacant by the death or retirement of its holder is available, the name may go unused for years or may even vanish completely. When Danjūrō XI took that name in 1962 he was the first living actor to bear it in almost sixty years. On the other hand, some actors holding top names occasionally choose while still alive to hand their name on to a successor, themselves either taking another established family name or coining a new one. For example, Danjūrō VII (1791-1859) handed his name over to his son, Danjūrō VIII, in 1832, himself becoming Ichikawa Ebizō VI, a name closely associated with the line and one that many actors held before becoming Danjūrō. Matsumoto Kōshirō VIII (1910-82), on the other hand, took the new name of Matsumoto Hakuō when he allowed his son to become Kōshirō IX in 1981.

Kabuki actors also may bear other names, including one for each artistic pursuit they follow. Thus an actor may also have a poet's name, a painter's name, a playwright's name, a dancer's name, and so on. He also has his legal name, the one by which he is known in private life. Danjūrō XI was Horikoshi Haruo off the stage and Horikoshi remains the private family name of actors in the line.

Danjūrō XI's career illustrates the procedures usually followed when a *kabuki* actor has no sons able enough to receive the father's name. The ninth Danjūrō (1838-1903) died without a capable stage heir. His son-in-law, Ichikawa Sanshō III (1882-1956), a businessman, tried to become a *kabuki* actor but never progressed beyond mediocrity, despite his powerful family connections. His life was devoted to preserving the Ichikawa family's prestige, mainly through his scholarly research and the revival of old plays associated with the family line. His efforts in this direction were so respected that, in 1956, he was posthumously granted the name of Danjūrō X, something that has also happened to a small number of actors in other lines. The actor who became Danjūrō XI was his adopted son, having been born the eldest son of the great star Matsumoto Kōshirō VII on January 6,

1909. The place of birth was Hama-chō, a street in the Nihonbashi section of Tokyo.

Figure 5: Danjūrō XI during his schoolboy years. (Photo: *Engekikai* [1966].)

The family into which Danjūrō XI was born is known in the world of Japanese dance as Fujima. At the time of his birth, Fujima Kan'emon II (1840-1925), was the headmaster (*iemoto*) of the Fujima school, and Danjūrō's earliest training, beginning at the age of five, was under his care. Kan'emon was the adoptive father of Kōshirō VII (who became Kan'emon III), making Kan'emon the future Danjūrō's grandfather. The boy was not a very diligent student and was sent to several family teachers before being brought into line by another dancer, Fujima Kanpachi, who took great pains to teach him how to dance. Although his father eventually became the Fujima *iemoto*, the eleventh Danjūrō never developed into a great dancer; his youngest brother, Onoe Shōroku II (1913-89), however, became the leading *kabuki* dancer-choreographer under the dance name of Fujima Kan'emon IV.

The young actor-in-training studied dance and the traditional *kabuki* singing style called *nagauta*, but he did not have the extensive childhood stage experience common among the sons of *kabuki* stars as famous as Kōshirō VII. He made a typically early stage debut at the age of five, however, playing the son of Kagekiyo in *Shusse Kagekiyo*, with his father in the title role. This occurred on a tour outside of Tokyo in 1913, his stage name at the time being Matsumoto Kōtarō.

Kōshirō VII was rather progressive. Wanting his sons to have the benefits of modern education, he did what was then almost unthinkable for a *kabuki* actor—he enrolled his eldest boy in a private school where he could learn everything *but kabuki* from a corps of foreign teachers. The boy appears to have been a less than mediocre student and was even something of a problem to his teachers. Of course, when we think of the life he had to lead, getting his general education in the mornings and afternoons followed by grueling *kabuki* training in the evenings, we can hardly be surprised at his poor academic showing. These scholastic problems were probably intensified when his young mother died in 1916.

He was only seven at the time. Other childhood tragedies saddened the boy. A sister, Hamako, died at eleven and the stepmother who came into the family following his mother's death died within the year.

In 1915, he made his formal debut on the stage of Tokyo's Teikoku Gekijō. His name was changed to Matsumoto Kintarō for the occasion, and his role was Kaidomaru in *Yamanba*. For years following this debut his Tokyo appearances were quite few, his major stage experiences as a child being on his father's annual summer tours. The rest of the year was spent in school.

Figure 6: A childhood performance of the dance *Sanja Matsuri*, the future Danjūrō XI kneeling, his brother, the future Kōshirō VIII, standing. (Photo: *Engekikai* [1965].)

Although his father hoped he would eventually go on to college, then unheard of in *kabuki* circles, by 1922 it had become evident that schoolwork was not his forte and he dropped out of junior high school. He now devoted himself to the task of becoming a first-rate actor.

Following the great earthquake of 1923, in which Kōshirō's Tokyo house was destroyed, the child actor now known as Kintarō went with his family to Osaka where they were aided by the great star of the Kamigata (or Kansai) region (Osaka/Kyoto), Nakamura Ganjirō I (1860-1935). Ganjirō and the boy became good friends, the latter undoubtedly learning a lot from Ganjirō's acting. Being at an awkward mid-teen age, he was limited in the roles he could play. His roles at the time were mainly lesser female ones, such as ladies-in-waiting.

The sojourn in Osaka did have some beneficial effects, though, as Kintarō learned much about the play *Kanjinchō* when he was allowed to be a *kōken* (formal stage assistant) during its performance by Ganjirō and his father. In the years to come he became one of the few actors to hold the distinction of playing every major and minor role in this most popular of all *kabuki* plays. During this period, he also studied the art of *bunraku*, chanting *gidayū* narratives with an Osaka master of the art. *Gidayū*, as the actors interviewed in the previous chapter insist, is an art that is essential to the vocal technique of a well-trained *kabuki* actor.

The family returned to Tokyo in 1924. Kintarō's stage appearances, however, attracted little notice for many years. Yet he displayed a diligence at his craft that differed greatly from his attitude when attending school. Together with his brother Junjirō (the later Kōshirō VIII) and Bandō Tamasaburō IV (later Morita Kanya XIV, 1907-75), he formed a "trial performance group" (*shienkai*) called the Tsubomi-za. The fathers and teachers of the actors concerned watched this group closely. Its members selected and cast their own plays and gave demonstrations of their work to invited members of the profession. Having received much early encouragement, in 1927 they gave their first public performance in a large room at the Imperial Hotel. Most of the works they performed were the so-called *shin kabuki* (new *kabuki*, plays written during the twentieth-century), but the vigor and freshness of their performances evoked much talk among contemporary theatre folk.

In 1929 Kintarō changed his name to Ichikawa Komazō V and appeared at the Teikoku Gekijō in a new play by the well-known dramatist Oka Onitarō (1872-1943). Hoping to live up to his new name, Komazō applied himself to his training with such fervor that he soon collapsed from the strain. The illness that resulted kept him off the stage for the next four years. These were four crucial years for the young actor, who was only twenty when illness struck. It seemed doubtful that he would ever amount to much as a *kabuki* actor. Even his father is said to have doubted that Komazō would attain to great heights. Indeed, upon returning to the stage in 1933, Komazō found it difficult to get anything but minor supporting roles.

Komazō's reappearance on the stage was noteworthy enough to be announced in a special ceremony (*kōjō*) incorporated into a production of the popular *Sukeroku* being performed by his father at the time. Such ceremonial events are fairly common in *kabuki* where there is an intimate rapport between actor and spectator. Tatsuya Ryū, a critic of the day, took Komazō to task for the faulty diction he displayed during this ceremony. The actor sent Ryū a letter in which he humbly asked the critic for a detailed description of his diction problems. This led to Komazō actually studying articulation with Ryū.

In 1936 Kobayashi Ichizō (1873-1957), the railroad magnate who created the world-famous all-girl revue known as Takarazuka (after the city in which it was born), founded a new theatrical company, the Tōhō Gekidan. Its idealistic program of theatre reform lured Komazō away from the until-then practically monopolistic *kabuki* producers, Shōchiku, for whom he had been playing, but his three-year term with Tōhō also failed to advance his career. Kōshirō, who felt a debt of obligation to Shōchiku, disinherited Komazō. The fathers of several other rising young actors who joined Tōhō did likewise with their sons. One of Tōhō's most appealing notions was that actors should be cast because of their true merit and not because of their lineage. Such antifeudal notions, however were soon forgotten in the daily struggle for survival.[1] Tōhō found the road hard going, and in early 1939 Komazō resigned and returned to his father's side.

The years with Tōhō, though not brilliant, had at least given Komazō the chance to play certain major roles for which he was not even considered when playing with his father's company. There were simply too many older stars still active, and the best roles always went to them. With Tōhō he got to play such classic parts as Yoemon in *Kasane* and Naozamurai in the play of that name; both became among his most frequently performed roles. He also played Yoshitsune in *Kanjinchō*, Raiko in *Tsuchigumo*, and Tomomori in *Yoshitsune Senbon Zakura*. Moreover, he got to play various leading roles in new plays. By the time Komazō returned to Shōchiku his brothers already had been taken under the wing of the families of other stars. Junjirō, then called Ichikawa Somegorō V, married the daughter of the great Nakamura Kichiemon I (1886-1954). His second son is now Kichiemon II (b. 1944). The other brother, Shōroku, had become the disciple of Onoe Kikugorō VI (1885-1949). Arrangements were now made for Komazō to be adopted into the family of Ichikawa Sanshō, the head of the main branch of the Ichikawa family who, as mentioned above, was posthumously awarded the name of Danjūrō X.

The Matsumoto and Ichikawa families had a long history of close relationships and, for this reason, the adoption was not an unusual event. There had been a previous Matsumoto family member who even had attained the name of Danjūrō. This was Matsumoto Kōshirō II (1712-78), who, in 1754, became Danjūrō IV. Since all Danjūrōs through Danjūrō IX were blood descendants of this actor it might be claimed that six generations of the Danjūrō line owe their origin to a Kōshirō. To be more precise, however, it should be noted that Kōshirō II was himself the illegitimate son of Danjūrō II; we may thus draw a direct line of descent from Danjūrō I to Danjūrō IX. The one exception was Danjūrō III, who was the son of a teahouse proprietor named Mimasuya Sukejurō, but who was adopted by Danjūrō II. When Danjūrō III died at the age of twenty-one, Kōshirō II left the Matsumoto family into which he had been adopted as a child and returned to the Ichikawa as Danjūrō IV.

Komazō's adoption was formally announced to the public in May 1940, along with his taking of a new name, Ichikawa Ebizō IX. Apart from exceptions, such as that of Danjūrō VII, mentioned above, Ebizō was a name that most actors who became Danjūrō held just before acquiring the latter name; it must therefore have been a perceptive eye that saw a future Danjūrō in the tall, somewhat awkward, and still unripe thirty-one year old actor. The play performed for the occasion was *Uirō Uri*, a rarely done piece included in the Ichikawa family's famous collection of eighteen *kabuki* plays, the *Kabuki Jūhachiban*, a collection announced in 1832 by Danjūrō VII and formalized in 1840. *Uirō Uri* is little more than a difficult tongue-twisting monologue delivered by a street peddler of a cure-all medicine, providing the actor with an excellent vehicle for elocutionary display. However, despite his prestigious new name, Ebizō still had to settle for unexciting roles. The better parts continued to go to the veterans in this star-studded period of *kabuki* history.

In order to grow as actors, the younger players of the time formed the
Kabuki Association to produce works in which they could play the roles denied them in the major companies. Ebizō played several principal roles
during the brief period of the Association, including a presentation of Act
VII of *Chūshingura*, Japan's most famous revenge drama. In this production Ebizō, his brothers Shōroku and Somegorō, and Bandō Shinsui VII (b.
1916; later Ichimura Uzaemon XVII), alternated daily in the roles of
Heiemon and Yuranosuke, to the frequent confusion of the spectators. The
outbreak of World War II forced the group to cease their activities, and
Japanese theatre in general had to face a period of increasing restrictions.

In 1943, while performing in the dance-drama *Ibaraki*, Ebizō received
his draft notice. He immediately left for home, but on arriving there came
down with a high fever. He was confined to bed for days, his life often
seeming to lie in the balance. Still, he insisted on reporting for duty on
January 7, 1944, the day specified in the draft notice. The officer in charge,
however, sent him home as soon as he saw the actor's condition. The illness
was diagnosed as typhus and intestinal bleeding. He required almost three
months of recuperation before he could act again. This disease was actually
a blessing in disguise. The transport ship on which he had been scheduled to
sail to Saipan was attacked by United States air power and was destroyed.

Returning to the stage was a dreary business during this time of ferocious air raids. Stages were often dark and actors were forced to make
"condolence" tours to factories and schools. Ebizō's home was destroyed in
the air raids of 1945, and he eventually had to evacuate to the country. In
May 1945, a bare three months before the end of the war, the chief *kabuki*
theatre, the Kabuki-za, was destroyed by bombs, as was the nearby Shinbashi Enbujō, another *kabuki* venue.[2]

In May 1947, Ebizō made the first giant step toward the fame he was
eventually to command. April had seen the first postwar revival of *Sukeroku*, produced at the Tōkyō Gekijō, which was the only usable *kabuki*
theatre in the immediate postwar years. It starred Ebizō's aged father, Kōshirō VII, as the dashing young hero of the title, and Kichiemon I as the
wicked old samurai Ikyū. Faubion Bowers, the American who had been
placed in the position of Occupation theatre censor after the first chief censor, Earle Ernst, resigned in 1946, was very much in favor of giving young
actors more opportunities. He felt that too many of the great roles kept going to the seniors. So he used his influence to have the April production
followed by a May production at the same theatre, but with young actors in
the leading roles and with the great veterans playing supporting characters.
In this way Ebizō got to play Sukeroku, one of *kabuki's* most popular heroes. He prepared so diligently that he developed a leg cramp on opening
day that almost prevented him from making his entrance, during which the
character performs an extended dance-mime sequence on the *hanamichi*.

The muscles in his face tightened up so severely that when an important dialogue was about to begin with Kichiemon and Kikugorō VI he could barely open his mouth and had to be coached *soto voce* by these veterans. But his performance was so inspired that audiences packed the Tōkyō Gekijō for days to see it. Most critics today feel that this production was the turning point not only in the actor's career but in postwar *kabuki* as well. The period is still remembered as that of the "Ebizō boom." Ebizō soon became the representative postwar actor as so many of his predecessors in the Danjūrō line had been the representatives of their eras. The late 1940s saw him make his first attempts at such classical roles as the title parts in *Narukami, Kochiyama,* and *Benten Kozō*. In addition, he performed Rokusuke in *Keya Mura,* both Togashi and Benkei in separate productions of *Kanjinchō,* Matsuōmaru in *Terakoya,* Izayoi in *Izayoi Seishin,* Gorozō in *Gosho no Gorozō,* and Moritsuna in *Moritsuna Jinya,* among others, most of which came to be steady favorites in his repertoire. He played in new works as well, including the role of the seventeenth-century romantic actor Sakata Tōjūrō in the *shin kabuki* play *Tōjūrō no Koi,* which was one of his major successes.

Figure 7. Danjūrō XI as Sukeroku. (Photo: *Engekikai* [1962].)

Ebizō's work during these years was mainly displayed at the Shinbashi Enbujō (reopened in 1948), the Tōkyō Gekijō, and the Mitsukoshi Gekijō, a new theatre opened in 1948 in the Mitsukoshi Department Store in Tokyo's Nihonbashi district. This period is often referred to as his "Mitsukoshi period."

It soon became clear that Ebizō had become *kabuki's* leading player of romantic young men (*nimaime*). Like most actors in the Danjūrō line, he specialized in history plays (*jidaimono*) although he also excelled in certain domestic dramas of every-day life (*sewamono*).

In March 1951, soon after the January opening of the new Kabuki-za, Ebizō's fame grew rapidly following his portrayal of the leading role in a new play, *Genji Monogatari,* a stage adaptation by Funabashi Seiichi of Japan's most famous classical novel. Ebizō's unusual stage beauty led the thousands of female fans who adored him to scream and shout "Ebisama!" whenever he appeared, much as though he were a performer in some more generally popular form of entertainment than *kabuki*.

The 1950s saw Ebizō's star constantly rising higher. He was skillful in new plays such as *Genji Monogatari* and, especially, in a long line of plays written for him by the prolific Osaragi Jirō (1897-1973). The most successful of these was *Wakaki Hi no Nobunaga,* first performed in October 1952, in which Ebizō played the famous historical figure Oda Nobunaga. Osaragi's *Edo no Yubae* was popular enough to be made into a film; as a consequence, in the summer of 1954 Ebizō recreated his stage role in his formal film debut. In 1955 he starred in one other film, *Ejima Ikushima,* playing the role of the romantic eighteenth-century actor Ikushima, whose notorious affair with the court lady Ejima in 1714 led to the permanent closing of one of Edo's four licensed theatres. This too was based on an earlier stage success. Actually, Ebizō had been seen on film before. In December 1943, he played a minor role as one of Yoshitsune's men in an outstanding production of *Kanjinchō* starring Kōshirō VII, Uzaemon XV, and Kikugorō VI, filmed during an actual stage performance at the Kabuki-za.

With the 1960s came the ultimate recognition of Ebizō's artistic achievements. In April 1962 the name Danjūrō was conferred upon him. He is said to have been offered the name several years earlier, but to have modestly declined it, feeling he was not quite ready for such an honor. Many Japanese commentators have remarked that among Danjūrō's various private demons was a rather persistent streak of weak self-confidence. By 1962 he had become so powerful a force in Japanese theatre that a controversial event in which he had recently figured did not have any effect on his receiving the coveted name. This event was signaled by his refusal to perform in a new play by Osaragi Jirō, shortly before its scheduled opening in May 1961. The reason for his refusal seems never to have been disclosed outside of the theatre, but Osaragi was sufficiently upset to break their alliance and never to write another word for the stage. As a result, Danjūrō's productions from outside the classical repertoire were by other modern dramatists. Danjūrō even starred in a work he had written himself, *Tonbi ni Aburage no Monogatari,* an uncommon event in modern *kabuki* history.

Most critics found it difficult to define Danjūrō XI's appeal. He was never considered a virtuoso at stage technique, nor, despite the many roles in his repertory, was he very versatile. He was even thought to be rather awkward and to have various flaws in his acting. His dancing was acceptable, but not brilliant—although perhaps this statement should be qualified: he was outstanding in dramatic roles that required some dance, such as Benkei in *Kanjinchō* (American casting descriptions would call him "an actor who can dance"), but pure dance roles were not his specialty. When it came to his performance in such roles, critics often claimed they preferred his presentation of them in the style called *su odori,* or "plain dancing." In *su odori* the dancer wears a formal kimono and *hakama,* but not the costume or makeup of the role as it would be presented in a full production.

Danjūrō's special stage charm seemed particularly strong in such perform-ances, although his angular unmade-up face was nowhere near as striking as when seen onstage in romantic makeup. His last fully costumed perform-ance was in a gentle dance-drama, *Yasuna,* in May 1965. His last performance of any kind was in July when, already eaten by the disease that soon would kill him, his gaunt figure was seen in a special *su odori* version of his most famous role, Sukeroku, done for the Theatre Festival of the Japan Theatre Association.

Figure 8. Danjūrō XI during his Ebizō period. (Photo: from *Ichikawa Ebizō Butai Shashin Shū.*)

Japanese critics are fond of expressing their appreciation of an actor's appeal in poetic terms; often these terms border on the mystical. Despite the many attempts to do so, stage presence has never been adequately defined either in the East or the West. In the West we frequently refer to the actor's charm as "stage magnetism," a term that is itself in need of defining. The Japanese sometimes use the term *oshidashi,* or "pushing out," to suggest the actor's projection of personal qualities. Obviously, an actor's stage person-ality cannot be measured by the same objective standards that we might apply to his technical accomplishments. Yet, so important is this elusive element that, even in a theatre form like *kabuki,* where technical accom-plishment is considered a *sine qua non* of acting artistry, the attractiveness of the player's personal qualities as reflected in his looks, his bearing, his voice, his movement, and his gestures may, as in Danjūrō's case, override strict critical censure on technical points and win for the actor a devoted following.[3] The very critics who, on the one hand, pan the actor for his shallowness, clumsiness, or vocal inadequacy may, on the other hand, find themselves giving in to such subjectively fascinating traits as "sex appeal," "dynamism," or "mystery."

It is interesting, therefore, to note the difficulty critics had in appraising Danjūrō's talents. Although almost everyone cited faults in his acting, critics were unanimously swayed by his strangely affecting charisma. At the time he was granted the name of Danjūrō one critic wrote: "There is a distinctive atmosphere of darkness within the showy brightness of *kabuki*: Danjūrō makes this darkness float over the stage. It is not the kind of darkness that causes you to bump into things; it has a bright and sparkling aspect to it. You can see it well without leaving your seat and yet it is somehow in the shadows. This refractable beauty is no doubt an inner one and floats from him as would the fragrance of aloes wood were it concealed within his pocket" (Hamamura 1962, 40).

Danjūrō, as we have seen, specialized in male roles, rarely playing females. His great stage looks were widely celebrated, especially in such roles as Sukeroku and Yosaburō in *Kirare Yosa*. In fact, his popularity in the latter role is one reason most critics liken his success to that of the tragic nineteenth-century star Danjūrō VIII (1823-54), who killed himself at thirty-one, and whom, above all other family predecessors, Danjūrō XI most closely resembled. Danjūrō XI even played the part of Danjūrō VIII in a play about the actor produced in 1964, a year before he died. Critics are also fond of comparing him with the late Ichimura Uzaemon XV (1874-1945) and with his father, Kōshirō VII. It was through his father, in fact, that he may be said to have inherited the stage traditions of Danjūrō IX, one of the most outstanding in *kabuki* history.[4]

Danjūrō possessed a powerful voice that was rich, resonant, and capable of a remarkable range. This served him in good stead in plays like *Kenuki* and *Narukami*, peformed in the flamboyantly exaggerated *aragoto* style, although, strangely, he never performed the leading roles in *Yanone* or *Shibaraku*, *aragoto* works traditionally favored by earlier Danjūrōs.

Danjūrō was a painstaking, fastidious artist. He gave his roles much study and brought great psychological depth to his portrayals. His several efforts at directing were marked by the same fastidiousness. According to one writer, Danjūrō felt that everything in a production should be carefully worked out prior to rehearsals, as in a symphony. Nothing was to be left to chance. He was scrupulous about putting all his production notes and revisions into the texts he used for the sake of those who might later desire to study his performances. Still, he was undogmatic about what worked on stage—as long as it did work—and he was quite tolerant of approaches other than his own.

Danjūrō the man was remarkably quiet, gentle, and unassuming. Interviewers sometimes complained about the difficulty of drawing him out and of the problem of interpreting his mumbling when he finally spoke. Unlike many starring performers of East and West, his career was scarcely spotted by rumor or scandal—nor did he create many enemies during his fifty-six years. He was an idealist, yet he knew how to live with the commonalties of life. This modest, gracious actor was even nicknamed "the bower" (*ojigi*) when he was young because of his obvious deference toward others.

In 1985, Ebizō X (b. 1946), son of Danjūrō XI, succeeded to his father's name. This star remains one of the most popular actors on the present *kabuki* scene, and is a worthy successor to his lineage, although he, too, has his detractors. He is handsome, possesses a trumpet-like voice (with which some critics find fault, though), and is skilled at a variety of roles. His son, Ichikawa Shinnosuke (b. 1977), already has a large following and, with his resemblance to his grandfather, shows every promise of continuing the Danjūrō tradition well into the twenty-first century.

NOTES

This is a revision of an article originally published in *Educational Theatre Journal* 29 (October 1977). Special commemorative issues of *Engekikai* magazine, published on the occasion of Danjūrō's assumption of his name and upon his death, were very helpful in preparing this essay.

1. *Kabuki* still casts only the sons of leading actors in major roles. Some effort to break this system down and to base casting upon merit has been attempted in recent years by Ichikawa Ennosuke III (b. 1939), but, outside of his company, it has not had much effect.

2. *Kabuki's* travails during World War II are discussed in Okamoto (2001).

3. The Japanese say of *kabuki* actors: "First the voice, second the face, and third the figure" (*hitokoe, nikao, sansugata*).

4. Danjūrō IX is the subject of the next chapter.

REFERENCES

Engekikai. 1962. Special commemorative Ichikawa Danjūrō XI issue. 20: 4 (April).

————. 1966. Special commemorative Ichikawa Danjūrō XI issue. 24: 2 (February).

Miyake Saburō. 1956. *Kabuki o Mirume*. Tokyo: Shinjusha.

Okamoto, Shiro. 2001. *The Man Who Saved Kabuki: Faubion Bowers and Theatre Censorship in Occupied Japan*, trans. and adap. Samuel L. Leiter. Honolulu: University of Hawaii Press.

Parallel Lives:
Henry Irving and Ichikawa Danjūrō IX

When theatre historians remember the name Clement Scott they usually associate it with a late nineteenth-century English theatre critic who objected violently to the plays of Henrik Ibsen, especially his controversial masterpiece, *Ghosts*. This critic was not always so obtuse, however, as he demonstrated when he journeyed to Japan in the 1890s, describing his experiences in a travel memoir called *Soiled Doves*. In those pages he remarked that "the chance of seeing Danjirō [*sic*], the great Japanese actor . . . was not to be resisted. He is the Henry Irving of Japan" (quoted in Longstreet 1970, 210). Scott, of course, without much further information, was basing his simple but perceptive statement on the relative esteem in which each of these stars was held by his respective countrymen. It is the purpose of what follows to go beyond Scott's metaphor and to offer a comparative discussion of the careers of these great contemporaries, England's Sir Henry Irving and Japan's Ichikawa Danjūrō IX, and to briefly illuminate some of the basic similarities and differences in the theatres they represented.

England in the late nineteenth century was enmeshed in the cultural-social matrix we know as the Victorian era (1837-1901), while the Japan of that time was experiencing the Meiji era (1862-1912). The words "Victorian" and "Meiji" have significant implications for the English and the Japanese. Simply put, to Englishmen, the Victorian age was a period when England gained a pinnacle of world power and prestige under a strong and dignified monarch; it is associated with a severe moral code and a consequent excess of unnatural decorum. The word "Meiji" reminds a Japanese of the restoration of a figurehead emperor to a position of actual sovereignty, after two and a half centuries of military dictatorship. It also suggests the astonishingly rapid and voluminous influx of Western culture into a nation that had followed an isolationist path for most of that period.

Both Irving and Danjūrō were born in 1938, and Irving outlived Danjūrō by two years, dying in 1905. The English actor was born to a poor Somerset farmer and his Cornish wife, and was raised by relatives, who provided a rudimentary education in rural schools. He never had much of a formal education. The English stage at the time was widely considered a social evil and was often lambasted by preachers' attacks. Irving's own mother never accepted her son's choice of a profession. However, had he been born to an acting family, it is unlikely that he would have made any other choice. Irving's leading lady, Ellen Terry, herself the child of actors, wrote that, in her youth, "theatrical folk did not imagine that their children could do anything but follow their parent's profession" (Terry 1969, 8) Consequently, there were a number of acting dynasties in England and America, such as the Kembles, Keans, Booths, Terrys, Drews, Wallacks, Sotherns, Mathewses, Powers, and Jeffersons.

Social prejudice against actors was even more pronounced in Japan.[1] Actors were called "riverbed beggars" (*kawara kojiki*) and the like, and were ultimately counted as less than human in the Confucian scheme. Within this world, actors had, by the nineteenth century, created a kind of artistic royalty of their own, and with few exceptions had to be born into or adopted by a dynastic line to have a chance at fame. The actor who would become Danjūrō IX was the illegitimate fifth son of the great star, Danjūrō VII (1791-1859), whose outstandingly talented and attractive eldest son was guaranteed to become Danjūrō VIII (1823-54). With others in line to the succession before him, our Danjūrō was adopted as a small child by an actor-manager named Kawarasaki (sometimes spelled Kawarazaki) Gonnosuke VI (1814-68), who had no likely successor. Thus Danjūrō's early years were, like Irving's, in the hands of foster parents. However, unlike Irving, he received what was then a remarkable actor's education because Gonnosuke's wife, determined that the boy become a star, gave him not only performance training, but had him learn various Japanese classical arts.[2] His stage debut came at age seven, under the name of Kawarasaki Chōjūrō, which he changed to Kawarasaki Gonjūrō in 1852.

Irving, however, had to work for poorly paid, long hours in order to pay for elocution and fencing lessons. He made his first London stage appearance in 1855, aged eighteen, in a semiprofessional performance of *Romeo and Juliet*, paying for the privilege of acting the lead. His real name was John Henry Brodribb, but, for the stage, he became Henry Irving. In 1855, the year of Irving's debut, Gonjūrō suddenly became eligible for the name Danjūrō, because of the death of two of his older brothers. But he was not yet considered ready for the honor. It was the first time in 175 years that *kabuki* had no Danjūrō.

Stage names were common in England, where actors wished to protect their families from antitheatrical prejudices. Irving's came from both the

American writer, Washington Irving, and the evangelist, Edward Irving. Fans nicknamed him "Crab," "Antique," "Spindleshanks," "Governor," "Chief," and so on. But *kabuki* actors' names are a far more complex matter, and the same actor may have many names, all of them more or less traditional, one for private use, one for the theatre, and one for each of the arts he practices, as well as a theatrical nickname called a *yagō*, traditional to his line. For example, the future Danjūrō's private name was Horikoshi, his *yagō* was Naritaya,[3] and his *haiku* penname was Saigyū.

Physically, neither actor seemed, at first, star material. Irving's face, like that of our *kabuki* actor, was long and thin, and only gradually acquired its ascetic beauty and theatrical adaptability. He had to pad his skinny legs and even suffered from a stammer. The Japanese player was known for his

"old woman's face," and was, in youth, sickly and physically unappealing.

(left) Figure 9. Irving in old age. (Photo: Irving, *Henry Irving*.)

Figure 10. Danjūrō XI toward the end of his life. (Photo: author's collection.)

Following Irving's debut, he worked for years in provincial theatres, and played over 400 roles in one two-and-a-half-year period. The future Danjūrō, meanwhile, spent most of his formative years on the stage of the principal city, Edo (later Tokyo), also playing numerous roles. Both actors developed in what were essentially stock company systems, which were more likely to provide frequent changes of bills than long runs. During the 1870s both Irving and Danjūrō rose to stardom.

In 1871, H. L. Bateman (1812-75), an impresario who managed the careers of his actress-daughters, Kate (1843-1917) and Isabel Bateman (1854-1934), took over London's Lyceum Theatre, hiring Irving as his leading man but hoping mainly to show off Isabel's talents. The Lyceum had been built in 1765, at a time when only two London theatres—Drury Lane and Covent Garden—were permitted to stage legitimate plays (a third would be added a year later). In order to circumvent these theatres' royal patents, other playhouses, like the Lyceum, invented various subterfuges. Only after 1843 could theatres legally produce any type of play they wanted. Not long after he assumed control, Bateman's Lyceum management was greeted with success when Irving starred in and directed a highly successful melodrama called *The Bells*, and he became the theatre's main attraction. In 1878, Irving took over the Lyceum as its actor-manager and inaugurated "the greatest era in the history of the modern stage," according to Alfred Darbyshire (1969, 95).

In Edo, eleven years earlier, Gonjūrō succeeded to his foster father's name as Gonnosuke VII[5] and was named actor-manager (*zagashira*) at the Ichimura-za. Although most *zagashira*—literally, "troupe leader"—were not producers, Danjūrō's hereditary position in the Kawarasaki line entitled him to this function, but he practiced it only briefly. In 1872, a year after Irving joined the Lyceum, Danjūrō joined the progressive producer Morita Kanya XII (1846-97) at the latter's theatre, the Morita-za, which had just moved to Tokyo's Shintomi-chō. From 1714, only three theatres had been officially licensed in the city, although there were many smaller, less well-equipped playhouses that operated under special rules for brief periods of activity, and were not unlike the host of minor (illegitimate) theatres competing with the majors in London.

After many years in the same Edo locations, the three big theatres—as an outgrowth of sumptuary regulations—were forcibly moved in 1841 to a specially designated theatrical district on the city's outskirts renamed Saruwaka-chō for the occasion. It is now part of Tokyo's Asakusa district, still known as an entertainment center. The loosening of restrictions following the Meiji Restoration allowed Kanya to take the bold step of moving the Morita-za to the heart of Tokyo, not far from where the Kabuki-za stands today. But a struggle by Kanya with his former backers, from whom he sought to become independent, forced him to release Gonnosuke VII, who took to touring the provinces to pay off his debts, a practice often followed by Irving in England, especially toward the end of his career. Our Japanese star returned to the Morita-za, now called the Shintomi-za, in 1876, having in the interim left the Kawarasaki family to return to the Ichikawas, who had granted him the name of Danjūrō IX in 1874. In 1878, the same year that Irving's brilliant Lyceum period began, the burned-down Shintomi-za was rebuilt, and a golden, eleven-year era of Meiji *kabuki*, called the "Shintomi-za Age," commenced, with Danjūrō as actor-manager.

The great stars were now in position to institute their respective views on the function of the stage in society. They arrived at a time when their national theatres were generally considered artistically moldy. Each developed reformist ideas for raising the theatre in public esteem. Each felt the need to present the stage as an educative and moral force. Irving wrote that the purpose of theatre was to act "as a constant medium for diffusion of great ideas, and by throwing new light upon the best dramatic literature, it largely helps the growth of education" (H. Irving 1969, 2). Danjūrō had similar views, being in complete accord with the orders dictated by the

Japanese government in 1872 that the stage should "disseminate moral teachings." At the 1878 opening of the Shintomi-za, Danjūrō said:

> There has been a tendency in the theatre during recent years to revel in the impurities of the world and to take pleasure in the rank odor of ig- nobility. The theatre has lost its wonderful property of encouraging virtue and admonishing vice, and has fallen instead into a wanton seeking after novelty. . . . I . . . earnestly hope that . . . we shall be able to free our art from this defilement (quoted in Komiya 1956, 188).

In England, Irving strived to regain the interest of the middle and up- per classes in a theatre that had lost their patronage. This had happened partly because of the increased numbers of working-class spectators who attended in the wake of the Industrial Revolution and to whose populist tastes the managements catered. Irving began campaigning for the honor of the stage in 1875, being determined to break down the prevailing prejudice "of puritans to the theatre and actors" (Laurence Irving 1952, 31). As a to- ken of the respect given him, Irving was invited to revive the old custom of playing before the Queen, the so-called "Windsor theatricals." In 1895, he became the first actor to be knighted.

The samurai class having been abolished, there were no such honors possible for Danjūrō at the time, but he was recognized for his ability to at- tract the services of important officials, scholars, and writers for the betterment of *kabuki*. Convinced that *kabuki* was a theatre of "fantastic ab- surdity" (Tsubouchi and Yamamoto 1960, 67), especially for its historical exaggerations and revisions, Danjūrō, influenced by newfound Western no- tions, campaigned vigorously for stage reform. Most importantly, in 1887, he and several of his greatest contemporaries were given an honor almost equal to that of being knighted when they performed before the imperial family on the grounds of a private mansion. The impact of this on raising the prestige of Japanese actors was immeasurable (See Komiya, 35-36).

Among Danjūrō's chief reforms was his support for the writing of new period plays that were true to historical facts and customs. Although still deriving their materials from the old romantic legends and tales that served as sources for the older plays, these plays provided authentic behavior, costumes, and character names, the latter previously having been forbidden because of shogunate proscriptions. *Kabuki* plays had evolved all sorts of intriguing methods of masking dramatized events related to the contempo- rary samurai class, such as by altering the characters' names and setting the action in similar circumstances of an earlier period. Productions were done in theatricalized ways that bore minimal resemblance to the historical peri- ods depicted. Danjūrō was convinced that this made *kabuki* primitive in Western eyes. In the effort to fix the problem, he became a devout anti- quarian in the mode of Victorian actor Charles Kean (1811-68), inspiring a genre called *katsureki* or "living history." His efforts, however, failed miserably at winning popular acceptance, and Danjūrō was widely urged to return to classical *kabuki*. With great reluctance, he did so, for the most part, in the mid-1880s. The chief influence of the *katsureki* plays, few of which are now revived,[6] lies in the genre of "new" or *shin kabuki*, which arose in the early twentieth century.

Figure 11. Danjūrō IX as Shigemori in the *katsureki* drama, *Shigemori Kangen* (1876). This was his representative *katsureki* role. (Photo: from Kawatake, *Nihon Engeki Zuroku*.)

Irving was also something of a "stage archaeologist," whose reforms suggest, but do not repeat, those of Danjūrō. His productions were famous for their visual authenticity, and he hired famous artists and archaeologists to design them. Because they were the outgrowth of earlier experiments by others, and were done with great taste, they had a readier public response than Danjūrō's, which met with the kind of criticism that greeted earlier reformers, such as the eighteenth-century actor Charles Macklin (1699-1797). Irving never became a slave to visual authenticity and always considered stage effect before historical truth. He said that he did not "think that servility to archaeology on the stage is an unmixed good" (H. Irving, 68).

Irving and Danjūrō stood on the cusp of the dawning of a new drama that they did not fully understand. Irving represented the kind of theatre in which the star's personal glory illuminated the stage in plays that cultivated emotional and sensational effects without an overwhelming regard for historical veracity. He was confounded by the new psychologically and socially realistic drama of writers like Ibsen and Shaw. The influence of these playwrights did not come to Japan until after Danjūrō's death, but the *kabuki* star did have to confront the newly arisen *shinpa* ("new school") theatre. This once progressive form, while following certain *kabuki* conventions—such as men playing women's roles, even on a stage shared with

actresses playing women—was much more realistic than *kabuki*, and was born in an attempt to combine politics with drama. Irving continued to perform in "parts worthy of him, parts of a certain stature; classic, historic, mythical, legendary, figures of dignity" (Saintsbury and Palmer 1969, 59). Danjūrō, sensing the threat of *shinpa*, returned to classic roles that might be similarly described, refusing to act in *shinpa*, whose new realism he found beneath contempt.

(left) Figure 12. Irving as Shylock. (Photo: from Irving, *Henry Irving.*)

Figure 13. Danjūrō IX as Benkei in *Kanjinchō*. (Photo: author's collection.)

Irving and Danjūrō shared in the practice whereby stars revised plays, often with great liberty, to suit their talents. Even today, *kabuki* actors adjust famous scripts for their own performances. In the nineteenth century, the practice was exacerbated by the common existence in both countries of resident playwrights, although this custom was more clearly systematized in Japan. Irving's chief writer was W. G. Wills (1828-91), creator of *Iolanthe*, *Charles I*, *Eugene Aram*, *King Arthur*, and other vehicles. Danjūrō's main collaborators were the prolific Kawatake Mokuami (1816-93) and, toward the end of the actor's career, Fukuchi Ōchi (1841-1906). Nevertheless, neither actor was ever satisfied in his search for new material. Danjūrō "could not find a suitable author—one who would write the kind of plays in which he wished to perform" writes one source (Komiya, 35), while Laurence Irving commented of his grandfather that "there seemed to be playwrights galore to supply everyone's needs but his own" (L. Irving: 637).

For all their versatility, these larger-than-life actors were best in a roughly similar dramatic genre, what might be called the history or period play, as opposed to domestic dramas of everyday life. In Irving's England, the Bancrofts were the preeminent domestic play performers, while in Japan, that honor went to Onoe Kikugorō V (1844-1903). Irving's greatest successes were in historical melodramas like *Richelieu, Charles I, Louis IX, The Corsican Brothers, King Henry VIII, Faust,* and *Becket.* He offered nine major Shakespearean productions at the Lyceum, the majority of which were historically or period oriented, such as *Hamlet, Othello, Romeo and Juliet, Macbeth, Cymbeline,* and *King Lear,* but his only true history productions were *Henry VIII* and *Richard III.* Danjūrō's greatest roles were in such classic history plays as *Chūshingura, Kumagai Jinya,* and *Takatoki.* Nor must one forget his preoccupation with historical dramas of the *katsureki* school, despite their popular and critical failure.

The theatres of Irving and Danjūrō loved to exploit the versatility of their stars, and doubling—the playing of multiple roles within a single drama—was not uncommon. Irving was outstanding playing dual roles in plays like *The Corsican Brothers* and *The Lyons Mail,* but Danjūrō might play three, four, or more roles in plays like *Chūshingura* and *Sugawara,* or display his virtuosity in dance plays like *Kagami Jishi,* where he was a beautiful, completely feminine, dancing maiden in the first half, and a mane-waving, powerfully masculine lion in the second. In Irving's early career, the English theatre allowed actors to appear in several pieces on the same program, while Danjūrō spent much of his career performing in similarly structured programs, whereby he might appear in three or more plays during a single day.

The rigid role-type (*yakugara*) system so familiar to Japanese audiences was paralleled in England by a long tradition of "lines of business." Stock companies hired actors to play one type of role, such as the "heavy father," "leading man," "light comic villain," "walking gentleman," and so on, while *kabuki* had its *oyajigata* (old man), *tachiyaku* (leading man), *katakiyaku* (villain), *onnagata* (female character), *dokegata* (comedian), and so on, each with many subdivisions. Danjūrō, who could effectively play female roles, excelled at upright, noble, and courageous heroes, such as Benkei in *Kanjinchō,* Yuranosuke in *Chūshingura,* Sukeroku in the play known by his name, and Gongorō in *Shibaraku,* while Irving was superb in villain roles, like Mathias in *The Bells,* Wolsey in *Henry VIII,* Shylock (whom he gave a famously sympathetic tinge), Mephistopheles in *Faust,* Iago in *Othello,* and Iachimo in *Cymbeline.* Some spectators were even unwilling to accept him as an honest man, like Hamlet.

Irving championed an inner, psychological approach to acting, expressed through many details of realistic by-play. He claimed that the actor's greatest effects are gained by an "electric quality" (see Coquelin 1958, 181) that brings forth the character's soul rather than mere externals. He called for an idealization of character and situation placed on the stage in a "picturesque" fashion, which he defined as "the selection of what is

pleasing and harmonious in illustration" (182). Yet he was convinced of the
need for inner conviction and truth. No matter how much the actor felt, the
audience could only understand his feelings through the proper external
signs. Still, the actor had to feel something akin to his character's emotions
during performance.

Danjūrō, for his part, sought "to perfect, on the basis of the traditional
Kabuki, a free technique for creating on stage a real human being" (Komiya
194). He was the exponent of a type of inner realism he called *haragei* (literally, "gut acting" or "stomach art"), defined by a Japanese theatre
dictionary as "an inner, restrained and quiet type of acting. . . . It is a type of
acting more realistic than stylized. . . ." (Yamamoto 1971, 255). Never de-
siring to avoid the "picturesque," he "considered it . . . more important to
the actor to express . . . the emotions he was playing" (Komiya, 234). He
therefore played down the traditional emphasis on stage business in order to
find more subtle means for communicating thoughts and feelings. Thus in a
play where a spider always had hung from the ceiling, Danjūrō eliminated
the spider and suggested its presence purely through his facial expression.
As with Irving, he paid little attention to traditional "points" (what *kabuki*
would call *kata*), but created his own by examining his roles from a fresh
viewpoint. He thus brought new ideas to the classics, as did Irving in
Shakespeare. His remarks on acting point out vividly the importance for
actors to express inner reality, even in formalistic theatres like *kabuki*.

Each of our subjects was an iconoclast who often broke with tradition
to serve the needs of increased stage reality. Each came from a theatre that
could claim a long historical tradition for certain roles. Some *kabuki* roles
use traditions dating back over two centuries, although today's theatre tends
to be more strict about these matters than in Danjūrō's time, when—with
kabuki's future somewhat in doubt—the process of "classicalization" of
kata began in earnest. Thus many of Danjūrō's own *kata* have dominated
modern *kabuki*, which is ironic considering his own tradition-breaking
methods.

Whereas Meiji *kabuki* began to fix and solidify the various *kata*, the
Victorian era saw a sharp break with traditional styles. This is partly explained by *kabuki's* continuation as a self-contained *type* of theatre, while
other forms arose to deal with modern developments. English legitimate
theatre (the spoken form as opposed to the musical), confined to a single
evolutionary strain, kept developing new styles, while retaining only certain
elements of the old. There is, therefore, much more of a singular tradition
from Shakespeare to Pinter than from Chikamatsu to Mishima. Still, there
was an apparently similar attitude toward a tradition-oriented approach to
acting in both nineteenth-century Japan and England, as can be seen by
contrasting the following statements. The first is from a *kabuki* dictionary
definition of *kata*:

When an actor created an appropriate way of acting the spirit of a play (in terms of movement, attitude, speech, etc.) and this was handed down from one generation to another, a *kata* was born. . . . In such cases either the entire *kata* is followed or part of it is inherited and then an actor adds new elements of his own. When this . . . occurs, the new actor's *kata* is passed on after him (Yamamoto 238; *see also* Leiter 1997, 289-91).

The next statement comes from Irving's contemporary, the American actor Lawrence Barrett (1838-91):

The so-called "business" of nearly all the commonly acted plays has been handed down through generations of actors, amended and corrected in many cases by each performer, but never radically changed. New readings of certain passages have been substituted for old, but the traditional "points" have been preserved, personal characteristics and physical peculiarities finding ample freedom of expression with the old readings of the play (Barrett 1969, 3).

Irving and Danjūrō each had disciples but no immediate successor. Despite Irving's objections, both of his sons became actors. One, Laurence Sidney Irving, was talented but died at forty-three. Irving's grandson noted that Irving "left no successor. The continuity of the Shakespearean succession was broken. . . . In the next generation, no supreme actor took the stage capable of transmitting the fiery message, through his genius" (L. Irving, 673-74). One reason for the lack of true successors was that Irving's iconoclasm tempted his disciples to create their roles afresh, as he did. Danjūrō's disciples were among the greatest actors of twentieth-century *kabuki*, and much of their success stemmed from their absorption of his famous *kata*. But, at his death, there was no actor of the right maturity and achievement deserving of his name. As noted in the previous chapter, he had no son and, although—as customary—he adopted his son-in-law, the man was a businessman and not an actor. He did try to become one, though, and, fifty years after Danjūrō IX's death, was posthumously named Danjūrō X because of his scholarly contributions on behalf of the family. The present successor is Danjūrō XII (b. 1946).

Danjūrō and Irving were the outstanding representatives of their national stages at precisely the same time. They raised the esteem of the theatre in the eyes of their countrymen and, in many ways, ennobled their profession. This brief description has pointed out not only some of their similarities and differences, but those of the theatres in which they performed. The words of the painter Delacroix, quoted by Laurence Irving for his grandfather, are remarkably appropriate for Danjūrō as well:

There was a sun in his head and storms in his heart who for . . . years had played up on the keyboard of human passions and whose brush grandiose, terrible and suave, passed from saints to warriors, from warriors to lovers, from lovers to tigers and from tigers to flowers.

NOTES

An earlier version of this paper was presented at the International Conference on Shakespeare and *Kabuki*, Nishinomiya, Japan, 1995.

1. This applies specifically to actors in *kabuki*, the popular theatre, and not to *nō* actors, most of whom were under the protection of the samurai class.
2. See Nakamura Utaemon VI's comments on this practice in this volume's "Four Interviews with *Kabuki* Actors."
3. Actually, while he was in Gonnosuke's care and used the name Kawarasaki, his *yagō* was Yamazakiya.
4. This subject is discussed below in "From the London Patents to the Edo *Sanza*: A Partial Comparison of the British Stage and *Kabuki*, ca. 1650-1800."
5. In 1868 Gonnosuke VI was murdered by a robber, one of *kabuki* history's most notorious events.
6. The best-known examples are Kawatake Mokuami's *Sakai no Taiko* (1873) and *Takatoki* (1884).

REFERENCES

Barrett, Laurence. 1969. *Edwin Forrest.* New York: Benjamin Blom.

Darbyshire, Alfred. 1969. *The Art of the Victorian Stage: Notes and Recollections.* New York: Benjamin Blom.

Irving, Henry. 1969. *The Drama: Addresses.* New York: Benjamin Blom.

Irving, Laurence. 1952. *Henry Irving, The Man and His World.* New York: Macmillan.

Kawatake Shigetoshi. 1956. *Nihon Engeki Zuroku.* Tokyo: Asahi Shinbunsha-kan.

Komiya, Toyotaka, comp. and ed. 1956. *Japanese Music and Drama in the Meiji Era,* trans. and adap. Edward G. Seidensticker and Donald Keene. Tokyo: Ōbunsha.

Leiter, Samuel L. 1997. *New* Kabuki *Encyclopedia: A Revised Adaptation of* Kabuki Jiten. Westport, Ct.: Greenwood Press.

Longstreet, Stephen, and Ethel. 1970. *Yoshiwara: City of the Senses.* New York: McKay.

Coquelin, Constant. 1958. "Actors and Acting." In *Papers on Acting,* ed. Brander Mathews. New York: Hill and Wang.

Saintsbury, H.A., and Cecil Palmer, ed. 1969. *We Saw Him Act: A Symposium on the Art of Sir Henry Irving.* New York: Benjamin Blom.

Salter, Denis. 1992. "Henry Irving, The 'Dr. Freud' of Melodrama." In *Melodrama, Themes in Drama*, ed. James Redmond. Vol. 14. Cambridge, Eng.: Cambridge University Press.

Terry, Ellen. 1969. *Ellen Terry's Memoirs: Being a New Edition of The Story of My Life, with a Preface, Notes, and Additional Biographical Chapters by Edith Craig and Christopher St. John.* New York: Benjamin Blom.

Tsubouchi, Shōyō, and Jirō Yamamoto, 1960. *History and Characteristics of Kabuki, The Japanese Classical Drama*, ed. and trans. by Ryōzō Matsumoto. Yokohama: Heiji Yamagata.

Yamamoto Jirō, Kikuchi Akira, and Hayashi Kyōhei, eds. 1971. *Kabuki Jiten.* Tokyo: Jitsugyō no Nihonsha.

II

PERFORMANCE

The Frozen Moment:
A *Kabuki* Technique

One of *kabuki* acting's most distinctive features is its crystallized acting patterns, handed down from generation to generation, and presenting the spectator with an almost Delsartian approach to the art of acting.[1] The conventions of *kabuki* acting are much more rigid than those of the Delsarte school, and leave today's actor little room for experiment, at least externally, in his presentation of a traditional role. During the Edo period, there was a far freer approach, but the opening of Japan to the West led to acting conventions becoming increasingly set as *kabuki* sought to preserve its artistic hegemony in the face of Western influence on Japanese theatre. These conventions range from vocal techniques and facial expressions, to costume colors and makeup.

One of the most important conventional aspects of *kabuki* acting is the frequent use of dramatic poses, held rigidly for a moment or two, in the course of performance. These poses are interspersed throughout the plays and come at specific moments set by tradition. The position of the actor's body and his facial expression are also traditional. These poses are sometimes called *omoire* ("expression"), a term that refers to the physical as apart from the spoken parts of a performance. *Omoire* are the corporeal attitudes taken by the actor to express his character's emotional state of being. They capture the essence of the character's thoughts and feelings at a specific point in time and draw the audience sharply into an immediate understanding of the character's state of mind. Scripts may say "free expression" (*jutsunaki omoire*), suggesting that the actor is at liberty to devise his own method of playing a moment, or they may say "irritated expression" (*haradatashiku omoire*), "mortified expression" (*kuyashiki omoire*), and so forth.[2] These moments often bear a resemblance to dance in that they are usually assumed after a rhythmical series of minor movements, accompanied by the beating on a floor board of the wooden clappers called *tsuke* or by other music, which accentuates the progression and climax of the actor's expression.

Bound up with the idea of posing is the element of silence or pause (*ma*), which many actors believe to be the most important part of *kabuki* acting. This silence occurs over and over in many of the *kabuki* techniques, but it takes on its greatest significance when considered as the moment of pause rendered through posture. All of the actor's physical and psychic energies are concentrated in that one brief moment when he draws himself up into a pose. Margaret H. Young wrote, "The highest points of dramatic expression in the Kabuki performance have little to do with words" (Young 1953, 162). Or, as the Stanislavski disciple, Eugene Vakhtangov observed, "there must be an inner dynamic in the externally static. A figure halting his movement must be expressive, must be dynamic in his immobility" (Vakhtangov 1947, 123).

The most powerful and characteristic poses are those that are termed *mie*. The phrase used for the performance of *mie* is usually *mie o suru* ("do a *mie*"), or *mie o kiru* ("cut a *mie*"), although some experts believe the most accurate phrase is *mie o kimeru* ("sets a *mie*"). These poses are taken at moments of intense emotion and the moments at which they occur are more or less fixed by tradition. Anger is often a good excuse for a *mie*, but many less dramatic emotions may lead to such posing, including surprise, curiosity, resolution, and the like. The convention that separates *mie* from other less exaggerated poses is the fierce glare—often with one eye crossed—frequently seen in old woodblock prints, which typically capture the actor's face at the climax of a *mie*. This staring, which reveals an enormous intensity of feeling and is not in the least humorous, is called *nirami*. The actor will close his eyes at the climax of his pose and then open them to display his crossed-eye technique. He may also, in certain *mie*, stare before him with eyes open and show the actual process of crossing to the audience.

In the old days, it is said, actors did not merely glare, but were able to make it seem as if their eyes had rolled back into their sockets.

Figure 14. Kutani-ware statue of Fudō, in author's possession. (Photo: Samuel L. Leiter.)

No one can be sure, of course, but the cross-eyed expression is believed by many to derive from the conventional representation of the fiery Buddhist god, Fudō, who is always shown with one eye looking upwards and one eye downward, and who has even given his name to the so-called *Fudō mie*, in which the actor poses like the deity. The *mie* pose itself has been likened to the appearance of Buddhist gods, Fudō included, depicted in ancient statuary with bulging muscles and ferocious attitudes.

One of the most famous *kabuki* moments comes when an actor assumes the greatly revered name of Ichikawa Danjūrō.[3] When important actors take a new name—whatever that may be—a special name-taking announcement ceremony (*shūmei hiro*) is held, and all the troupe members appear with the actor in formal costume to support this new step forward in his career. Because the Danjūrō line is most closely associated with the flamboyantly masculine acting style called *aragoto*, which requires many powerful *mie* poses, the high point of the ceremony comes when the actor announces to the audience, "I will now glare for you" (*kore kara nirande goran ni iremasu*) and, picking up a small, ceremonial wooden stand in his left hand, uses it to accentuate a dramatic crossed-eye pose with his right hand in a fist held near his chest and his right knee on the ground.

Mie are seen in all types of plays, but they reach their most elaborate form in *aragoto* and history plays (*jidaimono*), where the normally heightened nature of the acting tends to reach its climax in stylized poses. The *aragoto* character was said to represent the actor's superhuman power and his ability to strike down evil, thereby saving the innocent from danger.

Figure 15. The *nirami* pose. (From Toita, *Tsuzuki Waga Kabuki*.)

A *mie* may be one in a chain of poses by a particular character, each separated by a short space of time and differing from the others in form and rhythm. In *Kenuki*, Danjō is bewildered and chagrined at the mystical behavior of a huge pair of tweezers and a knife which dance before him, to his left and right. In consternation he strikes one pose after another to the beating of wooden clappers (*tsuke*) by a stage assistant kneeling down left. As usual, each pose utilizes the nature of the costume. Danjō is wearing an oversized pair of wing-like shoulder pieces (*kataginu*), and these figure in each *mie* as he clutches them or turns his body to emphasize their proportions. Thus the visual effect is emphasized and punctuated to the point where the actor freezes sharply and creates the "close up" effect mentioned by various writers. The final movement of the pose, which transfixes the audience's attention on the actor, zooming them in, so to speak, is the peculiar revolving motion the actor makes with his head, just before he snaps it to a rigid position in time to the clappers. This circular motion, called *senkai*, is used to a modified extent in non-*mie* poses as well.

Figure 16. Danjō (Danjūrō XI) performs a series of *mie* as he watches the tweezers. (Photo: author's collection.)

Though the *mie* is considered the single most impressive moment for a *kabuki* actor, it sometimes has to compete with other more spectacular stage effects being simultaneously performed. In *Meiboku Sendai Hagi*, for example, there is a scene in which an *aragoto* character (Arajishi Otokonosuke) rises on a stage trap with his foot on a large rat (the villainous wizard Nikki Danjō, under a self-imposed spell). Otokonosuke is dressed in a fantastic padded costume and his face and body are covered in red lines against a white background, a version of the spectacular makeup known as *kumadori*. (In modern performances, a skintight cotton garment serves for the body makeup.) His appearance is coupled with the simultaneous rising of an entire setting on a trap immediately upstage of him. The rat (played by a small, acrobatic actor, perhaps a boy) and the powerful man grapple in stylized fashion until the rat runs off and disappears swiftly into the *suppon*, the small elevator trap on the *hanamichi*. At this point, Otokonosuke, on stage, turns his back to the audience to allow attention to focus on the *suppon*, from which Nikki (changed again to human form) slowly rises. Otokonosuke performs a very strong *mie* here, as he spins around and takes a position with the left leg stretched out in a straight line and the right leg bent, the weight of the body resting on the right leg. He quickly shakes his left arm, encased in a huge sleeve, to free it, and it shoots out suddenly from the fold of his kimono at the breast, pushing the right sleeve up in a gesture of defiance as be revolves his head and crosses one eye. What is involved here is that the magical entrance of Nikki Danjō has drawn the spectator's attention to the *hanamichi*; as powerful as the *mie* at center is, it does not draw the attention usually reserved for so strong a pose. The curtain is soon drawn past Otokonosuke's figure, further negating his image. In this scene, the *mie* has served as a means of directing attention elsewhere, rather than upon itself.

Figure 17. Nikki Danjō, in *Meiboku Sendai Hagi*, rises on the *suppon*, left, as Otokonosuke cuts a *mie* at center. (Photo: Noguchi, *Kabuki*.)

A *mie* may be performed standing, kneeling, or sitting. A famous example with both standing and kneeling variations is the "stone-throwing pose" (*ishinage no mie*), performed by Benkei in *Kanjinchō*, Narukami in the play of that name, and Matsuōmaru in *Kuruma Biki*. When standing, the legs are held closely together, a position called *soku* ("sheaf"), which gives us the term *soku mie* for any pose in which the legs are so positioned. When the *ishinage no mie* is done kneeling, the legs are slightly apart, the body is turned somewhat to the side, and the left knee is on the ground. The actor holds his right hand above his head, fingers open, as if just having tossed a stone. The above-mentioned *Fudō mie*—done by Benkei, Narukami, and Fudō himself in a play of that name—may be done standing or sitting. The actor holds a sword at his right side, the point held upwards, while his left hand holds a Buddhist rosary.

(left) Figure 18. Benkei in *Kanjinchō* (Matsumoto Kōshirō VII) performs the *ishinage no mie*. (Photo: author's collection.)

Figure 19. Benkei (Danjūrō XI) poses with his feet in the *soku mie* position. (Photo: *Ichikawa Ebizō Butai Shashin Shū*.)

Although these examples have been taken from history plays, domestic plays of everyday life (*sewamono*), usually far more realistic than *jidaimono*, may also use theatricalized poses, although more selectively and with more restraint. A well-known example is a sitting *mie* seen after Benten's "unveiling" (*miarawashi*) in the Hamamatsuya scene of *Benten Kozō*.

When Benten's male identity is discerned beneath his female accoutrements he delivers a famous speech, seated center behind a tobacco box. He then pulls his left arm free from inside his kimono, revealing a body covered with tattoos. He waves his arm once above his head, pulls his left leg over his right, yoga fashion, and concludes by stretching his bared, tattooed left arm before him, hand in a fist, while with a revolve of his head he crosses one eye.

Figure 20. Benten Kozō (Ichikawa Somegorō VI, later Matsumoto Kōshirō IX) performs the *miarawashi mie*. (Photo: author's collection.)

In some cases, the actor may be seated on a high property so that it seems he is standing in a difficult pose while he is actually leaning against something for support. For example, when Nippon Daemon reveals himself to Kōbei in *Benten Kozō* he poses while leaning against a high chest, with one leg crossed over the knee of his other leg.

The *mie* may be further emphasized by a speech that ends on a violent and forcible note as the pose is struck, or it may be performed in silence punctuated only by the *tsuke*, as is the case with the *mie* in *Kenuki*, described above.

Hippari no mie is the term given to those moments when two or more actors perform *mie* in conflict with one another. The term signifies the "pulling" effect produced by their mutually varying attitudes. There is an example of this *mie* in the trial scene of *Meiboku Sendai Hagi*, when Nikki Danjō and Katsuyori face each other. Katsuyori is seated upstage center on the platform reached by a three-step unit at its center. Nikki sits down left of the platform, on his knees. A point in the acting is reached where they quickly shuffle on their knees in each other's direction to the accompaniment of the beating; suddenly, however, they stop and perform *mie*, crossing the eye that is furthest from the opponent. Nikki crosses his left eye and Katsuyori his right. This strengthens the line of contact between the two characters at the particular moment in which the pose is adopted. A similar effect occurs at the conclusion of *Musume Dōjōji*, when the demon queller character (*oshimodoshi*), portrayed as an *aragoto* hero, poses across the stage from a ferocious demon. The latter stands on a special platform, suggesting that the demon is the head of a huge serpent whose long tail is symbolized by a group of men dressed in identical scale-patterned garments, posing upstage from stage left to right. Although the contrasting emotions expressed are often antagonistic, this does not have to be the case, as witness the end of *Terakoya*, where the characters assume individual postures, each one's eyes having a different focus, but their body language emphasizing the upstage center position of the young lord, Kan Shūsai, and his regal mother. Such final tableau poses may also be called *emen mie* or "picture poses." *Emen mie* are sometimes seen when two or more characters rise in tableau on an elevator trap during the action. Interestingly, nineteenth-century Western melodrama typically employed dramatic tableaus reminiscent of *hippari no mie*. According to Gary Richardson, "The freezing of the action, most often at the ends of scenes and acts, furnished a spatial and pictorial distillation of a specific emotional moment, allowing the focusing arrangements of characters, their frozen attitudes, and the play of light and shadow to reiterate the participants' situations . . . " (1998,

281). And we might also remember the effect when the characters suddenly freeze at the end of Gogol's *The Inspector-General*.

Figure 21. *Hippari no mie* in *Musume Dōjōji*, with *oshimodoshi* (Bandō Mitsugorō VIII) posing opposite the demon (Onoe Baikō VII). (Photo: author's collection.)

Male roles dominate the field of the *mie*, although certain powerful female roles occasionally perform them as well. The most notable such example is the "prawn-shape pose" (*ebigaeri no mie* or *ebizori no mie*), in which the kneeling woman bends over backward, her spine curving gracefully, when threatened by a strong male standing over her. One of the rare occasions on which a male character performs this pose is in *Yoshitsune Senbon Zakura*. (See figures 47-48 in the following chapter.) More typically, female characters perform a gentle variation of the *mie*, sometimes

called *kimari*, which simply suggests a set position and can also refer to a
male pose.

Figure 22. *Hippari no mie* in *Terakoya*. Downstage, left to right, Chiyo (Nakamura Ganjirō II), Matsuō (Matsumoto Kōshirō VIII), Genzō (Kataoka
Nizaemon XIII), and Tonami (Nakamura Shikan VII). Upstage, Sono no Mae
(Nakamura Matsue V), Kan Shūsai (Iwase Kōshirō). (Photo: author's collection.)

Figure 23. *Torite* lined up behind Matsuō (Ichikawa Danjūrō XI), right, and
Genzō (Ichikawa Sadanji III) in the head inspection scene of *Terakoya*.
(Photo: author's collection.)

It is often said that the *kabuki* stage should always be so arranged that
if a photograph were taken at any moment in a performance the resulting
picture would have the quality of a beautifully planned composition. To enhance this compositional quality the actors move through their roles in
graceful poses, never permitting body or costume line to jar with the pictorial effect. When necessary, onstage assistants—either those dressed in
black (*kurogo*) and deemed to invisible, or those in formal costumes (*kō-*

ken)—assist the actor in keeping his costume and props in perfect alignment. Many poses are further accented by musical accompaniment though they are not technically called *mie*. The importance of extensive dance training for *kabuki* actors should be obvious. A specific tempo and rhythm runs through all *kabuki* movement and most *kabuki* speech. The effects may be produced with one or two actors alone on the vast stage or by a large, formally arranged, company.

Many of the poses assumed are characteristic of the roles in which they are performed. For instance, the *kabuki* policemen, *torite*, usually garbed in black, normally are arranged so that they all stand simultaneously in the same manner. Each man poses with feet together, right hand raised before the forehead, holding the short steel club (*jitte*) vertically with the left hand extended, palm outward, before him. Characters acted in the gentle *wagoto* style strike several typical poses; usually, however, their feet are arranged in a semi-pigeon-toed stance, so that one foot is kept straight with the other foot in front of it and turned inward.

(left) Figure 24. Yosaburō (Kataoka Takao, later Kataoka Nizaemon XV) in a *wagoto* stance during *Kirare Yosa* (Photo: *Engekikai* [1991].)

Figure 25: Jihei, the *wagoto* hero of *Shinjū Ten no Amijima*. (Photo: author's collection.)

(right) Figure 26. Heieimon (Ichimura Uzaemon XV) listens to a secret whispered by Okaru in *Chūshingura*. (Photo: *Jūgosei Ichimura Uzaemon Butai Shashin Shū*.)

When a character has to listen to a secret he ordinarily stands facing front while his informer whispers in his ear. Often crossing his arms, he leans his body over toward the whisperer as he extends his outer leg and bends the inner one. His face is completely front so that the audience can watch his reaction to the whispered secret.

There is a specific standing pose most often seen in fight scenes, but also used for every other type of scene. Variations can be seen in several of the illustrations in this chapter. It takes various forms and may be approached in many ways. This posture is seen when the actor stretches one leg taut and out to one side, toes pointing directly away from the body, while the other leg is bent at the knee with the weight of the body resting on it. The heel of the bent leg is normally perpendicular to the heel of the straight leg. The degree to which the body weight rests on the bent leg, the posture assumed by the torso and the arms, hands, and head, the distance between the legs, as well as the method of taking the pose, all determine the variations used. For example, the left foot may be brought strongly up into the air and kicked out before the actor to stamp sharply on the ground, at which moment the right leg is bent back at the knee, the distance between the legs being fairly wide apart. Or the actor may already be standing with legs apart when at a given point he leans his body to rest on one knee, which bends, while the other tightens in a straight line parallel to the body. A variation of the former method occurs when the actor inclines forward on the kicked leg, bending it, while the other leg straightens. These are poses that, though common to all *kabuki* forms, carry a constant sense of beauty through their bold and graceful lines. The *Genroku mie* (named for the Genroku period, 1688-1704), one of the most highly exaggerated poses, and used only by *aragoto* roles, is seen in such plays as *Shibaraku* and *Kanjinchō*. It uses the bent and straight leg pose as its essential linear component, as do many other *mie* forms.

Figure 27. Ichikawa Danjūrō IX performing the *Genroku mie* (see previous paragraph) in *Shibaraku*. (Photo: *Engekikai* [1957].)

Certain settings have elements used for effective posturing. Numerous scenes allow the actor to strike poses outside the sliding door entrances that are used with many interior sets. The actor may be waiting at the door for someone, or may be eavesdropping on the scene in the room to which the door leads. In *Kirare Yosa*, Yosaburō makes much use of the door to Otomi's house in a famous scene of that play, both while waiting to enter and after he is inside.

Figures 28-30. (left) Yosaburō (Ichimura Uzaemon XV) peers out the door in *Kirare Yosa*. (Photo: Kagayama, *Kabuki no Kata*.) (center) Katsuyori (Uzaemon XV) on the stair unit in *Honchō Nijūshikō*. (Photo: *Jūgosei Ichimura Uzaemon Butai Shashin Shū*.) (above right) Mitsuhide (Ichikawa Ennosuke II, later Ichikawa Eno) in *Ehon Taikōki*. (Photo: *Engekikai* [1959].)

Figure 31. Narukami's (Onoe Shōroku II) *hashiramaki no mie* in *Narukami*. (Photo: author's collection.)

Platforms and steps are frequently utilized for special poses, especially when the character is wearing the long, trailing trousers that trail down the steps, as do the warrior Kumagai's in *Kumagai Jinya* or the romantic young samurai Katsuyori's in *Honchō Nijūshikō*. In the former pose, Kumagai, wielding a wooden signpost, stands at the top of the steps while in the latter, Katsuyori, holding his sword, sits there. And house-supporting pillars are sometimes very useful for those famous "pillar-wrapping poses" (*hashira maki no mie*), in which potent characters like Narukami grasp a pillar with their arms and one foot to express their rage.

Two characters posing together is common, especially with one kneeling at the side of the standing other. This position is known as *tenchi* ("heaven and earth") and often involves one person restraining another from acting impulsively. A man may kneel beside a woman as in *Sukeroku*, or a woman beside a man as in the first *michiyuki* or "traveling scene" of *Chūshingura*. In *Soga no Taimen* the gentle older Soga brother, Jūrō, kneels throughout most of the play, while his younger brother, the hotheaded Gorō, stands. At a dramatic moment in *Kagamiyama* Lady Onoe strikes an attitude on her knees at the side of her tormentor, Lady Iwafuji, who beats her with a sandal. Three-person *mie* are known, too, among them the *tenchijin no mie* ("heaven, earth, and man *mie*"), in which one character is high, another on a middle level, and a third lower down, as seen in *Kanjinchō* when Benkei, Togashi, and Yoshitsune assume it.

(above) Figure 32. Gorō (left) and Jūrō (Nakamura Kanzaburō XVII) in *Soga no Taimen*. (Photo: *Engekikai* [1971].)

Figure 33. Sukeroku (Nakamura Kanzaburō XVII) and Agemaki (Nakamura Utaemon VI) in *Sukeroku*. (Photo: author's collection.)

An attractive element of many poses is the holding of some small property between the teeth. This may be seen in many scenes, such as when Sadakurō in *Chūshingura* strikes a famous *mie* with a purse in his teeth. A dagger's blade or the rope on its scabbard may be clasped by the teeth. Other props on which the actor may bite when posing include a wad of paper, perhaps before wiping a bloody sword; a fan in the various narrative monologues called *monogatari*; a corner of a hand towel (*tenugui*) to help restrain tears by biting on it or to keep it on the head when worn as a shawl; a sleeve when crying; and so on.

Because the kimono sleeve is a fairly substantial swath of material, it offers countless possibilities for posing. The sleeves may be held up by stage assistants for further effect after dramatic poses. Women's sleeves, in particular, are crucial acting aids, and the art of playing female characters is closely bound up with the myriad effects that can be communicated through skillful manipulation of the sleeves.

Among the many properties often used by actors when posing are various weapons, ladders, a straw mat carried around the shoulders as protection from poor weather, hats of several widths and heights, huge wooden sign posts flung effortlessly round in tight scenes, immense anchors, umbrellas, long scroll letters, pipes, rosaries, severed heads and head boxes, lanterns, and on and on.

Quite often a well-known pose in a certain role is equally familiar in another role. In *Kirare Yosa*, after Yosaburō reveals himself to Otomi he sits on the floor with legs crossed before him, forearms encircling his knees, and fingers intertwined, palms outward. This pose is duplicated in *Benten*

Kozō after Benten has revealed his identity, and is seen as well in *Naozamu-rai*, during the hero's scene of parting with Michitose. (Particularly striking is the similarity between the two-character poses seen in both the dance-drama *Kasane* and *Hakone no Shikabue*, an infrequently revived 1880 play in the *zangirimono* style that shows the influence of Western civilization, including short hair for men. The woman in both poses is on the ground at the left side of the man, clinging to his left leg, which is held in a straight line while his right leg is bent at the knee. The man threatens the woman with a weapon—in *Kasane* a sickle, in the other play a knife—held in his right hand. Both men pull the sleeve of their right arm upward with their left hand.

Figures 34-36. (left) Sadakurō (Onoe Shōroku II) in *Chūshingura* posing with a purse in his mouth. (Photo: *Engekikai* [1962].) (center) Tadanobu (Ichikawa Ennosuke III) in *Yoshitsune Senbon Zakura* poses with a fan in his mouth. (Photo: *Engekikai* [1968].) (right) Otowa (Ichikawa Shōchō VII, later Ichikawa Monnosuke VII) bites on *tenugui* in *Sumōtori Senryō Shiki*. Inasegawa Jirōkichi (Kawarasaki Gonjūrō III) sits next to her. (Photo: *Engekikai* [1961].)

No brief essay can hope to describe the myriad poses that form the visual backbone of so much *kabuki* performance. The more one examines photographs of stage productions the more one realizes how rich the topic is. The examples offered here do serve, however, to illustrate clearly how reliant *kabuki* is upon conventional stage postures. The inclusion of an inner technique in such apparently objective acting is an artistic phenomenon by no means limited to the *kabuki*; nevertheless, it is one reason why the actors of *kabuki* have never failed to amaze and delight the most diverse audiences.

Somewhat similar dramatic poses as are used in *kabuki* are observable in other classical Asian theatre forms. *Kabuki's* acting style is, on the whole, more realistic than those found in these other forms. It is the selective use of the pose within the framework of this fairly realistic mode that makes the "frozen moment" in *kabuki* stand out as a theatrical technique.

The technique thus becomes important not only because of its being a path to an aesthetic appreciation of the *kabuki*, but also because it is one of those too few elements of Asian acting technique that can, perhaps, be effectively transferred to the production of stylized Western drama.

(upper left) Figure 37. Naozamurai (Ichikawa Danjūrō XI) entwines his fingers in *Naozamurai*. Michitose (Onoe Baikō VII). (Photo: *Engekikai* [1962].)

(upper right) Figure 38. Yosaburō (Danjūrō XI) entwines his fingers in *Kirare Yosa*. (Photo: *Engekikai* [1962].)

(lower left) Figure 39. Yoemon (Danjūrō XI) struggles with Kasane (Baikō VII) in *Kasane*. (Photo: *Engekikai* [1962].)

Figure 40. Kurōbei (Danjūrō XI) fights with Oyosa (Baikō VII) in *Hakone Shikabue*. (Photo: *Engekikai* [1962].)

NOTES

An earlier version of this essay appeared in *Drama Survey* 6 (Spring 1967).

1. See MacKaye (1927, 269-70) for a discussion of Delsarte's principles as applied by American actor-director-playwright-inventor Steele MacKaye.
2. Brandon (2000) has subsequently taken up this subject in detail.
3. See the essays in this volume titled "Ichikawa Danjūrō XI: A Life in *Kabuki*" and "Parallel Lives: Sir Henry Irving and Ichikawa Danjūrō IX."

REFERENCES

Brandon, James R. 2000. "Performance and Text in *Kabuki*." In *Japanese Theatre and the International Stage*, ed. Stanca Scholz-Cionca and Samuel L. Leiter. Leiden, The Netherlands: Brill.

Engekikai. 1955, 1957, 1959, 1960, 1962, 1966, 1968, 1970, 1991. Miscellaneous issues.

Jūgosei Ichimura Uzaemon Shashin Shū. 1951. Tokyo: Wakei Shoten.

Kagayama Naozō. 1957. *Kabuki no Kata*. Tokyo: Tōkyō Sōgensha.

MacKaye, Percy. 1927. *Epoch, The Life of Steele MacKaye, Genius of the Theatre, in Relation to His Times and Contemporaries*. Vol. 1. New York: Boni and Livewright.

Noguchi Tatsuji. 1965. *Kabuki*. Tokyo: Bungei Shunka Shinja.

Toita Yasuji. 1948. *Tsuzuki Waga Kabuki*. Tokyo: Wakei Shoten.

Richardson, Gary A. 1998. "Plays and Playwrights: 1800-1865." In *The Cambridge History of American Theatre*, ed. Don B. Wilmeth and Christopher Bigsby. Vol. 1. Cambridge, Mass.: Cambridge University Press.

Vakhtangov, Eugene. 1947. "Preparing for the Role: From the Diary of E. Vakhtangov." In *Acting, A Handbook of the Stanislavski Method*, comp. Toby Cole. New York: Crown.

Young, Margaret Hershey. 1953. *Japanese Kabuki Drama; The History and Meaning of its Theatre Art Form*. Ph.D. diss., Indiana University.

Keren:
Spectacle and Trickery in *Kabuki* Acting

In Act IV of the classic play, *Yoshitsune Senbon Zakura*, the leading character, having revealed his true form as a magic fox, comes to the edge of the stage, below the curtain. Several stage assistants quickly attach wires to a rig he is wearing under his costume; a moment later, he flies aloft into the upper reaches of the huge *kabuki* theatre, far over the heads of those seated in the orchestra. Suspended in a horizontal position to emphasize his fox-nature, he cavorts with great energy as he moves along near the ceiling, following a course above the *hanamichi* runway passing through the audience from stage right to the rear of the auditorium. He eventually lands in a specially constructed booth on the theatre's top balcony.

Figure 41. The fox (Ichikawa Ennosuke III) in *Yoshitsune Senbon Zakura* performs *chūnori*. (Photo: author's collection.)

This technique, called "riding the sky" (*chūnori*), is a specialty of the extraordinarily dynamic and versatile star, Ichikawa Ennosuke III (b.1939). In the traditional exit for this role the actor bounds down the *hanamichi* in the vigorous leaping, bounding style called "fox in six directions" (*kitsune roppō*).[1] The innovative Ennosuke feels the *chūnori* technique is more startling to contemporary audiences and his popularity in the role, which is one of his artistic signatures, appears to bear him out.

Chūnori is one of a number of spectacular *kabuki* acting techniques, specialties of a small group of actors. The art of trick techniques is called *keren* and actors such as Ennosuke or the late Jitsukawa Enjaku III (1921-

91), who are contemporary masters of such effects, are called *kerenshi* (*"keren* masters"), while *keren* acting is *keren gei* and *keren* plays are *keren mono*. *Keren* is sometimes loosely applied to trick scenic and lighting effects, but the word more properly defines the special, almost circus-like effects that the actor himself performs.

Through much of the nineteenth century *keren* was considered one of *kabuki's* most popular, crowd-pleasing elements, and a number of major families such as the Onoe regarded the art as a family tradition (*ie no gei*). However, the influx into Japan in the late nineteenth century of Western theatre ideas with their concomitant sense of rationality led many of the most important figures in the *kabuki* world to attempt a reform of their traditional stage practices. This was in keeping with the trend toward modernity affecting all areas of Japanese culture. As a result of the reformist attitudes imposed on *kabuki* during the Meiji era, *keren* came to be looked on with scorn as the product of a naïve townsman culture that clamored for childlike fantasy in its popular theatre. This tendency was particularly marked in the Tokyo theatre world; in the Kamigata (or Kansai) area (Osaka/Kyoto), such actors as Ichikawa Udanji II (1881-1936) worked diligently to keep the tradition alive. Beginning in the 1960s, there was a resurgence of interest in *keren*. One of its first signs was the reintroduction of *chūnori* by Nakamura Kanzaburō XVII (1909-88) during a 1967 production, and its rapid adaptation by the two actors who came to specialize in it, Ennosuke III and Enjaku III. It is now as vital a tradition in Tokyo as in the past.

Ennosuke III has said:

These techniques probably began in the time of the playwright Tsuruya Nanboku IV. Audiences of the time were growing bored with the usual fare so these *keren* must have come as quite a surprise to them. Moreover, the audiences were overjoyed by these effects and applauded then wholeheartedly, Therefore, the producers began to turn them out more frequently. However, such works appeared far too often and the actors became too used to appearing in them so the roles gradually weakened in character depiction and degenerated into mere excuses for quick changes or speedy acrobatic acting; meaningful theatre was forgotten in the process (quoted in Katsuo 1970, 30-31).

Fully aware, therefore, of this aesthetic problem, Ennosuke notes that, "If the essential nature and emotional basis of the roles are missing there is no art" (quoted in Katsuo). He has described in detail how the various *keren* he uses in *Yoshitsune Senbon Zakura* are all a direct result of character interpretation and not a superimposition for the sake of effects alone.

The word *keren's* antecedents are somewhat unclear, as is suggested by its being written in syllabic characters (*kana*) rather than Sino-Japanese ones (*kanji*), scholars being unsure about which *kanji* would be appropriate. One view holds that the original form of the word meant to deceive or cheat, which then evolved into the meaning of surprising people through some illusionary skill. Another opinion holds that the word first gained theatrical use in *gidayū*, the narrative accompaniment used in *bunraku*, to refer to the performance of a work from another school in the style of one's own traditional school. In *kabuki* the word came to signify a decidedly unorthodox acting method. Though the word eventually took on derogatory overtones, those critics who feel that the Meiji reforms robbed *kabuki* of its vital energy as a popular theatre look more favorably on it than did many of their predecessors. They argue that *kabuki* cannot be viewed as a performing art that shares the lofty idealism of Japan's *nō* and *kyōgen* theatres. *Kabuki's* gradual ossification into a dusty museum relic can only be averted by a return to its original "side show" (*misemono*) quality. Recent use of *keren* is one manifestation of this kind of critical support. Since Western ideas were largely responsible for the demise of *keren* in the Meiji era, it is interesting to note that a 1970 Japanese periodical article on *keren* begins with a description of the stage tricks used in Peter Brook's famous production that year of *A Midsummer Night's Dream*, implying a justification of *keren* on the basis of Western usage.

Although *keren* came into their own in the nineteenth century, its techniques have been a part of *kabuki* for centuries, dating back to the early period of young men's or *wakashu kabuki* in the seventeenth century, when various acrobatic arts were performed, among them *kumo mai*, a kind of tightrope walking. By the Genroku period (1688-1704), acrobatics were a regular part of plays, so that a young woman might be transformed into a cat, jump onto a fence, and do a dance while standing on her hands. In an early version of the eighteenth-century dance *Musume Dōjōji*, the heroine might make a startling transformation into a fiery serpent and then fly off over the audience's heads. During these years, *keren* were considered the specialty of *onnagata*. After a period during which such methods lost favor for pandering to common tastes, they were brought back to popularity in the early nineteenth century by Onoe Matsusuke I (1744-1815), who teamed up with rising playwright Tsuruya Nanboku IV (1755-1829) to create a host of fascinating effects in a series of eerie ghost plays (*kaidanmono*). *Keren*—now becoming the special sphere of male-role actors (*tachiyaku*)—were further elaborated by Matsusuke's son, Onoe Kikugorō III (1784-1839), who created such effects as the *hashibako* and *butsudan gaeshi*, described below. Matsusuke himself was so adept at *keren* creation that he was even suspected of dabbling in Christian witchcraft.

Chūnori

The techniques of *keren* are usually divided into three main categories: *chūnori*, *honmizu* (the use of real water on stage), and *hayagawari* (quick-change techniques). Probably the most spectacular is *chūnori*. However, the present method of performing this technique differs from the way it was done in the past. The character performing the flying in *Yoshitsune Senbon Zakura* is attached to the flying rig only when he comes to the stage apron, below the curtain. Modern *kabuki* is played on proscenium stages so it is impossible for the actor to fly from an upstage position to a place near the ceiling over the spectators' heads. The presence of the proscenium arch impedes the rigging of the necessary wires. Even if such a rig were possible, the curtain, which moves horizontally, would be unable to close because of the wires passing through the proscenium. The modern method of flying an actor over the auditorium is to drill a hole high up in the proscenium wall and fix a system of wires from there to the theatre's third balcony. This allows the actor to fly all the way over the auditorium, providing everyone with a delightful frisson.

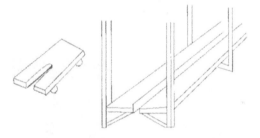

Figure 42. The *chūnori* devices of *geta* (left) and *kakesuji*.

In pre-proscenium theatres, a device called a *kakesuji* (hanging track) was used instead of a wire system. The track was suspended from the ceiling beams over both stage and auditorium (or wherever it was needed). The track consisted of wooden boards running horizontally in parallel lines with a one-inch space between them. A device called a *geta* (because of its resemblance to the similarly named Japanese clog) with a niche in its center and four small wheels on its bottom was placed on these boards so that it rode along them like a roller skate. To lift the actor into the air, a metal pole with a hook on its end (*sakigane*), was attached to a ring on the actor's flying harness. A ring on the pole's upper portion was attached to a hook connected to a flying rope and the actor was lifted off the ground from above. A collar or flange was affixed to the pole and when this was set into the *geta* niche it acted as a slip-proof device so that the actor could not fall. The rope that lifted the actor was released and a stagehand standing on the overhead board system pulled the *geta* along, allowing the hanging actor freedom of movement through the air. The problem of the front curtain was solved by the maneuverability of the horizontal boards. They could be thrust forward or backwards along their supports in accordance with the opening or closing of the curtain.

When the new system developed for proscenium theatres was first tried at Tokyo's Kabuki-za, it was not certain that the proscenium wall would hold the actor's weight. This postwar theatre (reconstructed from its bombed-out shell and opened in 1951) had not, after all, been built for the performance of *chūnori*. Those working on the flying project were unsure as to how thick the wires should be and what sort of winch to use, so an expert—an elevator maker—was brought in to devise the system. The wire selected was capable of holding 850 kilograms and was five millimeters thick. The actor, Ennosuke, weighed about 76 kilograms in full costume. However, at the peak of his flight he planned to cavort energetically, putting even more strain on the system and adding considerably to his weight. This, it was estimated, would increase his weight ten times. A meter was used to gauge the correct weight ratios. Ennosuke's heaviest weight came to 750 kilograms, which accorded well with the estimates.

(left) Figure 43. The unopened basket, with Ennosuke III hidden inside, for the *tsuzura nuke* trick in *Tenjiku Tokubei*. (Photo: from *Ennosuke no Kabuki Kōza*.)

Figure 44. Ennosuke III emerging from the basket. (Photo: from *Ennosuke no Kabuki Kōza*.)

The pulley system had to be devised so the character of Genkurō (also called Fox-Tadanobu because he is a magically transformed fox substituting for someone named Tadanobu) could fly in a horizontal position in accordance with his fox-nature. This contrasts, for example, with another famous *chūnori* of recent years, that performed by the Enjaku III as Goemon in Ishikawa Goemon when the character flies off with a huge basket strapped to his back. Since he does foot movements in the exaggerated and vigorous *roppō* style, he must fly in a vertical position. In Ennosuke III's version of this stunt, performed in *Tenjiku Tokubei*, the basket flies off on its own. In mid-flight the actor emerges from the basket and flies off with it on his back. This is called the *tsuzura nuke* ("out of the basket") effect.

The *chūnori* actor wears a parachute-like harness (*renjaku*). Ennosuke's harness for *Yoshitsune Senbon Zakura* runs under the armpits and crotch. One man in the balcony runs the main pulley, another controls the waist wire, and a third handles the crotch wire.

The winch was surprisingly difficult to operate when first used. It was not possible to make the wire lines horizontal because of the difference in height between the proscenium and the winch position in the balcony. This forced the wire to incline at an angle. Since Ennosuke had to be pulled quite high the problem of moving him was increased. A solution was to add extra gears; this, however, cut down the speed of the actor's movement through space.

Those involved worried daily about the possibilities of an accident. Ennosuke was lifted every morning before the theatre opened in order to test and re-test the system for safety. Obviously, the device was built specifically for this actor and would have to be re-rigged or built anew for anyone else.

Prior to a month's performances in which he must do this *chūnori* over the audience, Ennosuke sets up a temporary shrine on the *hanamichi* to pray for a safe production. Fortunately, none has occurred in the three and a half decades or so that he has been flying over *kabuki* audiences.

Though the wires that support his *chūnori* are clearly visible, Ennosuke feels that "there is a startling effect on the audience of seeing such slender wires support me at so high a height. Though it is high I can't afford to be afraid. If I allow even a slight fear to creep in, I won't be able to rise on the wires and move about. I place my trust in the mechanism and in the men who operate it" (quoted in Katsuo, 31).

Ennosuke has introduced a number of exciting *chūnori* variations. In a 1974 production of *Satomi Hakkenden*, Ennosuke appeared, among other roles, as the spirit of a magic cat. In one scene this cat flew across the stage riding on a huge log oddly resembling a horse. In another, even more visually exciting scene, Ennosuke and Kataoka Takao (b. 1944; now called Kataoka Nizaemon XV) were enacting the roles of the heroes. The magic cat appeared, a gigantic furry animal, twice the size of a human being. It flew in from above and, seizing Ennosuke and Takao by the scruffs of their necks, flew out with them as they kicked and thrashed frantically. The actors were each wearing harnesses, which quick-moving, black-garbed stage assistants attached to grips on the huge cat's claws. In a more recent play,

Ennosuke flew off on a capering white horse (embodied by two actors in a horse costume).

A famous *chūnori* occurs in *Kagamiyama*[2] when the ghost of the wicked Lady Iwafuji calmly flies over the stage and auditorium holding an umbrella above her head. She rides on a specially built contraption: the staff of the umbrella is fastened to a metal device which fits around the actor and under his armpits and which has a pedestal for the actor to stand on. Ichikawa Udanji I (1843-1916), an Osaka actor of the Meiji era, once performed an exit as the magical bandit Ishikawa Goemon in which a large drum placed on stage was raised in the air and flown over the *hanamichi*, at which point the drum opened and Goemon appeared from inside. The front skin of the drum flipped over, revealing an ox head, as the rear skin turned around, showing a tail, The actor had a pedal arrangement attached to his feet. Wings dropped on either side of the actor and, as he moved his feet rhythmically, the pedals made the wings flap up and down. The impression was of a flying ox with Goemon calmly riding it as it exited toward the rear of the *hanamichi*.

Hayagawari

Hayagawari, or quick-change techniques, can, when well performed, be a delightful theatrical experience. Few theatre forms anywhere have developed the art of the quick change to *kabuki's* level of perfection. The *hayagawari* classified as *keren* demonstrate the often mystifying skill with which a single actor can alter his appearance almost instantly and sometimes seem to be almost everywhere at once. A number of English-language books have described the onstage costume-change techniques known as *hikinuki* (pulling off) and *bukkaeri* (falling off), where the loosely sewn threads of a performer's costume are silently removed by stage assistants preparatory to their pulling the disconnected garment—or part of it—off the actor in a flash of movement, revealing a completely different costume underneath.[3] *Hikinuki* and *bukkaeri* are onstage techniques designed to reveal a new aspect of the same character. The latter suggests a change in the very nature of a character, as from villain to hero, or vice-versa. The former suggests a change of mood, as in the numerous examples of its use in the popular dance-play, *Musume Dōjōji*. Though these are forms of *hayagawari*, the examples described below are classified as *keren* because an actor changes from one role to another, baffling the audience by his surprising speed.

The art of *hayagawari* was given enormous impetus by a genre of dance plays that became tremendously popular in the nineteenth century. These were the "transformation pieces" (*hengemono* or *henge buyō*), multiscene dances that allowed the star to play from seven to twelve sharply contrasting roles, often after changing instantaneously from one to the other. Today, barely any such works survive, only certain of their discrete dance segments still being performed as one-act dances. Many are among *kabuki's* most frequently seen works. Their popularity also stimulated the already existing practice of doubling, that is, the playing by one actor of several roles in the same play; actors even began to demonstrate their versatility by playing most of the leading characters in various classic dramas, like *Sugawara* or *Chūshingura*, although not necessarily through the use of quick-change techniques.

An excellent example of doubling in which quick changes are vital occurs in the Kawatsura mansion scene in *Yoshitsune Senbon Zakura*. The central role is that of Satō Tadanobu, faithful retainer to the great general, Yoshitsune. As suggested above, Tadanobu's physical form has been assumed by a white fox, considered in Japan to have magical powers. Fox-Tadanobu appears whenever Yoshitsune's mistress, Shizuka Gozen, beats a drum made of the fox's parents' skins. Both Fox-Tadanobu and Satō Tadanobu appear in this climactic scene, which affords the actor playing both roles opportunity for some virtuoso acting as he switches from role to role in split-second transformations. The fox-role is especially difficult, as it demands a great deal of acrobatic acting.

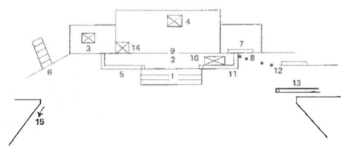

Figure 45. Groundplan for *Yoshitsune Senbon Zakura*.

A number of *keren* traditionally have been performed for this role but Ennosuke has doubled the number of tricks in his performance. The ground plan illustration printed above is numbered in accordance with the specific *keren* listed below it.

1. After appearing on stage dressed in the formal costume of a samurai at court, Tadanobu exits up center. Shizuka, alone, beats the magic drum and the fox appears miraculously, lying across the lacquered steps at center stage. This effect is created by the use of special revolving steps to which the actor clings as he is rotated into position from underneath. The audience's attention is distracted from the stage

to the brightly-lit *hanamichi* where the sound of the curtain being swished aside traditionally signals an entrance. During the instant in which the audience is looking left, the actor pops into position.

Figure 46. The revolving steps device in *Yoshitsune Senbon Zakura.* (From *Ennosuke no Kabuki Kōza.*)

2. Performing with fox-like movements, the actor does an acrobatic  "prawn-shaped" backbend (*ebigaeri*) while on his knees, his head directed backward toward the audience from the top of the steps. To do this he grips a special rope attached to the floor but unseen by the audience.

Figure 47. Ennosuke III practices the trick backbend in *Yoshitsune Senbon Zakura.* (Photo: *Ennosuke no Kabuki Kōza.*)

(right) Figure 48. The backbend as seen in performance. Fox-Genkurō (Nakamura Tomijūrō V); Shizuka (Nakamura Jakuemon IV). (Photo: author's collection.)

3. A trap swallows the actor as he seems to disappear.

4. Very soon afterwards he pops up through an upstage trap, dressed completely in a white, furry animal costume signifying his total transformation into the fox. (The costume actually makes him look more like a sheepdog than a fox.) His human face and wig remain exposed, although his wig hints subtly at his animal-nature.

5. The fox trots rapidly along a narrow railing to suggest his agility. In fact, the railing is made wider than normal, though this is difficult to discern from the auditorium.

6. The fox seemingly disappears by jumping through a trick paper lantern at stage right.

7. The true Tadanobu appears in a remarkably quick change (about ten seconds), looking through a window at stage left. We can see the upper portion of his body but his wig and costume are those of the Tadanobu first seen at the opening of the scene.

8. The fox's shadow is thrown where that of the cherry tree, at left, should be.

9. The fox tumbles out of a false transom overhead at upstage center where he somersaults to the stage below.

10. Further emphasizing his magic powers, the fox sits astride the gilt knob of the railing post, which is made so that it can revolve rapidly.

11. The fox disappears through a trap.

12. He appears behind the cherry tree at left, rising mysteriously until almost in its branches. The actor is standing on a small elevator platform attached to the rear of the two-dimensional tree.

13. The fox appears downstage left (this is really a double, played by Ennosuke's brother, Ichikawa Danshirō [b. 1946]).

14. The fox comes up through a trap and rises on a pillar, using a device like that described in item 12.

15. He flies off over the *hanamichi.*

Enjaku III once described his performance in *Chibusa no Enoki*, in which he played three roles: Shōsuke, Shigenobu, and Miyoshi. In the murder scene at Tajima Bridge, he entered in the role of the servant, Shōsuke, accompanied by a murderous masterless samurai (*rōnin*). He and the *rōnin* hid in a thicket. A moment later, Enjaku re-entered as Shōsuke's master, Shigenobu, on the *hanamichi*. Shigenobu soon after was slain on top of the bridge and covered with a blanket. The actor slipped out of the blanket and reappeared from the thicket as Shōsuke, wrapped himself in a straw mat, and left on the *hanamichi*. Just then, Miyoshi (played by a double [*fukigae*]), covering his face with an umbrella, ran in on the *hanamichi*. As they passed each other, the mat was wrapped around Miyoshi and Enjaku changed into Miyoshi as the double, looking like Shōsuke, made his exit. A similar technique is used in the popular *Osome no Nanayaku*, in which a single actor plays seven roles.

Enjaku described a scene in *Chibusa no Enoki* taking place at a waterfall:

> I enter as Miyoshi and go into a hut, then change to Shōsuke and enter from the *hanamichi*. A double takes my place on the stage at the rock grouping there and I enter from the falls as the ghost of Shigenobu. When I disappear I change again to Shōsuke. Then a double takes over as Shōsuke as I change to Miyoshi, from Miyoshi to Shōsuke, and back and forth any number of times. At the final curtain I am Shōsuke and leave on the *hanamichi*; the spectators are now totally confused as to which is the real me and which the double. Actually, for a mere instant in the performance, everyone is a double. Meanwhile, I run to the *hanamichi*. The audience has no idea as to which is the genuine actor (quoted in Hattori 1969, 165-66).

Enjaku emphasized that it is clearly the intention of the performance that the audience realizes that one or more of the actors are doubles. Almost invariably the double does not show his face full front; he usually faces upstage. Although it is important to have a double who resembles the star, it is even better for him to have a grasp of the star's manner of movement and gesture. He must, therefore, be a skillful performer in his own right.

Obviously, the actors in such scenes wear trick costumes and wigs to effect their changes. In *Chibusa no Enoki* Enjaku wore a wig with a movable section representing hair grown in on the normally shaved crown. When he changed from Shōsuke to Miyoshi the hairy crown section was pulled forward from a special compartment at the rear of the wig. When changing back to Shōsuke, this part was pushed in, giving the impression or a fully shaved crown.

Ennosuke's 1975 revival of *Satomi Hakkenden*, which he rewrote, had a striking scene of *hayagawari*. The scene takes place at a hermitage where Kakutarō (Ennosuke) lives as a priest. He is visited by his wife, Hinaginu, but soon after is called away to his injured father, leaving Hinaginu alone. Although it seems that he has been carried off down the *hanamichi* in a palanquin, the actor actually slips off unseen into the wings at right.

Soon after, Kakutarō's father, Ikkaku (Ennosuke), appears. Ikkaku's body is actually possessed by the spirit of a magic cat. His entrance, therefore, seems magical as he slides through the upstage doors while standing still. This is done by the use of a small rolling platform called the *shamoji* (ladle), used in several other plays, including the popular old classic *Yanone*, when Soga Jūrō appears during his brother Gorō's dream. The evil cat proceeds to torture Hinaginu. His cat-nature is suddenly signified when his wig shoots up two sprouts of hair shaped like cat ears. To further emphasize this feline element, his costume is swiftly changed onstage to one with black animal spots on it. A double emerges from behind an upstage standing screen to substitute for the tortured Hinaginu, who is made to perform a number of acrobatic tricks as the cat tortures her. The cat stabs Hinaginu, but a silver globe bursts forth from her supposedly torn abdomen and knocks out the cat, who falls behind the screen. The audience is absolutely astonished when, a mere thirty seconds or less afterwards, Ennosuke comes running down the *hanamichi* changed completely into his former appearance as Kakutarō. One can clearly see the similarity of this business to that described by Enjaku for his performance in *Chibusa no Enoki.*

After Kakutarō is joined by his friend Genbachi, the cat (now played by a double) reappears from behind the screen. Kakutarō, overcome by the cat's power, falls behind the screen but soon re-emerges (played now by Ennosuke's double). Kakutarō faints while Genbachi battles the cat. Going behind the screen, the cat double is replaced by Ennosuke, now dressed in his cat costume. (There is a trick escape hatch in the wall upstage of the screen. The actors make good use of it as they go in and out making their quick changes.) The action itself is extremely rapid and the changes from role to role so swift as to be nearly impossible to follow. The "double" Kakutarō battles with the cat and, during the following action, one or the other exits behind the screen several times, with Ennosuke switching in a flash from one role to another. At one point both Kakutarō and the cat are played by doubles, a technique also used by Enjaku.

One of the most interesting varieties of quick-change technique is that called "floating door" (*toitawatashi*) or "revolving door" (*toitagaeshi*). Used in the famous ghost play *Yotsuya Kaidan*, this involves a wooden raindoor to either side of which the murderous Iemon has lashed one of his victims before sending the board floating down a canal. When the door is lifted from the water by Iemon, who has been fishing from the canal embankment, and placed against the embankment side facing the audience, one dead body—that of Iemon's wife, Oiwa—is seen. Turned around, the other body—the servant, Kohei, whose hands move feebly as he asks for medicine—comes into view. The same actor plays both corpses, a man and a woman. A specially built door allows this weird effect. Through another device, Kohei's body soon turns into a skeleton.

The door used to have costumed dummies on either side, and a head section with a cutout hole. The actor, standing inside the embankment behind the door, thrust his head through the hole, changing his facial appearance for each role. It is more usual nowadays for the actor to be attached to one side of the door, as Oiwa, and for him to get off and thrust his head through the hole when the door is reversed. A dummy is used only for Kohei. The door itself is affixed to a specific place on the set where it is revolved by means of a fulcrum. Kohei's hands are made to move by the actor's thrusting his hands through holes in the door. Oiwa's gruesome makeup, depicting a horribly deformed face, is easily removable as it is attached to a headpiece, which the actor can don or remove.

Figure 49. Yoemon (Danjūrō XII), above, and Kohei (left) and Oiwa (right)—both played by Nakamura Utaemon VI, during the *toitagaeshi* scene of *Yotsuya Kaidan*. (Photo: *Genshoku Kabuki Shōsai*.)

Kohei turns into a skeleton when a stage assistant pulls a special cord releasing the dummy's costume. At the same time, the head hole is closed up and, by means of a spring, a skull moves up into position from its storage place in the rib area. The change, though, seems instantaneous.[4]

Honmizu

The third major type of *keren*, the use of real water (*honmizu*), is said to have originated in an attempt to provide a cooling image for audiences attending *kabuki* in summer's sweltering heat. The water was either meant to represent a canal, river, lake, or pond, or it was used as realistically falling rain. Pieces which featured its use were called "water plays" (*mizumono*), whereas the art of acting in such works was "water art" (*mizugei*). Though the use of real water has become rare in modern theatres it was common in the past, especially in the Bunka-Bunsei period (1804-1829). Almost every ghost play of Tsuruya Nanboku IV seems to make use of water in its action. Elaborate technical arrangements were often necessitated by this practice.

Premodern theatres were built on earth foundations, not concrete as is now the case. A large wooden trough was built into the stage at the front whenever required by the script. Leakage or spills presented no problem as the earth soon soaked up the water. Sometimes, the trough was not confined to the stage alone but was continued all the way down the *hanamichi*. Productions of *Yotsuya Kaidan* often had the door with the two bodies lashed to it float in on the *hanamichi* from the rear of the theatre. Sometimes the ghost of Oiwa would fly over the trough and then be released in order to drop into the water, where she would disappear. Moreover, various Kamigata (or Kansai) region (Osaka/Kyoto) theatres had a permanent trough (*karaido*) built at the junction of the stage and *hanamichi*. One can still be seen in *kabuki's* oldest theatre, the recently restored Kanamaru-za in Kotohira, Shikoku.[5] Such devices certainly provided interesting effects not possible in today's modern theatres.

The major problem presented in staging "water plays" today is the concrete floor beneath the stage, which presents the possibility of flooding. Since the floor beneath the modern stage is usually quite low, the trough must be built on an elevator platform set below one of the large stage traps. The great weight of the water-filled trough on the elevator presents a serious technical problem, which is further compounded when an actor jumps into the water.[6]

Once, when Enjaku presented a rare revival of a water play, he encountered an almost insurmountable technical obstacle. Fear ran high that the vat constructed for the task would burst its seams. If the lift on which it was situated broke under the strain or if the vat itself broke the theatre would be inundated. Enjaku saw that he had to compromise. He agreed to use a nineteenth-century method according to which he jumped into an empty trap, conventionally disguised to look like water (a blue cloth was placed over the area). A number of mattresses were set under the trap to break his fall. To simulate the effect of real water splashing, two stagehands under the stage tossed buckets of water up onto the stage at the appropriate moment.[7]

Enjaku played the spirit of a carp. As part of the action he was suspended over the stage as if on a fishhook and twirled there dizzily. When the line was cut he fell into the "water." An apprentice stood in for the star at a late rehearsal before the idea of using real water was abandoned. After going through the business the apprentice told his master that the trick was too dangerous and should be canceled, which it was.

This effect of being dropped from midair into a vat of water used to be performed by Udanji II during the early part of this century. Udanji required at least seven feet of water for a safe fall. This posed a problem, however, as a battle that ensues in the water could not reasonably be performed at such a depth. Therefore, a flat, grill-like piece was placed on the bottom of the trough; when the fight began it was moved up into a fixed position at a shallower depth where the actors could stand on it without sinking.

(left) Figure 50. Ennosuke III performing a *koitsukami* scene. (Photo: *Ichikawa Ennosuke*.)

Figure 51. Edo-period illustration of *koitsukami* performed in a trough in front of the stage. (From *Shibai Kinmōzui* [1803].)

Water fight scenes are conventionally carried out between a giant carp, about eight feet long, represented by a realistic property-costume worn by two actors, and a heroic character. The technique is called *koitsukami* (grappling with a carp) and is a major kind of "water art." In the old days, the fight might proceed all the way down the length of the *hanamichi*. Dormant for many years, the technique has been revived by Ennosuke on a number of occasions, although real water is not generally used. In fact, Ennosuke's innovations have included the use of special lighting and a movable, pillar-like stand with a raised base on which he can lie while making swimming gestures to suggest that he is underwater. But real water has not been totally abandoned. Kataoka Gatō V (b. 1935) performed *koitsukami* in an August 1973 production at Kyoto's Minami-za which, according to a review (*Engekikai* 1973, 15), removed the first four rows of the orchestra so that a trough could be built there for the use of a carp. When the traditional water battle began, the spectators seated in the rows nearest the trough covered their heads with clear vinyl provided by the management, to protect themselves from getting drenched.

A *koitsukami* scene was often arranged so that, at the proper moment, the carp's mouth would open and an actor dressed as a youth would emerge playing the flute and fly away. Most unusual was the fact that the actor appeared completely dry although the carp was immersed in water. This strange effect was created by building a chimney-like waterproof housing under the water where the actor sat and waited for his entry. The apparatus, called a *kama* (cauldron), could not be seen by the audience. Its upper portion was expandable like an accordion and a lid sealed off its top. When the cue arrived, the top of the *kama* would suddenly expand to reach the surface of the water. The lid would open to either side and a *chūnori* attachment would be lowered from above and hooked onto the actor's harness ring. When his body emerged, the lid would shut, the spring recoil, and the *kama* once more sink into the water.

A number of plays employed water art combined with quick-change technique. The actor would be seen falling or jumping into the water on stage only to emerge, a few moments later, rising on the small *hanamichi* elevator (*suppon*) in a completely different costume and wig. One famous example occurs in *Tenjiku Tokubei*. In some cases the reappearance was in *chūnori* style: one famous actor did a play in which, following his immersion, a cloud appeared in the sky, split to right and left, and revealed him floating there dressed as a beautiful princess. The escape methodology may be understood by examining the illustration below. The lip of the stage is extended over the trough with a vertical section acting as a masking element blocking the actor's exit movements from the audience, seated to the left. The arrows show the route taken by the actor in escaping.

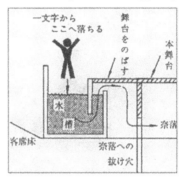

Figure 52. Diagram of escape methodology for water trick.

Miscellaneous *Keren*

All types of *keren* do not fit into the three established categories. Two are particularly interesting, though unclassifiable. The *hashibako* (chopstick box) technique gets its name from its resemblance to old-fashioned chopstick boxes with lids that slid in grooves. This device is used for a number of effects where a magical appearance is made by the actor's lying on his belly on a sliding board. The actor may appear through a lantern as in the "through-the-lantern technique (*chōchin nuke*). The lantern is burned up in a flash of fire, leaving only the framework exposed. The framework is made of metal, not the usual bamboo, and a portion of the lantern's paper is painted with a noncombustible substance. The actor slides through the burned-out aperture from behind the scenes, his timing in perfect accord with the man who does the burning. A thin rod with a handle rises in front of him and through the operation of this rod he can move eerily up and down. He emerges from the background as far as his feet in this ghostly trick. It is used in *Yotsuya Kaidan*, which has an abundance of these hair-raising effects.

One is the "revolving altar" (*butsudan gaeshi*). Chōbei falls under the spell of Oiwa's ghost and is pulled back by her power to the onstage house's Buddhist altar where Oiwa hovers weirdly. Directly behind this altar is a large, wheel-like device with cutout sections in it. Oiwa stands in one of these sections. When the wheel is tipped backwards the onstage actor can be pulled onto it from the stage and made to disappear through a trick wall.

Keren plays are among the biggest audience attractions in today's *kabuki*. Though the pall of intellectual disdain has long covered them, their ability to please has finally conquered even their most bitter critics. The number of such plays in the current repertoire is small but *kabuki* would do well to rescue more *keren* pieces from the shadows of oblivion to which they have been assigned. Ennosuke III has done wonders for these special effects, and, since the mid-1980s, has developed them even further in his spectacular "super-*kabuki*" productions, where they continue to evolve.

NOTES

This is a revised version of an article that first appeared in *Educational Theatre Journal* 28 (May 1976).

1. *Roppō* is a general term for a variety of bounding *hanamichi* exits, most of which are identified by a more specific name. Thus *kitsune roppō* suggests that the actor executes his leaping movements in a manner suggestive of a fox, while *tobi* ("flying") *roppō* means that the exit gives the impression of flying. The word *roppō* is usually written with the characters for "six directions," suggesting the actor's physical movements, but it is sometimes written as "six laws," which appears to have a Buddhist implication.

2. There are two important plays that are popularly known by this title, their more formal titles being *Kagamiyama Kokyō no Nishikie-e* (1782) and *Kagamiyama Gonichi no Iwafuji* (1860). The latter is referred to here.

3. See, for example, Ernst (1974), Scott (1999), Gunji (1969), Shaver (1966), and Leiter (1997) among others.

4. See this volume's "What Really Happens Backstage" for an illustration of how this effect worked in the nineteenth century.

5. See "The Kanamaru-za: Japan's Oldest *Kabuki* Theatre," in this volume. See also this volume's "What Really Happens Backstage: A Nineteenth-Century *Kabuki* Document," for illustrations of old-time water effects.

6. The popular play *Sukeroku* has long employed a scene in which the eponymous hero hides from his pursuers in a large vat of water set up on the stage as part of the environment. This use of water differs from the *keren* effects I am describing wherein the water is set into the stage and the effect created is that of a character situated in a natural body of water.

7. See this volume's "What Really Happens Backstage" for an illustration of this technique.

REFERENCES

Ernst, Earle. 1974. *The* Kabuki *Theatre*, 2d ed. rev. Honolulu: University of Hawaii Press. Originally published 1956.
Gunji, Masakatsu. 1969. *Kabuki,* trans. John Bester. Palo Alto and Tokyo: Kodansha, 1969.
Hattori Yukio, ed. 1969. "Natsu Kyōgen Han—Shin Okyōgen Gakuya Honsetsu." *Kabuki* 5. (Roundtable discussion.)
Ichikawa Ennosuke. 1984. *Ennosuke no Kabuki Kōza.* Tokyo: Shinchōsha.
Katsuo Shin'ichi, ed. 1970. *"Keren." Kabuki* 11. (Roundtable discussion.)
Leiter, Samuel L. 1997. *New* Kabuki *Encyclopedia: A Revised Adaptation of* Kabuki *Jiten.* Westport, Ct.: Greenwood.
Scott, A.C. 1999. *The* Kabuki *Theatre of Japan.* Mineola, N.Y.: Dover. Originally published 1955.
Shaver, Ruth. 1966. Kabuki *Costume.* Tokyo and Rutland, Vt.: Charles E. Tuttle.
Tomita Tetsunosuke. 1970. "Yoshitsune Senbon Zakura Saiken." *Kabuki* 9.

"What Really Happens Backstage":
A Nineteenth-Century *Kabuki* Document

In 1967 the Kokuritsu Gekijō (National Theatre of Japan) produced a facsimile version of *Okyōgen Gakuya no Honsetsu* (What Really Happens Backstage), a two-volume, four-part work published in Edo and written by Santei Shunba, with volume one (1858) illustrated by Baichōrō Kunisada and Ichieisai Yoshitsuya, and volume two (1859) by Ichiransai Kunitsuna. Despite its great value as a historical resource, this work had been barely known to the Japanese academic community, apart from one of its pictures being frequently reproduced after first appearing in Ihara Seiseien's [a.k.a. Ihara Toshirō] history of Edo-period theatre, *Kinsei Nihon Engeki Shi* (1913). The chief source of information concerning its contents was an entry in the six-volume encyclopedia *Engeki Hyakka Daijiten*, published by Waseda University (1961-1962). This entry contains several inaccuracies, such as the number of the book's volumes and its date of publication. *Kabuki* scholar Hattori Yukio, then of the Kokuritsu Gekijō—which was undertaking a project to reprint various forgotten texts—edited the material for publication. His task was complicated because its component parts had been scattered and it was impossible to find an entire well-preserved copy in one location. The work originally had been published in two pamphlet-size volumes, each divided into "upper" and "lower" sections, equivalent to parts 1 and 2. Copies of the respective parts, mostly intact, were eventually discovered in Tokyo's Hibiya Library, the Tsubouchi Memorial Theatre Museum Library at Waseda University, Tokyo University Library, and Osaka University Library. With the assistance of the Hibiya Library's Suzuki Shigezō, who also found pages missing from the available manuscripts, Hattori reassembled the book for reproduction.[1]

In the reprint, everything shown in the illustrations is numbered and listed with its corresponding page at the rear of the book. These listings are accompanied by the brief commentaries and labels accompanying the pictures in the original text. The original commentaries, in cursive brush strokes, are transcribed in the listings in easier-to-read modern characters. In many cases, as in the original, the commentary is no more than an identifying label. For the most part, the plays in which the techniques are used are not mentioned. The pictures show a number of things, such as scenic pieces (*ōdōgu*), properties (*kodōgu*), musical instruments (*narimono*), actors in rehearsal, and backstage workers facilitating stage tricks (*keren*).[2] In several cases the stage effect is first pictured as the audience sees it, while a succeeding picture shows how the trick was done.

There had been earlier illustrated guides to the workings of the *kabuki* theatre but none had exposed how *kabuki's* special effects worked. This book was exceptional in its breaking with the tradition according to which stage secrets must never be revealed to the public; just like a recent television series on magic acts, it laid bare the workings of what were then considered marvels of illusion. *Kabuki* had enjoyed visually deceiving and sexually titillating its audiences since its beginnings in the early seventeenth century, when its men often played women and vice versa. During *kabuki's* flowering in the Genroku era (1688-1704), stage trickery came into use, including pyrotechnical effects that allowed the spirit of a deceased character to emerge from flames into which prayers or love letters had been tossed. This fondness for spectacle was combined with *kabuki's* increasing emphasis on the dramatic power of transformation, perhaps stemming from widespread beliefs in supernatural powers operating beyond the realm of the empirical world. The theatre became a Pirandellian mindgame in which nothing could be trusted to be what it appeared—neither characters, costumes, props, environments, nor events. The *nō* theatre has also been an art of transformation, as seen in the many plays in which a living character who appears in the first half turns out to be a ghost or spirit in the second. But *kabuki* took this notion to unheard of extremes.

Dramaturgically, this often provided melodramatically effective scenes. For example, play after play exploited a convention in which a leading character of dignified status is forced to go underground, changing his name, appearance, and profession, as he searches for a missing heirloom. When he reveals his true persona (kept hidden from the audience as well as the other characters), he usually prefaces his remarks with "in reality" (*jitsu wa*), the name by which the device came to be known. Thus characters frequently had multiple personalities, rarely being who they seemed. In numerous other works, characters who appear to be inordinately wicked are revealed in a powerfully climactic scene to have been putting on an act because of some compelling need to disguise their virtuous selves. The moment of revelation was frequently accompanied by a sudden physical alteration of the character's makeup and costume, using *kabuki's* quick-change techniques (*hayagawari*). Furthermore, because of censorship, characters based on real life were typically given fictional names and their stories placed in the distant past. Audiences took pleasure in seeing how cleverly they had been dramatically transformed.

During the eighteenth century, advances in stage technology made the scenic world equally subject to transformation. Characters and sets could rise or sink magically on elevator traps and sets could revolve before the spectators' eyes to show new locales almost instantaneously. The stage became a world where anything was possible, where people could even fly or be changed into animals. The very stage boards could be replaced by water effects comparable to those of British nautical melodrama.

During the first third of the nineteenth century, Japan underwent considerable social and economic turmoil; the country was enveloped in what many writers have characterized as an aura of decadence. This was vividly expressed in the literature and art of the times, such as those works that exploited Japanese folk beliefs in (and fears of) spirits and ghosts. In the theatre, this atmosphere was best represented in the horror plays (*kaidanmono*) of Tsuruya Nanboku IV (1755-1829), who worked closely with the imaginative scenic technician Hasegawa Kanbei XI (1781-1841) to create an abundance of startling new effects: legless ghosts were suspended in midair, rose from water, or slid on their bellies through lanterns; bodies continued moving after being cut in half; people metamorphosed into skeletons; giant cats, frogs, and boa constrictors breathed fire; realistic rain fell in torrents; swords pierced characters' necks; sets changed in the twinkling of an eye; living heads rolled around in flaming wheels; buildings collapsed; and soon, as the century wore on, popular fascination with the means used to produce these effects became so strong that it was decided to abandon the secrecy surrounding them and to publish *Okyōgen Gakuya Honsetsu*. The present essay is the first non-Japanese account of this work, considered the prime source for knowledge of *kabuki* stage effects during the Edo period.

The book contains 150 pages, mostly illustrations, from which I have selected twenty-five for reproduction and commentary. The first dozen were originally published in *Theatre Survey* (1997). I have supplemented these here with an additional thirteen, which are placed following the original twelve. Fifteen (not counting illustrations that demonstrate the same illusion from a backstage perspective) of them picture actor-centered effects, showing such things as how to create the illusion of drowning, how to be a convincingly haunting ghost, how to rise up a waterfall, or how to be rapidly transmogrified from one role to another. Five display scenic techniques, including the collapse of a house, the sudden alteration of a backdrop, and the use of wave rollers. The remainder demonstrate trick props and the like.

Rather than use the letters or numbers that have been inserted in several of the pictures, I have made clear the parts of the illustrations, or the words they contain, by referring to them in expressions like "left side, bottom," and so on. I have done this, however, only in selective cases, where I thought it would be helpful. The first illustration (figure 53) contains no written explanation in the original, so I have provided my own. All comments in quotation marks are my translations of the original explanations. I have followed a different approach in the supplemental pictures, using a mixture of my own comments and a paraphrase of the original Japanese. Technical terms have been more or less literally translated. Some of the devices shown are no longer seen, and it is difficult to determine precisely how they would have been used.

These techniques are all native to Japan and, while they often resemble methods then in use in the European theatre, there is no strong evidence of intercultural influence, in either direction. Japan's contacts with the West from the 1630s to the 1850s were very restricted. Some information leaked out and in through Dutch traders, but how much of that information, if any, had an impact on the theatre is yet to be determined.

Figure 53: A stage trap (*seri*) being used without its elevator mechanism. Such openings are called *kiriana* ("cut holes"). A character is seen falling into the trap on a stage dressed to look like water. Ground rows of waves are set in front of the trap to disguise it. Below the stage is a group of stagehands holding a blanket ready to catch the actor, while another stagehand uses a fan to toss pieces of paper upwards, thereby suggesting splashing foam. Modern versions of this method sometimes have had the stagehands splash water from buckets. The stagehand at the bottom left in the illustra-

tion is dressed in a hood and robe designed to blend in with the waves, presumably because he is onstage at some point during the action. His blue costume (*mizugo* ["water robe"] or *namigo* ["wave robe"]), meant as camouflage, is still seen in *kabuki*, although today it is more likely to be without the wave pattern.

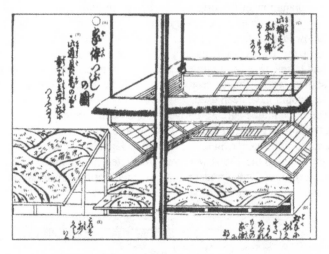

Figure 54: "Illustration of *yatai tsubushi*" [literally, 'room crushing']. The picture shows a scenic change that occurs during the choreographed fight scene (*tachimawari*) in *Kuzunoha*. The scene changes from an interior to an exterior before the audience's eyes. Upper part, right side: "These ropes are covered in black cotton." Lower corner, right side: "An embankment when flipped forward and, when flipped back, a house again." When the fringed flat (*harimono*) at the lower part of the interior (*yatai*) is flipped over (*uchigaeshi*), as seen along the lower edge at center and right, the wall at the left, an exterior representing a river embankment (*dote*), is revealed. When the scene ends, the process is reversed and the house returns. Bottom, left side: "This is called *uchigaeshi* ['overturned']." Today, flats that flip from top to bottom are called *patangaeshi* (*patan*=with a snap or bang, *gaeshi*=change, reverse). When flats open to the side, as in a book, the term used is *aorigaeshi* ("flap change"). There may be two, three, or even more surfaces. This method is used mostly in quick-change dances (*hengemono*). There was a very similar British scenic transformation device, the "Falling Flap" method, described in an 1803 account as "those double flat scenes, which are also used to produce instantaneous changes. The whole scene being covered with pieces of canvas, framed and moving upon hinges, one side [of each of these hinged flaps] is painted to represent a certain scene, and the other to represent one totally different" (unidentified source quoted in

Southern 1957, 957). Apparently, the flaps were raised and showed their obverse sides to the spectators; they fell when a catch was removed, revealing their other side, thereby presenting a new picture.

Figure 55: "A scenic vista [*tōmi*] overturned [*uchigaeshi*]." Lower part, right side: "Shrubbery overturned by the *dengaku* method." The landscape of trees and fields comes into view via the *dengaku* (also *dengakugaeshi*) technique, named after a popular bean curd food served on a skewer. *Dengaku* ("field music") also is the name of a theatre form that once rivaled the *nō* and exists today as a folk performing art. Two flat boards at either side of the platform are joined by a horizontal pole that runs through a thick scenic backdrop, which is made to revolve on the pole. The front of the platform, presently showing an interior facade, is simultaneously converted to an exterior appearance when a string, attached to pegs set in loops, is sharply yanked. *Dengaku*, a technique that originated in the puppet theatre in 1789, can also employ a vertical shaft, like the Greek *periaktoi*. In addition to changing the scene, such a method can be used by magical characters to appear and disappear through walls.

Figure 56 (next page): "Illustration of *dōgu nagashi* ['scenery flowing'] in *Imoseyama*." An elaborate scene in *Imoseyama Onna Teikin*, a Romeo and Juliet-like drama, in which two seemingly hostile families live on opposite sides of the Yoshino River, represented by a perspective effect in which the water seems to rush toward the spectators. After a tragic reconciliation, the lady on the left is sending the head of her daughter—placed in a ceremonial case—across the river to the household of the daughter's lover on the other side.

Figure 57 (below): "Illustration of the same scene from the rear. The former picture shows a cutout in the water cloth over a stage trap in which a stage-hand dressed in a wave costume (*namigo*) passes the head from one side to the other. As the present picture shows, to represent the Tani River, a *takiguruma* ('waterfalls wheel') has been set up, and it is revolved from behind." This device, of course, is remarkably similar to one then being used for the same effect in Europe. It can still be seen in use at the court theatre of Drottningholm, Sweden.

Figure 58: This is probably the book's best-known illustration (and the first to be reproduced in another work). It explains the famous *toitagaeshi* quick change used in the embankment scene of Nanboku IV's great ghost play, *Yotsuya Kaidan*. The scene is shown from upstage, behind the embankment, whose internal structure (and the hidden step unit leading to its top), is visible behind the actor (right) and stage assistant, hiding in its shadows. In a previous scene two murders have occurred, that of the cruelly disfigured wife, Oiwa, and that of the manservant, Kohei. (See figure 49 in the previous chapter.)

Their corpses have been lashed to either side of a rain door, and then set adrift down a river. In the present scene, the door floats into view and comes to rest against the embankment. During the eerie scene, both Oiwa and Kohei appear on the door. The same actor plays both corpses. This door—seen at the left—is constructed with a head-size hole, where the corpse's head is placed. There is a corresponding hole in the face of the embankment, visible in the picture. A headless dummy represents the bodies. When the door is leaned against the embankment, the actor inside the embankment puts his head through the hole to reveal Oiwa. By means of a rapid makeup change, shown in progress in the picture, the same actor appears as Kohei when the door is flipped around. He also thrusts his hands through to ask feebly for medicine. The original description reads: "The embankment scene. The embankment uses hemp palm leaves for grass.

They should, though, be finely torn. The *toitagaeshi* [is seen] in this scene. A dummy is placed on both sides of this door, and a hole is cut in it big enough for a head to poke through. Doing this allows for the quick change of Oiwa and Kohei." Written on the circle into which the actor will place his face are the words, "This hole is hidden by grass."

Figure 59 (next page): "*Niwatori musume* ['chicken girl']. As shown in the illustration, there is a central shaft in the stone lantern, with a thick rope coiled at least one hundred times around it, and this should be yanked via a pulley. However, there should be scenic pieces to hide the trick mechanism. A [prop] chicken should be affixed to a long pole [*sashigane*] and its wings made to flap via a string. A fan should be flapped rhythmically to simulate the sound of flapping wings." The technique is used in *Sanshō Dayū*, in which a character has a mysterious affliction that turns her into a fowl. The illustration reveals a device for the actor to display some bizarre birdlike behavior when the pulley system causes him to spin wildly. The bamboo *sashigane* pole manipulated by a stagehand is one of *kabuki's* most common devices, and is often used to introduce birds, butterflies, and the like.

Figure 60: "Someone wearing an official or foreign dignitary's costume is changed into bones by donning a skeleton costume sewn together by the

stagehands, with the head part separate and placed at the rear. When the outer costume is whisked away by the *hikinuki* trick the mask is instantly pulled forward over the head to cover it. In other words, as in the illustration." The *hikinuki* technique, by which an exterior costume is swiftly dismantled before the audience's eyes by stagehands to reveal another one underneath, is one of *kabuki's* best-known tricks and is described in the previous chapter. In this picture the actor's original costume is seen dangling from his left arm, while he now appears in the guise of a skeleton, although his mask, attached to the back of his costume, is not yet fully in place. An interesting sidelight on this picture is that it shows the stagehands in costumes other than the traditionally black ones that provide one of the names they now go by (*kurogo*). Many other Edo-period pictures show stage-hands dressed thus, suggesting that, unlike today, they did not invariably appear in black.

Figure 61: "The appearance of a ghost from out of the water." The actor is standing on a plank: "This plank is used as a crossover to the stage. Moreover, after the ghost appears it is removed." He is held in place by a vertical shaft: "This shaft [not visible] is secured to the actor through his sash as he rises. When appropriate, it descends." The picture tells us: "The water is about four feet deep." At the end of the plank on which the actor is standing are the words: "This elevator-post rises to the water level" and nearby it says, "The elevator-post is hidden by water lilies. Water laps against this board. If you pass under it you come to beneath the stage." We are told of the rectangular water area to the left of center: "This water basin [*mizubune*] is covered with a lid so that it cannot be seen." On the flooring adjacent to this basin at the left, it says, "There is a water basin under here, too." Elsewhere, we learn that "The actor who appears from under the water enters it via an opening in the musicians' room [*geza*], passes under the backboard against which the water is lapping, is hidden by the water lilies, rises into view on the elevator shaft as he breathes in air, while a drum beats out the *dorodoro* sound associated with ghosts, and, as he seems to weep, he wipes away the water from his nose and eyes, crosses the plank to the stage, and performs in an appropriate fashion." And at the extreme left, upper part, it says: "In this corner of the musicians' room, there is a passageway leading to the water basin. It is only about two feet, four or five inches square." There used to be a well-like opening called the *karaido* ("empty well") at the stage left side of the junction with the stage of the *hanamichi* runway. The *hanamichi* segment nearest the stage can be seen in the lower left corner. The front of the stage is at the extreme right, where a footlight bracket is affixed to it. The *karaido* was associated with theatres in the Kamigata (or Kansai) area (Osaka/ Kyoto) and may still be seen at Japan's oldest *ka-*

buki theatre, described later in this book in "The Kanamaru-za." The *karaido* could be flooded when necessary, as here. When filled with mud for certain scenes it was the *dorobune* ("mud basin") and when used with water it was, as noted above, the *mizubune*.

Figure 62: "Illustration of a horizontal flying [*chūnori*] effect." (A) "There is a loop attached here so that it can be hooked to a narrow, hanging rod. In the illustration, [the actor] rides along a constructed unit with a vertical shaft set into his sash to hold him steady as four or five men pull a rope affixed to a pulley system." (C) "They pull him along to the appropriate spot, and a hooked pole descends from above, connecting with the loop on his

collar. The mechanism below enabling this effect is hidden with a cloud curtain." Although the book adds nothing further, it is assumed that the actor may now "fly" without benefit of the platform. The earlier part of the trick is very similar to the old English "Ghost Glide" method.

Figure 63: "This ghost emerges from a box used to hold a shamisen and rises about three feet on an elevator shaft to loom over a nearby mosquito netting. The shaft is hidden by the ghost's costume He leans forward over the netting, grasping a cross brace as his elevator shaft descends. He makes an upside down entrance into the mosquito netting through a secret hole cut in its roof while a stage hand simultaneously removes the cross brace, as in the picture." In the upper portion, left, it says: "The opening in the mosquito net's roof through which the ghost disappears." In the lower portion, center, are the words: "The legs [of the cross brace] are fitted into the stage floor." A note in the lower right corner adds, "When the ghost grasps the cross brace within the netting, the elevator shaft is instantly withdrawn." *Kabuki* actors were often skilled acrobats and were able to perform tricks like this without harm.

Figure 64: "Illustration of the trap mechanism." This is the machinery under the stage for raising the shaft in the previous picture.

Supplementary Illustrations

The following pictures are supplements to those that appeared when this essay originally was published.

Figure 65: A scene in *Kuzunoha* where the main character, a magical fox who has been masquerading as a woman, is rapidly transformed back into her animal form. The picture shows a small, hinged opening having been cut in the stage floor so that, at the proper moment, the actor can turn away, stoop down, and take the mask from a stagehand in the basement. There is no need for the actor to use his hands because the mask has a protrusion he grips between his teeth, allowing for an instant transformation. When the mask is no longer needed, it is disposed of through the same opening.

Figure 66: An actor standing in a scenic waterfall and effortlessly going either up or down. His clogs rest on small wooden platforms. To his side is a vertical, rocky crag that hides him until he rises into view. The audience, then, is probably somewhat to the left. The effect is created by men beneath the stage manipulating a shaft attached to pulleys that allow it to go up and down through a hole in the stage floor. A hook-like piece of metal affixed to the shaft is inserted in the rear of the

actor's sash to secure him in his place. The waterfall and crag are at the left, where the actor-less shaft and steps are clearly seen. This effect was used in one of the several plays about a bandit named Jiraiya, who had magical powers. Other Jiraiya play effects are described in subsequent illustrations.

Figure 67: A number of other effects used in Jiraiya plays. At the right is a group of vertically positioned snakes made to move by pulling a number of strings seen near their nether ends, behind an arrangement of flowers. A spotted waistband (*shigoki*) affixed to the end of a *sashigane* pole is at the bottom, center, the thin black pole being on the right. Three or four hooks are fixed to the bottom of the large snake head at right center. It works in conjunction with the spotted waistband, which seems to turn into a snake: while the snake's head and neck remain hidden, a stagehand manipulates the *sashigane* so that the waistband makes snake-like movements; when one of the hooks catches on to the waistband, the *sashigane* is detached and the head is now manipulated as if the waistband were its body. Two spider techniques are depicted on the left page, but are unexplained.

Figure 68 (next page): Some more Jiraiya devices. At right, a trick scroll whose picture panel has two layers. The outer one, seen here partially obscured at the top, can be lifted instantaneously to reveal a different picture underneath, thereby creating the effect of a sudden transformation. At right center is a pot that spews forth money (oblong gold coins), with its interior exposed. Strings are attached to a small internal pot so that when they are pulled the money pours out. At left, a way to simultaneously extinguish many votive flames set up on a table before a wall. The wick in each oil lamp is attached to a white cotton thread, all of these being threaded through holes in the wall so that when the threads, joined together 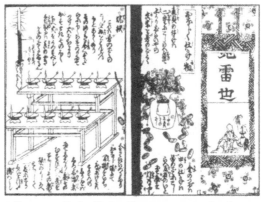 on the other side of the wall, are pulled, all the flames go out. At the extreme left, a red-hot poker effect. The top half of the poker is painted red and filled with many small slivers of tinder set into it. When the poker is removed from a brazier, the tinder burns. Seen from afar, the smoking prop looks red hot. The lower half of the rod is painted red.

Figure 69: The *renribiki* ("entwined pulling") convention whereby a person trying to escape from a spirit is prevented from making progress, and is pulled back magnetically by the spirit's weird hand movements, suggested in the illustration. Ghosts are often shown suspended from the collar in midair, their lower half without legs—Japanese ghosts have no legs—so that the kimono seems to fade into a trailing wisp of cloth. The device for raising the ghost (and moving him from side to side) is shown here. It is based on the very similar Japanese method of using a stone to counterbalance a pail on a long horizontal beam supported near its center on a vertical pillar, in order to dip the pail into a deep well. Such non-theatrical contriv-

ances are called *hanetsurube* ("well sweep"), by which this technique is also known. At the extreme left is a *sashidashi* with its phosphorescent flame suggesting the presence of a soul.

Figure 70: Among *kabuki's* more bizarre conventions, no longer seen, are the *tobi kubi* ("flying head") and *kasha kubi* ("wheel of fire head"). The *tobi kubi*, seen at the top, left center, employs a folding screen covered by a black cloth. The actor, dressed entirely in black, sits on a platform that moves from one side to the other, with his head thrust over the screen, giving the impression of a living head moving under its own volition. More unusual is the *kasha kubi*, left, which presents the illusion of a flaming wheel—in which a living head is encased—rolling across the stage.

Figure 71: The secrets of the *kasha kubi* trick revealed. The wheel is a sturdily built contraption, resembling a Japanese spinning wheel, with ropes attached for a stagehand to grab when turning it. Inside the wheel is a hole for the actor's face, as well as grips for the actor to hold on to. The wheel is saturated with the phosphorescent *shōchū* mixture, so that it emits green-blue flames as it revolves. The actor, all in black, sits inside the wheel in a cross-legged position. A note recommends that, because of the flames, it is best if the actor's hair not be too long.

Figure 72: The secrets of the *tobi kubi* trick revealed. An elevator (*seriage*) platform (*tsukitoi*) is set up behind the black screen. The platform is split down the middle by a channel or groove in which rides a circular seat (*tsukidai*) pushed from one side to the other by a stagehand using the extension seen at the left. The table has a center support not shown because of the break between the picture's halves. The actor—whose outline is barely visible—sits on the seat holding on to two vertical grips and with his head sticking out just above the screen. At lower right, the actor as he looks when sitting on his seat. At left, halfway up, the side-moving seat, shown outside of the platform. The actor sits on a chevron-shaped base, which fits into the channel. The distance between the *tsukitoi* platform and the floor is about two feet. At right, a descending elevator shaft (*seriage*). At extreme left, a descending elevator shaft. Apparently, the actor—visible on the stage left side of the screen—rose on the *seriage* seat, moved onto the *tsukidai*, was pushed across the screen, shifted to the *serisage* seat, and then descended.

Figure 73: A ghost appears through a street lantern. Because the overhead area is filled with tree branches, the slender pole attached to the actor from the grid can barely be seen, as is appropriate. Soul-fires burning at the ends of *sashidashi* are visible at the left.

Figure 74: The technique for creating the effect in the previous picture. The actor (not shown) lies prone in a box attached to a plank pushed on through the lantern by a stagehand. The steps to the plank are apparent. When the actor emerges, a thin pole descends and is attached to his collar. This allows a stagehand on the grid to quietly raise and lower the actor, which, given the actor's position, would be quite difficult to otherwise achieve. The plank is pushed forward approximately one foot. The box moves forward with the actor. Because the plank covers the light in the lantern when it is pushed forward, it becomes rather dark while the ghost is thrust in that direction, but when the ghost withdraws the flame lights up again.

Figure 75: A method of making a small hill appear instantly on the *hanamichi* or stage. The hill is constructed of two pie-shaped segments that are hinged together and can be swung from a hidden position to a visible one at a moment's notice. The hill has steps built into it for the actors' freedom of movement. Box at upper left: the hill, beneath a stage opening, waiting to be used. Box at upper right: the hill as it looks in use. At bottom, the stagehands can be seen beneath the stage pushing the hill into place. Protruding from the right side of the hill in the upper portion is one of the two small clips, used to connect the two sections. These clips attach to the latches on the opposite side. When the hill is in position, a peg is placed in the hole (and three others like it) seen in the center of the horizontal floorboard on the right side of the picture. This firmly secures the unit.

Figure 76: This appears to be the legendary bandit Ishikawa Goemon, subject of many plays, flying through the air (*chūnori*) with a wicker basket (*tsuzura*) on his back. The actor, wearing a brace attached to a heavy wire, is pulled from the stage level to a higher altitude and flies in a straight line. There are other techniques using overhead tracks for more convoluted flying paths. A photograph of this *tsuzura nuke* technique in use today can be seen in the previous chapter's figures 43-44.

Figure 77: A character who has been sliced in half during a fight. He stands in a cutout section of a staircase.

NOTES

1. I am indebted for this background to the commentary in Hattori (1967, 151-54).

2. For more information on the various trick effects mentioned in this chapter, see "*Keren*: Spectacle and Trickery on the *Kabuki* Stage" in this volume.

REFERENCES

Southern, Richard. 1957. "Trickwork on the English Stage." In *Oxford Companion to the Theatre*, ed Phyllis Hartnoll. 2d ed. London: Oxford University Press.

Hattori Yukio, ed. 1967. *Okyōgen Gakuya no Honsetsu, Kabuki no Bunken*. Vol. 2. Tokyo: Kokuritsu Gekijō.

Beautiful Cruelty:
Suicide, Murder, Torture, and Combat in
Kabuki

Kabuki, as Donald Keene observes (1964, 332-351), is a harmonious blend of realism, as we know it on the representational Western stage, and highly abstract stylization. The eclectic nature of *kabuki* permits the plays of its repertoire to vary widely, one from the other, in their conventional production styles. Some plays are rather realistic, in the Western sense, while others are extremely unrealistic and exaggerated, and still others may differ markedly from scene to scene, fantasy following hard upon the heels of naturalism, and vice-versa.

This mixture of realism and theatricality is used to express a wide range of dramatic scenes, not the least powerful of which depict suicide, murder, torture, humiliation, bullying, and combat. One or more of these appeared in practically every *kabuki* play (or the puppet plays from which so many *kabuki* dramas are derived), although those parts of the plays that survive do not necessarily reflect this. When such events are enacted, it is in a way that reveals the action's inherent cruelty while also serving visually and aurally to beautify the horror. Many of us have watched the scariest scenes in fright films by peeking at them through the fingers covering our eyes, wanting to experience shudders of fear but afraid that things may get too difficult to bear. Remember, for example, Laurence Olivier drilling into Dustin Hoffman's teeth in *Marathon Man*? These films are often more concerned with increasing our heartbeat than with eliciting aesthetic appreciation. In *kabuki*, beauty and cruelty go hand in hand and, no matter how intense, pain and fear are never presented purely for their own sakes. *Kabuki* star Bandō Mitsugorō VIII (1906-75) observed that whenever *kabuki* seems preoccupied with cruelty, the fault lies with particular actors, not with *kabuki* itself, which, over the centuries, has created conventions to prevent such a fixation (Bandō 1974, 21; see also Gunji 1972). This fascination with making horror beautiful has been given a name, *zankoku no bi*, or the aesthetics of cruelty.

The violence and cruelty that remain in today's *kabuki* are more restrained and infrequent than in the premodern period. During Meiji, the *kabuki* reform movement wished to remove those things that might be considered inappropriate for a nation attempting to catch up with the standards of Western civilization. Among things on the discard list were plays of cruelty; had the reformers succeeded, *kabuki* would have become an anemic version of itself. Still, various modern and Western influences continued to affect *kabuki* and scenes of mental and physical suffering became less frequent or were modified, the use of stage blood was decreased, staging methods were altered to make the action seem less vicious, and some plays simply dropped out of the repertory. However, enough of the old-time violence and cruelty survived so that one can still witness, even if in smaller and more infrequent doses, what so worried the Meiji reformers.

This chapter looks at a number of ways in which *kabuki* cruelty is manifested. Although wide-ranging it stops short of being comprehensive, and only selected examples are used. It does not look at all instances of physical or psychological suffering, nor does it examine various other manifestations of *kabuki* terror, from rape to ghostly bedevilment, a subject worthy of a study of its own. It is subdivided into five principal subsections. One deals with blood, decapitation, and dismemberment, the others with suicide, murder, torture, and combat, although several of these clearly overlap.

Suicide

Kabuki deaths usually occur after some act of violence such as murder or suicide. The feudal society that produced *kabuki* was a pressure cooker that often drove people to kill themselves when they could not abide by strict ethical standards. Such suicides—which the government tried to control through very strict laws—became a stock-in-trade of *kabuki* dramaturgy, which time and again turned to self-destruction as a character's response to impossible demands. Playwrights depict two principal types of suicide (*jigai*), those committed by a pair of lovers, which use various fatal measures from drowning to self-stabbing to hanging, or those committed by a single individual, which typically involves some form of disembowelment (*seppuku*). Double suicide (*shinjū*) is common to the genre of domestic dramas of everyday life (*sewamono*), first popularized by Chikamatsu Monzaemon (1653-1724) in his puppet plays and later adopted by *kabuki*. These include *Sonezaki Shinjū* (1703), *Shinjū Ten no Amijima* (1720), *Shinjū Yoi Gōshin* (1722), and many others. Dramatized double suicides, themselves invariably based on real-life cases, were the impetus for many additional real-life copycats—so many, in fact that the government banned such plays in the 1720s.

The suicidal couple normally consists of a young married man, of weak moral character, and his courtesan or geisha mistress. Unable to reconcile their human feelings (*ninjō*) with their duty (*giri*) to family and society, they choose suicide as the most effective alternative. As Buddhists, they frequently believe that they will find a happier existence in the next world, where they can share paradise together. A lyrical dance-mime, the *michiyuki*, often precedes the suicide scene. Played with bittersweet pathos, it shows the state of mind of the lovers as they journey to their deaths. The suicide itself is often grotesquely beautiful—the man usually kills the woman before taking his own life—and the actors must evince the necessary elements of somberness and the doomed unfortunates' hope for a future life.

Now and then, the suicides go awry and the participants survive attempted drowning, each unaware that the other is alive until circumstances bring them together. One version of this pattern is visible in Tsuruya Nanboku IV's (1755-1829) *Sakura-hime* (1817), which begins with an attempted double suicide when homosexual lovers, a priest and his acolyte, attempt to drown themselves, but only one—the delicate young acolyte—leaps into the water. He is reborn, however, as a beautiful princess and, years later, meets his lover, now an important priest, the clue to their former relationship being a memento that the princess has held clutched in her fist since birth.

Figure 78. Izayoi (Sawamura Sōjūrō VII) and Seishin (Ichimura Uzaemon XV) prepare to die in *Izayoi Seishin*. (Photo: *Jūgosei Ichimura Uzaemon*.)

This type of pattern suggests the power of fate in human affairs, a concern that dominated not only many of Nanboku's plays, but those of his successor, Kawatake Mokuami (1816-1893), who wrote so many dramas of this nature that they formed a subgenre called *inga mono* or "fate dramas." The pattern can be seen, for example, in Mokuami's *Izayoi Seishin* (1859), where the hapless lovers, Izayoi and Seishin, jump into the Inase River, yet both survive and take up separate lives until fate once more reunites them. These scenes always take place at night, with evocative music playing and lonely-sounding temple gongs periodically being beaten in the background. The poetic feeling of Izayoi and Seishin's attempt is suggested in Frank Motofuji's translation. Notice the use of the highly conventionalized "pass-along" dialogue (*watari zerifu*) in which the same speech is divided between the two characters, and the presence of the narrator, who sings an ethereally beautiful accompaniment from a musicians' platform visible at stage right.

> SEISHIN *(in despair)*: An evil karma prevents our union in this world.
> IZAYOI: We have made up our minds to die.
> SEISHIN: Before we run into the searchers from the quarter . . .
> IZAYOI: . . . let us leap hand in hand into the river . . .
> SEISHIN: . . . in a love suicide that will be a scandal . . .
> IZAYOI: . . . for tomorrow we will be the gossip of the world.
> SEISHIN: When he hears that gossip . . .
> IZAYOI: . . . how grieved father will be.
> SEISHIN: Think of that, too, as having been foreordained.
> IZAYOI: . . . father, and our unfilial act of dying before you . . .
> SEISHIN: . . . will you forgive?
> NARRATOR: They look toward the west, and the hands they press in supplication freeze. They leap into the icy river and notoriety as lovers separated not even by death seems to be theirs (Motofuji 1966, 48-49).

While attempts at killing oneself (or others) by drowning do not always succeed in *kabuki*, *seppuku*—or *harakiri*—always does. *Seppuku* is written with Chinese characters for "cutting belly," while *harakiri* reverses the same characters to read "belly cutting." It was a form of death technically permitted only to samurai, was considered an honorable way to die, and when commanded as a method of execution was carried out with many ritualistic touches. However, *seppuku*—usually without the attendant ritual procedures—is also the suicide of choice for characters who find that circumstances demand their death, and there are numerous historical incidents dating to the early middle ages in which real people thus ended their existences.

The Edo period, when feudalism was at its height, was an age in which self-chosen *seppuku* was particularly common. The military government had a hard time halting the practice, especially when it was exercised as an act of *junshi*, killing oneself to follow one's master in death. This latter was eventually ended in the late seventeenth century and does not appear in any surviving *kabuki* or puppet play. Nor does *kanshi*, committing *seppuku* to admonish or caution one's superior. *Kanshi* appears to have been the motive for the 1970 *seppuku* of writer Mishima Yukio, who sought to bring national attention to his conservative political ideas. *Munen-bara*, in which one disembowels oneself to express anger or resentment toward someone else, is also not a *kabuki* device. The form of *seppuku* that constantly reappears in *kabuki*—and was quite frequent during the Edo era—is *sokotsu-shi*, expiatory *seppuku*, in which the individual kills himself for some breach of his responsibilities. The term seems to be applicable whether the *seppuku* is ordered by a superior or imposed by the one doing the deed.

Enya Hangan's *seppuku* in Act IV of *Chūshingura* (1748) represents the only surviving example of a dramaturgical suicide ordered as an act of execution (others are reported by dialogue or narrative), but, for all its ritualism, its performance does not accurately mirror a real-life execution by disembowelment by command. Much as *kabuki* was frequently a realistic reflection of contemporary practices, theatrical needs took precedence over literal replication. Hangan's *seppuku*, while lengthy, slow, and very specific in its ritualistic details, would take far longer and involve many more procedures if it were enacted precisely in the fashion described by early Meiji period eyewitness A. B. Mitford (Mitford 1966; see also Seward 1968). Still, Hangan's suicide is the only *kabuki* suicide that attempts to produce anything like the kind of ceremony and atmosphere associated with the authentic kind. It is said to be have been retained because of its dramatic centrality to the events that follow. This makes sense since *Chūshingura* is one of the few plays that still regularly receive full-length productions.

The scene incorporates a very specific sequence of ritualistic actions, during which the actor sits on his knees on a double layer of *tatami* matting over which a white cloth has been spread and at each corner of which is a branch of anise. Hangan, who first keeps his back to the audience (during which he paints blue makeup over his red lips), turns around and removes his vest-like upper garment (*kataginu*), raises a ceremonial wooden stand holding the dagger to his head, and wraps the dagger in paper, so that only the point protrudes. He then mimes pulling the blade across his abdomen from left to right; at the right side he gives a quick upward jerk to the sword. Shortly before he dies, his retainer Yuranosuke, for whom he has been waiting, arrives and Hangan hints to him that he must seek revenge. Finally, Hangan, so weak that he must grasp his right wrist with his left to keep his hand steady, cuts his own jugular vein and falls forward, being extremely careful about the angle at which his upper body lands. There follows a funeral ceremony replete with the ritual burning of incense.

Actually, apart from the other freedoms it takes, little of this accords with the historical suicide that inspired the action. In the first place, the drama's scene occurs within a palace room, while the suicide of Lord Asano (dramatized as Enya Hangan), was enacted in the palace garden, which was then considered an unusual setting for a daimyo's death and which Asano considered unworthy, although he kept his peace about it. In most such formal *seppuku* situations, an assistant or second (*kaishaku*) was assigned to decapitate the victim the moment the sword was inserted in the belly, thus limiting the amount of pain actually suffered. And thus did Lord Asano meet his end, the *kaishaku's* sword, in fact, removing his head before Asano's dirk even touched his skin. The play does not depict the eventual suicides of Asano's loyal retainers, who avenged his death, but their noble vendetta was honored by their being decapitated the moment they reached forward to pick up their suicide blades. Mishima Yukio employed a *kaishaku* for his own self-immolation.

Figure 79. Hangan (Onoe Baikō VII) hints to Yuranosuke (Danjūrō XI) that he must seek revenge. (Photo: *Engekikai* [1966].)

Because of the esteem in which Japanese audiences held the participants in the historical event on which the play is based, it was traditional during the Edo period for the death of Hangan to be performed as if it were really happening and as if the audience was present to both witness and mourn his death. Although *kabuki* audiences were known for their volubility and interaction with the actors, as well as their proclivity for eating and drinking during performances, for this scene—and this scene only—audiences remained absolutely silent, taking neither food nor drink, and not entering or leaving the auditorium until the scene was over. In a sense, such audience behavior suggests the sacred atmosphere surrounding scenes of Christ's Passion as experienced in Western medieval drama; indeed, Hangan may be said to have had—in a secular sense—a Christ-like aura for the Japanese, who could not get enough of this play and countless others that recreated (and still do) the story of the forty-seven *rōnin* who avenged his death. Thus the presentation of Hangan's *seppuku* must be played with an exquisite sensitivity to the formalities embracing it, leading to a stage suicide that is truly a work of theatrical art. The sense of formality is heightened by not a hint of blood being present, despite the whiteness of Hangan's robes and the mats on which he sits. Moreover, unlike most other scenes of *kabuki* death, it is played in relative silence, with only the barest minimum of musical accompaniment, provided by sparsely distributed shamisen chords and *gidayū* narrative, which only intensifies at the moment of the blade's insertion.

Figure 80. Kanpei's (Ichimura Uzaemon XV) *seppuku*. (Photo: *Jūgosei Ichimura Uzaemon Butai Shashin Shū*.)

In contrast to Hangan's *seppuku* is that shown later in the same play, in Act VI, when Kanpei takes his own life in penance for not being at Lord Hangan's side when his presence might have prevented the act that led to Hangan's suicide. It is one of several *kabuki* suicides caused by regret (*kaikon*) for falling down in one's duty to a superior, among them Sakuramaru's in *Sugawara* (1746), by the same authors who wrote *Chūshingura*. In fact, Sakuramaru was also spending time with a young woman friend when he should have been attending to more serious duties. Kanpei's demise contrasts vividly with that of Hangan by being set in a humble, rather naturalistically depicted farmhouse, and its enactment lacks all refinement. Although he employs such conventionalized touches as finishing himself off—as did Hangan—with a symbolic jab at the jugular, the scene is performed with a realistic use of stage blood, which not only spreads across Kanpei's white belly band after he impulsively thrusts his blade into it, but even has him wipe his goredrenched hand on his pure white cheek, leaving a striking red handprint there. This, too, is strangely beautiful, not disgusting, because of the scene's various stylized elements, such as the narrative music and recitation that is combined with the actor's speech, Kanpei's theatricalized beauty, his rhythmic dialogue, and so on.

The *seppuku* of Sokan in *Tenjiku Tokubei* stems from a different sort of regret, and suggests the range of motives open to characters who must atone for some misdeed by taking their own lives. Sokan is a dignified old man who is, in reality, a Korean general who has failed in his attempt to overthrow the Japanese government. His suicide is meant to redeem him from the crime of treason.

An egregious example of a *seppuku* carried out because the persons involved feel they must shoulder responsibility for various events occurs in the "Sannin Warai" scene of *Shin Usuyuki Monogatari* (1741): two fathers, whose loyalties have been called into play, appear onstage after already having sliced open their own bellies offstage, but they do not reveal this until the proper moment. At that point, they show their bleeding wounds, and, realizing each other's sacrifice, laugh painfully but loudly, joined by one of their wives. This laughter gives the scene its name, which means "Three People Laughing."

Even a child may commit *seppuku*, as Koshirō does in *Moritsuna Jinya* (1769). In a war that pits Moritsuna against his brother Takatsuna, Kōshirō is a captive of the former. Moritsuna fears that Takatsuna's concerns for the boy's well being will influence him to act dishonorably, and—since the boy is otherwise protected—he desires the child's suicide to keep Takatsuna from disgracing himself. Koshirō waits until Moritsuna is inspecting a head said to be Takatsuna's, calls out to the head as if it is his father's, then leaps from a veranda to the stage floor. He rapidly strips off his upper garment and stabs himself in the stomach. By this sacrifice he succeeds in convincing his uncle to declare the head Takatsuna's, which it is not. Koshirō thus belongs to that group of *kabuki* children—like Kojirō in *Kumagai Jinya* and Kotarō in *Terakoya*—who willingly give up their lives (although not necessarily by suicide) for the sake of feudal loyalties in which their parents are entwined. In the case of Koshirō, the awful sight of a young boy killing himself as a calculated act of deception embodies the most extreme form of feudalistic behavior, but the demands it places on the child actor, who continues to speak in a traditional rhythmic falsetto as he dies, help to elevate the scene to artistic heights.

Figure 81. Moritsuna (Ichimura Uzaemon XV) with Koshirō, who has just committed *seppuku*, in *Moritsuna Jinya*. (Photo: Kagayama, *Kabuki no Kata*.)

The physical circumstances of such self-sacrifices sometimes occur under rather novel, highly dramatic conditions. Gonpachi in *Ukiyozuka* (1823), for example, cuts his abdomen open while standing in a rocking boat, and Benten Kozō in the play of that name (1862) thrusts the blade into his stomach while standing on a temple roof where he has just fought off a host of attackers. As he stands there with sword in belly, the entire temple roof begins to tilt backwards as the gorgeous red and gold temple beneath it

rises from the stage basement on a giant elevator trap, a spectacular technique called *gandogaeshi*.

Figure 82. Gonpachi's (Danjūrō XI) *seppuku* in *Ukiyozuka*. (Photo: *Ichikawa Ebizō Butai Shashin Shū*.)

Seppuku is a male suicide, and *kabuki* women do not perform it, although they do commit suicide when circumstances drive them to it. Samurai women often kill them-selves by sticking a short sword or a large hairpin through their body under the heart. Tomomori's wife in *Yoshitsune Senbon Zakura* (1754) and Onoe of *Kagamiyama* (1782) are the victims of such painful deaths. The dying Onoe's anguish is made worse by the sadistically bitter treatment she receives at the hands of the iniquitous Lady Iwafuji.

Occasionally, a character—aware of his or her responsibility for various problems—wishes to be absolved by allowing someone else to kill them. In a sense, this, too, is a kind of suicide. These characters often deliver some sort of powerful speech before they die. Their acting in such scenes is classified as *teoigoto* ("wounded business"). When, in *Ehon Taikōki* (1799), Mitsuhide thrusts a bamboo spike through a paper screen, believing he is slaying his enemy Harunaga, he discovers that he actually has speared his mother, Satsuki. She uses the opportunity—which she has deliberately arranged—to deliver a powerful speech of admonishment at him, reviling him for his treacherous behavior. (TAKEMOTO in the following refers to the chanter who narrates some of the action, accompanied by a shamisen player.)

> SATSUKI *(With great effort)*: Don't fret, don't fret. It's only right that I'll die this way because I'm a member of the Takechi clan, who killed Lord Harunaga. You have fouled the fair name of this upstanding family with your treachery and corruption. You are unfilial, cruel, and *(Striking the floor and squeezing these words out with her last strength.)* more wicked than words can say.
> TAKEMOTO:
> "Ill-gotten power is ephemeral, like floating clouds. (SATSUKI *gestures toward* MITSUHIDE.) / You wear a prideful master-killing face and / even if you become shogun, / don't you know

you're nothing more / *(She rises a bit, weakly.)* than a villain in a tiny farmhouse?"

(She collapses, leaning on her right hand.)

SATSUKI: If only you hadn't betrayed your lord, had served your mother, and followed the path of humanity, justice, fidelity, and filial piety, even your share of prison rations would . . .

TAKEMOTO:

"Exceed one million rice bales."

SATSUKI: Your attitude might have changed everything. *(Places her hand on the spear and tapping it.)* But, as it is, look, this is what happened. There are many blades with which to kill a warrior, but the one you use to slay your mother is this handmade, bamboo, boar-killing spear!

(Painfully, she shifts position to move directly to MITSUHIDE's *left. She feebly smacks his thigh, then crumples again.)*

TAKEMOTO:

"The retribution for killing your lord," she says, / "is thus delivered upon your parent," / and she grabs the spear to drive it deeper. / Suffering intensely, she maintains her bravery and pride. / Misao is choked with tears (Leiter and Hibino 2002).

When dying characters deliver a speech of repentance for their previously evil behavior, the convention is called *modori* ("return"). Tamate Gozen, apparently guilty of incestuous feelings for her stepson, Shuntokumaru, reveals the real motives for her actions after Gappō stabs her in *Gappō ga Tsuji* (1773). Tamate's death stems from her wish to die so that her lifeblood—magical because of the star under which she was born—can be used to cure Shuntokumaru's disfiguring illness. A similar pattern of dying to provide magical blood occurs in several other plays as well, as in *Imoseyama* (described below) and in *Tenjiku Tokubei* (1804), in both of which the goal is to foil a villain's sorcery.

Other famous *modori* appear in *Yoshitsune Senbon Zakura's* (1747) "Sushiya" scene, when the hitherto nasty Gonta unburdens himself after receiving a mortal blow delivered by his father. Equally famous is the *modori* of Senō in *Sanemori Monogatari* (1749). Here is his death scene, as translated and described by Katherine Saltzman-Li. Senō, having allowed himself to be mortally wounded by his grandson, young Tarōkichi, speaks:

SENŌ *(Slowly)*: He has brought down a hereditary Heike samurai, Senō no Jūrō Kaneuji. It's a great feat and benefit to you. Although he is not yet of age, please retain him. In truth, long ago when I was still a dependent, there was a serving woman who became pregnant. The child she bore was taken unknowingly to Katada Bay and abandoned by its Heike father, who was, in fact, me. . . . As proof of its origins, I placed this sword with the infant, and now these many years later, my own grandson has stabbed me in the side with it. . . . *(Looking at his grandson.)* When I first became a retainer, I hated being tied to the Heike. When you first become a retainer, hatred of your Heike bonds could cloud your future and harm your chances. Serve well for seven years and you will be able to join Lord Kiso's inner circle. *(Turning with effort.)* Sanemori, please help him achieve a matchless level of service. *(Speaks with increasing difficulty.)* Now, for my head. *(To* TARŌKICHI.*)* Help me by performing another early service for your master.

(SENŌ pulls the dagger out of his side, then grasps his long sword. He leans on it to raise himself up, but falls down again.)

TAKEMOTO:

This warrior, so rooted in the ways of cruelty, / easily unsheathes his sword.

(He raises himself again and leans over to TARŌKICHI, *looking at him and leaning down in a gesture of love. Then he unsheathes his sword and looks at* TARŌKICHI *who grabs hold of it with him. In a special piece of business designed to suggest his self-decapitation, he and* TARŌKICHI *lift the sword over his head to rest on his neck. He makes ferocious facial expressions as they move the sword back and forth across his neck. Then he tumbles forward to the ground, his head hidden. As he does this, the* STAGE ASSISTANT *behind him tosses forth a property head and* TARŌKICHI *strikes a pose holding the sword to his side)* (Saltzman-Li 2002).

Figure 83. Senō (Bandō Mitsugorō VIII), right, and Tarōkichi cutting off the former's head, in *Sanemori Monogatari*. (Photo: author's collection.)

Thus Senō, after expressing his guilt for past behavior, with the help of a young boy, actually chops off his own head, followed by his performing a forward somersault from a sitting position (called *heimagaeri* or "flat-horse flip"). As is usual when a head is lopped off, a head prop is quickly introduced through the services of a black-robed stage assistant (*kurogo*), and a black cloth is thrown over the actor's own head. Stage assistants hold up a black "disappearance" curtain (*keshi maku*) that allows the actor of Senō to exit behind it.

A variation of *modori*, called *teoi no jukkai* ("wounded memories"), is sometimes used when the character has committed suicide. Kanpei's suicide contains this method. The character need not have been a really bad person in such a case, but, like Kanpei, must have done something for which repentance is necessary before leaving life.

Murder

Kabuki murders, which are generally the cruelest scenes, are similarly heightened by a host of theatrical techniques, and the term *koroshiba* ("murder scene") was coined to categorize such harsh events. Like all else in *kabuki*, *koroshiba* may be grim and fairly lifelike, or they may be boldly stylized, even grotesquely comical. A play's period and genre also make a big difference in the way such scenes are played.

Even sadistic murders designed to chill spectators may have a touch of comedy, as in the case of Motoemon's merciless killing of his brother Yasuke in *Tengajaya Mura* (1781). Alan Cummings's translation contains a description of this semi-comical, but nonetheless deadly business, performed to the offstage chords of a shamisen, a drum playing a wind pattern, and a temple gong, to which the movements—exaggerated because of the presumed darkness—are perfectly timed. Motoemon, dismissed from the service of the Hayase brothers, Genjirō and Iori, steals into his former masters' humble dwelling to kill and rob Genjirō of the money he has just raised by selling his wife into prostitution. He eventually chooses to kill Yasuke, who has remained a faithful servant to the Hayase.

(He places the lantern within the upstage curtained area, thus darkening the stage. Pausing, he takes down and drinks . . . sake from the altar. With a pot of oil . . . he greases the runners of the downstage sliding doors, and stealthily slides them open to reveal the sleeping GENJIRŌ. *Then he carefully lifts them off their runners and sets them aside. He slips his hand beneath the mattress and removes the packet of gold pieces. Offstage bell. Gingerly stepping over* GENJIRŌ, *he takes a sword and unsheathes it. He attempts to sever* GENJIRŌ's

head, but on the upswing strikes it against the lintel. Startled by the noise, MOTOEMON *briefly hides behind the upstage curtain. Reassured that neither of the sleepers has awakened, he wavers between killing* GENJIRŌ *or* YASUKE, *eventually deciding on the latter. Offstage bell.* MOTOEMON *pauses to take a drink of water from a dipper in the kitchen area, then raises the dipper as though to strike* YASUKE. *Offstage bell. He realizes at the last moment that he has mistaken it for his sword. Finally, he straddles the sleeping* YASUKE *and, to a loud* tsuke *beat, stabs him)* (Cummings 2002).

When he does so, by thrusting downwards on his sword, Yasuke's hand suddenly appears, flailing, above the screen that hides him. Such an approach to murder objectifies the horror and make it somehow more digestible. But even the most sadistic murders are tempered by stylized movement, music, and other conventions. In many cases, the complex choreography of the murder sequence makes it classifiable as a *tachimawari*, *kabuki's* dance-like combat scenes, discussed below.

That is not quite the case, however, with the murder of Hayase Iori, later in *Tengajaya*. Iori was crippled by Motoemon's sword when he came upon the scene of Yasuke's murder. He has been reduced to living in a hovel, but he and his brother continue to seek vengeance against their father's killer, Tōma, whom Motoemon now serves. Motoemon and another flunky, Udesuke, find Iori at the hovel late one night, and, despite his being paralyzed below the waist, attack him with their swords, although he manages to hold them off. But Tōma, hiding at the rear, wounds him from behind and an attenuated scene of physical and psychological abuse ensues, until the kicked and wounded cripple is held from either side by Motoemon and Udesuke as Tōma plunges his sword into Iori's breast. Even this vicious scene is modified by the use of stylized poses, vocalizations, and accompanying music. It also represents a classic example of the *kaeriuchi* convention, in which a would-be avenger is slain by the villain himself, which never fails to produce a stab of pain to audiences wishing justice to prevail. Only the strange beauty of the performance saves the action from being unwatchable.

Typical murder victims in *kabuki* die by being either stabbed, shot, poisoned, strangled, or drowned, or a combination of these. The killer is usually a man, although in a small number of cases, as with Otomi in *Kirare Otomi*, discussed later, it may be a woman as well. (For convenience, I use the male pronoun in what follows.) A classic example is the killing of Giheiji by Danshichi in *Natsu Matsuri* (1745), a play that epitomizes the aestheticization of cruelty. While the murder of Iori gains sympathy for the victim, here it is the killer with whom the audience commiserates. *Natsu Matsuri's* murder is representative of those in which the slayer—who originally has no intentions of killing or even harming the other person—finds himself in a very difficult position with a stubborn antagonist, or one who misinterprets his motives. In such cases, the slayer tries to silence his opponent, often by placing one hand over his mouth. This leads to a struggle and, through one misstep or another, the drawing of the slayer's weapon and the accidental wounding of the opponent. The opponent, enraged and frightened, only entangles the slayer in further struggle, and the scene culminates in the killer's having no alternative but to finish off the opponent, perhaps with a fearsome coup de grace in which the victim lies on the ground, face up, with the killer standing astride him before thrusting his sword downwards into the victim's neck. This basic pattern is crystallized in the murder scene of *Natsu Matsuri* when the hateful Giheiji lashes into his son-in-law Danshichi with a continual barrage of invective that escalates into the old man's murder.

(left) Figure 84. Danshichi (Nakamura Kanzaburō XVII) stifles Giheiji in *Natsu Matsuri*. (Photo: Kagayama, *Kabuki*.)

Figure 85. Mitsugi (Ichikawa Jukai) stifles Manno (Onoe Taganojō III) in *Ise Ondo*. (Photo: Kagayama, *Kabuki*.)

In this memorable scene, set on a muddy back street embankment on a hot summer night, with local houses seen in the distance at the rear, Danshichi gradually strips off his boldly striped rust and white kimono, and reveals his white body, naked but for a bright red loin cloth, and covered with a bold blue and red pattern of tattoos. As the scene progresses, the half-naked Danshichi—whose physical beauty should only increase the horrendousness of his actions—strikes one murderous pose after another, performing a virtual dance of death as he kills the crusty old man.

During the fight, they become covered not only in stage blood, but in mud, which Danshichi later washes off with water from a nearby well. And throughout this grimy, gory, watery scene, the terror of the action is underscored and made even more mesmerizing by the ironic counterpoint of lighthearted festival music in the background. In fact, the use of festive or even lyrical music as a background to scenes of slaughter is one of the distinguishing characteristics of *kabuki's* aesthetic of cruelty. (The only similar scene still performed of characters struggling in grime as a murder is committed comes in the *kabuki* version of Chikamatsu's *Onna Goroshi*, where the hero kills a woman in an oil shop and they slip and slide in the dark liquid used to provide this delightfully abhorrent scene with unforgettable verism.)

Figures 86-88. A sequence of Danshichi's famous poses in *Natsu Matsuri*. (From Toita, *Waga Kabuki*.)

The murder of Manno, the hateful head brothel maid in *Ise Ondo* (1796), bears a certain resemblance to the slaying of Giheiji, in that this middle-aged woman is as tauntingly derisive as the old man. Both almost seem to beg for their target to lose his temper and injure them. The butt of Manno's scorn is the young hero, Mitsugi, with whom she is in conflict over the possession of his sword. He warns her that he will strike her but she sneeringly invites him to go ahead and do it. Unable to control himself, he lightly strikes the sitting woman on the back of her shoulder with the sheathe, but she only dares him to do it again. When he does so, again not strongly, she repeats her demand that he hit her. Once more he hits her, but this time so sharply that, without his knowledge, the scabbard splits and the blade wounds her. When Manno touches the injury, her hand—to her shock—comes away with blood on it and she loudly accuses him of being a murderer. Putting his hand to her mouth, he tries to silence her and only then notices the exposed weapon. An ominous gong sounds, the broken scabbard slides off the blade, and the bloodthirsty sword takes possession of Mitsugi, who cuts Manno down. Then, to heighten the scene's theatricality, Mitsugi pulls down the long half-curtain decorating the upstage area, and poses with it over his shoulder as another gong sounds. Languid offstage singing and shamisen playing begin. An innocent maid appears and Mitsugi cannot help himself from fatally slashing at her as she passes. A brothel guest enters and is wounded, but continues to fight as the stage revolves. When it stops, the bloodied Mitsugi thrusts his way through a round paper window, holding a victim around the head at his side, and posing with his sword raised high. The ruthless killing of two men who try to stop him ensues. The scene is carried out within the exquisite back garden of the brothel, with its bridge-like passageway spanning the state, and remains incomparably theatrical and dance-like from first to last.

Another interesting variation of a murder that does not start out to be one occurs in Kawatake Mokuami's *Izayoi Seishin*, quoted from above. One night, a youth named Motome encounters the impoverished romantic hero, Seishin, on a river embankment. Motome has an attack of cramps and Seishin, attending to him, discovers that the boy is carrying a large sum of money. He attempts to rob Motome, but the latter strikes back with his sword, which Seishin fends off with Motome's umbrella. During their dance-like struggle in the dark, Motome's head hits a paling and he dies. Seishin, overwhelmed by guilt at having unintentionally killed the youth, prepares to commit suicide with the sword. He soon experiences a change of heart, however, and decides to make the best of the situation, even disposing of the body by tossing it in the river.

One must, of course, sympathize with Motome, but it is impossible not to empathize with Seishin, who finds himself a killer by default, and, as a result of the suffering he already has experienced, chooses a path he believes is fated. There can be no sympathy at all for those who commit premeditated murder, though, a powerful example being the eponymous priest-bonze in Mokuami's unrelentingly dark *Murai Chōan* (1862). In a nighttime scene during a downpour, with temple bells resounding gloomily in the distance, melancholy music playing, and eerie drums beating, Chōan, dressed in black with a scarf around his head, lies in wait for his victim, the farmer Jūbei, and unhesitatingly butchers him, treating the corpse with utter disdain, and leaving behind someone else's umbrella to implicate them in the crime.

Nineteenth-century works, especially those of Nanboku, often introduce the element of the supernatural into their murder scenes. One of the most distinctive examples is the dance-drama *Kasane* (1823), cowritten with Matsui Kozō. Set at night along the banks of the Kine River, it begins as an apparent *michiyuki* of two beautiful young lovers, Kasane and Yoemon, on their way to commit double suicide, but descends into a hellish nightmare when a skull floats into their sight, a sickle thrust through an eye socket. The skull, we learn, is that of Kasane's late father, Suke, slain by Yoemon, who was having an affair with Suke's wife, Kasane's mother. When Yoemon withdraws the sickle, Suke's spirit possesses the girl and she turns lame and horrifically repulsive. She clings to her wicked lover, who forces her to look at herself in a mirror. Even after learning of his crime, she refuses to abandon him and he goes after her with the deadly sickle, finally killing her. But her tenacity remains and she comes back to haunt him as a vengeful spirit. This work's bone-chilling violence is aestheticized and refined through the lovely lyrics—suggestive of nature images of beautiful flora on a folding screen—sung by the *kiyomoto* musicians, whose melancholic melodies play throughout, and by the ravishing appeal of the lovers, especially when played by highly attractive actors.

Figure 89. The murderous struggle between Kasane (Onoe Baikō VI) and Yoemon (Ichimura Uzaemon XV) in *Kasane*. (Photo: *Onnagata Shashin Chō*.)

One of the principal causes of women's deaths in nineteenth-century plays stems from the device of *enkiri* (separation) introduced at the end of the previous century by playwright Namiki Gohei I (1747-1808). In these works, a courtesan or geisha, believing she is acting on her lover or client's behalf, publicly insults him and asks him henceforth to leave her alone. She may wish to tell him her true feelings later, but she never gets the chance, as the man, seething with rage, returns and murders her. These works—including *Godairiki* (1794), *Ise Ondo, Edo Sodachi Omatsuri Sachichi* (1898), *Gosho no Gorozō* (1864), and *Kagotsurube* (1888)—always draw great sympathy for the misunderstood heroine, whose efforts to help the man turn so quickly to ashes. Few scenes can be as heart wrenching as those where a sword or dagger-bearing angry lover, who will stop at nothing until she breathes no more, relentlessly pursues a beautiful courtesan.

In *Godairiki*, the handsome Gengobei, thinking Koman has betrayed him, kills her without qualms at the brothel, slices off her head (she is lying behind a low screen), and—chanting from a *nō* play—somberly, but feeling no guilt (for the moment), walks off into the night, an umbrella over one shoulder and Koman's head in a bag dangling at his side. (In one version, her sliced off arm continues to cling to his lapel.) The scene in *Edo Sodachi*, where Sashichi slays Koito, is as notable for its heroine's anguish as it is for its gloomily atmospheric staging, in which Sashichi, dressed in a polka-dotted headband and a workman's vest and trousers, kills the girl in the dark with a carving knife and only then learns of her true feelings when he reads her farewell note by a lantern's light.

Even more devastating, though, is the action in *Gosho no Gorozō*, where the intended victim, Satsuki, the courtesan wife Gorozō believes has betrayed him, turns out to be Oshū, mistress of his former master, to whom he is obliged. As is so common with murder scenes, the scene (here outside a brothel) occurs in the darkness of night, when all sorts of mistakes can occur, and Gorozō does not realize until too late that the woman he has attacked is wearing his wife's over-robe. Shamisen and vocal music play, a large drum pounds loudly, and a gong sounds periodically as the tragedy transpires. Oshū is returning to the brothel accompanied by henchmen in the service of Gorozō's enemy, Doemon. Gorozō, wearing a scarlet under-kimono, engages the henchmen in a brief choreographed combat and drives them off. Alan Cummings's description provides a compelling picture of this scene's *zankoku no bi*.

(ŌSHŪ tries to flee but in the darkness she bumps into GOROZŌ: he thrusts her back and slices viciously at her shoulder with his sword. She cries out and collapses in the gateway. GOROZŌ strikes a mie *with the sword concealed behind him. Slow offstage vocal, large drum, and shamisen music as he searches for the attackers. ŌSHŪ staggers toward him from behind, and they confront each other in languid and erotic slow motion. He slices at her repeatedly; she collapses to the ground, hurling tissue paper into the air to distract him. It flutters down slowly, forcing him backwards. They strike a* mie, *ŌSHŪ lying on the ground, one hand held out protectively, he with the sword poised to strike. A bell tolls once. Back to the audience, she grabs his kimono from the front, imploring him to stop, but he shakes her off. She moves to embrace him from behind, slipping out of her outer-robe as he takes one end of it. They strike a* mie, *the robe stretched out between them, and his sword arm raised threateningly. She pulls the robe from under his feet, sending him tumbling to the ground. Sitting, bodies touching, their* mie *is a grotesque parody of a love-scene. When she stands, he stabs at her again and again, missing in the darkness. At last he pulls her toward him and runs his sword deeply into her breast. Screaming, she falls behind the water barrel. He goes to check, then staggers backwards and falls to his knees in anguished contrition.)* (Cummings 2002).

As mentioned earlier, women do not have to be victims, however; a few cases show them as the murderer. There is, in fact, a category of roles developed during the nineteenth century that exemplifies female wickedness, although such characters always act out of affection for some man and not out of pure malice or a desire for power. These women are called *akuba* ("evil woman") or *dokufu* ("poison woman"), and a principal representative is the scarfaced heroine of *Kirare Otomi*, a play written so that a popular roguish hero, Yosaburō of *Kirare Yosa*, could be played as a woman, Otomi. At the end of the play, Otomi murders "Bat" Yasu in order to take from him a large sum of money that she wants to give to Yosaburō, her lover. The killing is enacted in the suitably dismal precincts of a graveyard, and the pair engage in an extended fight, she wielding a carving knife, he an umbrella, until she finds an opening and brutally thrusts the blade into his side. Throughout, they strike a series of dynamic poses, highlighted by one in which he sits on the floor, his open umbrella over his shoulder, and Otomi stands behind him, tearing open the umbrella and posing with the glittering blade held high. Shortly later, it should be noted, a formal stage combat ensues in which a band of attacking police also use only umbrellas to fight the knife-wielding Otomi. What was necessity for Yasu, who had no other weapon, becomes a stroke of pure stylization when employed by the police.

Figure 90. Otomi (Onoe Kikugorō VI) poses threateningly over "Bat" Yasu in *Kirare Otomi*. (Photo: *Onnagata Shashin Chō.*)

Other Death Scenes

Characters sometimes die by violent means other than suicide and murder, of course. The killing of major villains cannot be considered murder, but simply the administration of just punishment. Such characters, whose evil knows no bounds, get to express their death agony in nearly operatic terms. A good example is Nikki Danjō of *Meiboku Sendai Hagi* (1785). Nikki has been engaged in a fight to the death with the old samurai Geki, whom he has wounded with his dagger. He finally pins the old man to the ground and sits astride him, trying to deliver the final blow, but Geki, armed only with a fan in his right hand, keeps waving it in Nikki's face, distracting him. Nikki pins Geki's hand down only for the fan to be transferred to Geki's left hand. This too is pinned down and Geki is about to receive the coup de grace when other samurai rush in. Nikki stabs one, but the others grab Nikki. The old man, supported by another, takes the opportunity to stab Nikki deeply, twisting the blade over and over. The villain holds out his hands, groping and clawing wildly at the air, his face contorted in a series of exaggerated grimaces, until he finally falls, twisting slowly on one foot and lying on his back, his head toward the audience. To guarantee that he is dead, Geki crawls over and slices Nikki's jugular vein.

Figure 91. Nikki Danjō (Danjūrō XI) expresses his anguish as he dies in *Meiboku Sendai Hagi*. (Photo: Kawatake T., *Kabuki Meibutai*.)

Sometimes the dying character is still alive as the curtain closes on his or her agonized figure, surrounded by others in a final tableau. For example, when Lady Yashio is stabbed by Masaoka in *Meiboku Sendai Hagi*, she is still standing with Masaoka kneeling at her side holding the blade in the wound, with several other ladies grouped around them, as the curtain closes. Yashio gropes and grimaces through it all.

The onstage deaths of Yashio and Iwafuji (in *Kagamiyama*) may bring melodramatic closure to their respective dramas, but along with Nikki's death, they are actually among the few examples where vengeance is successfully carried out against a villain before the audience's eyes. In the case of Iwafuji, her evil is so powerful, that she manages to return as a ghost. It is more common for the villain's death not to be enacted. At the end of *Ehon Taikōki*, for instance, a familiar pattern is presented when the villain, Mitsuhide, is confronted by someone both capable and desirous of disposing of him. The scene ends, however, with the characters vowing to meet again in a more appropriate place—on the battlefield.

Accidents happen, too. Several sympathetic characters end their lives by chance, although there are always circumstances that conspire to create these fatal mishaps. Consider, for example, the death of Oiwa in Nanboku's famous ghost play, *Yotsuya Kaidan* (1825). A victim of her unfaithful husband's betrayal, Oiwa has been poisoned through his agency. Not only has her former beauty become repugnant, but her hair has begun to fall out and to drip blood when squeezed. Panicked and angry to discover this she rushes right into a sword sticking through a wooden pillar and is impaled at the neck. Like Kasane, she took will soon wreak havoc as a ghost.

Blood, Decapitation, and Dismemberment

Although bloody effects are fairly common in *kabuki*, they were not used in this theatre's early days. Actors performing *seppuku*, for example, would strip off their over-garment to reveal a white silk kimono to which a piece of red cloth would be attached for blood. The earliest known use for stage blood was in 1752 although it proved an anomaly until 1777, when the idea caught on. Scenes that formerly were played without blood, like some described here, now began to redden. Toward the end of the century a realistic substance made from sappan wood (*suō*) was employed, and by the nineteenth century, when increasingly oppressive social and political conditions inspired an age of growing unrest and decadence, the use of stage blood became de rigeur. Some effects approach Grand Guignol gruesomeness, as seen with Kanpei in *Chūshingura* and Giheiji in *Natsu Matsuri*. When Tomomori enters wounded at one point in *Yoshitsune Senbon Zakura*, arrows protrude where they have penetrated his white armor, and he is prominently smeared with blood on hands, arms, legs, and head. The sight is surprisingly beautiful, not horrific. When Mitsugi in *Ise Ondo* goes on a killing spree, his white summer kimono, as well as his face, become splattered with gore.

One of the most powerful blood effects appears in Act V of *Chūshingura* when Sadakurō is shot. He bites on a concealed tablet that allows a red liquid to trickle from his mouth, down his chin, and onto his exposed knee. This is particularly effective because of the contrast between Sadakurō's dead white face and body, his black kimono—which is tucked up behind, exposing his legs—and the bright red liquid. His subsequent death agony, by the way, closely resembles that of Nikki Danjō.

Just as some violent scenes show blood realistically, others—like Hangan's *seppuku*, the death of Nikki Danjō, and even Murai Chōan's savage murder of Jūbei—display either no outward signs of a character's wound, or—as in early *kabuki*—offer a simple conventionalized representation of it. Sometimes the blood is purely symbolic, as when a small red crescent represents a wound to the forehead of Benten in *Benten Kozō*. In Chikamatsu's *Kokusenya Kassen* (1715), the outcome of an important scene is to be signaled to other characters by Kinshojō's releasing either white or red rouge into the water. She resolves the scene's dilemma by killing herself, substituting her blood for the rouge, but the actor indicates this by pouring a long red cloth out of a silver bucket.

One other technique of inflicting death must be mentioned—that of head severing. Heads play an important part in *kabuki*, especially for *kubi jikken*, scenes of head-inspection (to determine the identity of the victim), and the property heads used are of varying qualities according to the character that is killed or the use to which the head is put. Although the use of a *kaishaku* for *seppuku* is not seen in *kabuki*, heads often do roll, usually in fight scenes. The severing of a head is usually done in a manner quite as symbolic as other deaths inflicted by a sword slash in *kabuki*, that is, the blade does not come especially close to the intended victim. A simple stroke suffices to convince the audience of the act's validity. Generally, like the above-described Senō in *Sanemori Monogatari*, the actor playing the victim lies so that his head is hidden from the audience's view. A cloth hides the place where the head would normally be. Occasionally, a character is parted from his head as the actor playing him runs offstage. In this case a stage assistant hands a dummy head wrapped in red to the severer, as in *Kiichi Hōgen* (1731) and *Benkei Jōshi* (1737).

Figure 92. The prop used for Kotarō's head in *Terakoya*. It sits on a base that forms the lid of the head box, right. (Photo: author's collection.)

Such heads may be rather realistic, even sculpted of wood in the likeness of the "decapitated" actor, or they may be the comical cotton balls—which may have cartoonish faces painted on them—used when a superman hero acted in the flamboyantly masculine *aragoto* style slaughters a corps of exaggerated villains. In *Shibaraku* (1697), for example, it takes one swipe of the Kagemasa's gigantic sword to loosen a dozen or so heads, while in the latter, the heads cut off by Benkei are tossed up to him as he stands astride a huge water barrel into which the heads are dropped. He then mixes them with two large poles, in what is likened to the washing of potatoes (*imo arai*). The killing in such *aragoto* plays, which is childlike and exaggerated to the point of amusement, dates back to the mid-seventeenth-century *kinpira jōruri* genre (named for the violent character Kinpira) of early puppet theatre, in which the narrator was likely to be as brutal in his storytelling as any of the superhuman heroes.

For true comical grotesquery, however, few scenes match the fight scene killings in *Suzugamori* (1823), when a pack of grisly bearers—far more individualized than the usual stage fight attackers—set upon the handsome young swordsman Shirai Gonpachi. Each meets a different fate, one's face being sliced off, another losing an arm, someone else a leg, someone having his head pushed into his body, and so forth, all represented by an assortment of traditional, nonrealistic stage tricks, all of which clearly epitomize *kabuki's* stylization of violence. Moreover, as in *aragoto*, the results to the victims are really secondary to the display of the hero's beauty or martial skill, displayed in a series of powerful or graceful moves and poses.

The grisly, laugh-producing effects of *Suzugamori*, it might be mentioned, are reminiscent of one in the otherwise very serious *Ishikiri Kajiwara* (1730) where the hero tests a blade's sharpness by slicing through two corpses, represented by dummies whose bright red innards are exposed when their severed halves are removed from the scene.

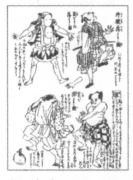

Figure 93. Illustrations of various techniques used in *Suzugamori*. Top: a face is sliced off (left) and an arm is severed. Bottom: a head is decapitated (left) and eyeballs pop out. (From *Shibai Kinmōzui* [1803].)

Torture

Just as *koroshiba* became crucial dramaturgic components of *kabuki*, so did *semeba* or "torture scenes," which have an even longer heritage. During the Genroku period (1688-1704), a theatrical pattern emerged in which a wicked stepmother would torture her pregnant stepdaughter with a red-hot roasting grill (*tekkyū*). It brings to mind a vivid moment in *Natsu Matsuri* when the beautiful Otatsu, wishing to be trusted in the company of a handsome young man, scars her face with a red-hot iron to rob her of her beauty. These, of course, are prime examples of physical pain being inflicted, but *kabuki* is also replete with scenes of psychological torture. The early torture scenes—inspired by the sermon-like tales recounted in the musical-narrative art called *sekkyōbushi* and in the pre-Chikamatsu puppet theatre called *kojōruri*—are said to have been based on Buddhist religious, as well as folk beliefs. The victim was expected to suffer great physical anguish as a necessary step toward achieving salvation. The convention was that a benevolent deity would—in a dramaturgical pattern called *migawari* (substitution)—take the place of the suffering maiden. These early *semeba*—performed to an accompaniment of suitably pathetic music—became an *onnagata* specialty during Genroku, and female characters continued to be the prime victims of such suffering throughout most of *kabuki's* history. This aspect gradually faded and, by the early nineteenth century, when a decadent quality increasingly permeated *kabuki*, torture was exploited for the additional horror it added to scenes of murder. Such scenes depicted pitiless cruelty amidst an atmosphere of doom and gloom, and—like the above-cited examples of Oiwa and Kasane—frequently led to the victim's return in the form of a vengeful ghost.

Among classical examples of tortured, bullied, or abused women are Omiwa in *Imoseyama* (1771), Onoe in *Kagamiyama*, Akoya in *Akoya no Kotozeme* (1732), and Princess Chūjō in *Hibariyama* (1740), all of them in plays first performed in the puppet theatre. Omiwa is a beautiful city girl in love with Motome, a high-ranking samurai, whom she follows to his palace by holding on to a white thread attached to his clothing. When she arrives she is brutally mishandled and mocked by the court ladies, all of whom are played, not by *onnagata*, but by *tachiyaku*, whose strongly masculine faces and voices give an extremely threatening tone to their contemptuous treatment of the poor girl.

Figure 94. A sequence showing Omiwa (Nakamura Utaemon VI) being bullied by the palace women in *Imoseyama*. (Photo: Tobe, *Kabuki no Mikata*.)

A gang of similarly rough women is found in other plays set at court where a gentle maiden must be mistreated by her superiors, as in *Kagamiyama*. In that play, however, the maidservant Ohatsu is able to fend off her tormentors because of her martial skills. But the threatening power of the chief court lady, Iwafuji, also played by a baritone *tachiyaku*, is sufficient cause for believing in the mental torment endured by Iwafuji's true victim, Ohatsu's mistress, Onoe.

Omiwa and Onoe are not so much tortured as bullied, but the discomfort produced by their plight is not unlike that felt when women are put to more overt forms of torture. However, each eventually experiences a climactic form of suffering leading to redemption. In Omiwa's case this happens when she is killed by the retainer Fukashichi so that—because of the auspicious star under which she was born—her lifeblood can be used in a potion to kill the charmed villain Iruka. Onoe, for her part, experiences one of the most potent forms of humiliation in *kabuki*, being beaten with a sandal. The pain of the beating is irrelevant; in a society where no one ever dared to walk into a private home in their shoes, the disgrace of being struck by a sandal was almost too intense to bear. Such scenes—which have several variations—even have their own name, *zōri uchi* (sandal beating). Ohatsu finds satisfaction for her mistress's humiliation when, following the latter's suicide, she manages to avenge Onoe's death by killing Iwafuji, and beating her mercilessly with the ill-used sandal, now smeared with Onoe's blood.

Figure 95. Onoe (Nakamura Utaemon VI, seated) and Iwafuji (Nakamura Ganjirō II) in *Kagamiyama's zōri uchi* scene. (Photo: Tobe, *Kabuki no Mikata.*)

Far subtler is the *kotozeme* (koto torture) experienced by Akoya in *Akoya no Kotozeme*, where this beautiful courtesan is questioned about the whereabouts of her lover, the warrior Kagekiyo. Her inquisitor believes he can tell from the way she plays the Chinese fiddle (*kokyū*), shamisen, and koto whether she is telling the truth when she says she does not know where Kagekiyo is. This musical polygraph scene truly exemplifies *kabuki's* sublimation of cruelty in its depiction of a woman's being subject to psychological torture through the delicate test of having her display her performative skills. The scene allows a musically skilled *onnagata* to display his talent on three different instruments, but the actor's attitude as he plays also permits him to express the mental pain experienced by the character.

In several plays the heroine is tortured while forced to stand in the snow, which is depicted in *kabuki* with considerable realism, as thousands of tiny white paper triangles continue floating from above over a stage already whitened by a ground cloth. This pattern of snow torture (*yukizeme*), too, derives from medieval tales as handed down through religiously oriented *kojōruri* in which wicked stepmothers caused young women to endure punishment in the snow. One obvious example is Princess Chūjō in *Hibariyama*, who, as the flakes swirl about her, is ruthlessly questioned by Iwane Gozen, her stepmother, about a stolen religious statue's whereabouts. She eventually faints, although some think she has died. Later, she becomes a nun in order to redeem the crimes of her stepmother—who has died by now—and is rewarded with a manifestation by Amida Buddha.

Another snow torture is found in *Akegarasu* (1851), where the courtesan Urazato is tied to a pine tree in a garden and beaten with birches after she has secretly met with her forbidden lover, Tokijirō. She, too, eventually faints. Although not meant to be funny, the scene is considered a parody of the one in *Hibariyama*. It is an example of a *chōchaku ba* or "beating scene," although even this kind of torture usually stresses the psychological rather than the physical aspects of suffering. Indeed, the mental pain endured by some characters can only be understood when one considers Ruth Benedict's assessment of Japan as a "shame culture" rather than a "guilt culture" (Benedict 1946). Consider the relentless taunting of Hangan by Moronao in *Chūshingura*, which begins early in the play and never lets up until Hangan's sudden loss of control. The shame of being openly ridiculed, beaten with a sandal, and publicly cross-examined causes these characters to suffer outrageously, and leads Japanese audiences to share their distress in a palpable way.

A variation of the snow torture, raised to an even more obviously aestheticized level, is the scene in *Kinkakuji* (1757) where Princess Yuki is punished by being tied to a cherry tree, whose blossoms fall on her in a blizzard of petals. The artistically heightened atmosphere is exemplified by Yuki's escape, when the rats she draws in the petals at her feet come to life and gnaw her free.

Figure 96. Princess Yuki (Onoe Baikō VII) in *Kinkakuji*, tied up as the cherry blossoms (seen on the floor) fall around her. (Photo: *Onnagata Shashin Chō.*)

While we cannot call them scenes of torture, there are moments in *kabuki* when the dramatic circumstances force the leading characters to endure heart-crushing distress while being forced to keep a stoic countenance. In *Terakoya* (1746), for example, Matsuō must serve as inspector of a decapitated head that is actually that of his own son, Kotarō, whose death he has prearranged; he must accept the head as that of someone else while not giving away to the others present that the head is Kotarō's. In *Meiboku Sendai Hagi*, Masaoka must coolly stand by as Yashio sadistically murders Masaoka's child before her eyes. Only later, when it is safe, do these characters get to express the anguish that has been pent up in them, yet even during their scenes of seemingly stoic indifference the actors must somehow convey the pain being felt inside. Of course, the more they have held in their feelings, the greater the sense of sympathy felt for them when they give way to release.

Equally harrowing for the participants are scenes of separation, lover from lover, parent from child, husband from wife. In *Shigenoi Kowakare* (1751), for example, the court lady Shigenoi and the young packhorse driver, Sankichi, discover that they are mother and son, but Shigenoi is unable to keep the long-lost boy with her and must bid him farewell, neither of them even revealing to one another their names. In both *Banzui Chōbei*

(1881) and *Sakura Sōgo* (1851), the title characters must bid their wives and children farewell as they themselves depart to a certain death.

Figure 97. Masaoka (Nakamura Utaemon VI) stands by, left, as Yashio (Ichi-kawa Sadanji III) murders Tsuruchiyo in *Meiboku Sendai Hagi*. (Photo: author's collection.)

Combat

Mortal wounds are often inflicted upon characters participating in the styl-ized battles called *tachimawari*, to some of which I have alluded. When the (usually) nameless attackers who figure in these scenes are killed, they normally indicate this by performing a somersault or otherwise falling to the ground. However, in rare cases, as in *Banzui Chōbei*, described below, the hero may also die after first putting up an admirable show of martial skill. In fact, this scene—like many other *tachimawari*—can as easily be considered a *koroshiba*, since its successfully realized intention is to kill someone. The different styles and varieties of possible fight scenes, as cal-culated by Kagayama Naozō (1965, 56), add up to between 220 and 230. However, only 30 to 50 types are still used. Some are large scale, others are restricted to only two or three combatants.

An excellent example of a large-scale *tachimawari* is seen in *Hira-gana Seisuiki* (1739) where Kanemitsu battles with a large crowd of attacking boatmen. After some vividly stylized maneuvers punctuated by the performance of difficult somersaults by several attackers, the entire company, using only its bodies and wooden oars, strikes a spectacular tab-leau in the shape of a huge boat. At either end, a boatman does a headstand supported on the shoulders of an equally erect fellow boatman. In the center of the "boat," the hero assumes a climactic *mie* pose as he stands on the back of a boatman and brandishes an oar over his head. This scene contains many of the typical elements found in *tachimawari*: musical accompaniment, the rhythmic beating of oak clappers (*tsuke*) on a flat board, a deliberate and nonrealistic tempo, acrobatics, powerful *mie*, and beautiful tableaux.

Figure 98. Kanemitsu (Matsumoto Kōshirō VIII) poses in a fight with boatmen in *Hiragana Seisuiki*. (Photo: *Engekikai* [1975].)

Another famous large-scale *tachimawari* is in *Igagoe Dōchū Sugoroku*, which has a revenge scene during which Masaemon must duel with an enormous number of pursuers, while very casually carrying on a conversation with another character who is on the *hanamichi*. As he talks, a blade slices at his knees but he simply jumps high above the sword while still conversing. He pays scarcely any attention to his attackers and at one point nonchalantly takes a throwing knife from his headband and flings it in the direction of an enemy who stands about fifteen feet upstage of him. Through sleight of hand the other catches it near his forehead as if it has pierced his skull. Masaemon, meanwhile, continues chatting.

The origins of *kabuki* stage fights are not clear, though some believe that the first example was introduced in a 1655 performance when a band of fourteen or fifteen armored warriors did acrobatic battle with cudgels six feet long. Such fights developed into a basic pattern intended to set off the play's hero, acted by the troupe's leading player. A major factor was the appearance in Edo during the late seventeenth century of the exaggerated martial style called *aragoto*, created by Ichikawa Danjūrō I (1660-1704).

A powerful adversary was always provided in order to set off the hero's martial prowess. Obviously, the hero's powers could be demonstrated more vividly if his enemy were not one man but many. As the crowd of attackers fell back under the hero's merciless onslaught, the audience gasped at the display of so superhuman and admirable a show of strength. Later, this method of the one against the many was used in non-*aragoto* plays as well. In those cases the hero is not so exaggeratedly ferocious, but the aesthetic principle remains the same. No matter what the style, mood, or tempo of the scene, the central figure must be dominant: he or she must be physically attractive and graceful, even if is fighting with only one hand—as does the injured hero in *Kyō Ningyō* (1847), a dance play requiring special skill—and appear strong and courageous.

Figure 99. Jingorō (Onoe Shōroku II), one arm in a sling, poses during the fight in *Kyō Ningyō*, which is fought with carpenter's tools. (Photo: author's collection.)

An extraordinary scene that fits the pattern of a hero fighting his attackers with bare hands, or whatever he can grab, appears in *Banzui Chōbei*, when the brave title character, a townsman, about to enter a bath, is set upon by a band of samurai. He is clad only in a summer kimono and, having no weapons but his hands, uses judo to send his enemies flying, ending the sequence with his foot on an attacker's back. The evil leader of the attackers, Mizuno, then enters with a spear. After setting themselves for battle, Chōbei and Mizuno engage in a powerful verbal sparring match, following which Mizuno attempts to kill Chōbei with his spear. Chōbei fends him off, tosses a bath implement at him, and then challenges Mizuno with a wooden spike. As they battle, a Mizuno man rushes in and slashes Chōbei from behind with a sword, after which he presses the wounded hero to the ground. A moment later Mizuno plunges his spear into Chōbei's side. In mortal pain, Chōbei performs a *mie* as the curtain closes on his writhing figure.

The stage must always present a well-composed picture during fight scenes. Beauty of form is more crucial than mere external vigor. Once again, *kabuki* aesthetics lift it above the plane of mere realism, and the hero's sheer power is made far more evident through stylization than would be possible in a more naturalistic context.

The stylized character of *kabuki* fight scenes is further heightened by the use of musical accompaniment, especially by the use of the *tsuke* clappers. The clapper specialist (*tsukeuchi*) watches the action on his knees at stage left and, striking the board at crucial moments with specific patterns, produces a sharp, non-reverberating sound. Among the onomatopoetically named patterns is *battari*, which is produced at the culmination of *mie*, and *batabata*, which is produced when a character comes running into a scene in a state of excitement. When a full-scale tableau ends a scene, with the characters glaring at each other, the *tsuke* are beaten even louder, *bata*, *bata*, *bata!* The beating of the *tsuke* during the *tachimawari* emphasizes the action and suggests the sounds of battle.

The more traditional fight scene music is produced from the stage right room called the *geza* or *kuromisu*, which is screened off from the audience's view, although the musicians can see the action through slits. The *geza* music, especially the use of drums, is designed to further emphasize the action and can also heighten the emotional atmosphere, as when the lonely wail of a flute or the boom of a gong is heard floating over the scene.

It is obvious that *kabuki* fight scenes, because of their strict reliance on formal picturization and rhythmic accompaniment, must be staged carefully to achieve the desired results. The responsibility for fight scene choreography falls to the *tateshi*, an actor-specialist. He must know the hundreds of traditional patterns (*kata*) which may be used in choreographing a combat. He arranges all the different kinds of fight scenes, from those like the boat scene described above, which may employ twenty or more attackers, to the small scale "grappling" (*karami*) scenes. Some fights must be imbued with a tragic air, others with a comical one. The *tateshi* must decide where to incorporate *mie*, and where to use somersaults. He then has to determine how all these elements will be tied in with the music and *tsuke*. To some degree, his task is lightened by the existence of certain classical forms that must always be used in specific plays. He may also compose new arrangements for a scene, provided that the classical components remain intact as a framework. Ultimately, he is concerned with two major elements, *tate* and *tachimawari*. Although these words are used interchangeably, there is a distinction that can be made between them.

Strictly speaking, *tate* refers to the performance of the movements of the attackers. *Tachimawari*, on the other hand, which is used as an umbrella term for stage fights, may refer specifically to the fighting of the individual. Another important term, *shinuki*, refers to the individual movements when the leading character is assaulted by one, two, or three men at a time. These characters usually step out of the crowd to make their attack and, when they are routed, a fresh force appears to repeat the pattern. After several repetitions, a mass battle ensues. Actually, even before the *shinuki* occurs, there is a moment when the hero is suddenly surrounded by the attackers, who form a background pose around him. They then divide into two groups and line up at either side in a formal pattern with the hero at center. They aim their weapons and pose. Meanwhile, the hero spreads wide both his hands and cuts a *mie*. This typical pattern acts as a prelude to the *tate*. The *shinuki* are now presented and, in the end, the group is dispersed. They may run to the *hanamichi* with the hero in pursuit, perhaps placing his foot on an attacker's back as he performs a powerful *mie*.

Figure 100. A sampling of the combat moves diagrammed by the late *tateshi* Bandō Yaenosuke. (From Gunji, *Kabuki Colour Compact.*)

These patterns are more or less fixed but, as with the individual *shinuki*, may benefit from the new and imaginative devices introduced by the *tateshi*. The *tateshi* has studied the various forms of martial arts, such as sword fighting, judo, and sumo. He is skilled at handling the long pole, sword, halberd, and dagger. He knows the possibilities for staging presented when the weapons are ordinary props pressed into service for fighting. But though he borrows from the formal movements of the martial arts in arranging his effects, he enhances them so as to make them more visually attractive; he tailors them one by one to the needs of the fight scene. He occasionally alters the normal methods of classical fighting so as to help conserve the energy of the star, and those around the latter are made to do most of the movement. The *tateshi's* skill, however, makes it seem as if the star is very active.

Among the weapons used in fights are those just mentioned, as well as *jitte* (short, metal, pronged rods carried by policemen to ward off sword blows), *sasumata* (a two-pronged weapon used by police), axes, ladders, and wooden buckets, as well as a variety of fanciful props that may be cleverly deployed. In some scenes, for example, the fighters battle with only flowering branches. A woodcarver may fight with carpentry tools and even saw an attacker in half. Another character, assaulted while eating, may strike back with eating utensils. In *Igagoe Dōchū Sugoroku*, Masaemon proves his fighting ability with a roll of paper. Even fans may be used to fight with, both paper ones and those with iron ribs; also umbrellas, bamboo poles, boat oars, sign posts, pillars, and anything else available. Some characters, like Banzui Chōbei, fight with only their bare hands, using judo or sumo methods.

Figure 101. Ranpei in *Ranpei Monogurui* fights on a ladder handled on the *hanamichi* by his attackers. (Photo: author's collection.)

Other props may be used for interesting staging effects. In a famous scene of *Yoshitsune Senbon Zakura*, Kokingo fights a band of police and—spider-like—ends up, sword raised, in the center of a net made up of ropes held by the twenty men surrounding him. The tall ladder used in *Ranpei Monogurui* (1752) allows the hero to climb it, weapon in hand, as it is held up high over the heads of the audience by the attackers who gather for this effect on the *hanamichi*. There are also fights that make abundant use of water effects, a popular one being found in *Shin Usuyuki Monogatari* (1747), when the liquid is used to douse someone.

The numerous large-scale fights still performed include a variety of classical patterns. The attacking crowd usually belongs to the class of char-

acters called *yoten*, a name derived from that used for their costume. There
are several types: the black or *kuro yoten*, worn by conventional policemen
(*torite*); the gold thread or *kinshi yoten*, costumes sewn with shining gold
thread; and the flower or *hana yoten*, who appear in spectacular scenes,
bearing flower-bedecked spears or the blossoming branches mentioned
above. The appropriate number of such attackers appear as needed and may
range from four to twenty. Non-*yoten* attacking groups may be retainers,
boatmen, or pack bearers, among other possibilities.

> Figure 102. A *hana yoten* fighter. (From Toita, *Waga
> Kabuki*.)

A number of dazzling fight scenes end with the hero
mounting a three-step, scarlet-covered platform (*tennōdai*),
brought to center stage. Standing atop this platform, which is
there merely to make him look grand, the hero performs a
mie. At the end the two-person battle that concludes *Seki no
To* (1784), one of the combatants, a ghostly woman, mounts the platform
holding high a flowering branch, while her ferocious male opponent, bearing a huge ax, poses at her side, his lower position suggesting that she has
got the better of him. At this point, regardless of how many are in a scene,
the curtain closes on a tableau pose.

As in *Seki no To*, some scenes show only one or two attackers battling
with the leading figure. Although the attacker in this dance play is a major
character, lesser attackers who are not themselves important characters, are
called *shinobi* ("spy"), referring here to someone with no or little significant
relation to the plot and whose appearance is used to provide the play with
strong movement and variety by putting the chief character in jeopardy.
Such scenes often have been cut in recent years because of time considerations and a lack of sufficiently trained acrobatic actors. A popular remaining
example is in *Keya Mura* (1786), where a black-robed man suddenly appears and attacks the heroine, Osono. This delightful scene helps to convey
Osono's Amazonian qualities, which the actor (a man, of course) suggests
while remaining as feminine as possible under the circumstances.

Another such conventional figure is the *karami* ("grappler"), who appears briefly in some dance plays. He may also be a *rikisha* (wrestler) or
gunbei (soldier), or have no designation at all.

Like the holds and throws in sumo wrestling, each movement pattern
has a name. Important examples include the *tenchi* where two adversaries
cross weapons above and below; the *bunshichi*, where the weapon is thrust
to either side of the enemy as the one attacked steps away from the thrusts;
the *yanagi*, where one receives the sword blow of one's opponent by
thrusting one's sword out to the side and over the shoulder in a straight line;

the *furikomi*, a method of whirling one's pole while striking with it; the *yamagata*, where the two opponents make a mountain shape by the profile of their bodies as they bring their weapons down on either side of the other party; the *nijiyori*, where the enemies advance toward each other by a shuffling foot movement; the *kubinage*, a method of throwing the opponent over one's shoulder by grabbing his head; and the *chidori*, where the hero is faced by a lineup of attackers who are dodged one by one as they go by to left and right, in alternating patterns.

Figure 103. An actor, gripping hand towels held by others, practices *tonbo*. Below, an actor performs a *tonbo*. (From Toita, *Tsuzuki Waga Kabuki*.)

The performance of somersaults (*tonbo*) is necessary to most fight scenes, although the hero rarely executes them. For instance, in *Yoshitsune Senbon Zakura*, the fox, Genkurō, has supernatural powers so that when a large group assails him he needs only to flick his paws to knock out his opponents. When "struck," they perform somersaults to depict the force of the blow.

About twenty varieties of somersault exist, though their number was once even higher. In the past, even leading actors diligently trained in acrobatics, but this is becoming rare nowadays. Great old stars like Ichikawa Danjūrō IX (1836-1903) and Onoe Kikugorō V (1844-1903) and VI (1885-1949) were capable of performing *tonbo* even in their later years. It is said that Matsumoto Kōshirō VII (1870-1949) could perform a perfect flip in midair, landing in the same position from which he started, even in his seventies.

Kabuki somersaults have a special style. Typically, at the moment when the acrobat is about to do a front flip, he stops and stands still for a second, places his hands, palms outward, before him—one hand stretched slightly further than the other—and then executes his *tonbo*. He lands with one leg extended and the other foot bent under it at the knees, lying on his back.

Chinese classical theatre is known for its remarkable acrobatics, but a leading *tateshi*, the late Bandō Yaenosuke (1909-87), pointed to a major difference between acrobatic fighting in Chinese theatre and *kabuki*. In Chinese theatre the plot seems to exist to show off the acrobatics, whereas in *kabuki*, the acrobatics are an integral part of the plot and are included so as to demonstrate the hero's prowess. Also, Chinese somersaults are executed from a stance using both feet, whereas *tonbo* begin on one foot, which Yaenosuke claimed was more difficult.

A number of other conventions inform fight scenes. One is the use of mime to suggest props that are not actually used. For example, at one point in *Yoshitsune Senbon Zakura*, a villain, Tōta, is trying to escape and Genkurō mimes tossing a lasso after him. This "lasso" ensnares Tōta, who stops short and comes hurtling backwards in circles as Genkurō winds in the "rope."

When an attacker is killed or wounded he usually runs offstage, only to re-emerge later as another assailant when he may be killed once more. The attackers rush at the intended victim shouting *"Nao!"* but are effortlessly turned aside or struck down. Actually, blows rarely make contact in these scenes although there is occasionally light touching, and even weapons may briefly come in contact. However, the swing of the sword or other weapon and the reaction of the stricken attacker are enough to convey the impression of an actual blow.

The only time that an actor falls hard on the ground is after performing a somersault. Otherwise, he merely takes a position such as when pleading for mercy, on one knee with one hand outstretched. Often the main character holds a man in this position with his sword or with one foot pressed on the man's back, while posing and delivering a speech.

In several cases those pursuing the hero help him change his costume in the middle of the scene, posing with him while they do so. Changing the costume onstage allows the character to show his readiness for action by the rearrangement of his clothing into a style more suitable for fighting. The change is done in dance-like fashion, punctuated by poses, in which assailant and attackers strike several tableaux.

Though the tempo of fight scenes is faster today than formerly, it still seems slow by Western standards. The tempo does, however, vary from play to play and a sense of roughhouse and violence manages to emerge regardless of the actor's deliberate rhythm. In fact, the unhurried music of the shamisen and big drum (*ōdaiko*) played offstage during fight scenes is meant to counteract the brutality of the fights.

Although the most common stage battles consist of one character defending himself against many others, there are scenes that show several major characters involved with a much larger group. This type affords excellent opportunities for scenic tableaux and colorful choreography, with fighting on stage and *hanamichi* at the same time. The brief but very colorful fighting scene at the Inase river in *Benten Kozō* in which five principals figure, and the closing scene of *Sannin Kichisa* (1860) with the three principals involved in a fight in the snow near a fire tower, are two examples.

Conclusion

Kabuki's aesthetic of cruelty is a prime reason for the form's popularity. It demonstrates the power of art to sublimate the most painful of situations and to turn them into pleasurable experiences. Suicide, murder, torture, and mortal combat may seem unlikely subjects from which to derive artistic enjoyment, but *kabuki* has been demonstrating for four centuries how universal their appeal can be.

NOTES

Some of the material in this chapter appeared in "The Depiction of Violence on the *Kabuki* Stage," *Educational Theatre Journal* (May 1969), and "Tachimawari: Stage Fighting in the *Kabuki* Theatre," Monographs on Music, Dance and Theater in Asia, Vol. 3. New York: Performing Arts Program of the Asia Society 1976.

REFERENCES

Bandō Mitsugorō VIII. 1974. "Koroshi no Gei." In *Kabuki-Bunraku-Nō Zankoku no Bi*, ed. Hattori Yukio. Tokyo: Hōka Shobō.

Benedict, Ruth. 1954. *The Chrysanthemum and the Sword: Patterns of Japanese Culture*. Tokyo and Rutland, Vt.: Tuttle. Originally published 1946.

Cummings, Alan, trans. 2002. "The Revenge at Tengajaya." In Kabuki *Plays Onstage: Villainy and Vengeance, 1773-1799*, eds. James R. Brandon and Samuel L. Leiter. Honolulu: University of Hawaii Press.

_____. 2002. "Gorozō the Gallant." In Kabuki *Plays Onstage: Darkness and Desire, 1804-1864*, eds. James R. Brandon and Samuel L. Leiter. Honolulu: University of Hawaii Press.

Engekikai. 1966, 1975. Miscellaneous issues.

Gunji Masakatsu. 1971. *Kabuki Karā Konpakutu*. Tokyo: Zayūtama Kankōkai.

_____. 1972. "Zankoku no Bi." In *Kabuki no Bigaku*. Tokyo: Engeki Shuppansha.

Ichikawa Ebizō Butai Shashin Shū. 1954. Tokyo: Wakei Shoten.

Jūgosei Ichimura Uzaemon Butai Shashin Shū. 1951. Tokyo: Wakei Shoten.

Kagayama Naozō. 1965. "Enshutsu to Engi." *Engekikai* 14 (August).

_____. 1957. *Kabuki no Kata*. Tokyo: Tōkyō Sōgensha.

Kawatake Toshio. 1971. *Kabuki Meibutai*. Tokyo: Zenkoku Jūshō Shinshin Shogaiji (sha) o Mamoru Kai.

Keene, Donald. 1964. "Realism and Unreality in Japanese Drama," *Drama Survey* 3 (Winter).

Leiter, Samuel L., and Kei Hibino, trans. 2002. "The Picture Book of the Taikō." In Kabuki *Plays Onstage: Villainy and Vengeance, 1773-1799*, eds. James R. Brandon and Samuel L. Leiter. Honolulu: University of Hawaii Press.

Mitford, A.B. 1966. "An Account of the Hara-Kiri." In *Tales of Old Japan.* Tokyo and Rutland, Vt.: Tuttle. Originally published 1871.

Mokuami, Kawatake. 1966. *The Love of Izayoi and Seishin*, trans. Frank T. Motofuji. Tokyo and Rutland, Vt.: Tuttle.

Onnagata Shashin Chō. 2000. Tokyo: Engeki Shuppansha.

Saltzman-Li, Katherine, trans. 2002. "The Sanemori Story." In Kabuki *Plays Onstage: Brilliance and Bravado, 1697-1767*, eds. James R. Brandon and Samuel L. Leiter. Honolulu: University of Hawaii Press.

Seward, Jack. 1968. *Hara-Kiri: Japanese Ritual Suicide.* Tokyo and Rutland, Vt.: Tuttle.

Tobe Ginsaku. 1973. *Kabuki no Mikata: Gihō to Miryoku.* Tokyo: Daiichi Hōki.

Toita Yasuji. 1945. *Waga Kabuki.* Tokyo: Wakei Shoten.

_____. 1948. *Tsuzuki Waga Kabuki.* Tokyo: Wakei Shoten.

Female-Role Specialization in *Kabuki*: How Real is Real?

Kabuki's female-role specialists (*onnagata*), who originated in the seventeenth century, were only the latest in a long tradition of men playing women in Japan's performing arts. Unlike earlier examples, best represented by the *nō* and *kyōgen* theatres, however, what might be considered realistic—or representational—performances of feminine manners, movement, or vocalization were not highly developed until the appearance of *kabuki*. The beautiful boys who played so important a part in early *kabuki*, and who were often called upon to play female parts, were also same-sex prostitutes. They therefore learned to exploit the more overt aspects associated with femininity in their attempts to appear as sensually inviting as possible, but the images they projected were probably purely of a physical nature, rarely suggesting the complexity of women as three-dimensional human beings. Their performances were mainly limited to dancing, flirting, and acrobatics, not to fleshed-out characterizations. Only when the boys—like actresses before them—were banned did the emphasis turn from gay to *gei* (art). This was in the days of so-called *yarō* ("mature male") *kabuki* in the 1650s.

It was not long before the actors began to seriously explore the ramifications of feminine behavior. According to a hint in *Matsudaira Yamato no Kami Nikki*, the diary of a daimyo who regularly viewed *kabuki* from 1658-95, and in which the first use of the word *onnagata* appears, we may surmise that characters other than beautiful young women were beginning to appear by 1658 (Leiter 1997, 499). Danced women seem gradually to have been replaced by dramatized women for whom physical beauty was not their first prerequisite. The actors responsible were those who originally had starred in boys' or *wakashu kabuki* and were now maturing not only in age but also in artistic perception and dimensionality. Various stars of the day were described in contemporary critiques for qualities that went beyond their physical or vocal beauty, demonstrating that audiences were finding other qualities to praise in *onnagata* than had previously been the case. The greatest leap, however, occurred in the last decade of the seventeenth century, during the Genroku period (1688-1704), a time of spectacular artistic growth, when a number of outstanding *onnagata* appeared, none more so than the brilliant *onnagata* Yoshizawa Ayame I (1673-1729).

Ayame was the first to articulate the importance of psychological distinctions in the art of acting women. For example, he observed that a samurai's wife, who might find herself in various circumstances in which she would be forced to draw her sword and fight, should do so differently depending on the nature of the situation. If she is attacked by a group of armed men and must battle to defend both her life and that of her lord's daughter, she must—because of the intensity of her samurai loyalty— display martial skills even better than those of a man. If, however, the circumstances pit her against an enemy in a drawing room, her manner must be calmer than in the other situation. This kind of advice—coming at a time when *kabuki* acting was still in a relatively simple state and when actors tended to display the same bellicosity regardless of the conflict—was considered a breakthrough in making *kabuki* more believable (see Dunn and Torigoe 1969, 50).[1]

Ayame's comments on this and other matters were posthumously published in the *Ayamegusa*, known in English as "The Words of Ayame" and for many years revered as the *onnagata's* bible (see this volume's "Four Interviews with *Kabuki* Actors"). His greatest contribution lay in his belief that the key to becoming a convincing *onnagata* artist was to live one's life as a woman, both offstage and on. He says, for example, that if the *onnagata* loses his femininity when fighting, or seems consciously to be making his acting elegant, the result will be inferior.

> For these reasons, if he does not live his normal life as if he was a woman, it will not be possible for him to be called a skillful *onnagata*. The more an actor is persuaded that it is the time when he appears on the stage that is the most important in his career as an *onnagata*, the more masculine he will be. It is better for him to consider his everyday life as the most important (Dunn and Torigoe, 53).

The practice of living as a woman, even if married and even if a father (as Ayame was), became de rigeur for all important *onnagata* until modern times and the influence of Westernization. Iwai Hanshirō VIII (1829-82) and Onoe Kikujirō III (1882-1919) were among the last *onnagata* stars to have followed this procedure, at least in their public lives. Such actors believed that only by a process of complete self-deception could they acquire the requisite artistry that would enable them to convey artistic sex appeal (*iroke*).

Ayame felt that if one were to live as a woman offstage, it would have to be not just as any woman but as a virtuous woman, the kind of gentle, gracious, modest woman revered in traditional Japanese culture. Moreover, it was only such women that should appear in plays, he averred, and an *onnagata* artist should refuse to play women whose virtue was questionable. This has nothing to do with *keisei* (courtesan) roles, as *kabuki* courtesans are typically women who have not chosen their profession but have been sold into it because of financial need; they are just as virtuous—in the broad sense—as women in ordinary life. In fact, they are often more virtuous because of the dramatic interest thus established between their characters and the general perception of the world they inhabit. In other words, *kabuki* prostitutes, like those in so much Western drama, typically have hearts of gold. Nevertheless, despite Ayame's advice to *onnagata* to refuse the roles of immodest women, *kabuki* would never have progressed dramatically if only the kind of women he admired were put on its stage. Here is one area where the reality that Ayame sought was very selective; clearly, any truthful representation of Japanese society would have necessitated the depiction of all kinds of women, which is exactly what post-Ayame *kabuki* went on to do.[2]

Also extremely important to the *onnagata*—and closely related to *iroke*—is the concept of *tashinami* ("etiquette"), originally referring to the linguistic and behavioral choices made by the *onnagata* in his daily life as a woman. A famous, but possibly apocryphal, anecdote illustrating *tashinami* concerns Sawamura Kodenji I (1665?-1705?), a contemporary of Ayame's, who, after being bounced around all day in a palanquin while on a religious pilgrimage, referred to his physical unease by saying he was having his period (*chi no michi*). His companions laughed at his woman's locution but the great Genroku novelist, Ihara Saikaku (1642-1693), whose story was reported years later in the encyclopedic *Kokon Yakusha Taizen* (1750), found it touching, given that Kodenji had been raised since childhood to play female roles, and Saikaku insisted that *onnagata* should use only female language from the time they began their training (quoted in Hirose 1978, 78).

Another example comes from Ayame himself, where he notes that he refused to eat a certain sweet potato concoction (*tororo jiru*) when dining with the male-role actor Arashi San'emon II (1661-1701), who was impressed by Ayame's singleminded devotion to female etiquette. According to later commentators, it seems that the food was objectionable to a proper lady either because eating it required an objectionable sucking noise or because it was somehow used in male lovemaking (Dunn and Torigoe, 51).

A much later example, recorded in his memoirs by Onoe Kikugorō VI (1885-1949) and often referred to by Japanese commentators, occurred when Kikujirō III (1882-1919) played the prostitute Michitose against Kikugorō's romantic hero Naozamurai, in the play popularly known by the latter character's name. The scene required Michitose to greet Naozamurai when he came to visit her during midwinter as he fled from the police. Having overheard Kikugorō say that "When one meets a woman with cold hands, one will want to warm up those hands," Kikujirō prepared for the scene offstage by dipping his hands in ice water so as to stimulate his character's own desire to have her hands warmed and his theatrical partner's desire to warm them (Onoe 1947, 119-20). The business, which suggested the urgency with which Michitose wanted to greet her lover and gave Naozamurai something real to respond to, may be an example of the appropriate etiquette for an *onnagata* vis-à-vis his regular onstage partner, but it also conveys to us the realism with which actors in this highly conventionalized theatre often approach their roles.

Not a few modem critics believe that the quality of *onnagata* acting has declined with the abandonment of the custom of living offstage as women. But there are also those who argue that a *kabuki* woman is a theatrical construction, an idealization, a stylization, and not reality, and that it is a mistake to think you must live like a woman to effectively inhabit this construction. Another reason for what is perceived as a weakening of the *onnagata's* art is the practice of *onnagata* occasionally playing male roles, which—following the epochal success of Iwai Hanshirō V (1776-1847) in playing multiple role-types—gained popularity in the nineteenth century when versatility took precedence over specialization. Ayame himself attempted to switch from female to male roles, but his failure in this line only confirmed his own oft-stated belief that those *onnagata* who attempt such boundary crossing could not do so successfully. Fukuoka Yagoshirō, the amanuensis through whom Ayame's words were handed down, noted: "I have come to the conclusion that this is because essentially there can be no person who can be both a man and a woman" (Dunn and Torigoe, 54-55). And Ayame is quoted as saying that "A real woman must accept the fact that she cannot become a man. Can you imagine a real woman being able to turn into a man because she is unable to endure her present state?" (Dunn and Torigoe, 55). Whatever Ayame's reactions to modern surgical miracles might have been, when he says these things he seems to conflate the idea of a "real woman" with the true *onnagata*, the player of female roles who takes so seriously his psychological transformation from man to woman that he is, to all intents and purposes, just that, a woman. He conveniently overlooks the contradiction that the *onnagata* he idealizes is a "real man" who has become a woman, because what concerns him is the need to emphasize the technique required to make the *onnagata*—an artist who has trained in this line since childhood— achieve as high a level of conviction in it as possible. If you are an *onnagata*, he is saying, don't imagine that you can also play men and still preserve the quality of your art.

Until the mid-nineteenth century, the *onnagata* took a backseat in the *kabuki* hierarchy to the actors of male roles, just as women did with men in the nontheatrical world. Now, with their appropriation of male roles, the *onnagata* began to claim increasing power within their troupes, even having female versions of the great male roles written for them. Also, the nineteenth-century development of a line of female characters—the *akuba* or "evil women"—known for their rough-edged qualities, led some *onnagata* who played such roles to assume crude characteristics in their offstage lives, like the mid-nineteenth-century actor Matsumoto Kosaburō (fl. 1834-60): "There's a story that when he went flower-viewing at Mukōjima dressed as a maiden in a long-sleeved kimono, a country samurai thought him a real girl and snuggled up to him. He thereupon raised himself a bit from his seat, lifted his hem, took a leak, and went off just like that . . . " (quoted in Tobe 1971, 146). Of course, an *onnagata* from earlier years would never have been so uncouth as to deflect a man's unwanted attentions by choosing to urinate.

Today, only a few *onnagata* devote themselves to complete (or nearly complete) specialization, although most of their roles are female. Ayame admits that he made a big mistake at one point in his career when he attempted to switch to male roles; he cautions others not to try the same thing, but his advice eventually went unheeded. The devotion of an old-time *onnagata* to playing only females is represented by a story dating from around 1805 when Segawa Kikunojō III (1751-1810) was asked to play a male page in a new play.

> He faced the playwright and said, "I'm an *onnagata*. I should play female roles. A page is definitely a male. I therefore can't play it and am turning it down." The writer replied, "I wrote this as a rare opportunity for you to play a youth and if you don't play it my efforts are in vain." "Well, well," [asked the actor], "if you revise the play so that the boy really is the female character—Lady Yamabushi—who, because of her fear of the Genji clan, has disguised herself as a boy, I'll play the part; I'll play it if she's really a woman" (quoted in Hirose, 79).

One of Kikunojō III's disciples, Segawa Kikujirō (dates unknown), declared, "If you pay attention to the Chinese characters in the word '*onnagata*,' you'll be a very bad actor. My advice is never to look at the 'gata' ['person' in this example] part of *onnagata*" (quoted in Hirose, 79). In other words, the actor should concentrate only on the part of the word using *onna*, or woman.

Even an actor's name, said Ayame, should not suggest too much strength; an actor named Karyū spelled it with the characters for "perfumed dragon," but Ayame argued that "dragon" was too strong a character for an *onnagata's* name and the actor subsequently changed the characters to those for "song stream," which can be pronounced Karyū (Dunn and Torigoe, 50).

Further weakening the position of pure *onnagata* acting has been the practice of great male-role actors now and then choosing to play female roles, which became increasingly popular from the time of the late nineteenth century stars Ichikawa Danjūrō IX (1838-1903) and Onoe Kikugorō V (1844-1903). This is not unlike our seeing Dustin Hoffman playing Tootsie-like characters as a regular practice. What this has done, it seems, is to replace the emphasis on lifestyle with one in which pure skill is demonstrated, so that *onnagata* acting becomes a technical achievement instead of the natural byproduct of training and personal behavior totally dedicated to the embodiment, both externally and internally, of a feminine ideal. Because of the traditional nature of *kabuki* acting in which an actor hands his art on to his son, the handing on of *onnagata* performances by a nonspecialist father, like Kikugorō VI, to a specialist son, like the late Onoe Baikō VII, whose private life was conventionally masculine, leads, some believe, to a diminution of the art.

We should recall that the original intention of Ayame and his peers was not to *act* as women but to be women, at whatever cost, in the interests of art. They were not necessarily thinking of themselves as men playing women but sought to be as true as they could to women as they understood them. This was not a conscious process of observation but a lived experience. Ayame told his followers such things as to hide the fact that they were married, to blush if their wives or children were mentioned, to observe female rules of decorum when eating in their dressing rooms, to treat their stage lovers with the proper respect, and so forth. Here is a famous example from the *Ayamegusa*:

> The *onnagata* should continue to have the feelings of an *onnagata* even when in the dressing room. When taking refreshment, too, he should turn away so that people cannot see him. To be alongside a *tachiyaku* [actor of male roles] playing the lover's part, and chew away at one's food without charm and then go straight out on the stage and play a love scene with the same man, will lead to failure on

both sides, for the *tachiyaku's* heart will not in reality be ready to fall in love (Dunn and Torigoe, 61).

This comment suggests that not only is the *onnagata's* art affected by his offstage behavior, but so is that of his onstage partner. If the *tachiyaku* can't believe in the total femininity of his partner, he will be unable to give a truly believable performance. Thus stage reality will suffer in general if the *onnagata* is anything less than completely faithful—at least while in the presence of other actors—to the ideal of femininity he represents. In fact, there are stories like that of Sakata Tōjūrō I, the great Genroku-period actor, who fell in love with his "leading lady," Kirinami Senju I (1679-?), whom he found overwhelmingly believable as a woman.

Ayame's comments are contained in a literary form known as a *geidan*, which essentially means a "commentary about art," in this case, the art of acting. Many later *geidan* also focus on the problems and techniques of the *onnagata*, but the one that most modern scholars use to contrast with Ayame's is that of Segawa Kikunojō I, a younger contemporary of Ayame's who achieved greatness in his field. This actor's *geidan*, called *Onnagata Hiden*, reveals how discussions of *onnagata* acting evolved from Ayame's preoccupation with the authenticity of female experience and how this could be translated into effective performance. Kikunojō, of course, also lived like a woman offstage, but by his time this was a given, so his principle concerns were with the specific technical details of performance rather than with (like Ayame) the personal experiences that had led to various insights. This ultimately became the foundation upon which subsequent *onnagata geidan* were and still are written. These writings tell you how to look beautiful, how to hold your lover when sincere and when insincere, how to do your makeup, how to hold and maneuver your fingers, how to differentiate between character types, how to manipulate the kimono's hems and sleeves (which, by the way, are among the most crucial aspects of *onnagata* acting in conveying the essence of different character types), how to hold a pipe, and how to play specific roles. They may even be concerned with the way an actor crafted his career in terms of fan interest. For example, Kikunojō's *Onnagata Hiden* has this statement:

It's bad for an *onnagata* to have female fans. It would be inconvenient if one wanted to marry him. He should have many male fans who wish there were a woman like him. If he is going to receive female support, he should work to get them to admire the kinds of hair ornaments, combs, headdresses, and so forth, that he likes and that palace maids, prostitutes, and city girls will emulate. He should be setting his sights on making fans of those women who see in him a woman like themselves (Suwa 1979, 36).

The increasing tendency, especially after the end of the Edo era, to formalize the male actor's technical observations of feminine behavior reveals a need that was not as necessary in a time when the *onnagata's* behavior flowed naturally out of his female lifestyle. What Kikunojō set in motion, apparently, was a concern with form that led to a gradual ossification of stage behavior in set patterns (*kata*) rather than a naturalness that grew out of a fundamentally realistic approach to spirit and character (*shōne*). The modern actor, therefore, strives to be an *onnagata* rather than to be a woman. Because it is no longer possible to observe the type of female behavior available during the Edo period, today's actors have no opportunity to do anything but repeat the patterns they have learned. But it was not unusual during the Edo period for serious actors to make special attempts to observe women with whom they might not ordinarily come in contact, such as when Hanshirō IV, preparing to play a cheap whore, went with his playwright collaborator to a real lower-class brothel to study the women and to copy their coarse speech mannerisms. This was part of a nineteenth-century trend away from the idealized female characters who had come to dominate *kabuki* and to expand the repertory in the direction of more naturalistic effects. It also serves to remind us once again of how even the most formalistic acting traditions must be based on truth derived from observation. The Moscow Art Theatre's famous visit to a dross house to prepare for *The Lower Depths* is actually a late example of the kinds of things great actors have always done, in Japan as well as elsewhere.

The practice of male actors living as women suggests that, for all the stylization associated with *kabuki* acting, these early actors—unlike the dancing women and boys who had pioneered *kabuki* in the first half of the seventeenth century—believed that realism was at the core of their art. Ayame refers, for example, to *jigei* (literally, "ground art"), which was an early term for realistic acting as opposed to dance (*shosagoto*). His comments continually underline the need for complete believability in acting. If the actor is to achieve femininity beyond femininity, he must first be completely feminine, as much like a woman as possible. Ayame and his peers felt that anything they did to betray their masculinity was a weakness in their acting. Unless they believed themselves to be women they could not express the feminine truth of their characters. Thus, to compensate for their innate maleness, the women they created had to be even more overtly feminine than real women, although the latter were in turn influenced by the stage performances and borrowed many items of behavior and appearance from the actors. The importance of being completely believable as a woman may even have superseded the quality of one's acting. We are told of one Kyoto actor, Yamamoto Kamon (1682-?), contemporary with Ayame, whose acting, dancing, and looks were not especially impressive but whose popularity was tremendous. According to the *Kokon Yakusha Taizen*, he was beloved because "He was like a real woman and had absolutely nothing rough about him. The first thing for an *onnagata*, said [the great Genroku actor] Sakata Tōjūrō I, is to be a woman, the second is his acting" (quoted in Hirose, 77).

As several of the stories I've presented reveal, *kabuki* actors have a long history of attempting to make their characters as realistic as possible within the conventions of the form. They often examined each motivation of their characters for its psychological truth. When appropriate, they made an effort to observe real people whose behavior could be appropriated for authenticity in performance. And, despite their frequent use of obviously artificial conventions, the *onnagata's* female characters were no more artificial than the similarly stylized men of every description who appeared on stage with them. I thus find it hard to accept Peter Hyland's remark that "A man who plays a woman on the stage is always playing 'a kind of woman,' not a realistic woman" (1987, 6-7). There is little to suggest that, if women had created these roles, they, too, would not have been playing "a kind of woman." As Mette Laderierre wrote, "The actor must not symbolize a woman, but must create the illusion that he is a woman on stage" (1989, 31).

NOTES

1. Kawatake (1972), offering a brief comparative survey of the history of theatrical female impersonation, East and West, claims that the acting (not the writing) of women's roles in the West, from the Greeks to the Italian castrati of the eighteenth century, was more conventionalized and less psychologically dimensional than that of the *onnagata*. He suggests that the Western actors' primary function was to express the values of poetic drama, whereas Japanese actors of female roles—once such acting began to be taken seriously in the light of Ayame's breakthroughs—were more concerned with the depth and quality of their acting as art. He notes, for example, the absence of any known "artistic path" (*geidō*) associated with classical acting of women's roles in the West. Kawatake also provides a concise examination of the history and development of female-role playing in Japan, and its relationship to the tradition of male-male sexual relations (*shudō*).

2. For an overview of *onnagata* roles (apart from those of old women) and their relationship to Edo-period women, see Leiter (2001).

REFERENCES

Dunn, Charles J., and Bunzō Torigoe, eds. and trans. 1969. *The Actors' Analects*. Tokyo: University of Tokyo Press.
Hirose Chisako. 1978. "Onnagata no Geidan." *Engekikai* 36 (June).

Hyland, Peter. 1987. "'A Kind of Woman': The Elizabethan Boy-Actor and the *Kabuki Onnagata.*" *Theatre Research International* (Spring).

Kawatake Toshio. 1972. "Onnagata no Kiseki." *Kabuki* 19.

Laderierre, Mette. 1989. "The Early Years of Female Impersonation in *Kabuki.*" *Maske und Kothurne* 35.

Leiter, Samuel L. 1997. *New* Kabuki *Encyclopedia: A Revised Adaptation of* Kabuki Jiten. Westport, Ct.: Greenwood Press.

_____. 2001. "From Gay to *Gei:* The *Onnagata* and the Creation of *Kabuki's* Female Characters." Originally published in *Comparative Drama* (Winter/Spring 2000). Reprinted in *A* Kabuki *Reader: History and Performance,* ed. Samuel L. Leiter. Armonk, N.Y.: M.E. Sharpe

Onoe Kikugorō VI. 1947. *Gei.* Tokyo: Kaizōsha.

Suwa Haruo. 1979. *Kabuki no Denshō.* Tokyo: Senninsha.

Tobe Ginsaku. 1971. "Onnagata no Gihō to Seishin." *Kabuki* 12.

Kumagai Jinya:
Form and Tradition in *Kabuki Acting*

Unlike the presentation of a *kabuki* play, when the lights come up on a production of a Western classic, chances are no one in the audience will have any idea of what they are going to see. Although certain traditions are associated with the canon, the specifics of production are newly invented for each mounting. In the case of Shakespeare's *Henry V*, for example, knowledgeable audiences are concerned with many factors: the play's relative emphasis on the romantic or antiromantic view of war; the degree to which the central figure is drawn as an icon of nobility or one of human dimensions; the extent to which the production exemplifies current political concerns; how much of the original text has been cut or altered by the director's blue pencil; how specific highlights will be delivered; and what combination of staging devices have been used to bring the text to life. When it comes to revivals of Shakespeare, anything goes. While it is precisely this flexibility in interpretation that keeps Shakespeare alive in the modern world, such freedom of interpretation often leads to artistic catastrophe.

The same does not hold true in *kabuki*, however, where self-regulatory mechanisms prevent such laissez-faire inventiveness. This is not to say there is no freedom in the *kabuki* tradition. If we may say, despite their obvious differences, that *kabuki* is the closest thing in the classic Japanese tradition to Shakespeare, we may have a basis for understanding the artistic license with which Japanese audiences are confronted when they see a revival of a famous *kabuki* play. To begin with, the concept of a director, the guiding artistic force in a Shakespeare revival, is practically nonexistent in traditional *kabuki*. For the most part the functions we typically associate with the director in the West are taken by the leading actor of the play. It is he who decides on the fundamental interpretation and guides the other actors.

Kabuki plays are produced in what might be called a modified repertory system. The most popular works are seen on a fairly regular basis. Tokyo's Kokuritsu Gekijō (National Theatre), used to make it a regular practice to produce nearly complete, "all-day" (*tōshi*) dramas, but in recent years it has taken to the more common procedure (called *midori*) of offering only the principal scenes and acts from several famous plays on a single bill. For example, the three-act drama *Ichinotani Futaba Gunki* (1751) by Namiki Sōsuke and others is represented by two scenes, the "Suma Ura Kumiuchi" scene from Act II and the "Kumagai Jinya" scene from Act III. Plays such as *Ichinotani* are frequently revived; a two-year span rarely passes without at least one major revival of the play, which actors know by heart. But that alone does not explain the reason for the lack of importance accorded the director in the typical *kabuki* revival. The true reason resides in the emphasis placed on acting traditions in the performance of these plays. Indeed, the situation is reminiscent of the nineteenth century in Western theatre before the rise of the director. Although the Western tradition was never codified to the same extent as *kabuki*, there was a time when popular Shakespeare plays could be staged with a minimum of rehearsal, usually under the guidance of the leading actor, because of a set of conventional production techniques. The traditional nature of *kabuki* performance is further underlined by the hereditary nature of the actor's art, whereby he learns the approach to a role from an older actor and only adds refinements when he is himself of sufficient stature. These refinements too may then become part of the tradition.

Nevertheless, one should not be lured into thinking that all productions of classic *kabuki* plays are essentially mirror images of each other. Although *kabuki* productions do not begin to approach the diversity of original interpretations given to Shakespeare's plays, radicalized versions of famous works are in fact staged, if rarely. In 1959, for example, the left-wing theatre group Zenshin-za staged a version of "Kumagai Jinya" that emphasized its essentially antiwar theme more than conventional productions. The text was revised so that Kumagai actually kills the enemy Atsumori and Kumagai's son Kojirō dies in battle—major events that are not in the original script.[1] Strictly speaking, this was more an adaptation than a revival. Ten years earlier, Takechi Tetsuji (1912-88), an avant-garde director-critic, staged a series of experimental productions of *kabuki*, including an unusual mounting of *Ichinotani*. Such productions are the exceptions that prove the rule. The variety one finds in different productions of a *kabuki* play is usually concerned less with themes than with details in the acting of major roles. These details are normally the result of careful thought about certain aesthetic as well as psychological aspects but may also stem from such practical considerations as the size of the theatre and the need to alter traditional business to suit narrower stages or shorter *ha-*

namichi. At any rate, diversity does exist and it is in detecting and appreciating it that *kabuki* aficionados find much of their pleasure.[2]

Kabuki and Kata

To enjoy a *kabuki* play fully, one must be familiar with the all-important concept of form or *kata* (see Brandon 1978 and Leiter 2000). A simplified definition of *kata* (which is sometimes rendered as "pattern") is the myriad conventions of *kabuki* production, comprising every feature of the performance, beginning with acting and extending to sets, makeup, costumes, and props. After the Meiji Restoration (1868), *kabuki* underwent many changes as Japan struggled to catch up with the Western world in all facets of life. *Kabuki* eventually began to lose ground to new theatrical forms, and what was once an actively evolving art reflecting the interests of its society (although always within a certain traditional framework) started to settle into a rigid system of traditional *kata* for the presentation of classic plays.

The *kata* system allows *kabuki*-lovers to study the differences in approach among actors playing principal roles. To the uninitiated such differences may appear minute, but to the experienced observer they are of great significance and provide a useful gauge for assessing the quality of the performance at hand. Indeed, much *kabuki* criticism consists of descriptions of productions in light of other productions seen or read about by the writer. The "Kumagai Jinya" scene of *Ichinotani* is an excellent example of how this latter concept works. What follows here is an account of the scene's most famous *kata* highlights with a description of the chief options open to *kabuki* actors in handling their traditions. The focus is on the acting of Kumagai.

There are basically two *kata* traditions for the performance of "Kumagai Jinya," both of them established in the late nineteenth century and solidified during the twentieth. The first tradition, by far the more widely practiced, was developed by the actor Ichikawa Danjūrō IX (1838-1903); the other was established by Nakamura Shikan IV (1830-1899). Critics disagree over which *kata* are the most appropriate, but on the whole Shikan's *kata* are considered to be more concerned with theatrical values than realistic ones, while Danjūrō—under the influence of Western ideas—was famous for adding psychological insight to his interpretations and injecting throbbing life into the external form.[3] Some actors prefer to work within the general outlines of one or the other of these traditional *kata,* but others mix and match them or add variations of their own at certain points.

The two principal traditions will be contrasted in much of what follows. Most of the descriptions of Shikan *kata* are based on an account of Nakamura Utaemon V (1866-1940) made in 1905 (Shunbō 1927) when he was still known as Shikan V. All page references are to James R. Brandon's translation (1992); frequently there will be differences from the stage directions given in Brandon. In brief, General Kumagai of the Genji clan secretly seeks to protect the life of Atsumori, a prince of the enemy Heike clan, by killing his own son, Kojirō, in Atsumori's place. Kojirō's mother, Sagami, and Atsumori's mother, Lady Fuji, must conceal their feelings when they are shown the severed head of "Atsumori" (in reality Kojirō) before Kumagai's lord, Yoshitsune. In fact, Kumagai has acted under Yoshitsune's secret orders; in contrition he renounces his military rank and departs to wander as a Buddhist monk, praying for the soul of the son he has murdered.

Kumagai's Entrance (*De*)

In some critical eyes Kumagai's entrance is the crux of his performance, more important even than his famous speech describing the slaying of Atsumori. Such mimetic entrances on the *hanamichi,* called *de,* are among the most noteworthy skills in a *kabuki* actor's bag, as they must silently convey a great range of feelings pertinent to the situation. Typically an actor stops at the trapdoor (*suppon*) on the *hanamichi*—a spot known as *shichisan*—and enacts a piece of highly expressive mime. Without being too obvious, Kumagai must communicate the essence of his decision to resign the military life and become a wandering monk; as the action will make clear, he has already become a monk, but the audience does not know

this. If he goes too far and reveals his decision too clearly, there will be no surprise at the end of the play, so the acting must be extremely subtle. In fact, Kumagai's behavior during the ensuing action is sometimes made more brusque and more militaristic than usual as a way of heightening the contrast and disguising the fact of his decision.

Figure 104. Kumagai (Matsumoto Kōshirō VIII) at *shichisan* position. He hides the rosary in his right sleeve and grips the cuff of his sleeve with his left hand. (Photo: author's collection.)

There is thus great significance to the narrator's line, "Does Kumagai Jirō Naozane, slayer of Atsumori in the flower of youth, understand life's impermanence?" (191), as Kumagai's mind is already immersed in thoughts of Buddhahood. When he arrives at *shichisan* his rosary is wrapped around his left wrist, his arms are folded inside his sleeves, and his eyes are practically closed in deep concentration. Realizing that he has reached the camp, he opens his eyes and allows the rosary to slip off his wrist and hang from his grip as he withdraws his arms from his sleeves. He starts upon seeing it, places the rosary in his right sleeve while looking up again sharply toward the stage as a chord of shamisen music is struck, grips the cuff of his right sleeve with his left hand, and slowly closes and reopens his eyes as he realizes that no one has seen the rosary and that his secret is still safe. He then proceeds to the stage. All this business is established by tradition but is not carved in granite. Personal taste may suggest variations. Ichikawa Sadanji I (1842-1904) did not enter with his arms crossed, and he liked to put the rosary in his left sleeve instead of the right; he then would place his left hand on the sword hilt. Moreover, important differences may emerge from the timing necessary to make the entry in different theatres, since each gesture occurs on a specific line of the narrator. In other words, Kumagai will make his entrance on a different line according to how much time it will take him to reach *shichisan*.

In addition to Kumagai's *hanamichi* acting, his costume and makeup signal which tradition is being employed. Both traditions display Kumagai's "double-pigeon" crest (*mon*) on the breast and sleeves, but the costumes themselves are notably different. Danjūrō actors wear a light-brown kimono under a predominantly brown and gold brocade dress of wide skirtlike *hakama* trousers and *kataginu* vest with stiff pieces projecting winglike from the shoulders. Shikan actors, on the other hand, wear a black velvet kimono with red *hakama* and *kataginu* dominated by an embroidered silver pattern. Shikan actors wear yellow *tabi*, Danjūrō white. Even the swords and scabbards worn by the two traditions differ. Both utilize a version of stylized makeup (*kumadori*), but with differences. The Shikan coloration is reddish while Danjūrō actors use light brown. In addition to the pair of reddish-brown lines drawn up from the outer ends of the eyebrows to the sidelocks of the wig, Shikan actors may also draw a separate pair of lines upward from the outer corners of the eyes. It is interesting to note that today some actors otherwise adopting the Danjūrō *kata* have adopted the Shikan makeup.[4] All told, the Danjūrō-style appearance is the more subdued and considered an example of what Japanese taste calls *shibui* (astringent). In fact, the Shikan tradition is truer to the older, flashier, style of *kabuki* performance, whereas the Danjūrō approach is more modern and realistic.

Kumagai Notices Sagami

When Kumagai arrives on the stage proper, he stops momentarily to read a signboard near the stage right gate before passing through the gate. Kneeling near the gate are his retainer, Gunji, and, half-hidden by him, Sagami, who knows that her husband will be upset at finding her at a battle camp (*jinya*) in the midst of war. In the usual presentation, the narrator sings, "He looks at his wife Sagami with stern displeasure and goes to sit without speaking" (191). As Kumagai walks past her, he realizes that she is there, and, with an expression combining amazement and consternation, stops to glare at her for being where she does not belong. Onoe Shōroku II (1913-1989) once added a new touch of his own on his entrance. After reading the signboard, and while still outside the gate, he noticed with the conventional expression of surprise Sagami's presence within. With Shōroku noticing Sagami from outside the gate, rather than after walking by her, the actor playing Sagami had to alter his position so he was no longer cringing in Gunji's shadow but was instead in a much more exposed position that allowed Sagami to greet her husband as he entered the camp. This change seems to have softened Kumagai's annoyance with Sagami and to have increased sympathy for her, at an earlier point than usual in the play That it was not retained in subsequent revivals suggests that it is more desirable for

Kumagai to show annoyance here because of the contrast it sets up with his later behavior.

Figure 105. Kumagai (Matsumoto Kōshirō IX) stops to stare at Sagami. (Photo: James R. Brandon.)

In the Danjūrō *kata*, when Kumagai sees his wife he slaps his thighs briskly before proceeding up the steps to sit at the center of the platform. Some actors—such as Kataoka Nizaemon XV (b. 1944)—grasp the *hakama* trousers and then release them before slapping their thighs. Since Shikan actors do not turn around to glare at Sagami until Kumagai has his right foot on the bottom step leading to the upstage platform, his position—with his back to the audience—is strikingly different from that of Danjūrō actors at this moment. As he frowns at her, the wooden clappers (*tsuke*) are struck, highlighting the emotion.

The Pipe or the Fan

When Kumagai sits, he must withdraw the longer of his two swords and place the sheathed weapon at his left side. He sits holding his battle fan erect in his right hand, resting it on his lap. Gunji and Sagami take up positions on the stage right side of the platform. According to the Shikan *kata,* Gunji pushes a tobacco box in Sagami's direction before leaving at Kumagai's command and Sagami busies herself with the box, lighting Kumagai's

 pipe, as he is turned slightly upstage during Gunji's exit while the narrator sings, "Watching him go, Kumagai speaks" (192).

Figure 106. Kumagai (Ichikawa Ennosuke III) sits while holding his battle fan vertically in his lap. (Photo: Tobe, *Kabuki no Mikata.*)

Kumagai berates Sagami for coming to the camp, and she explains how her poignant concern for Kojirō drew her there. Queried as to Kojirō's welfare, Kumagai responds harshly at first but then softens and seems saddened when he tells her that the youth behaved valiantly in battle and was slightly wounded. When Sagami asks whether it was not a fatal wound, Kumagai cuts into her last syllable, saying *"Sore, sore, sore,"*[5] an expletive that might be rendered, "There, there, there" (it does not appear in Brandon's translation). Actors following the Danjūrō *kata* tap the handle of their battle fan on the floor before them in three rapid beats, one for each *sore,* to stress the words; some then thrust it sharply toward Sagami on the words, "Would you grieve?" (193). As mentioned, the Shikan tradition holds that Sagami should placate Kumagai by lighting his pipe from the tobacco box. Furthermore, since Kumagai would then have the pipe to smoke, he could use it instead of his fan to tap on the floor, thus adding variety to the role by diminishing the use of the fan, which is later used extensively. But Nakamura Kichiemon I (1886-1954), one of the greatest Kumagais and the actor most responsible for the transmission of the Danjūrō *kata* to the present, could not shake the feeling that, for all the domesticity implicit in the action of Sagami handing her spouse the pipe, the business reminded him too forcibly of a stage prostitute's behavior, and he refused to use it (Kawatake 1955, 407). Various Shikan actors, among them Nakamura Utaemon V (1866-1940) and Shōroku (in his Shikan performances), felt similarly and preferred tapping with the fan instead of the pipe. Even when Utaemon used the tobacco box in his performance, he chose to emphasize his words with the fan.

Lady Fuji Attacks Kumagai

Kumagai tells Sagami that he placed the wounded Kojirō safely in camp
and then struck off the head of Atsumori, finishing his speech in a tone of
exultation. At this, Atsumori's mother, Lady Fuji, overhearing from within
the small room at stage left, rushes out, dagger in hand, to dispatch her
son's killer. A complex series of moves and countermoves follows during
which Kumagai—who is on his knees during most of the scene—dodges
Lady Fuji's blows, subdues her, realizes who it is he is restraining, and
again must overcome her wild slashing. Finally, as the narrator sings,
"Meeting so unexpectedly, he leaps back and bows in respect" (193), he
demonstrates that he means no harm by sliding his short sword toward her
and by performing an ostentatious bow of obeisance.

The principal variations in the *kata* during this active mimetic scene
are worth noting. Shikan actors disarm Fuji by knocking her dagger from
her hand with the fan; Danjūrō actors prefer to use their fist. Toward the
end of the sequence, many Danjūrō actors push their short sword toward
Fuji, who is to their left, and, facing front, point to it with their left hand.
But Danjūrō XII (b. 1946) faces upstage after pushing the sword, a gesture
that allows him to point to the sword with his right hand as he looks up at
the standing Fuji over his right shoulder; he then withdraws his right knee
so that he may face forward to make his grand bow. Shikan actors, however, do not point to the sword at all. Instead, they grasp their *hakama* at the
thighs, step back rapidly while extending their left hand toward Fuji in a
strong gesture of restraint, and freeze in a climactic *mie* before engaging in
the business of prostration.

The *Monogatari*

Further into the scene, Fuji pressures Sagami into agreeing to assist in re-
venging herself on Kumagai but the women are overcome with emotion.
Kumagai reluctantly agrees to explain his slaying of Atsumori. In his famous narrative speech (*monogatari*), to the accompaniment of the narrator
and shamisen player, he employs his fan to act out the alleged slaying of
Atsumori. This dramatic highlight is roughly equivalent in theatrical impact
to the "St. Crispian's Day" speech in *Henry V*, although it is perhaps more
appropriate to think of it in light of a messenger speech from Greek tragedy.
Unlike other famous *monogatari*, it is made up entirely of falsehoods. The
speech, which lasts nine minutes, is spoken with the actor positioned on the
platform at center and seated on one or both knees throughout.

There are at least twenty-five points in the *monogatari* that allow for a
comparison between the Shikan and Danjūrō. Here I describe only the more
obvious variations. One such moment occurs on the narrator's line,

"Holding the fan, he motioned him to return"
(194), as Kumagai pulls the fan open to reveal its
gold circle on a scarlet background (the colors
are reversed on the other side) and does a *mie*
with it held over his right shoulder as the *tsuke*
clappers crack. The Danjūrō actor poses with the
left foot thrust forward while looking off to the
left. The Shikan *kata* does not seem to be much
different, but Ichikawa Ennosuke III (b. 1939),
one of the few contemporary actors to provide
several of his own *kata* for specific highlights
(while in other respects selecting from
whichever tradition he finds more appropriate),
performs it while leaning back on his left knee,
his right knee raised, his gaze directed to the right.

(top) Figure 107. Kumagai (Kōshirō VIII) cuts a
mie on "Holding the fan . . . " This is the Danjūrō
kata. (Photo: Shōchiku.)

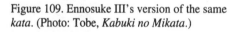

Figure 108. The same *kata* performed by
Ichikawa Danjūrō XII. Note the slight differences
in his position and the direction of his gaze.
(Photo: author's collection.)

Figure 109. Ennosuke III's version of the same
kata. (Photo: Tobe, *Kabuki no Mikata*.)

A strong pose is taken on the line "until he
turned his horse's head" (194), when—as if whip-
ping the animal—Kumagai lightly strikes the
back of his left hand twice with the open fan and
mimes steering his horse's head by holding the
open fan upside down by its outer ribs in the
"mountain" position. In the Danjūrō *kata*, the actor's right knee is raised and the fan is held out to
the left side, while Shikan actors hold it out to the
right against their raised right knee.

Another important moment involving a
significant technical difference comes at the narrator's line, "brushing off the
dust" (195). Here Danjūrō actors raise the short sword in a vertical position,
lift the fan, snap it open, and flick it once near the sword as if brushing the
dust off Atsumori. Shikan actors, instead of holding up the sword, strike the

left sleeve two or three times in a manner that is said to resemble the dusting off of straw sandals.

(left) Figure 110. Kumagai (Kōshirō VIII) mimes steering his horse's head. (Photo: Tobe, *Kabuki no Mikata*.)

(above, right) Figure 111. A variant of the head-steering *kata*, performed by Danjūrō XI. Ennosuke III uses the same *kata*. (Photo: Shōchiku.)

Figure 112. The *hirayama mie*, with the actor (Onoe Shōroku II) not using the top step for the pose. (Photo: Umemura Yutaka.)

Then one of the more controversial *monogatari* passages appears, the one in which the narrator sings, "Then I heard! From the mountain-top behind me, routed Hirayama cried out!" (195). Danjūrō IX, thinking of the physical layout of the scenery and action in the "Suma Ura" scene which precedes "Kumagai Jinya," decided to revise this to read "from yonder mountaintop," and instead of turning upstage he saw "the routed Hirayama" by looking "yonder" (out front). He then stared at Sagami while pointing with his fan to "yonder mountaintop," snapped it open, and held it upside down near his chest in his left hand, throwing his right leg out, stamping with it on the top step, and bringing his right fist near his chest in a grandiose *mie* accompanied by the beating of the *tsuke* as he stared out over the top of the fan. This famous pose is called the *hirayama mie*. Danjūrō's disciple, Kōshirō VII (1870-1949), kept the original line (as have most post-Danjūrō actors) and, as the words "behind me" suggest, looked over his shoulder to the rear while performing the *mie* with his left instead of his right foot. In the Shikan version of the pose the actor turns upstage to see where Hirayama's voice is coming from, but the sequence of other movements is a bit different both from that of Danjūrō and the revised version of his followers. Most crucial is the final *mie* position, in which the right foot, like that of Danjūrō, is placed on the top step but—instead of holding the upside-down fan near the chest in his left hand—the Shikan actor holds it over his head in the right while extending his left hand to the side with splayed fingers. This is the most marked variation between the Danjūrō and Shikan *kata* in the entire *monogatari* section. A major variation in the Shikan pose is that of Ennosuke III. Rather than extending his empty left hand out to the side, he thrusts it out while gripping the upside-down fan. Both Kōshirō VIII and Nizaemon XV appear to have used a similar pose in some of their revivals. Shōroku II once claimed that the actor can intensify the Shikan *hirayama mie* by opening his mouth as wide as possible and curling hack his tongue to hide the teeth, which is apparently how such poses were done in the candlelit days when dim lighting made it hard to see the actors' faces (Fujino 1961, 147).

The *monogatari* concludes as the women weep loudly and Kumagai glares at his wife, bows humbly to Fuji, and poses looking ahead. The chief

difference between the Danjūrō and Shikan *kata* here is the fillip added by the former with the extra phrase, "Thus I fulfilled the custom of the battlefield!" (196), delivered with great vocal power as Kumagai raises his right knee, brings his right hand in a circular gesture to rest on it, and thereby completes the *monogatari*.

Figure 113. The Danjūrō-style *hirayama mie*, with Kōshirō IX as Kumagai. Compare Kumagai's pose here with his foot on the top step to that in figure 112, where the top step is not used. (Photo: James R. Brandon.)

The women lament, and Kumagai asks Sagami to take Fuji away from the camp. With great dignity, he rises and takes his leave through the upstage sliding doors. A feeling of deep gravity pervades his acting as he prepares for the inspection of "Atsumori's" captured head. In the following scene the women mourn Atsumori's death. When Fuji attempts to play Atsumori's keepsake flute she thinks she sees his shadow on the *shōji* doors, but opening them reveals only his suit of armor.

The Head Inspection

The Danjūrō actor, having had a few minutes to change costume, now appears for the second time, entering through the upstage doors wearing a formal pine-green costume of long trailing trousers (*nagabakama*) and *kataginu*. The Shikan *kata* calls for the same costume that Kumagai wore earlier, although Shōroku II changed into a long-trousered, heavily brocaded costume. Kumagai bears a cylindrical wooden box—Danjūrō actors carry it against the left breast and Shikan actors against the right—that contains the head to be inspected. Such boxes are standard in head inspection (*kubi jikken*) scenes (see figure 92).

(left) Figure 114. Kumagai (Kōshirō VIII) cleans off the shaft of the signboard. (Photo: Tobe, *Kabuki no Mikata*.)

Figure 115. In a variant of the previous *kata*, Kumagai (Ennosuke III) wipes off the signboard itself. (Photo: Tobe, *Kabuki no Mikata*.)

Kumagai's every movement is burdened with his preoccupation concerning the inspection. Momentarily detained by Fuji and Sagami, he pushes them off and heads for the *hanamichi*, but he is stopped by Yoshitsune's offstage voice asking him to present the head for verification. The upstage sliding doors now open to reveal an exterior vista that was not there before; Yoshitsune, dressed in gorgeous armor, enters with his retinue and sits in a camp chair placed up left center. Kumagai moves up the steps and expresses his reverence for his master, who demands to see the head. Shikan actors here slip off their right shoulder wing to signal their preparation for physical activity. Kumagai then moves stage right and leans over the platform to pull up the signboard he had examined during his first entrance. He withdraws a wad of paper from the breast of his kimono and brushes the dirt from the base of the pole. Ennosuke III dusts off the written portion as well, presumably to show respect for this important message.

The signboard is then placed on the floor before Yoshitsune and the speech beginning "A short time ago at the Horikawa Palace" (200) is spoken. As Kumagai lifts the lid of the box, the startled Sagami begins to rise but he forces her down the steps to the right with the signboard. Then Fuji is similarly forced down to the stage left side. Kumagai moves forward and places his right foot on the top step, his right trouser leg trailing down the steps. He turns the signboard upside down, holding it against his left shoulder with his left hand on the upper part of the pole and his right on its lower portion as he stares down right and freezes in the climactic "signboard *mie*" (*seisatsu mie*). This is one of the most powerful *mie* in the entire *kabuki* repertoire and certainly the most famous in this play.

Figure 116. Kōshirō VIII performs the "signboard *mie*" (*seisatsu no mie*) in the Danjūrō style, with the sign pointing downwards. (Photo: Shōchiku.)

The principal alternative version of this pose belongs to the infrequently seen Shikan tradition. Here the signboard is held right side up against the left shoulder, as in the original puppet version. It has been argued that this is the most appropriate pose because it is irreverent to hold so important an item as this signboard upside down and Kumagai, of all people, would treat it respectfully.

With great emotion, Kumagai then asks Yoshitsune if he has interpreted the ambiguous words on the signboard correctly. His actions now perfectly match the dramatic rhythm of the narrator's words, "He cries out!" (201), as he removes the lid, puts his right hand on the topknot of the head, and thrusts the head on its stand toward Yoshitsune. The latter, staring at it through the ribs of his fan, accepts it as Atsumori's. The staging question faced here is whether Kumagai should be angled slightly upstage to face Yoshitsune, or whether both Kumagai and Yoshitsune should be positioned three-quarters facing front: most actors (Danjūrō and Shikan) do the former, but Ennosuke III does the latter. At least one actor has even played the scene facing full front, holding the head to the side as if unable to look at it.

Figure 117. The "signboard *mie*" in the Shikan style, performed by Shōroku II. Note both the position of the signboard and the striking difference in Kumagai's costume as compared to the Danjūrō costume in the previous and following pictures. (Photo: Fujino, *Maruhon Kabuki: Gikyoku to Butai*.)

Figure 118. The mixing of two *kata* is seen here with Kumagai (Kataoka Gatō V) wearing the Danjūrō-style costume but holding the signboard in the Shikan pose. (Photo: *Engekikai*.)

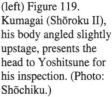

(left) Figure 119. Kumagai (Shōroku II), his body angled slightly upstage, presents the head to Yoshitsune for his inspection. (Photo: Shōchiku.)

(right) Figure 120. An alternate *kata* according to which Kumagai (Bandō Jūzaburō) holds the head to his side while continuing to face front. (Photo: *Engekikai.*)

(left) Figure 121. The head is placed on the edge of the platform for Sagami to approach on her own as Kumagai (Kōshirō IX) watches. (Photo: James R. Brandon.)

(right) Figure 122. A *kat kata* in which Kumagai (Ennosuke III) hands the head to Sagami. (Photo: Tobe, *Kabuki no Mikata.*)

Kumagai now allows Sagami to hold the head (in truth her son's), telling her to show it to Lady Fuji. The actor playing Kumagai will then ask himself whether he should, like most players in the two major traditions, place the head on the edge of the platform for her while retreating up center or place the head in Sagami's hands, thereby expressing his parental and marital affection. Ennosuke III, who stresses the husband-wife relationship, chooses the second approach.

Sagami's *Kudoki*

In both *kabuki* and the puppet theatre the sequence that follows is a scene of lamentation (*kudoki*). It is one of the most bathetic in all *kabuki* and is designed to show off the female impersonator's emotional technique. During Sagami's business Fuji realizes that the head is not her son's and that a substitution has been arranged. Meanwhile the grieving Kumagai sits impassively, although his eyes must somehow betray his deep pain. Utaemon V, at the end of the *kudoki*, did a bit more than sit impassively when the narrator sang, "The husband does not even blink before his lord, though tears stream from his eyes" (203). He allowed the fan resting on his right knee to slip, then, as he caught himself, he and Sagami looked in anguish at one another followed by a glance at Yoshitsune suggesting deep embarrassment. Finally, offstage music representing the sounds of battle is heard and Kumagai begins to collect himself. Ordered to prepare for battle, he deferentially takes his leave of Yoshitsune through the upstage doors.

Kumagai Takes the Tonsure

Figure 123.
Kumagai (Kōshirō
IX) appears in a full
set of armor. (Photo:
James R. Brandon.)

Kumagai, having once more made an extensive costume change, enters up center; he is dressed from head to toe in armor, including a horned helmet. A large box bearing Atsumori's armor (Atsumori himself is supposed to be secreted inside) is placed by retainers on the stage proper. Kumagai kneels to Yoshitsune's right, requests the leave the latter has promised him, and presents him with a sheaf of paper containing his sheared-off topknot. He subsequently removes his armor and—to his wife's great surprise—reveals that his recent experiences in war have persuaded him to give up the warrior's life and become a monk.

At this point, immediately after Kumagai's line, "My Lord, please grant the leave I have requested" (210), there is an important narrator's line omitted in most Danjūrō *kata* productions (including the one translated in Brandon): "As he removes his helmet, he reveals the partly shorn head of a priest" (*Kabuto o toreba. Kiriharautaru uhatsu no so.* Fujino, 136).[6]

The line signifies that Kumagai still has most of his hair; only his topknot has been removed, implying that the actor's long sidelocks should remain, but loosened and gathered into a ponytail. Indeed, this is precisely how Shōroku II's wig was arranged when he performed the Shikan *kata*. Most actors since Utaemon III, however, have followed the tradition of showing a completely shaved head when their helmet is removed. The contrast between the fully armored warrior and the priest's round dome is visually striking. Actors differ in whether they remove the helmet before or after they take off their armor; the majority remove the helmet only after they are already revealed in their priest's robes. Some critics consider it more aesthetically effective for the actor to remove the helmet first. They argue that the sight of a man in monk's robes wearing a warrior's helmet looks silly, the head being so greatly out of proportion to the body. Among the few contemporary actors who do remove the helmet first—thereby creating the interesting look of a priest-warrior—are Ennosuke III and Nizaemon XV. Utaemon V removed the helmet first, as well, suggesting that it is a Shikan *kata*.

Figure 124. Kumagai (Ennosuke III) in the Danjūrō style, with his shorn head shown while he is still in armor. Usually, the helmet is not removed until after the armor is doffed. (Photo: Tobe, *Kabuki no Mikata.*)

As might be expected, Danjūrō and Shikan actors differ in their approach to the monk's costume. The Danjūrō costume is considerably more realistic, reminiscent of the garb worn even today by itinerant beggar monks in Japan. Over a gray silk under-robe is worn a black outer robe, white cotton half-gloves covering only the backs of the hands, and straw sandals without *tabi*. The Shikan actor wears a white satin, key-patterned kimono, a priest's black neck stole, and white *tabi* with double-thick white silk thongs. Invariably actors wearing the black robes of the Danjūrō *kata* appear with their heads shaved, but those wearing the Shikan costume prefer the ponytail wig. The decision seems to be based on the level of theatricality involved. As noted earlier, the Danjūrō tradition is more attuned to a realistic, subtle flavor in makeup and costuming, while the Shikan actor prefers a more flamboyant effect. A completely bald, *tabi*-less monk in gray and black with only touches of white is far more restrained in appearance, and makes a much more dramatic contrast with Kumagai's earlier appearance, than does the shift to a full-length shiny white kimono, which is normally accompanied by an eye-catching shoulder-length ponytail wig. Interestingly, Kōshirō VIII once appeared in a combination of ponytail wig and black and gray robes, presumably seeking to strike a balance between the two traditions.

Figure 125. A version in which Kumagai (Kōshirō VIII) wears the Danjūrō-style priest's garments with the Shikan-style partially shorn head. (Photo: *Engekikai*.)

Figure 126. In the Shikan *kata*, Kumagai (Shōroku II) wears the priest's robe with a partially shorn head. He is in position for the final tableau in the version, which does not require a *hanamichi* exit (see below). (Photo: Tobe, *Kabuki no Mikata*.)

Yoshitsune grants Kumagai his wish to become a monk; the latter is no longer a proud and valiant samurai but a humble seeker after enlightenment who has renounced this world of vanity.[7] Shikan actors remain on the upper platform, but in Danjūrō versions Kumagai descends the steps, puts on his straw sandals, hangs a monk's alms bag around his neck, and takes a thin bamboo staff and a round wicker hat. From this point to the final curtain the Danjūrō and Shikan traditions sharply diverge.

Figure 127. The complete Danjūrō *kata* for Kumagai (Kōshirō VIII) as a monk. (Photo: author's collection.)

Kumagai's Final Exit

The Danjūrō exit—one of *kabuki's* best known—employs the *hanamichi* runway according to the convention called "outside the curtain exit" (*makusoto no hikkomi*), while the Shikan *kata* ends the play with a company tableau and completely ignores the *hanamichi*. In Danjūrō-style revivals, the stage business is designed to portray a Kumagai who is torn between the life he is leaving behind and the one he is entering. His exit begins when Yoshitsune, standing up center with the exposed head, speaks of consecrating the head at Suma Temple; meanwhile, everyone freezes in a tableau. A section of "passed-along dialogue" (*watari zerifu*) follows in which the assembled characters express their sadness at what has transpired. At the conclusion Kumagai, who is down right, bows to Yoshitsune and Fuji. After a glance at his wife, he moves quickly to the *hanamichi* where he is stopped at *shichisan* when Yoshitsune—holding forth the head—calls out to him. Kumagai turns slowly and gazes back at it. As he ponders the transience of life he slowly utters the line, "Sixteen years have passed like a single day. It is a dream, a dream!" (210). Weeping profusely, he slowly rubs his shaven pate in a circular motion, from back to front, as the narrator compares him to various natural images of transience. The head rubbing must be done with discretion. Moving too abruptly or placing the hand directly on top of the dome may strike the audience as laughable.

Danjūrō IX, a master at justifying stage business, short-circuited any latent humor in the gesture by taking a step, absently straightening up, passing the hat from his right hand to his left (which also held the staff), and curling his right hand into a fist. The fist somehow seemed to energize his warrior spirit; as he spoke the words "sixteen years" with deep nostalgia for the vanished past, he vacantly raised the fist shoulder high as if handling a weapon. And then—gathering himself—suddenly opened the hand while sighing, "Ahh!" With his mouth wide open, he slapped the back of his head with the open hand, a gesture that led him, quite naturally, to rub the rear of his head and then, finally, the entire head.

Figure 128. Kumagai (Kōshirō VII) on the *hanamichi* stops to rub his shaved head. (Photo: Tobe, *Kabuki no Mikata.*)

Kumagai then looks toward the head once more and starts toward the stage. Overcome with feeling, he staggers backward several paces and turns away from the sight as he falls to a cross-legged position on the *hanamichi* and claps his straw hat over his head, pressing its sides to his face to block his vision, the staff trembling in his hand. The curtain closes behind him, and the wooden clappers (*ki*) are heard as he sits with his face hidden in his hat. A *shamisen* player now appears from behind the curtain, stands at the juncture of runway and stage, and places one leg on a small box to balance his instrument. When Kumagai hears martial music coming from the battlefield he hurriedly rises, almost unconsciously, still gripped by the warrior spirit, and looks off into the distance (toward the rear of the auditorium), only to catch himself, realizing that he has abandoned the martial life for one of prayer.

Figure 129. Kumagai (Kōshirō VIII) sits on the *hanamichi* and covers his ears with his hat. (Photo: James R. Brandon.)

Standing there with hat and staff in his left hand, he lets his head fall forward with grief, notices his soiled robe, and lightly brushes off his knees. He takes the staff in his left hand and slowly turns to face the rear of the *hanamichi*. He begins to depart, but, as if in the grip of an irresistible force, he stops, deliberately turns to face the stage, and moves inexorably back in the direction from which he has come. He manages to pull up short of the stage, however, knowing it is too late to return, and once more is drawn by the martial music heard in the distance. Several short steps pull him to *shi-*

chisan, where he halts momentarily. Fighting back his tears he puts the hat on his head with great resolve, pressing it against his ears to drown out the sounds. (The round hat has now served to shut out both sight and sound.) Trembling violently, he forces himself to depart as the tempo rapidly accelerates. This complex exit exemplifies the deep psychological realism with which Danjūrō IX is said to have infused *kabuki's* otherwise highly stylized acting.

Figure 130. Kumagai uses the hat as blinders. (Photo: Tobe, *Kabuki no Mikata*.)

The Shikan IV *kata,* although it is based on the puppet performance, requires a slight rearrangement of the dialogue from the puppet original. Directly following Kumagai's prayerful invocation on the platform, "Namu Amida Butsu" (208), he skips forward to what are usually his final words, "Sixteen years have passed like a single day!" and, overcome with sadness, completes the line, "It is a dream, a dream!" (210). Then follows a version of the head rubbing business, at which point the narrator delivers his final passage about the snow and the sunlight while Kumagai faces right and fingers the rosary in his left hand. With downcast expression he removes several sheets of paper from his robe with his right hand and presses them against his face as he breaks out in loud sobs.

It is at this point (and not earlier as in the Danjūrō version) that he speaks his lines about standing "apart from the bloody carnage" (208) and helping both the Heike and the Genji souls. He descends to stage right on the speech about "a monk's black robes," and a tableau is formed of Sagami and Kumagai right, Midaroku and Fuji left, and Yoshitsune up center. The latter declares, "Live your lives in good health," and Kumagai faces left, joining in on the last line of the "pass-along" dialogue section. He bows to Yoshitsune, grasps his rosary on the line "tears cloud their voices," prevents Sagami from impulsively moving toward the head, and, while the sound of the *ki* clappers is heard, the curtain closes.

This kind of curtain is known as a *hippari no mie* or "pulling tableau," named after the multiple angles of the stage picture which "pull" the various characters toward one another in terms of their mutual emotional attachments. Such a "company picture" is more in keeping with the theatricality of old-style *kabuki* endings than the psychologically detailed method of the Danjūrō tradition in which the star demonstrates the depth of his realistic technique. Kichiemon I remarks in his memoirs that although he generally followed the Danjūrō *kata,* he occasionally felt inclined to alter his approach and twice used the *hippari no mie* ending for his performance. He admits, in fact, the superiority of the Shikan ending because it allows Kumagai to share his wife's grief rather than deserting her (Kawatake, 409-410).

Figure 131. Ennosuke III's exit in which Sagami accompanies her husband on the *hanamichi.* (Photo: Tobe, *Kabuki no Mikata.*)

Two other experiments with the exit are of interest. In the production directed by Takechi Tetsuji in 1949, two *hanamichi* were used. Kumagai and Sagami departed down the main runway while Midaroku and Fuji left on the other. In one of his stagings, Ennosuke III had Sagami join Kumagai in his *hanamichi* exit, although he did not use the other runway for Midaroku and Fuji. Critics have praised this innovation because it focuses on both bereaved parents, not just the father. It also brings into focus the often neglected marital affection between Sagami and Kumagai.

Although the "outside the curtain" exit continues to predominate in contemporary performances, some critics insist that since the Danjūrō variant reeks of sentimentalism, the Shikan tableau ending is more authentic. This is because Kumagai is no longer torn between his passion for battle and his indignation to renounce worldly things. His mind is made up before his first entrance, and from the moment he appears it is clear that he has resolved to follow the way of Buddha. Furthermore the Shikan method allows Kumagai to share his grief with his distraught wife, in contrast to the preceding "Suma Ura" scene, which Kumagai ends by himself. According to this reasoning, the "outside the curtain" exit may result from the actor's wish to show off his individual acting technique, since it is not so true to the spirit of the text as the Shikan *kata*.[8]

The Uses of *Kata*

These details reveal not only the importance of *kata* in *kabuki* but also the degree of flexibility the tradition permits. An actor following one or the other *kata* does have the freedom to make selective use of *kata* from an alternative tradition when it suits his purposes. And, depending on the actor's taste, there are many minor variations even in the established *kata*. In many scenes, however, including "Kumagai Jinya," the dominant tradition too frequently holds the stage; indeed, when a major actor attempts an alternative *kata* it is considered a noteworthy occasion. Shōroku II presented Shikan *kata* revivals of "Kumagai Jinya" only a handful of times during the last three decades of his life; apparently the pull of the Danjūrō tradition and the expectations of audiences were too strong to resist. While specific Shikan *kata* may crop up here and there in another's performance, one is unlikely to come across a fuller version than that of Shōroku. Only Ennosuke III's approach has offered theatregoers some original *kata* and Ennosuke has been careful to present them within what is otherwise a blend of Danjūrō and Shikan techniques. This is as far as one can expect a *kabuki* actor to take his innovations in a classic play. No matter how unique the interpretation of individual moments or even the overall mood of a performance, the traditional outlines must remain intact.

One should not resent the *kata* system, which does preserve the traditional interpretations, so much as the lack of performances that take full advantage of the options open to performers. The late nineteenth century produced a number of actors—such as Shikan and Danjūrō—whose experimental interpretations were so exceptional that they eventually became traditional. Why should a contemporary actor not have comparable freedom to investigate new approaches to the classic roles? Even if he develops only one recognized improvement in an interpretation, that innovation should encourage others to seek similarly exciting insights. Certainly the readiness of audiences to accept a revitalization of the *kata* has been demonstrated by the popularity of Ennosuke III over the past few decades.

Without ongoing experiments with new *kata* or a serious attempt to revive periodically those *kata* that have fallen out of favor, *kabuki* will edge ever closer to the point where the only difference between one production of a play and another are the personalities of the stars. In fact, Shōroku's revivals of the Shikan *kata* are said to have been imperfect because he had no living teacher to transmit them and probably had to depend instead on textual and pictorial research. Unless the alternative as well as the standard interpretations are continually transmitted, even the limited artistic freedom of which I have spoken will eventually disappear.

NOTES

This chapter, originally given as a paper at "Theatre East and West," a National Endowment for the Arts seminar at the University of Maryland, July 1989, was first published in *Asian Theatre Journal* 8 (Spring 1991) as "'Kumagai's Battle Camp': Form and Tradition in *Kabuki* Acting." The present version is slightly revised.

1. Not only did the Zenshin-za revise the story, but it set the action at the ruins of an old temple and called the piece "The 'Don't Cut Off a Finger' Kumagai's Battle Camp" (*Isshi o Kiranai Kumagai Jinya*). The idea was to stress the tragedy of two mothers and a father who had lost their sons at war. The play was performed in semi-*kabuki* style and included the use of the narrator and *shamisen* player. The Takechi version of 1949, given in Osaka, gives a fairer idea of the kind of experimentation one is likely to encounter in *kabuki*. It sought to produce the play strictly according to the original puppet play style: avoiding the special metrical rhythm of *kabuki* verse, using a speaking pattern as close to that of the puppet theatre narrator as possible, eliminating most of the *kabuki*-style offstage musical accompaniment, and working toward an ensemble performance rather than one geared to the star. See, for example, Tobe (1973, 178)

2. This is, admittedly, the purist point of view. As I point out later, however, too often the standard approach is preferred to the alternative one. See Bach (1989).

3. Neither actor actually created all the *kata* associated with his name. Rather they codified *kata* that had already been created—in Danjūrō IX's case by Danjūrō VII (1791-1859) and in Shikan's case by Nakamura Utaemon III (1778-1838) and taught to Shikan by Utaemon IV (1798-1852).

4. The Shikan *kata* are rarely seen anymore. Among the few twentieth-century actors who are known to have attempted the Shikan method are Nakamura Utaemon V (1866-1940) and his pupil Ōtani Tomoemon (1886-1943), both of whom played the *kata* with considerable integrity, and Onoe Shōroku II, who first tried the Shikan *kata* in the mid-1950s but, aside from one or two later occasions, returned to the Danjūrō style in subsequent presentations. Several actors have tried combinations of the two styles. Shōroku's father, Matsumoto Kōshirō VII, for example, once used Shikan's costume and makeup but mainly

followed the stage directions of Danjūrō. Nakamura Ganjirō I (1860-1935) played Kumagai once by using mostly Danjūrō *kata* but switching to the Shikan *kata* for the play's final scene. A similarly hybrid approach was tried by Kōshirō VIII in 1961, but like his brother Shōroku II he reverted to the Danjūrō *kata* in later productions. Another *kata* tradition for the play once existed as well, that of Ichikawa Danzō IV (1745-1808)—but it has vanished. There are some surprising, if subtle, variations in this makeup from actor to actor. Apart from details concerning eyebrows, eyes, and lips, differences appear in the relative darkness of the hue used for the *kumadori* temple lines, the position and angle of these lines, and whether lines are even worn at all.

5. Shikan actors often say "*korya, korya, korya*" ("here, here, here").

6. This is a good example of the textual variation one finds in *kabuki* scripts. In most Danjūrō-style revivals the line about the removal of the helmet is changed to one in which neither helmet nor partly shorn priest's head is mentioned. Instead, the line simply declares that Yoshitsune is offered Kumagai's lopped-off topknot (*kiriharautaru no motodori*) and is sung as the action is performed.

7. The original text also calls for Sagami to cut her hair with her dagger to signify her own renunciation of worldly matters. This is rarely done nowadays.

8. Ennosuke's infusion of new *kata* into *Kumagai Jinya* is indicative of his position as perhaps *kabuki*'s most innovative actor. In his review of Ennosuke's 1973 performance of the play, critic Numa Kusaame (1973, 62) noted: "Shikan's were the Edo-period *kata*, Danjūrō's were the Meiji period *kata*, Kichiemon's were the Taishō period [1912-1926] *kata*, such actors as Kōshirō, Nizaemon, the late Bandō Jūzaburō, and others transformed the Kichiemon *kata* into the Shōwa period *kata* (1926-1989), while Ennosuke's may be said to be the *kata* of the 1970s."

REFERENCES

Bach, Faith. 1989. "New Directions in *Kabuki*." *Asian Theatre Journal* 6: 1 (Spring).
Brandon, James R. 1978. "Form in *Kabuki* Acting." In James R. Brandon, William P. Malm, and Donald H. Shively, eds. *Studies in* Kabuki*: Its Acting, Music, and Historical Context*. Honolulu: University of Hawaii Press.
————, trans. 1992. "Kumagai's Battle Camp." In Kabuki*: Five Classic Plays*. Honolulu: University of Hawaii Press. Originally published 1975.
Engekikai, unidentified issues.
Fujii Yasuo. 1978. "*Ichinotani Futaba Gunki*." *Engekikai* 36 (April).
Fujino Yoshio, ed. 1961. *Maruhon Kabuki: Gikyoku to Butai*. Tokyo: Sekigaku Shobō.
Hamamura Yonezō. 1921. *Kabuki no Mikata*. Tokyo: Hagino Yasha.
Honma Hisao. 1960. *Kabuki*. Tokyo: Shohakusha.
Kagayama Naozō. 1968. *Kabuki*. Tokyo: Yazankaku.
Kawatake Shigetoshi. 1955. *Nakamura Kichiemon*. Tokyo: Toyamabō.

Kawatake Toshio, ed. 1982. *Genshoku Kabuki Shōsai.* Tokyo: Gurafusha.

Leiter, Samuel L., trans, and ed. 2000. *The Art of* Kabuki: *Five Famous Plays.* Rev. ed. Mineola, N.Y.: Dover. Originally published 1979.

Numa Kusaame. 1973. "Shinro Sen no Kabuki." *Engekikai* 31 (February).

Suzuki Shunba. 1927. *Kabuki no Kata.* Tokyo: Kabuki Shuppanbu.

Tahara, Mildred, trans. 1969. *"Kumagai Jinya."* In souvenir program of touring *kabuki* troupe. New York: Program Publishing Company.

Tobe Ginsaku. 1973. *Kabuki no Mikata: Gihō to Miryoku.* Tokyo: Daiichi Hōkji.

Toita Yasuji. 1981. "Hōru Hirayama no Mie." *Engekikai* 39 (April).

Authentic *Kabuki*: American Style

"In 1958 the Institute for Advanced Studies in the Theatre Arts (IASTA) was chartered by the Board of Regents of the University of the State of New York. It was founded by John D. Mitchell and Miriam P. Mitchell in the belief that American actors and directors could benefit their own stage art by practical study of the theatre of other countries. To this end a program was launched whereby every year master theatre directors from different countries are brought to IASTA for a period of six to ten weeks to work with the American professional actors who are enrolled in IASTA. The cast is selected by auditions and the director works with his company on an English version of a play indigenous to his own country. The play is analyzed and explained, special techniques and styles to be used are studied, and finally the production is given before an invited audience." *IASTA Bulletin*

In January 1968 I learned that IASTA was planning an English-language production of the classic *kabuki* play *Kanjinchō* under the direction of two renowned *kabuki* actors, Matsumoto Kōshirō VIII and Nakamura Matagorō II. Remembering that the organization had produced English-language productions of the *nō* play *Ikkaku Sennin* and the *kabuki* play *Narukami* (this latter staged by Onoe Baikō VII) in 1965, I asked Dr. John Mitchell, IASTA's president, if I could attend rehearsals. Not only did he agree, he invited me to participate in the project as a *kōken*—a formal stage assistant.

It was not difficult to grasp why the position of *kōken* had gone begging among IASTA members. The *kōken's* job is to aid a major actor with his props and costumes without drawing attention to himself. (He is also supposed to be an understudy, but I was not.) It's a thankless job; much of the *kōken's* time is spent sitting motionless upstage on his knees in a formal position, his back three-quarters to the audience. Nonetheless, it provided me with an ideal vantage point from which to view impartially the methods the Japanese used to teach the *kabuki* style.

Figure 132. The author as *kōken*. (All photos Arthur Tress.)

Kanjinchō is one of the *Kabuki Jūhachiban* (Eighteen Famous *Kabuki* Plays) collection associated with the Ichikawa Danjūrō line of actors. IASTA had chosen it primarily because of its great popularity in Japan, where it is produced more frequently than any other dance play. But there were other points in its favor. Aside from the chorus and *kōken*, it has eleven roles, a relatively small number for a *kabuki* play. (IASTA reduced this number to nine.) The set, an adaptation of the formal setting for *nō* plays, consists simply of a back wall with a stylized painting of a pine tree, and two side walls, each with an entrance opening. In Tokyo's Kabuki-za the rear wall is upstage of an approximately 90-foot proscenium opening, but IASTA's stage was only about 21-feet wide—about the size of a *nō* stage—so the organization used the rear wall saved from a *nō* production it had staged.[1]

Figure 133. Benkei, Yoshitsune, and followers on the *hanamichi*.

To conform to traditional *kabuki* practice, IASTA built a *hanamichi*, although the physical layout of the theatre required some adaptation from the original models. Instead of running through the audience with spectators seated on both sides, IASTA's *hanamichi* abutted the wall at the audience's left, and ran from the down right corner of the stage, through the house, and into a large rehearsal room directly behind the auditorium.[2] One of the sliding doors that separate the rehearsal room from the auditorium was left open so that the actors, as in Japan, could enter and exit through a curtain strung across the opening. For those actors who had to enter via the *hanamichi*, the rehearsal room became a convenient dressing and make-up room.

The *kabuki* chorus traditionally sits upstage on raised levels that run the width of the rear wall. IASTA's stage, however, was too small to accommodate a chorus, so it built a special chorus platform below the down left proscenium wall. But aside from this, and the fact that the audience sat on only one side of the *hanamichi*, the set-up was essentially authentic.

Kanjinchō tells the story of how the priest, Benkei, helps his master, the nobleman Yoshitsune, pass an enemy barrier. Benkei makes him assume the disguise of a lowly porter. The group is supposedly on a pilgrimage to raise funds for a temple. Benkei is not only a formidable warrior, he is also a brilliant improviser when the guards suspect him and his men of being the enemy. One of his masterstrokes is to improvise a list of subscribers to the temple's welfare, even though the subscription list (*kanjinchō*) he reads from so fluently is blank. When Yoshitsune's disguise becomes apparent to an enemy soldier, Benkei beats his lord before the eyes of the barrier guard, Togashi. So unspeakable an act is striking his lord that, as a program note pointed out, "a Western audience may choose to think of the electrifying shock were there a play in which the disciple Peter were to strike Jesus in order to save his Master's life."

The play contains no female characters, but IASTA, wishing to give its actresses a chance to work in *kabuki* style, decided to use two casts, an all-male one and an all-female one. Authentic *kabuki's* female roles are played by *onnagata*, so this decision was unorthodox. But the directors were not adverse to the experiment. They probably rationalized that, after all, *kabuki* was originated by a female dancer, Okuni, and that today many women study *kabuki* dancing. In fact, their assistant on the production, Miyoko Watanabe, is a distinguished *kabuki* dance teacher in New York.[3]

The audition method, which IASTA had devised for previous Asian productions, was unique. A group of actors (all IASTA members) were drilled for a two-week period in all the aspects of *Kanjinchō*. First they studied how to walk in the style demanded by the play; then they learned the dance pieces in the sequence in which they appear in the play. After ten days or so, the directors blocked them and introduced scripts, making everyone study both major and minor parts.

When the two-week period was up, the casting sessions started. The directors ran through the play several times, interchanging roles at various points, to see which actors showed the best aptitude for the foreign style. At this stage I came into the production. Having seen *Kanjinchō* many times in Japan, I knew that though they still had far to go, the Americans had come quite a distance in the training period. Of the twenty-five actors who stayed with the training for the full two weeks, almost all got a role.

In the end four casts were chosen, two male and two female. There are only three major roles in *Kanjinchō*—Benkei, Togashi, and Yoshitsune—so most of the actors were cast as retainers or barrier guards. The plan was for the leading actors to play minor roles on the nights that their alternates were performing the important parts and vice-versa. But because of the limited number of women auditioning, and the lack of an appropriate type, only one female was chosen for Togashi.

In view of the outside professional obligations of various company members, a multiple cast system seemed a necessity. But from the beginning it presented problems. The schedule was set up to allow males to rehearse in the morning and females in the afternoon. Since several actors knew more than one role, there were usually enough people around to conduct a full rehearsal. However, it was rare that a pure female or male cast assembled in toto for a rehearsal.

What developed was that the duplication of roles forced the directors to work over and over with new actors, instead of polishing one performer. Most actors only got a chance to do their parts every other day. (Some of the leading actors, when playing minor roles, would duplicate, in a subdued manner, the complex movements being performed by their alternates.) It soon became evident that a few actors were greatly in need of extra rehearsals and that cast changes would have to be made. By the time the play opened the original concept of separate male and female companies had been modified to mixed companies with an all-male or all-female cast in the leading roles.

The directors taught the Americans the movements and postures of the play by using demonstration and imitation—in other words, by sheer rote. (Both, at one time in their careers, had played every role in the play.) Since the cast had learned the fundamentals of their movements and blocking in the training period, at each rehearsal the directors allowed them simply to run through the play. This procedure became standard: two run-throughs a day, one in the morning and one in the afternoon. As the entire play runs only about an hour, the procedure was a practical one.

Figure 134. Kōshirō VIII and the company bowing to each other.

Rehearsals, as in Japan, began and ended formally. The directors (called *sensei*, or master, by the actors) nearly always appeared in kimono. When they entered, making their acknowledgment, all made obeisance by getting on their knees and bowing low. This ritual was repeated after the note-giving sessions that followed each run-through. If an actor wanted to leave early, he had to catch the *sensei's* eye and then bow low before making his exit.

Of the two directors, the late Kōshirō, since he was a major star of the Japanese stage, had the more prestige. But the diminutive Matagorō, one of *kabuki's* most wide-ranging character actors, who can play women as well as men, is a master teacher of *kabuki* style and was the more active and demonstrative of the two in rehearsals. Matagorō's reputation as *kabuki's* leading teacher was enormously strengthened when he took over the training responsibilities for the *kabuki* acting program opened a few years later at the Kokuritsu Gekijō. He has even helped train and direct student actors at the University of Hawaii on several occasions.

(left) Figure 135. Kōshirō VIII demonstrating the *roppō* style of bounding exit.

Figure 136. An actress playing Benkei performing the *roppō*.

Although he would occasionally take an active part in the training, Kōshirō was more likely to sit calmly watching the proceedings, beating time with his fan and giving notes to an assistant. Matagorō would be right on stage with the actors, going through the motions with them, correcting mistakes. Gradually Matagorō left them more and more on their own, but he was always ready to jump on the stage to help an actor whose memory or technique had failed.

Although Matagorō and Kōshirō knew no English and the actors no Japanese, the language barrier was easily surmounted. An interpreter, of course, was always present, but the *kabuki* actors communicated so effectively through voice and gesture that words were seldom necessary. As Matagorō put them through their paces, the Americans could sense exactly what he wanted.

Figure 137. Matagorō II teaching Benkei's movements.

The actors, conditioned to Western practice, confessed in private that they would prefer fewer run-throughs and more polishing rehearsals. The directors seemed to take an almost completely external approach to the play, rarely interrupting to explain something, or to work on a difficult point. I do not, however, believe they did this out of a preference for form over inner conflict; as this book's chapter, "Four Interviews with *Kabuki* Actors," demonstrates, *kabuki* actors say that their art, despite its rigidly prescribed conventions, demands emotional and intellectual involvement. I think that, given only six weeks of rehearsal time, the directors simply did not want to confuse the actors with too many details. True diplomats, they seemed willing in the name of international good will to settle for something less than perfect.

Merely the idea of teaching Americans in six weeks a style the Japanese actor studies from early childhood would deter most *kabuki* players from attempting such a project. Yet rarely did Matagorō or Kōshirō display signs of temper, impatience, or disappointment; never did they refuse to spend additional time with an actor who requested it. Their reserve, diplomacy, and courtesy endeared them beyond words to their brother thespians at IASTA. If the latter had a criticism, it would be that their *senseis* were too kind, too undemanding.

After about a week and a half, rehearsals, which had begun in the special rehearsal room, moved to the stage. To give IASTA's pine floor the sheen and smoothness of a *kabuki* dance-play stage (made of cypress) the entire company, following Japanese custom, frequently got down on hands and knees and scrubbed it with bean curd. The bean curd, a cheeselike substance that the actors wrapped in rags and applied with elbow grease, secreted an oily substance that actually did make the floors easier to walk on. This was extremely important since actors in *Kanjinchō* do not wear shoes: they must glide gracefully along the floor in white *tabi*. Needless to say, no one was permitted to walk on the stage in shoes at any time—not before, after, or during rehearsals and performances.

The four choral parts in IASTA's production were to be delivered over music taped by a professional *kabuki* orchestra. (The tape, made specially in Japan for IASTA, cost about $500.) Raymond Hargrave, a professional musician, and Seiko, Kōshirō's lovely, talented wife (her father was the great actor Nakamura Kichiemon I), were in charge of training the Americans.

Though they made no effort to duplicate the musical patterns of a Japanese chorus, they did want to retain a chanting effect. One of their major problems was to rid the chanting of any associations, for Westerners, with the Catholic mass and, for Japanese, with Buddhist liturgy. They chose actors, rather than singers, for the chorus, and got them to achieve a recitative effect based upon timing rather than upon musical range.

In Japanese productions Yoshitsune is usually played in falsetto, Togashi in a lower though still somewhat high range, and Benkei in a forceful bass. But except for slipping in one or two minor Japanese phrases, Matagorō and Kōshirō made no attempt to get the Americans to approximate these vocal qualities. Several actors, disappointed by the neglect of so important an aspect of *kabuki*, attempted on their own to duplicate the authentic vocal style in their line readings. However, in those pre-videotape days they could only base their efforts on an old film of *Kanjinchō*, shown early in the training period and twice during rehearsals, so they mostly groped in the dark.[4]

Interpretation of lines also presented a problem. With several actors playing each leading role, obvious differences of approach were bound to occur. But since the directors didn't know English, they bypassed the all-important area of dialogue readings. And since none of the performers, because of professional ethics, dared discuss such matters with their alternates, some very strange readings were allowed to pass. Here the need for an English-speaking director was evident. However, several actors had so much difficulty with the dances and movements, I doubt they could have worried about interpretation in any event.

Early in the training period, when the film was first shown, the actors didn't understand it. At that point, I suspect, most of them didn't know the difference between *kabuki* and *nō*. But at the second screening, mid-way in rehearsals, they greeted it with applause. The Americans had come to know something about the essence of *kabuki* that could not be learned from books. After working for four weeks under Matagorō and Kōshirō, they were able to catch nuances in the film that none but an aficionado would notice. At this stage in rehearsal the value of the film to the actors was inestimable. The production took on new life as the actors strove to achieve an iota of the power displayed by the actors in the film.

As the actors watched the film they also noticed that the *senseis* had made several directorial changes in their production. For instance, the film showed three guards and a child swordbearer accompanying Togashi; IASTA eliminated the child and used only two guards, one of whom bore the sword. In the film, the three guards were seated upstage of Togashi, parallel to the footlights, but at IASTA the guards were placed downstage on either side of Togashi, their backs to the stage left wall. The reason for these and other minor changes was the smallness of IASTA's stage.

Figure 138. Togashi (Zeke Berlin) manipulates his trailing *hakama*.

Full dress rehearsals started as early as January 27, a little more than a week after rehearsals began. The expansive *hakama*, the divided trousers traditionally worn by Benkei and Togashi, were introduced even earlier as they required the most getting used to. Togashi's *hakama* was especially difficult. It encased the actor's legs and feet with voluminous folds of stiff material that trailed for several feet, and the actor had to learn to kick the material as he walked so it would fall on the stage floor in a designated aesthetic manner.

But the other costumes were complicated enough. Authentic in every detail (they had been rented from Japan), each consisted of undergarments, kimono, sashes, and over-garments worn outside the kimono, not to mention the accessories—hats, wigs, and *tabi*. The various components of the costumes were held together by the obi tied around the middle, each with a different formal knot. These obi put extreme pressure on the abdominal muscles, and the actors had to pad themselves with turkish towels. The Japanese also use padding, not only to absorb the pressure but also to give the actor a larger-than-life appearance.

To help the actors get into their voluminous, sculptured costumes, several outsiders, including a few Japanese women living in New York, volunteered to learn how to serve as dressers. The actors also had to learn the dressing procedures so they could help their fellow actors in an emergency. But the Japanese demand absolute symmetry in the way their costumes lie, and even the combined efforts of volunteers and actors often failed to please the *senseis*. On these occasions the directors would walk on stage and take an actor's costume apart, piece by piece, and dress him over again before everybody's eyes.

The headdresses, or wigs, present the Japanese actor with difficulties comparable to those faced by the Chinese thespian. In Chinese traditional theatre and *kabuki* the actor draws a piece of silk tightly around his head to increase the breadth of the forehead and draw the eyebrows and eyes up at an exaggerated angle. Over the silk he places the wig, made of hair sewn to metal plates. The tight silk together with the metal plates puts great pressure on the temples. One IASTA actress began to vomit from the pressure and thereafter had to forego her wig.

Makeup was done as authentically as possible—some of the ingredients had been brought from Japan. Although the makeup in *Kanjinchō* is not as exaggerated as in certain other *kabuki* pieces, the different eyeline, eyebrow, and mouth styles were sufficiently strange to the Americans to require much practice. At first the teachers painted the actors faces for them. Later, the actors received pictures of the different makeups and these were taped on the makeup mirrors.

The production opened in New York on February 14 and was presented a total of twelve times through March 3. Two more performances were given on February 19 and 20 at the Coolidge Auditorium in the Library of Congress. As the stage there is much wider, the set and curtain had to be expanded and the actors got a taste of what acting on the wide-open spaces of a real *kabuki* stage would be like.

Because of the steep rake of the Coolidge Auditorium, a real *hanamichi* could not be built. Instead, an apron was built below the regular stage; and below the down left and down right proscenium walls, abutting the apron, platforms connecting with the backstage area were constructed. The chorus was seated down right, and the apron became a *hanamichi*, entered from the down left platform, through a specially erected curtain. I think this method of staging a *kabuki* play would be effective in any theatre where no other solution for the *hanamichi* is available. The actors took the same positions they took on the IASTA *hanamichi*, except they now lined up across the apron before entering the stage proper.

The production made a tremendous impact on all the participants. But I believe no one expressed the meaning of the experience better than Kōshirō himself. Some of his program comments are repeated below:

> *Kanjinchō* encompasses all of the essentials of *kabuki*: *ka*-song, *bu*-dance, and *ki*-acting. Moreover, it includes elements of the *nō* theatre. It would be possible to spend a year rehearsing *Kanjinchō* and still not achieve all its nuances. So what we lacked in time, we tried to compensate for in hard work and spirits. . . . Our prayer was that the younger generation understand and learn, even a little, about *kabuki*. Our IASTA actors responded to our prayers with untiring effort. . . . Many young *kabuki* actors in Japan today are enriching their art by studying and performing in Western plays . . . and at the same time studying and performing *kabuki*. By the same token I commend American actors' and directors' efforts to enrich their art by studying and performing *kabuki* as well as plays growing out of the tradition of other nations. . . . It is our earnest hope that this *Kanjinchō* will serve as a bridge for the young professionals of the American and Japanese theatrical world.

NOTES

Reprinted from *Theatre Crafts* magazine (now *Entertainment Design*). © Copyright. Courtesy of Intertec Publishing Corporation, 32 W. 18 Street, New York, 10011. (The article has been slightly revised from its original publication in October 1968.)

1. *Kabuki* plays adapted from *nō* plays, like *Kanjinchō*—based on the play *Ataka*—and staged in a manner reminiscent of *nō* performance are called *matsubame mono* (pine board plays) because of their upstage wall with the pine painted on it.

2. The need to make architectural adaptations that allow for the placement of a *hanamichi* in theatres that normally do not use them is common in Japan as well. There are a number of theatres in Japan that position their *hanamichi* along the audience left wall when staging *kabuki*. Such runways are usually dismantled when other types of theatre are produced.

3. Ms. Watanabe was still teaching in 2002. In addition to having been founded by the female dancer Okuni, *kabuki* has a history of female performers. Even during the Edo period, when it was illegal for women to perform professionally, there were *kabuki* actresses who played for the women of the shogun's court, where male actors were forbidden to appear. There have been several modern attempts at establishing *kabuki* actresses, beginning with the mixed company that opened the new Teikoku Gekijō in 1911, and including the famous Ichikawa Shōjo Kabuki company of the 1950s and the Nagoya Musume Kabuki company, which performs today.

4. This black and white film, made in 1943, preserves an actual performance at the Kabuki-za starring Matsumoto Kōshirō VII as Benkei.

Terakoya at Brooklyn College

The previous chapter points to one of the most striking developments in Western interest in *kabuki* over the past half century, that is, the interest in staging English-language productions of *kabuki* plays, usually in an attempt to more or less replicate the vocal and visual aspects of a Japanese version. While the stagings at schools like Pomona College, the University of Kansas, and the University of Illinois, Champagne-Urbana have been, for the most part, exceptional, few—in their search for authenticity—have spent the kind of money or gone to the lengths that IASTA did in the 1960s or that is common practice at the University of Hawaii, Manoa campus. Hawaii usually prefers to bring in as actor trainers and co-directors distinguished *kabuki* actors, like the same Nakamura Matagorō II who played so prominent a role in IASTA's *Kanjinchō*. Stirred by my own experience at IASTA and by reports of other productions, I offered my own modest contribution to the trend in May 1976, when I staged my translation of *Terakoya* at Brooklyn College for a two-week run. This production was at the opposite end of the spectrum from Hawaii's *kabuki* and was produced with a tiny budget ($1,500) in a small black-box theatre. The following is an account of what was involved in mounting this production.

Rehearsals began early in February and lasted for three months. This long rehearsal period for a relatively short play (running time is about one and a half hours) was necessitated by the desire for a production that would be as technically precise as possible given the inherent difficulties of working with an undergraduate student cast without any experience of *kabuki* whatsoever. Fortunately, soon after rehearsals began, a recently enrolled Japanese theatre student, Kensuke Haga, somewhat older than the other students, showed up. Since he had studied acting in Japan, as well as modern dance, and knew something of classical Japanese dance and sword fighting, his presence became invaluable and he was soon made assistant director; he also performed in the black robes of an onstage, black-garbed assistant (*kurogo*) and appeared as a policeman (*torite*) as well. Another

193

Japanese student, Hori Hagi, whose major was not theatre, soon joined the production as well. She, too, worked as a *kurogo*. Although her theatre training was nil, she was quite helpful in working with the actresses in the company on such behavioral things as bowing, sitting, and walking. Her help with the putting on of costumes and tying of obis was also considerable.

There were no auditions in the usual sense. An announcement was posted informing all interested students that anyone who wished could participate in the production and that casting would be determined after a month or more of workshop activity. Since three months of rehearsal and workshop were planned most students did not wish to involve themselves in something which might lead to their playing only a walk-on role; therefore, all students were told that if they became active participants they could be assured of receiving an important role. This approach necessitated the use of a double casting system, not unlike the IASTA experience. Though this seemed at first a foolhardy experiment, it eventuated in a situation where only those students actually capable of playing the various roles remained in the company at the time of production. In other words, a good many students, after working with the company for a month or more, found themselves unsuited to the style of the play and the methods of rehearsal and, on their own initiative, dropped out. Several others had to leave because they could not keep up with the extensive rehearsal schedule or because they were promised a role in another play and could not wait to find out if they would get the role they desired in *Terakoya*. The end result was a company considerably smaller than had been hoped for but one far more cohesive and flexible than would have been the case if all the original people had stayed with the show.

The roles of Genzō, Tonami, Chiyo, Sansuke, and Yodarekuri—a clownish student—were all double-cast. An actor playing Genzō at one performance gladly went on in the role of a policeman at the next, while an actress in the role of Chiyo made no complaints about appearing as a farmer. The decreased number of available actors, however, made it necessary to change the gender of the farmers from male to female and to reduce their number from eight to three (with a consequent cut in the dialogue). Another cut was made in the number of children used: in addition to Kan Shūsai and Kotarō, only two other actual children were employed. A typical *kabuki* production will use at least eight. Because of the difficulty of securing young boys, these roles, including Kotarō, were played by girls. The children participated only in the last three weeks of rehearsal. Kan Shūsai was played by my then seven-year-old son, Justin.

Since casting was not decided upon for the first month and a half, early rehearsals saw each of the actors assuming a variety of roles. It thus became possible to work without some members of the company when they were unable to attend rehearsal. The men all became accustomed to performing the various male roles (as well as the parts of the children) as did the women for the female roles. This method allowed the actors to become more familiar with the play than they might have had they been confined to one role from the beginning. It also allowed them to keep their interest from flagging during the long rehearsal period.

Rehearsals were organized with respect for Japanese customs of social etiquette. Proper respect for the director ("*sensei*") had to be shown as it did for all other members of the company. Each student was given a list of Japanese expressions such as the equivalents of "hello," "goodbye," "thank you," and the like. Japanese theatre people say "good morning" for "hello" so the *Terakoya* company also used this expression (*ohayō gozaimasu*). Each rehearsal period began when I, as director, took a position on my knees, Japanese style. Seeing this, the company would sit on their knees, facing me in a semicircle. The company would bow to me, I would bow back, and then address them regarding the work to be done.

All participants, aside from the crew, had to attend each rehearsal in a kimono. Some students spent as much as forty dollars on a summer-weight kimono (*yukata*), obi, sandals, and fan, which was not inconsiderable for struggling theatre students in the mid-1970s. The average cost per student was about twenty dollars. It was felt that the student could not begin to approach the proper way of moving sitting, and standing unless he wore a garment that approximated the restrictions associated with traditional Japanese dress.

Rehearsals were conducted at a slow and careful pace, as the company worked its way through my translation of the play. *Terakoya* is actually a long scene from a much longer play, *Sugawara* (*Denju Tenarai Kagami*), one of the three great puppet dramas of the 1740s, all of which became *kabuki* staples. It tells the story of Matsuōmaru (Matsuō for short), a samurai who, because he is in service to the evil lord Shihei, is considered a villain by those who serve the wise and noble Sugawara. Shihei has risen to power at the expense of Sugawara, who has been exiled, and Shihei—fearful of a later vendetta—wants Sugawara's young son, Kan Shūsai, slain. It is learned that the boy is a student at the village school (*terakoya*) run by Takebe Genzō, a disciple of Sugawara's, and his wife, Tonami. He is also Kan Shūsai's benefactor and is passing the young lord off as one of his students. Genzō, ordered to behead the child, is confronted by Matsuō, sent by Shihei to verify the head's authenticity. However, Matsuō owes a secret debt of loyalty to Sugawara; therefore his wife, Chiyo, enrolled their own son, Kotarō, in the school earlier in the day with the hope that Genzō would kill him in place of Kan Shūsai and use his head as a substitute. Thus the head that Matsuō eventually inspects—unbeknownst to the others present—is actually that of his own son, which gives the actor powerful acting opportunities. The substitution works effectively and Genzō and Tonami are satisfied that they have done their duty, even though an innocent boy had to die. Soon after, Matsuō and Chiyo return to the school and reveal the truth of their deception, followed by a moving memorial service for the slain child.

The play was divided into eight sections, as it is in Japan: each of these was considered a unit equivalent to a scene or act. These divisions are *terairi* (Kotarō's admission into the school); *Genzō modori* (Genzō's return); *terako aratame* (the inspection of the schoolchildren); *kubi jikken* (the head inspection); *goshiki no iki* (the multi-colored breath); *Chiyo nidome no de* (Chiyo's second entrance); *Matsuō honshin* (Matsuō's true character); and *iroha okuri* (A-B-C funeral ceremony).

Figure 139. Matsuō (Jimmy Smits) strikes a *mie* during the head inspection scene. (All photos: Mark Prusslin.)

In order to approach as close to the authentic style of production as possible, frequent use was made of numerous production photographs I had collected in Japan. Videotapes, of course, were not available in 1976. The photos allowed the actors a relatively clear picture of what they were expected to enact physically, at least as far as static tableaux were concerned. All stage directions, of course, were taken from my notes, written in Japan.

In achieving vocal effects similar to those heard in a true *kabuki* performance, much recourse was had to a recording of a production starring Onoe Shōroku II as Matsuō. Although there were slight differences between the text of the recorded production and that of my translation, this use of a recording proved to be of immense value in getting the actors to produce tonal and emotional qualities which could not otherwise have been arrived at. A large number of the actors made their own tapes of this record for their private rehearsal needs. One rehearsal a week was devoted exclusively to vocal work. The actors attempted to approximate in English a style and rhythm that would convey the same aural effect as the Japanese. Naturally, the result was an approximation but I believe it was close enough to the original to give a strong suggestion of what *kabuki* dialogue sounds like.

I should point out that I have never really been satisfied with English-language approximations of *kabuki's* vocal style. That style is predicated upon linguistic values that are peculiar to Japanese and that cannot simply be transported into English. Some American director-translators of *kabuki*—like James R. Brandon—often attempt to duplicate in English the metrical values of the original, especially when the speeches are given in the "seven-five" (*shichigochō*) meter. Professor Brandon is especially clever at this and often manages to carry the task off with brilliant results. Still, when a language—in terms of stage verse—that sounds most comfortable when spoken in iambic pentameters is employed to speak *shichigochō*, the effect falls somewhat short of the "natural" ring it has in the original. Similarly, the forced falsetto most Western directors elicit for female voices (even when played by actresses), always manages to draw undue attention to itself. In Japan, the combination of *onnagata* speaking their own language—artfully constructed to exploit the *onnagata's* unique vocalizations—and the depth of meaning and emotion with which the actors are able to invest their speeches makes this highly artificial falsetto actually sound natural within the context of *kabuki* acting and dramaturgy. I have not yet, however, heard an actress—no matter how good—speak *kabuki* lines in English so that they not only sound highly stylized but natural. (I am not talking about realism, of course, but of the naturalness we expect of all elements within a well-executed artistic construct, no matter how artificial, abstract, or stylized.) At any rate, my production, for want of something better, followed the usual methods and asked the actresses to emote vocally in the characteristic falsetto tones. And it was, for what it's worth, closer to *kabuki's* spoken quality than IASTA's *Kanjinchō*, where voice and speech work was given short shrift.

Major problem areas were in the actors' movements and sitting. The women had to learn to move in that peculiarly delicate and rhythmical fashion developed in *kabuki* by three and a half centuries of female-role specialization by men. The men had to learn the proper manner of walking with a pair of swords at the waist so that they did not seem an impediment, but a natural part of their accoutrements. Actors had to sit for long periods of time on their knees, which was probably the most difficult thing to get used to. All company members were asked to sit at rehearsals in strict Japanese fashion, even when not on stage, to accustom their legs to the position. For a few this was an unbearable ordeal. Some resorted to kneepads, but this too proved futile since kimono have a way of parting down the front and revealing the wearer's knees. In the end, one actor of Genzō had to be

supplied by the stage assistant with a small stool on which he could sit so that the pressure was taken off his knees. Since a good many male roles (other than Genzō) often employ such stools, and since this liberty did have some basis in *kabuki* tradition, I felt justified in using it.

Figure 140. Genzō (Elliott Nesterman) confronts Matsuō (Jimmy Smits) when the latter returns.

In addition to dealing with the technical demands of *kabuki* acting style, it was also necessary for the actors to learn something about the world of the play. The cast read as widely as possible about Japanese history and feudalism and even did a number of improvisations to help bring the situations in the play to life. This is an area I wish we had more time to explore but, unfortunately, the exigencies of time and students' schedules allowed only for a cursory exploration of historical and thematic issues.

Terakoya—being a *kabuki* adaptation of a puppet play—makes considerable use of the kind of narrative musical accompaniment called *takemoto* or *gidayū*. I wanted this aspect of the presentation to be as authentic as possible, but did not wish to have the narrative speeches delivered in English. The style of delivering these passages in *kabuki* is so unique and aurally exciting, and so integral to the aesthetic values of *Terakoya*, that I sought a means of providing a performance as close as possible to one given in Japan. We did not have at Brooklyn the kind of local population that might have provided someone with musical and vocal skills gained from practicing *gidayū*, something that often has benefited productions at the University of Hawaii. A partial solution to this problem was found when I decided to use the music and narrative passages heard on the recording of the Japanese production of the play. A pair of able sound technicians lifted the pertinent passages from the long-playing disc and placed them on tape. Some minor cutting was required since portions of the recorded performance revealed an overlapping of actor's dialogue with background music and narrative recital. I had purchased in Japan a set of recordings, *Geza Ongaku* (Music from the *Geza* Room), which contains brief passages from most of the important offstage musical accompaniments used in *kabuki*. These records were used in finding background music similar to that played on the recording during the bulk of the dialogue scenes. Because of the brevity of the selections, loops were made to extend their playing time. This procedure worked very well and the production was pretty close to capturing the aural effect of a Japanese presentation. To solve the problem of making clear the meaning of the Japanese recited passages, I at first thought of flashing slides of the English translation on screens set up at the sides of the proscenium, a kind of primitive surtitle effect. When this was attempted during technical rehearsals the effect was distracting and technically deficient. Necessity being the mother of invention, I decided to seat myself at the rear of the auditorium with my script before me; a microphone was set up so that I could narrate in English as the Japanese was played on tape. I was told that the effect was not distracting and actually enhanced the presentation.

Figure 141. Chiyo (Susan Spindel), left, speaks with Tonami (Madeleine Nemirow). Upstage are the sleeping servant, Sansuke (Larry Berrick), and one of the schoolchildren (Diana Smits).

As I have mentioned, the play was performed in a small black-box theatre that—by using movable risers—allows for variable actor-audience arrangements. Space was limited, with room for less than 150 persons. This room was selected because I thought it appropriate to the play's intimate atmosphere. Risers were placed only at the rear of the room. The space in which the first five or six rows of risers might have been placed was filled with pillows and the willing audience members were invited to seat themselves on these. The stage and *hanamichi* runway were a mere foot above the level of the floor so the arrangement with the pillows allowed the people seated there to feel a closer relationship with the action than might have been the case had they been looking down on the play from risers.

Given our minuscule budget, we were fortunate to have the services of two very bright graduate students in design to overcome the limitations imposed on sets and costumes. Wigs were made by a member of the acting company, who almost single-handedly created each of the more than twenty wigs required. His method was borrowed from an article in *Theatre Crafts* describing the use of acrylic fur in the creation of period wigs. The results, while certainly nowhere nearly as beautiful as authentic *kabuki* wigs, served well enough to satisfy our requirements.

The production turned out to be such a success that the college's Television and Radio Department made the unprecedented decision to videotape it for possible sale to PBS. But since portable color taping equipment was not yet widely available it was necessary to take the set apart and rebuild it in the television studio. Unfortunately, the pressures involved in striking and reconstructing the set, the limited time allotted for rehearsal under the new conditions (the studio was in continual use and we had to get in and out quickly), and the inexperience of the graduate students assigned to direct the camera work led to a product with which I was not entirely satisfied and I requested that no attempt be made to sell the tape for public broadcasting. Ironically, however, the actor who played Matsuō, Jimmy Smits, later became a major film and television star, and clips from the tape eventually made a number of appearances on national television shows doing features on him.

To date, *Terakoya* has never been produced outside of Japan by any of the major *kabuki* tours abroad. Perhaps this is because the Japanese theatre world considers the theme of loyalty, in which a parent sacrifices his child for the sake of his master's boy, too feudalistic for Western tastes. *Terakoya*, after all, was once considered by the Occupation forces under Gen. Douglas MacArthur to be so dangerous an example of feudal tendencies that—in a notorious incident of military censorship—a production of it was closed down in November 1945.[1] I can only reply that the emotional impact our production had on audiences was a powerful one, and that it demonstrated to me, at any rate, that this play—for all its outlandish demands on a conflicted samurai's faithfulness—definitely can affect a non-Japanese audience in a dynamic and positive way. The subject is not so much feudal loyalty, after all, but the way humans react to adversity. And when the circumstances of the play lead to a father's having to sacrifice his own son because his code leaves him no alternative, there is rarely a dry eye—of whatever shape—in the house.

NOTES

This is a revision of an essay that originally appeared in *Asian Theatre Bulletin* IV:2 (Fall 1976).

1. The story is told in Okamoto (2001).

REFERENCES

Okamoto, Shiro. 2001. *The Man Who Saved* Kabuki: *Faubion Bowers and Theatre Censorship in Occupied Japan*, trans. and adap. Samuel L. Leiter. Honolulu: University of Hawaii Press.

III

THEATRES

Suwa Haruo's "The Birth of the *Hanamichi*"

Of all the various features associated with *kabuki*, few are as well known outside Japan as the *hanamichi*, the raised runway joined to the stage at the actors' right and proceeding through the auditorium to a curtained room at the rear. Used for major exits and entrances, it is also the site of important acting sequences. Because the *hanamichi* brings actors and spectators into close proximity without abandoning a stage-auditorium relationship similar to that in Western proscenium theatres,[1] it has been of considerable interest to international theatre artists.[2] Although its aesthetic and practical uses have been described in various Western sources, little attention has been paid to the *hanamichi's* origins. Among Japanese scholars, there is nearly as much contention surrounding this question as there is among Western scholars regarding the origins of the proscenium arch, the Elizabethan theatre's alcove, or the classical Greek theatre's use of a raised stage.

The few English-language sources (including works translated from the Japanese) that even mention the *hanamichi's* origins fall into three camps. One claims that the *hanamichi* originated in the *hashigakari*, the covered rampway used in the *nō* theatre and attached at an oblique angle to the upstage right corner of the *nō* stage. Early *kabuki* theatres were almost identical to *nō* stages and used a *hashigakari*, although at a right, not oblique, angle. During the seventeenth century, the *hashigakari*, used for entrances and exits, widened in a downstage direction until it was no longer distinguishable from the stage proper. According to many, the disappearance of the rampway led to its replacement with another, this being the runway through the audience.[3]

A second widely held theory argues that the *hanamichi* was an elaboration of the three steps placed in front of *nō* stages, originally used as a means for the actors to leave the stage in order to be presented with gifts (*hana*) of clothing by noble patrons. This theory links the name *hanamichi* (flower way, flower path) with the idea that the steps (or some other pathway) were used to offer gifts to the actors: a commoner, rather than a

205

nobleman, the donator would approach the actors and offer cash or flowers. *Hana,* an old word for "gift," is homonymous with that for flower, although written with a different Chinese character.[4] Finally, there is the suggestion that the *hanamichi* evolved from the use of flower-lined walkways (also called *hanamichi*) used for the entrance of wrestlers in sumo wrestling, a sport that predates *kabuki* by centuries. (See Bowers 1952, 144-45.)

Similar differences exist in Japanese-language scholarship. Professor Suwa Haruo's 1991 book, *Kabuki no Hōhō* (*Kabuki* Methods), contains an essay entitled "*Hanamichi no Tanjō*" (The Birth of the *Hanamichi*), which sums up the existing scholarship, noting the existence of—and variations on—the three theories of origin mentioned above, describing three more, and then arguing for a seventh. Professor Suwa, who teaches at Gakushuin University in Tokyo, does not pursue all the issues related to the *hanamichi,* among them the later development of the secondary *hanamichi* (usually called the "temporary" or *kari hanamichi*) or the appearance of the *hanamichi* elevator trap (*suppon*), but focuses on demonstrating that the seed from which the main runway evolved was a forestage (*tsuke butai*) introduced in the seventeenth century. Apart from several line drawings, Suwa does not provide illustrations, so I have added a number mentioned in his text from various sources.

I have abridged the first and adapted the second of the original essay's seven sections. The remaining portions are, I hope, faithful to the original although I have made a few minor adjustments for purposes of clarity.[5] The translation includes many of Suwa's notes although these, as in his original, do not include page numbers. To these notes I have added a number of my own.

Entrances and Exits from the *Tsuke Butai*

The famous *Actors' Analects,*[6] a collection of actors' commentaries and anecdotes of the Genroku period (1688-1704), contains a provocative passage about the use of a forestage. This passage describes an *onnagata* named Kokan Tarōji who, during a play in which he was appearing as a middle-aged woman, "came down from the forestage . . . and went and stood below the boxes at the back of the theatre." He was so convincing, it is reported, that another actor in the company, who was not in the scene and happened to he nearby, mistook him for a female spectator "and pinched her bottom" (Dunn and Torigoe 1969, 113).

This passage raises questions about the relation between the "forestage" (*tsuke butai*) and the "boxes at the back of the theatre" (*mukō sajiki*).[7] Usually, the *tsuke butai* is explained as an extension of the front of the *kabuki* stage during its early years, when—having come into existence as a reflection of the *nō* stage—it was found to be too shallow. The *mukō sajiki* were the box seats at the rear of the theatre, facing the stage on the other side of the pit (*hira doma*). Did the costumed Kokan Tarōji thrust his way through the pit in order to reach the boxes at the rear? Let us look for further examples of the *tsuke butai*. According to the script for Kojima Hikojūrō's play *Kōshoku Fumidenju*, produced at Kyoto's Hayakumo-za[8] (1693) and published that year with the rare inclusion of stage directions, there was a central scene in which a wicked samurai, Tachibana Ōkura, having gained power over the Tachibana clan, was celebrating his victory when the loyal samurai Asano Kazuma appeared in disguise. The stage direction states: "At this point, Asano Kazuma, dressed as a courtesan, enters the scene from the *tsuke butai*" (quoted in Shuzui 1928). If, as usual, the *tsuke butai* is considered the extended apron of the main stage, it becomes difficult to explain what sort of performance this entailed.

Several other stage directions in *Kōshoku Fumidenju* also point to the *tsuke butai*'s use for entrances and exits. For example, in Act I: "Kazuma, Naminosuke, Ganbei, and Utazō, all bearing a net, enter from the *tsuke butai*." According to the script, the actors not only used the *tsuke butai* but the old *hashigakari* runway and the stage left entranceway. And there is no mention of the *hanamichi*.

The *tsuke butai*'s use for exits and entrances can be seen in other documentation as well. For instance, there is no mention of the *hanamichi* in the oldest extant *kabuki* play in manuscript form, *Shinjū Kimon no Kado* (1710), produced at Osaka's Ogino Yaegiri-za, but there are several references to the *tsuke butai*, as, for instance, in:

"Yaegiri, Jōnosuke, Sōzaemon, and Saburōsuke[9] enter on the *tsuke butai* . . . " (quoted in *Kabuki Daichō Shūsei Daiikkan* 1983). Osome, daughter of an oil shop proprietor, and the shop's apprentice, Hisamatsu, are out shopping and stop to visit at the home of Hisamatsu's uncle, Okamura Gonzaemon. This first appearance of Hisamatsu (Jōnosuke), Osome (Yaegiri), the clerk Kyūbei (Sōzaemon), and the maidservant Oito (Saburōsuke), all entering together, takes place on the *tsuke butai*: "Jōnosuke, until now on the *tsuke butai*, goes from it onto the stage proper (*hon butai*)."

Jōnosuke joins the scene in progress. The four characters who have appeared on the *tsuke butai* talk for a bit, after which the clerk and the maidservant leave and Hisamatsu and Osome have a light romantic scene together. All of their acting has taken place on the *tsuke butai*, so this forestage seems to have been wide enough to allow for the maneuvering of at least two actors.

Everyone leaves by the *hashigakari* and Jōnosuke remains behind alone, looking off after them and leaning dejectedly on a pillar outside. Hisamatsu's father, coming from the country and carrying a large white radish, hands a package to [his servant] Nagamatsu, and enters via the *tsuke butai*. (Act II)

It is New Year and the family members have gone out. Hisamatsu, left alone, is visited by his father. The oil shop inhabitants exit via the *hashiga-kari* and the entrance to the stage is made via the *tsuke butai*. In what direction did the *tsuke butai* face and what did it look like?

Figure 142. Scene from an early *kabuki* performance in an unroofed theatre showing four actors entering on the *hashigakari* from curtain (*agemaku*) at left. Seated on his knees below the stage near the curtain is a servant holding the gift of a branch of bamboo with a note attached to it. The picture, from Nakagawa Kiun's *Kyō Warabe* (1658), shows clearly the *nō*-style stage of mid-seventeenth-century *kabuki*. The downstage extension was not yet called a *tsuke butai*. That term was added later, after the *hashigakari* became indistinguishable from this *nō*-style platform and another extension was added. See the plan in figure 142. (From collection of National Diet Library.)

Explanations of the *Hanamichi*

There are six basic explanations of the origins of the *hanamichi*.

(1) The principal theory is that it developed out of the *hashigakari*. One version of this argument holds that the *hanamichi* was formed in the Genbun era (1736-41) following the roofing over of the theatres during the previous Kyōhō era (1716-36), when their interiors became narrower, thereby shortening the *hashigakari*.[10] With less light available the acting on

the *hashigakari* became harder to see for those in the theatre's left-side boxes. Therefore, the *hashigakari* was shifted to a ninety-degree angle from the stage to create the *hanamichi* as "the *kabuki* theatre's new *hashigakari*."[11] Hattori Yukio (1980) feels that—along with the creation of a *tsuke butai* acting extension to alleviate the crowding of the actors necessitated by the narrow, three-*ken* wide (about eighteen feet) main stage, squeezed between the two front stage pillars—the *hashigakari* was gradually being widened in a downstage direction until its unique qualities as an entrance and exit path were lost. Therefore, the *hanamichi* was added on to replace these old functions.

(2) Imao Tetsuya (1979) makes a major addition to these theories. Following Hattori, he places the events in the Genroku period, and agrees that, as a result of the enlargement of the stage space, the *nō*-style arrangement was altered, the *hashigakari* lost its original purpose, and a need arose for an entrance-exit ramp through the audience. However, he believes that as a preamble to the *hanamichi's* arrival, there was a period in which there existed a temporary "attached" or *tsuke hashigakari* or—separated from the front of the stage—a temporary *tsuke butai*. Imao believes that the *tsuke butai* served here as an earlier form of the *hanamichi*.

Figure 143. Scroll painting, "44 Genroku Ōgimai," showing a temporary *hanamichi*, with low side railings, at an unidentified theatre sometime during the Genroku era. (From collection of Tokyo Idemitsu Museum of Art.)

(3) Another theory, with which several scholars concur, asserts that the *hanamichi* evolved as a pathway (*michi*) for the presentation of gifts (*hana*). This *hana no michi* ("path of flowers") notion was first proposed by Gotō Keiji (1925), who argued that the *hanamichi's* origins had nothing to do with the *hashigakari*, and that even after the *hanamichi* had come into existence, references were being made in Osaka to both the *hanamichi and* the *hashigakari*. He emphasized that when spectators wished to present gifts of flowers to the actors, they used the *hanamichi*, a provisional version of which already had been set up in the Jōō period (1652-55).

(4) A fourth theory insists that there is a fundamental relationship between the *nō*-style steps at the front of this stage and the *hanamichi*. Having been created when *nō* moved away from serving the gods to an association with men of rank, these steps may be considered *a hanamichi* for the *nō* stage (Hayashiya 1931).

Figure 144. *Yanone Gorō* at the Nakamura-za (1740), in a print by Okumura Masanobu. The *hanamichi* is placed obliquely at the left and at its center protrudes into the pit, with the "name-saying" platform (*nanoridai*, see below) at its end. Although not mentioned in the text, this picture shows an unusual temporary structure—a sort of forestage-forestage—added at the front of the stage and with an actor enclosed in a scenic unit set on it. It suggests the diversity of architectural approaches being experimented with in the theatre of that time. (From Toita, *Kabuki Kanshō Nyūmon*.)

(5) Next is a theory that sees the origins of the *hanamichi* in the entrance path used by performers in ritualistic *ennen*[12] dances and in the ritualistic performances called *hana matsuri* or "flower festival" presented in Mikawa and other rural places. This argument avers that because the performer progresses through the audience to the stage in *ennen* and *hana matsuri*, the *hanamichi* of *kabuki* and sumo are akin to the pathways used in these forms. The existence of children called *kajō no chigo* ("boys who carry a flower-staff") in a 1440 performance of *ennen* and of a child's dance called *hana no mai* ("flower dance") in *hana matsuri* suggests the origins of the *hanamichi* in the route taken by these child dancers (Yasaburō 1956). Related to this is the idea that the *hanamichi's* origins lie in an Indian festi-

val held in Kashi (now Varanasi), where a pathway connects a priestess's house with a sacred space used in *a hana matsuri*-like festival. In both India and Japan, it is thus believed, the local deity emerges on the pathway to appear among the people. If so, after the *aragoto* style of *kabuki* was established in late seventeenth-century Edo, the *hanamichi* arose as an avenue for the entrance of *aragoto's* god-like or superhuman characters (Aoe 1971).

(6) Finally, some believe that the sumo *hanamichi* led to the *kabuki* runway. A twelfth-century work, *Gōke Shidai*, contains a comment concerning a sumo tournament in which wrestlers entering through the crowd from the left and right were adorned with artificial floral decorations, thus spurring speculation that *kabuki's hanamichi* stemmed from the sumo version (Origuchi 1976).[13]

Apart from the first two theories, which concern the alteration of the *hashigakari* and the evolution of the *nō* stage's steps, the remaining four address not only the establishment of the bridgeway but the derivation of the term *hanamichi*. In other words, *hana* comes from the presentation of gifts on a pathway, or it derives from the use of floral accessories.

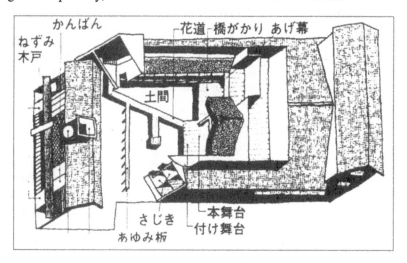

Figure 145. A modern plan of an eighteenth-century theatre like that depicted in figure 139. The *hanamichi* runs at an oblique angle from the *tsuke butai*, which is clearly visible downstage of the *nō*-style pillar supporting the gabled roof over the main stage. The unroofed portion of the stage right side of the interior gabled roof is the *hashigakari*. Extending into the pit from the *hanamichi* is a short pathway with a small platform at its end, the *nanoridai*. The narrow passageway extending into the pit to its left is a walkway used for vendors and audience members going to their seats. The entrance to the theatre is at the left. (From Suwa, *Kabuki e Dōzo*.)

In addition, some have speculated that the term *hanamichi* may derive from its use as a pathway for brilliant stars (*hana no yakusha*, literally, "flower actors"). As Nishiyama Matsunosuke (1969) explains it, combining the two given meanings of *hana,* an actor who collects gifts of flowers is a popular actor, and the *hanamichi* was, accordingly, a pathway for an actor who was a flourishing and blooming flower. Somewhat similar is an explanation declaring that the pathway gets its name from the beauty it represents as a flower-like (*hana no yō na*) or gorgeous (*hanayaka na*) path.

There are thus six explanations of the origins of the term *hanamichi:* (1) a path on which gifts of flowers were offered, (2) a path for "boys with flower-staffs," (3) a path for *hana matsuri's* "flower dancers," (4) the sumo *hanamichi,* (5) a path for popular actors (*hana no yakusha*), and (6) a path of beauty.

There exist rebuttals to each of these theories. For instance, the argument that the *hanamichi* emerged from the *nō* steps creates problems. Logically, if the *hanamichi* is an outgrowth of the *hashigakari*, then the place for all actors' entrances and exits would probably have to be on the *hanamichi.* In fact, actors' entrances on the *hanamichi* are not universal and, from the standpoint of dramatic structure, are limited to those moments when special notice must be made of them. Then there is the argument that the *hanamichi* and the *hashigakari* never coexisted within the same stage. The facts, however, state the contrary; while the term *hashigakari* disappeared quickly as stage construction was transformed in Edo, it continued to coexist for sometime with the term *hanamichi* in Osaka. Each of the other theories also has been carefully refuted.

The Word "*Hanamichi*"

It is now clear that the first known use of *hanamichi* may be found in the work *Dōtonbori Hanamichi,* which bears this imprint of date and place of publication: "Auspicious day, eleventh lunar month, 1679 (Enpō 7), Fushimi Gofuku-chō, Osaka, Bookstore Fukaeya Tarōbei (publisher)." It is a compilation of haiku poems gathered by the playwright Tominaga Heibei, who used the pen name Tatsuju. According to the preface, a group of actors, including young ones, had enjoyed themselves writing poems, and Tominaga collected them in a single volume. Beneath the title were the phrases, "New Year's production" (*hatsu shibai*) / "face-showing production" (*kaomise*)[14] / poet fellowship (*hokku tsukeai*)." One hundred and thirty-six poems read at the New Year's and *kaomise* performances and written by the theatre personnel of Osaka's Dōtonbori playhouse district were included. The published version mentions the word *hanamichi* four times, including the title.[15] In the preface we read:

I felt that it would be easy to collect the first lines of linked verses produced on the second day of ordinary performances and, moreover, at the time of the *kaomise* and New Year's productions. From single verse the number of lines grew to many and before long a collection was created making a *hanamichi* of diverse, individual pieces viewed by an audience of hopeful persons.

In the collection are the two verses: "The New Year's production and last year's dramatics on the *hanamichi*" and "The New Year production with the sandal-bearer [depicted as a kind of youthful strongman] forcing his way throng on the *hanamichi*." In addition, the book contains the line: "The dramatics began between the sexes during the *kaomise*."[16]

From these examples it can be seen that the word *hanamichi* was hardly unusual at the time, and it may be firmly accepted that *hanamichi* was a term that theatrical personnel and people familiar with *kabuki* would naturally have known. The question remains, though, as to precisely what portion of the stage arrangements this "*hanamichi*" refers.

We encounter the first mention of the *hanamichi* in a comment on Kosakawa Jūemon in an early volume of the yearly compendium of actors' critiques or reviews (*yakusha hyōbanki*): "During the *kaomise*, in the play *Chiyogasane Kiku Shinpai*, he appeared as Matsugane Dōjirō and it was wonderful. Moreover, he entered from the *hanamichi*, lumbering along without a word, which was certainly striking" (*Yakusha Gan Hodoki* 1716).[17] It was the first published use of the word in thirty-seven years, not having been seen in print since 1679.

Then, in *Yakusha Toshi Otoko* (Kyoto, 1729), in a critique of Sakakiyama Shirōtarō, is the statement: "Suddenly he appeared on horseback and made an energetic entrance onto the *hanamichi*. After some acting, he went off and returned, gripping a freshly severed head, and reciting the story of his father's lineage."

In the critique of Matsushima Moheiji is this line: "With his kimono thrown off, exposing his arm, he rushed onto the *hanamichi* and attempted to rouse the audience's laughter, all in the old fashion. The current style is hasty."

The other examples are from 1731, when the critique called *Sangoku Rōei Kyōbutai* had the phrase, "The *hanamichi* is the flower of the travel scene (*michiyuki*)," while 1734's *Kyō Sakakiyama-za Hyōbanki*, under the entry for Arashi Koroku, reads, "As he entered along the *hanamichi*, the spectators' hearts palpitated and the faces of the girls and ladies-in-waiting blushed noticeably."

All these references suggest a pathway through the audience like today's *hanamichi*, but in the entire eleven-volume collection of critiques, *Kabuki Hyōbanki Shūsei*, only these five examples can be found. Compared to the number of citations of the *hashigakari* and *tsuke butai*, this is extremely low. Until the Kyōho era, then, one must believe that either the use of the *hanamichi* actually was rare, or its existence so common that the authors of the critiques simply took it for granted.

The *Hanamichi* in Pictorial Evidence

When was the *hanamichi* set up in *kabuki* playhouses? As we have seen, the term itself existed at least as early as 1679, in *Dōtonbori Hanamichi*, but pictures do not appear until the Jōkyō period (1684-88). A definite picture of one is known from a scroll painting, the *Kita Zakura Oyobi Gekijō Zukan*, in the possession of the Tokyo National Museum. It shows Edo's Nakamura-za during a performance of *Ninin Saruwaka*. It was signed by Hishikawa Moronobu in 1687, and gives an almost unimpeded view of the stage during this period. The picture shows maids and wet nurses in the company of upper-class women taking their ease on straw matting. In front of them are two comical dancers, a male Saruwaka and a female Saruwaka.[18] At stage left *a hanamichi* is connected at a right angle to the stage proper, and on the runway is a palanquin whose passenger is being carried home by two bearers. Since the *hanamichi* is situated at stage left, it can be assumed that this is a temporary arrangement.

Figure 146. *Ninin Saruwaka* at the Nakamura-za in 1687. Part of scroll painting, *Kita Zakura Oyobi Gekijō Zukan*, by Hishikawa Moronobu. The *hanamichi* can be glimpsed at the audience's right, but the action on it described in the text is not visible. (From collection of Tokyo National Museum.)

There is also a scroll painting for a play, *Kinpira Rokujō Gayoi*, at the same theatre, made by an artist of the Hishikawa school, in 1687, and it, too, depicts the *hanamichi*. This picture offers new evidence little known in the academic world.[19] Despite the picture's title declaring it to be of a performance in the riverbed at Shijō, Kyoto, the theatre shown is the Nakamura-za in Edo's Sakai-chō district. I have only seen the picture once and cannot write of it in detail, but on the posters bearing the actors' names is written, "Nakamura Akashi, Saruwaka Kanzaburō, Nakayama Sayonosuke." The three posters read, "*Wakoku Hanaikusa* (Japanese flower battle)[20] / *Shimoyo no kaze* (A frosty night's wind):[21] Kinpira Rokujō Gayoi Sanban Tsuzuki (Kinpira Rokujō Gayoi in Three Acts)." On a board hanging stage left, at the "minister's pillar" (*daijin bashira*), is the inscription that the scene presented is of the middle act, titled "Rokujō no Sata" (Incident at Rokujō). The *hanamichi* is set up at stage right; two prostitutes are entering on it, and a character suggesting the powerful hero Kinpira is observing them. It. is reminiscent of a famous pleasure quarters scene in Kawatake Shinshichi III's popular 1888 play,[22] *Kagotsurube*, when the bumpkin Sano Jirōzaemon falls in love at first sight with the courtesan Yatsuhashi. It is very likely that the great Ichikawa Danjūrō I (1660-1704) is playing this Kinpira figure. A passage in the section on Danjūrō I in the 1702 actors' critique *Edo Zakura* says, "In *Kinpira Rokujō Gayoi*, when Danjūrō displayed *aragoto* . . . " while in the 1710 critique *Yakusha Kura Gotatsu* the section on Danjūrō II (1689-1758) notes, "Twenty-five years ago, his father played Sakata [Kinpira] in *Kinpira Rokujō Gayoi*, which was the beginning of his father's *aragoto*. . . . " This makes it probable that Danjūrō I played Sakata Kinpira in *Kinpira Rokujō Gayoi* in 1685.[23]

Although the *hanamichi* is affixed to stage right in the aforementioned picture it cannot be thought of as having been a permanent stage feature, yet, two years later a *hanamichi* was pictured at stage left in the same theatre for *Ninin Saruwaka*. Moreover, in a screen painting of the Nakamura-za by Hishikawa Moronobu made during the Genroku period, and now at the Tokyo National Museum, no *hanamichi* can be seen.

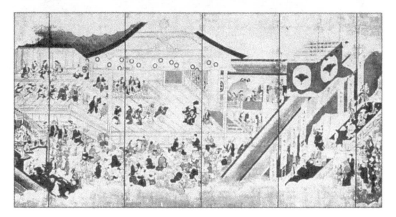

Figure 147. Nakamura-za during the Genroku era, from a screen painting by Hishikawa Moronobu. No *hanamichi* is visible. (Collection of Tokyo National Museum.)

There is one more picture of a *hanamichi* among the theatre pictures of Genroku. In my 1970 book, *Kabuki Kaika* (The Flowering of *Kabuki*), I introduced a screen painting, named "44 Genroku Ōgimai" (44 Genroku Fan Dances), presently in the Tokyo Idemitsu Museum of Art (see figure 143). It shows six young actors dancing, center stage, with fans over their heads in front of two shamisen players and a singer, with a *hanamichi* joined to the stage. The theatre represented cannot be determined but the *hanamichi* is at stage right and, from the fact that a railing has been built along both sides, it should be considered temporary.

Sometime later, the play *Hanabusa Bunshin Soga*, which opened on the second day of 1733, was depicted on a screen now in the collection of the Tsubouchi Memorial Theatre Museum at Waseda University. The scene depicts the younger Soga brother, Gorō—having learned that his brother, Jūrō, is in danger at a drinking party—rushing down the *hanamichi* with his *sakaomodaka* armor[24] carried in his left hand. This *hanamichi* is at stage right, at the same height as the stage proper, and may be considered standard. The difference from the three pictures previously described is its lack of side railings.

Figure 148. A print by Torii Kiyotada of the interior of the Nakamura-za during the *Shibaraku* sequence from *Mitsugi Taiheiki* (1743). The leading character is standing on the *hanamichi* at left. A *nanoridai* can be seen in the central part of the pit. (From Lane, *Images from the Floating World*.)

In pictures from the late 1730s on, the *hanamichi* is a regular feature on the stage right side. These pictures include, for instance, an anonymous view of the Ichimura-za interior showing *Shibaraku* in 1739;[25] one by Okumura Masanobu from 1740 of *Yanone Gorō* (see figure 144) during a *kaomise* performance (Shuzui and Hami, 1977); another by Torii Kiyotada of the inside of the Ichimura-za showing *Tsurukame Mitsugi Taiheiki*; and a fourth from 1765 by Torii Kiyotsune depicting the Nakamura-za during *Kanadehon Chūshingura* (in *Genshoku Ukiyo-e Daihyakka Jiten Daikkan* 1982).

On the basis of this pictorial evidence, the *hanamichi* depicted during the 1680s can be thought of as a temporary arrangement, while the permanently installed version becomes visible toward the end of the Kyōhō period. This confirms the written documentation.

The Ebb and Flow of the *Hashigakari*

Let us now examine how the words *hashigakari*, *tsuke butai*, and *hanamichi* were employed in the annual actor critiques. This examination will reveal the following:

(1) Examples of the word *hashigakari* appear through all periods.

(2) Related terms such as *hashi butai* ("bridge stage"), *tsuke hashikakari* [*sic*], *tsukuri butai* ("built stage"), *ayumi* ("walkway"), and so on, disappear during the Genroku period.

(3) *Tsuke butai* first appears in 1692 and vanishes after 1714.

(4) *Hanamichi* first appears in 1716.

Year	Actor Critique	Hashigakari	Tsuke Butai	Hanamichi	Other
1676	*Shibai*	*			
1677	*Shinasadame*				
1686	*Naniwa Tachigiki*	*			
	Mukashibanashi				
1687	*Yarō Tachiyaku*	*			*hb*
	Butai Daikan				
1688	*Yarō Yakusha*	*			*th*
	Furyūkan				
1692	*Yakusha Daikan*	*	*		
1697	*Yakusha Daikan*	*	*		
1701	*Arashi Hyakunin*		*		
	Katsura				
1702	*Edo Zakura*	*	* [O]		
	Yakusha Gozen				*a/tb*
	Kabuki (O/E)				
1705	*Yakusha Sanzesō* (E/K)	* [K]			
1708	*Yakusha Iro Shōgi*	*			
	Daizen Kōmoku (E)				

Year	Actor Critique	Hashigakari	Tsuke Butai	Hanamichi	Other
1710	*Yakusha Kura Gotatsu* (E)				
1711	*Yakusha Daifukuchō* (E)	*			
1712	*Yakusha Sengoku Dōshi*	*	*		
1712	*Yakusha Hako Denju* (K/F)	* [E]	* [K]		
1713	*Yakusha Za Burumai* (E)	*			
1714	*Yakusha Mekiki Kō* (E)		*		
1714	*Yakusha Iro Keizu* (E/O)	*			
1715	*Yakusha Futokori Zetai* (E)	*			
1716	*Yakusha Gan Hodoki* (K/E)	* [E]		*	
1716	*Shibai Hare Kosode* (E)	*			
1717	*Yakusha Iro Chayū* (E)	*			
1717	*Yakusha Kake Sugoroku* (E)	*			
1718	*Yakusha Sanpukutsui* (E)	*			
1718	*Yakusha Shoku Gataki* (E)	*			
1719	*Yakusha Kin Keshō* (E)	*			
1720	*Yakusha San Futagasa* (E)	*			
1720	*Yakusha San Meibutsu* (E/O)	*			
1721	*Yakusha Waka Ebisu* (E)	*			
1721	*Yakusha Uso Furo* (E)	*			
1723	*Yakusha Kiku Furumai* (E)	*			
1724	*Yakusha Tatsu Koyomi Gei Shinasadame (E)*	*			
1724	*Yakusha Mitsu Tomoe* (E) *				
1729	*Yakusha Toshi Otoko* (K)	*			*
1729	*Yakusha Niwa Zakura* (E) *				
1730	*Yakusha Wakami Tori* (E) *				
1731	*Sangoku Roei Kyō Butai Yakusha Harukoma* (E)	*			
1732	*Yakusha Mitsu Mono* (E)	*			
1734	*Kyō Sakakiyama-za Hyōbanki*	*			*

O=Osaka edition/K=Kyoto edition/E=Edo edition; *hb=hashi butai*; *th=tsuke hashi-kakari*; *a=ayumi*; *tb=tsukuri butai*

Most suggestive of the items listed prior to this table are numbers (3) and (4). In other words, citations of the *tsuke butai* are clearly replaced by the *hanamichi,* yet there are no examples of their coexisting. However, as we have already seen, the *tsuke butai* was used for actors' entrances and exits and the evidence proves that the *hanamichi* was used for precisely the same function.

Following is a table noting instances of the relevant terms in *kabuki* scripts of the period. It displays a pattern similar to that of the actor critique table. The "other" column is for references to the rear box seats (*mukō sajiki*). When the word *mukō* appeared in the scripts, it implied the place of entrance and exit facing these seats, that is, the *hanamichi*. In this table, too, the *hashigakari* appears throughout the given years, but the *tsuke butai* and the *hanamichi* are never mentioned on the same occasion.

Year	Play Title	Hashigakari	Tsuke Butai	Hanamichi	Other
1710	*Shinjū Kimon no Kado* (O)	*	*		
1712	*Matsukaze* (K)	*			
1729	*Keisei Kenninji Kuyō* (K)	*		*	
1731	*Shintokumaru*	*		*	*
	Konodegashiwa				
1732	*Keisei Tsumagoi Zakura*	*		*	*

Three Types of *Tsuke Butai*

Here is the current standard explanation of the *tsuke butai*:

> A stage term from the mid-Edo period. The early *kabuki* stage was modeled after the *nō* stage but, during the Kanbun era (1661-72), along with the maturation of the contents of scripts and acting, a draw curtain (*hikimaku*) was introduced and the stage was widened downstage below the *nō*-style stage pillars (*daijin bashira*). This extension was called the *tsuke butai* and the pre-existing stage was called the *hon butai* ("Tsuke Butai" 1962).

The most common view of the *tsuke butai* is that it was an extension of the front portion of the *hon butai* and *hashigakari*. It is indisputable that the *tsuke butai* was originally an enlargement of the stage. We will call this the A-type *tsuke butai*.

Figure 149. Dancers on 1692 *tsuke butai* separated from and parallel to main stage. (From *Yakusha Daikan*, 1692.)

In addition to this A-type, two other types of *tsuke butai* existed. In the *Yakusha Daikan*, published by Izumiya Saburōbei in the second month of 1692, there is a picture of a *tsuke butai* set up downstage of the regular stage but temporarily separated from it. The printed description says: "Illustration of the *tsuke butai* with dancers and chorus." On the regular stage there is a small platform on which three men are standing and singing: as they sing, three actors are dancing on a *tsuke butai*. The same picture appeared in the *Yakusha Daikan* published in the second month of 1697. This B-type *tsuke butai* accords with Imao Tetsuya's previously introduced theory of the *tsuke butai* as an earlier form of the *hanamichi*. It would have been impossible, however, for actors to have used this B-style *tsuke butai* for entrances and exits without passing through the audience seating.

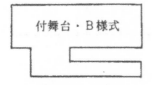

Figure 150. B-type *tsuke butai*, separated from and parallel to main stage. This plan is based on figure 139.

Examples of the *tsuke butai* used for entrances and exits have been cited above from *The Actors' Analects*, *Kōshoku Fumidenju*, *Shinjū Kimon no Kado*, and so forth. Here are several examples of entrances taken from actor critiques: "Coming onto the *tsuke butai* to the accompaniment of the shamisen. . . . " (from 1704's *Yakusha Gozen Kabuki* description of the comic actor Kanazawa Goheiji); "Takii Hanshirō, playing Soga no Jūrō, appeared from the *tsuke butai* wearing his hair in the *chosen kami* style and dressed in a *haori* jacket. . . . " (from 1702's *Yakusha Sengoku Dōshi*); "The entrance of these three, at the *kaomise* performance, in the Shinoda play,[24] when he appeared as Ukijima Tanshō and came on from the *tsuke butai* with Ōtani and Ikushima. . . . " (from 1702's *Yakusha Sengoku Dōshi* description of Ichikawa Danjūrō). The following is a reference to an exit:

> During the second play of the year, he played Jinen Sekijūrozaemon in *Keisei Nehan no Toko*. In the scene when he called the young lord Jūshirō a counterfeiter who had been ordered into exile, Jūshirō went to the *tsuke butai*, stopped, sighed, and spoke his lines while crying. . . . " (from 1712's *Yakusha Hako Denju* description of Nishimura Yaheiji).

As these quotations demonstrate, the *tsuke butai* was used for entrances and exits, so this stage extension must have served the same functions as the *hanamichi*. We will term this *hanamichi*-like *tsuke butai* the C-type.

付舞台・C様式

Figure 151. C-type *tsuke butai*, with *nanoridai* extension. This plan shows the *hanamichi* at a right angle to the main stage, but, as seen in figures 141, 142, and 145, the angle was actually oblique.

Until now, many historians have not accepted the existence of this C-type *tsuke butai*, but on the basis of the evidence, there can be no doubt that such a stage appendage was used for entrances and exits. The C-type *tsuke butai* was added to the B-type *tsuke butai* walkway and extended through the audience to connect with the rear box seats. This *hanamichi*—as seen in the above-described and/or shown pictures of the 1739 Ichimura-za, the 1740 production of *Yanone Gorō*, and the Genbun era Ichimura-za—is shown in the plan for the C-type *tsuke butai*.[27]

This Genbun *hanamichi* differed considerably from the *hanamichi* shown in the Nakamura-za during the Meiwa period (1764-72). It had, thrusting out into the center of the auditorium and parallel to the stage proper, a so-called "name-saying platform" (*nanoridai*), which had vanished by Meiwa. Here is today's generally accepted view of this *nanoridai*:

> Also called *masukata* ("box-shaped"), it was the name given to a stage feature during the Genbun era, but was soon dispensed with. It had a 1.8 meter square platform thrust into the seating in the pit and was connected via a walkway to the middle of the *hanamichi*. The actor, emerging from the age*maku* room at the end of the *hanamichi*, came to this place and spoke a formal monologue (*tsurane*), announced his name, and demonstrated his acting ("Nanoridai" 1962).

However, as can be seen from the 1739 picture of the Ichimura-za, this 1.8 square meter platform connected to the *hanamichi* by a walkway is a later alteration; at first, it was like the B-type *tsuke butai* and ran into the pit, parallel to the stage proper, as a rectangular or oblong stage. Concerning this *nanoridai*, a temporary construction of the Genbun era, Suda Atsuo (1949) insists: "The *nanoridai* (a term derived from the *nō* convention of 'naming' [*nanori*] oneself) was a temporary construction that lasted from the Genbun to the Kanpō (1741-44) era. Certainly, to the extent that existing pictorial evidence makes apparent, the *nanoridai* was depicted only in Genbun prints; since there is no previous or later pictorial evidence, we must follow Suda's assertion.

Still, if we put pictorial evidence aside and look at the written documentation, we may see in the above-mentioned 1710 play, *Shinjū Kimon no Kado*, that four people—Hisamatsu, Osome, the clerk Kyūbei, and the maid Oito—entered on the *tsuke butai* and stopped to converse, after which the clerk and the maid exited and Osome and Hisamatsu remained alone on the *tsuke butai* to perform a light love scene. The *tsuke butai* of that time had room for the expressive acting of only two actors. If we consider this *tsuke butai* as the C-type, the *hanamichi* equipped with the *nanoridai* appears to be this C-type *tsuke butai* with its terminology changed, and we can view the previous form of the *nanoridai* as a combination of both the B- and C-types of *tsuke butai*.

It boils down to this: there were two direct sources for the permanently installed *hanamichi*. One was the temporary version created prior to the Genroku era and whose existence has been confirmed. When this temporary bridgeway—set up from time to time either at stage right or left as needed by the performance—came to be limited to stage right, and the railings down its sides were abolished and its height established on a level with that of the stage proper, the regular *hanamichi* was born.

The other source was the C-type *tsuke butai* we have looked at. With the coming of Genroku, the B-type, whose presence has been determined, was further extended and, during the mid-Genroku period (sometime in the I690s), the development of the new C-type *tsuke butai* became one with that of the temporary *hanamichi*.

That the B-type evolved into the C-type is made even clearer by reference to the following passage in the section on the Kamigata actor Kataoka Nizaemon in *Yakusha Gozen Kabuki* (1704):

> First, this actor sometimes skillfully set up a large stage device. This time, the acting area has been thrust forth along the area in front of the audience right box seats, and an oblique walkway (*ayumi*) has been attached to a place between the onstage pillars. Further, the front of the right side box seats has been closed over with a "mirror board" (*kagami ita*) on which a young pine tree is painted. Running as far as the audience right side of the rear box seats (*mukō sajiki*) is a *hashika-kari* [*sic*] and from its curtained entrance Nizaemon appeared in formal court dress and headgear, presenting a haughty demeanor.

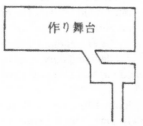

作り舞台

Figure 152. The anomalous temporary *tsukuri butai* described in 1704's *Yakusha Gozen Kabuki*. It is situated on the stage left side of the pit and has a small stage between it and the main stage.

This passage reveals that a temporary stage was erected on the audience right side of the theatre, in front of the side box seats: from a position between the stage pillars was a walkway running into the house at an oblique angle, and along with it a *hashigakari* progressed to the rear box seats. Certainly, this arrangement resembles the permanent stage right C-type *hanamichi,* only at the stage left side. Still, such sources as 1693's *Kōshoku Fumidenju* already made it apparent that, although the C-type *tsuke butai* was not permanent, it had been constructed, so that, to differentiate it from this temporary stage left runway, it was called the "built" or *tsukuri butai.*

The *shichisan*—"seven-three"—position on today's *hanamichi,* where important moments of acting occur, is so named because it is located approximately three-tenths of the distance from the stage and seven-tenths from the rear of the theatre. It is claimed, though, that *shichisan* originally was seven-tenths of the distance from the stage, and three-tenths from the back of the house, and that it was later moved to its present location (Imao 1979). An examination of Edo-period scripts reveals no reference to *shichisan,* but shows that the middle portion of the *hanamichi* was used for unique acting highlights: "[the actor] stops in the dead center (*mannaka*) of the *hanamichi.* . . . " (in 1742's *Narukami Fudō Kita Yama Zakura*); "at a good position dead center on the *hanamichi,* [the actor] faces the stage and sits. . . . " (in 1756's *Keisei Sato no Kaeru*); "[the actor] stops and delivers his speech dead center on the *hanamichi*" (in 1758's *Sanjikkoku Yofune no Hajimari*); "[the actor] goes to the middle of the *hanamichi* and acts with a smile" (in 1810's *Kachizumō Ukina no Hanabure*). Thus the *hanamichi* was not simply a pathway but was also a place for significant acting. Moreover, we can confirm that, with *shichisan's* beginning at the center of the runway and its later transference to its present position, today's *hanamichi* inherited its functions from the C-type *tsuke butai.*

The Birth of the *Hanamichi*

The *hanamichi* was not limited to *kabuki* but was also constructed in puppet theatres. In Uji Kaganojō's published script, *Genji Rokujō Jō* (1704) there is a stage illustration showing the *hanamichi.* A walkway about one meter wide and called the *soto butai* ("outside stage," the term used in the text for *tsuke butai*) runs through the center of the spectators in the pit. It is separated from them by a low fence on the left and right. As in the pit, there is no covering over its earthen floor, and three pine branches are set up at separate places along the way. This is in imitation of the three small pines along the *nō* stage's *hashigakari,* and can also occasionally be seen in pictures of early *kabuki,* which, as mentioned, was indebted to the architecture of the *nō* theatre. This fence and the trees could be removed, and the *hanamichi* was a temporary stage adjunct.

In the explanatory accompanying text are such comments as: "Oyama Zenemon uses it," "a place used to pass through among the spectators," and "courtesan Oshū's travel scene" [*michiyuki*]." As these comments demonstrate, the *hanamichi* was used for the special performance of the

courtesan's *michiyuki,* enacted by the puppet handler Zenemon as he manipulated Oshū's puppet in passing along it.

Another picture of the *hanamichi,* presumably published in the late
Genroku or early Hōei years (1704-11), can be seen in the script for *Aizen
Myōō no Matsu by* the same Uji Kaganojō, produced at his theatre. It says,
"The puppet Murakami Buhei was manipulated on its way on the *hanami-
chi.* It was a big hit." The word *hanamichi* is very much in evidence here.

There is another work picturing the *hanamichi,* this being in a play
called *Sukeroku Shinjū Nami Semi no Nukegara,* performed at a Kyoto puppet theatre in 1716. It shows *a* puppet handler on the *tsuke butai,* with two
pine trees at the front of the *tsuke butai.* Tsunoda Ichirō suspects that this is
a hanamichi (Ningyō Butai Shi Kōhen 1980) and we should follow his
opinion.

These two pieces of evidence show without question that *a hanamichi*
was used in the puppet theatre. They cover the years from 1703 to 1716,
and both may be thought of as temporary phenomena. However, it is positive that a permanent *hanamichi* was eventually set up in the puppet theatre,
as depicted both in words and an illustration in a work published in 1802,
the *Gekijō Gakuya Zue Shūi.* Its "Ayatsuri Shibai Butai Meimoku" section
about puppet theatre stage terms states: "*Hanamichi:* when the puppet tra-
verses the *hanamichi* and reaches the stage, the *tesuri* border[28] is opened
and it goes onstage from here. It is so well known a place that description of
it here is curtailed."

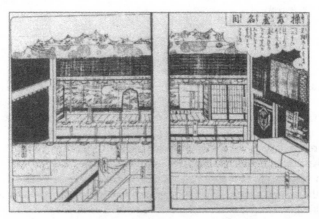

Figure 153. 1802 illustration of a puppet theatre showing the *hanamichi* in the
lower portion, left. The sides of the pathway are raised enabling the handlers
to hold the puppets so that their feet seem to be treading the grounds, suggested by the top edge of the panels. (From *Shibai Gakuyazue,* 1801.)

In the modern age, the *hanamichi* has been abolished in the puppet theatre, except for special instances, but it could be seen until recently in performances of regional folk theatre (*minzoku geinō*). The puppet stage in Kisawa Village, located in the furthest mountain recesses of Nachi province in Tokushima prefecture, has a long and narrow board walkway that runs through the open-air auditorium seating. It has no special name today but, according to an elderly inhabitant, it was called the *hanamichi* in the old days, and was used by spectators to bring flowers to the stage. This stage is said to have been built in the Meiji period (*Nihon Butai Shi Kōhen* 1980).

It is thus obvious that the *hanamichi* existed both in word and fact in the puppet theatre, and it is therefore necessary to reconsider the origins of the term. The clearest ideas on its etymology see it deriving from its use either as (1) a pathway for the presentation of gifts (or flowers), (2) a path for *ennen's* "boys with flower-staffs" or *hana matsuri's* "flower dance" performers, (3) the flower path of the *hana matsuri*, (4) the *hanamichi* in sumo, (5) the path for star (flower) actors, or (6) a path of beauty. The explanation that it comes from its employment by star actors is questionable when we see that it was used for puppet plays, just as the notion of it as a path of beauty is difficult to respect when the puppet theatre version is acknowledged as a rough, temporary arrangement with side walls set up in the midst of the pit.

Certain terms used in the puppet theatre, such as *daijin bashira* ("minister's pillar") and *hashigakari*, are the same as those in *kabuki*. If they were born under the influence of *kabuki*, the term *hanamichi* could be thought subject to the same possibility. Nevertheless, we should notice that *daijin bashira and hashigakari* came to both the puppets and *kabuki* from the *nō*, and that the *hanamichi* probably shares a common origin in both later forms of theatre.

The difficulty of seeking an etymological origin in *ennen*, *hana matsuri*, or sumo is that it is impossible to find any reference to the *hanamichi* in these presentations before the *kabuki hanamichi* itself. When the word appeared in the poetry collection of 1679, its significance and use were already limited. At that time, the *hanamichi* was still a temporary stage construction. The theory of its origins in sumo has attraction, but as there is no reference to the word before the Edo era, this explanation must be put aside.

Because of the limits of today's available evidence, the origin of the word must be sought in the idea of a pathway used for the offering of gifts. There are several early *kabuki* illustrations showing actors being offered money and inventories of gifts affixed to bamboo leaves, tree branches, and at the tip of long poles. These include a screen painting of riverbed performances at Shijō, Kyoto, owned by the Idemitsu Museum of Art; a screen painting of Edo customs, also owned by the Idemitsu; and a scroll of Kyoto riverbed performers, in the possession of the Hosomi family.

The same scene can be seen in the puppet theatre. There is an illustration thought to be from the late Genroku period, and shown on the reverse side of Uji Kaganojō's play, *Nan Daimon Aki Higan*, depicting a theatregoer on the *tsuke butai* in the act of presenting flowers to Uji. The caption, part of which is illegible, notes that the gift is made by an admirer enamored of his work, that the flowers are being given in gratitude, and so forth.

In these pictures, no path through the audience for the purpose of giving flowers is shown. Instead, the givers of gifts approach the stage from various directions. However, to the theatre personnel of the time, the presentation of gifts from patrons was a very important source of income indeed. When crowds of theatregoers packed the playhouses, creating a chaotic scene, consideration was given to the convenience of admirers bringing gifts, making it more than likely that the *hanamichi* was constructed for this purpose. Of course, it was not a permanent arrangement, and no consideration was given to its use for performance, so its height relative to the stage was variable.

The *hanamichi* ultimately came to be used as an entrance and exit for actors during the Kanbun (1661-73) and Enpō (1673-81) periods. It evolved into the C-type *tsuke butai* that was born during the Genroku years, and by the Kyōho period the permanent *hanamichi* was born.[29]

NOTES

This is a slightly revised version of an essay that first appeared in *Theatre Research International* 24:1 (1999). All notes aside from numbers 15 and 20 are those of the translator.

1. The premodern *kabuki* theatre, which had additional features that would require too much space to detail here, used what might be called a combination endstage and thrust arrangement. In the nineteenth century, the thrust was eliminated, and, finally, under Western influence, a proscenium was installed .

2. There are a number of examples of the *hanamichi's* influence on leading Western practitioners. One of the earliest attempts to employ it was Max Reinhardt's pantomime *Sumurun* (1910), which, after being shown in New York, is believed to have inspired similar ramps in vaudeville and burlesque. More recently, Ariane Mnouchkine's *Les Atrides* (1992) used a moving ramp through the audience that seemed to me a modern reconceptualization of the *hanamichi*, For an excellent discussion of the ways in which the *hanamichi* figured in the development of modern Western theatre, see Fischer-Lichte (1997).

3. For supporters of the *hashigakari* into *hanamichi* theory, see Cavaye (1993, 24), Scott (1999, 277), and Ernst (1974, 49-50). Ernst, whose work is

based largely on the writings of Japanese scholar Suda Atsuo, provides a good account of the *kabuki* theatre's architectural history.

4. Those who support one or another version of the idea that front steps used for gift giving evolved into the *hanamichi* include Toshio Kawatake in Inoura and Kawatake (1981, 184), and Gunji (1969, 45). Donald Shively (1978, 16) refers not to steps but to a small frontal platform for the placement of gifts.

5. I wish to thank Professor Torigoe Bunzō (Waseda University), Professor Masako Yuasa (Leeds University), and my graduate assistant Mr. Ikawa Yasukazu for very helpful suggestions regarding translation problems.

6. This famous book is known in Japanese by the title *Yakusha Rongo* and *Yakusha Banashi*. It is available in an English translation by Dunn and Torigoe (1969).

7. For background on these architectural features, see Ernst (1974, 24-66), and Leiter (1997, 49-53). Professor Suwa's article provides background on the *tsuke butai* not found in any English-language source. All technical terms used by Suwa are described in Leiter.

8. "Za" means "theatre" in this context, but I prefer to keep the original Japanese usage rather than to say Hayakumo Theatre.

9. These are references to actors, not the characters they are playing.

10. Theatres were lit by daylight streaming in from windows high up at both sides of the interior. These can be seen in most woodblock prints of theatre interiors.

11. The *kabuki* stage of the seventeenth and eighteenth centuries, being under the influence of *nō* architecture, long retained the *nō* theatre's front pillars, and the roof that—under the theatre's regular roof—they supported.

12. *Ennen* is a still surviving medieval ritual dance that played a role in the formation of *nō*.

13. Bowers's explanation of sumo's connection with the *kabuki hanamichi* is slightly different from this.

14. The *kaomise* production was the first of the season. Held in the eleventh month, it was the most gala event of the *kabuki* calendar, as it introduced the actors (thus the term "face showing") making up a theatre's new company.

15. According to a volume in the Japanese Literature Study Archives of Gakushuin University. There are portions missing from the book.

16. This quotation does not include the word *hanamichi* and I was going to exchange that word for *kaomise*, suspecting a misprint; Professor Torigoe has suggested to me, however; that the original is correct. He says it implies the use of the *hanamichi* because it was there that, during the *kaomise* production, male and female characters interacted.

17. Variously titled volumes containing critiques of all actors worthy of billing were published annually in Edo, Osaka, and Kyoto from the late seventeenth century to the years shortly after Japan was opened to the West. These provide a detailed record of theatrical accomplishments unparalleled in any other culture.

18. Saruwaka was a major comical character in early *kabuki*, appearing in numerous works.

19. It was introduced in Narasaki (1989).

20. *Hanaikusa was a* kind of colorful game involving fighting with flowers.

21. The phrases *Wakoko hanaikusa / Shimoyo no kaze* were part of a tradition in which characterizing expressions were painted on the theatre's billboards preceding the actual title as a way of summing up the dramatic contents. This tradition was called "horn writing" or *tsunogaki*.

22. Translated by Richie and Watanabe (1963).

23. Professor Suwa is especially interested in the relation between Danjūrō I and his performances of Kinpira, the character most instrumental in the development of *aragoto*-style acting.

24. *Sakaomodaka* is a kind of armor braiding.

25. Professor Suwa does not mention the fact that, once it became a permanent feature, the *hanamichi* in Edo theatres was first installed in the auditorium at an oblique angle, while in Kamigata theatres it ran at a right angle, which is how all *hanamichi* soon were built.

26. A reference to plays such as *Ashiya Dōman Ōuchi Kagami* (1734), also known as *Kuzunoha,* in which a fox takes the form of a hunter's absent wife, and lives with him.

27. In the woodblock prints, unlike in Suwa's diagram, what he terms the C-type *tsuke butai* is shown running through the audience at an oblique, not a right, angle.

28. The *tesuri* is the low, horizontal flat behind which the puppet manipulators stand, pretending that the upper edge of the flat is the floor on which the puppets they hold are standing or sitting.

29. Following his endnotes, Professor Suwa adds a postscript. He notes that, subsequent to the completion of his essay, he was given the opportunity of a single viewing of a rare manuscript in someone's (unidentified) private possession. Dated 1674, the manuscript shows a captioned illustration of the interior of a temporary *nō* theatre. Remarkably, this *nō* theatre is equipped with a *hanamichi* and is labeled as such. A bamboo railing runs along both sides of a ramp that is about two and a half feet wide and that extends from the front of the approximately eighteen square foot stage to the boxes at the rear. Because the ramp is somewhat lower than the stage, Suwa concludes that it would have been inconvenient for entrances and suggests that it may more likely have been used for gift presentations. He also wonders whether this document does not contain the first recorded use of the word *hanamichi*.

REFERENCES

Aoe Shunjirō. 1971. "Hanamichi Shiko." In *Nihon Geinō no Genryū*. Tokyo: Iwasaki Bijutsusha.

Bowers, Faubion. 1974. *Japanese Theatre.* Tokyo and Rutland, Vt.: Charles E. Tuttle. Originally published 1952.

Cavaye, Ronald. 1993. Kabuki: *A Pocket Guide.* Tokyo and Rutland, Vt.: Charles E. Tuttle.

Dunn, Charles J., and Bunzo Torigoe, eds. and trans. 1969. *The Actors' Analects.* Tokyo: University of Tokyo Press.

Ernst, Earle. 1974. *The Kabuki Theatre.* 2d ed. rev. Honolulu: University of Hawaii Press. Originally published 1956.

Fischer-Lichte, Erika. 1997. *The Show and the Gaze of Theatre: A European Perspective.* Iowa City: University of Iowa Press.

Genshoku Ukiyo-e Daihyakka Jiten Daikkan. Vol. 2. Tokyo: Daishūkan.

Gotō Keiji. 1925. *Nihon Gekijō Shi.* Tokyo: Iwanami Shoten.

Gunji, Masakatsu, with Chiaki Yoshida. 1969. *Kabuki.* Tokyo and Palo Alto Ca.: Kodansha.

Hattori Yukio. 1980. "Hanamichi Kō." In *Edo Kabuki Ron.* Tokyo: Hōsei Daigaku Shuppan Kyoku.

Hayashiya Tatsusaburō. 1931. "Kabuki no Gekijō Kōzō no Shinka." In *Kabuki Gashō.* Tokyo: Tōkyōdō.

Ikeda Yasaburō. 1956. "Gekijō (Kankyaku, Seki, Sajiki, Butai, Hanamichi) Sono Geinō Shiteki Kōsatsu." In *Kabuki Zensho Daiichi Ikkan.* Tokyo: Tōkyō Sōgensha. Reprinted in *Nihon Rekishi Shinsho: Edo Jidai no Geinō,* 1960. Tokyo: Shibundō.

Imao Tetsuya. 1979. *Kabuki o Miru Hito no Tame ni.* Tokyo: Tamagawa Daigaku Shuppanbu.

Inoura, Yoshinobu, and Toshio Kawatake. 1981. *The Traditional Theater of Japan.* New York and Tokyo: Weatherhill.

Kabuki Daichō Shūsei Daiikkan. 1983. Tokyo: Benseisha.

Lane, Richard. 1978. *Images of the Floating World: The Japanese Print.* New York: Konecky and Konecky.

Leiter, Samuel L. 1997. *New* Kabuki *Encyclopedia: A Revised Adaptation of* Kabuki Jiten. Westport, Ct.: Greenwood.

"Nanoridai." 1962. In Tsubouchi Memorial Theatre Museum, ed. *Engeki Hyakka Daijiten.* Tokyo: Heibonsha.

Narasaki Muneshige. 1989. "Saruwaka Kanzaburō Shijō Gawara Shibai Kōgyō Zukan." *Kokka* 1127 (October).

Ningyō Butai Shi Kōhen: Daini Bunsatsu: Kaisetsu no Bu. 1980. Tokyo: Kokuritsu Gekijō.

Nishiyama Matsunosuke. 1969. *Hana—Bi e no Kōdō to Nihon Bunka.* Tokyo: Nihon Hōsō Shuppan Kyōkai. Reprinted in *Nishiyama Matsunosuke Chosakushū Daihakkan.* 1985. Tokyo: Yoshikawa Hiroshi Bunkan.

Origuchi Shinobu. 1976. "Muromachi Jidai no Bungaku." In *Chū Kobun Gura: Origuchi Shinobu Zenshū Daijūnnikan.* Tokyo: np.

Richie, Donald, and Miyoko Watanabe, trans. 1963. *Six Kabuki Plays.* Tokyo: Hokuseido.

Scott, A.C. 1999. *The* Kabuki *Theatre of Japan*. Mineola, N.Y.: Dover. Originally published 1956.

Shively, Donald. 1978. "The Social Environment of Tokugawa *Kabuki*." In *Studies in Kabuki: Its Acting, Music, and Historical Context*, eds. James R. Brandon, William P. Malm, and Donald Shively. Honolulu: University of Hawaii Press.

Shuzui Kenji and Akiba Hami, eds. 1931. *Kabuki Zusetsu*. Tokyo: Manyōkaku. Reprinted in *Shuzui Kenji Chosakushū Bekkan*. 1977. Tokyo: Kasama Shoin.

Shuzui Kenji, ed. 1928. *Nihon Meicho Zenshū; Kabuki Kyakuhonshū*. Tokyo: Nihon Meicho Zenshū Kankōkai, 1928.

Suda Atsuo. 1949. *Nihon Engeki Shi no Kenkyū*. Tokyo: Sagami Shoten.

Suwa Haru. 1970. *Kabuki Kaika*. Tokyo: Kadokawa Shoten.

————. 1991. *Kabuki no Hōhō*. Tokyo: Benseisha.

"Tsuke Butai." 1962. In Tsubouchi Memorial Theatre Museum, ed., *Engeki Hyakka Daijiten*. Tokyo: Heibonsha.

Yakusha Gan Hodoki. 1716. Kyoto: np.

The Kanamaru-za:
Japan's Oldest *Kabuki* Theatre

In March 1995, while in Tokyo for a week of conferences, I saw a new film by Shinoda Masahiro called *Sharaku*. One of the most striking features of this colorful movie, which purports to explain the still-unknown identity of the eponymous late-eighteenth-century *ukiyo-e* artist, is the scenes set in a *kabuki* playhouse, Edo's Nakamura-za, as it might have looked in the 1790s. Standing in for the Nakamura-za is a theatre that actually was not built for another four decades and exists not in Edo's successor, Tokyo, nor even in one of the two other major *kabuki* cities, Kyoto and Osaka, but in the small town of Kotohira (or Konpira-San) in Kagawa prefecture, Sanuki province, on the island of Shikoku, several hours by train from Osaka. Previously, I had seen this theatre, the Kanamaru-za (or Konpira Ōshibai), only in photographs. Its screen presence was stunning, packed as it was with a simulated eighteenth-century audience, even though the theatre had been dressed up and somewhat altered from its regular appearance to conform with earlier architectural features.[1] The most obvious revision was the addition of a thrust stage (*tsuke butai*), an element that did not vanish from *kabuki* until well into the nineteenth century, somewhat later than it did in contemporary English theatres as the apron shrank to make room for more audience seating. When I returned to Japan several months later, I visited the theatre to photograph it and describe its features. Barely anything about it had ever appeared in English although it had received some Japanese coverage in recent years.

Kotohira's alternate name of Konpira-San derives from a famous shrine best known for its veneration of the Indian and Buddhist deity Kunphira, of which Konpira is a corruption. Konpira, conceived of as a fish or crocodile with the body of a snake, is revered as a deity who protects seafarers and other travelers, and is known for his miraculous deeds (Fujiya Hotel 1950, 475). Shrines to Konpira are found throughout Japan, although that in Kotohira is Japan's largest and most often visited, being a sort of once-in-a-lifetime mecca for pious citizens. Interestingly, early *kabuki* and Japanese puppet theatre produced a number of revenge dramas centered on Konpira.[2]

(top) Figure 154. Slope leading to Kanamaru-za. (All photos: Samuel L. Leiter.)

(lower left) Figure 155. Stone marker saying "Konpira Ōshibai."

Figure 156. Stone supporting wall with wooden staircase to left.

Pilgrims, who have visited the town en masse for hundreds of years, climb a seemingly endless flight of stone stairs, lined on either side by countless souvenir shops, before reaching the shrine—and its glorious view—at the top of a mountain. Those who, for one reason or another, are unable to make the ascent can hire sturdy men to bear them aloft in a kind of lightweight palanquin. Shortly after beginning the ascent there is a road to the theatre leading off to the left. It takes one up a less arduous slope (figure 154), past red lanterns and vertical stone markers on each of which one of the theatre's names, Konpira Ōshibai (Konpira Big Theatre), has been chiseled (figure 155). The walker then arrives at a stone supporting wall, with a wooden staircase (figure 156) that one can climb to reach the elevated plateau on which the playhouse is situated. Before the steps, though, is a public signpost on which is stated in Japanese (figure 157):

National Designated Important Cultural Property

Old Konpira Big Theatre[3] (Kanamaru-za)

Japan's oldest *kabuki* theatre (*shibai goya* [*koya*]), Old Konpira Big Theatre, was built in Tenpō 6 (1835). Before then, temporary theatres were built here as needed to serve not only as regular playhouses but to function as lottery (*tomigushi*) halls as well.

During the Edo period, Japan's greatest actors (*sen ryō yakusha*)[4] appeared in this theatre, which resulted in its name becoming renowned among the playhouses of the land.

Sparked by the theatre's selection in 1970 as a National Designated Important Cultural Property, a fund-raising drive lasting four years was instituted in 1972, and over $2,000,000 was collected. In April 1976 the theatre was restored to its original form on this site.

Every year since 1985 a *kabuki* production is held here and a great deal of attention is focused on it throughout the nation.

Kotohira City Board of Education[5]

Actually, the theatre had been officially recognized somewhat earlier, when the prefecture's board of education announced its designation as a Prefectural Important Cultural Property in 1953. Although most sources give 1835 as the date for the original theatre, official records note its completion in 1836. According to Kusanagi Kinshirō (1955, 1),

Figure 157. Public signpost.

the date of 1835 derives from an inscription on a no-longer extant overhead beam that was part of the theatre's supporting structure, and was visible until the theatre was renovated in 1898.[6] The older date is understood to have been the year in which construction was begun, with completion reached the following year.

Kabuki theatres, now usually called *gekijō*, were normally referred to in the past as *shibai goya*, meaning something like "play huts," the second word suggesting a makeshift and temporary structure. This may be, it has been said, because theatres were usually flimsy firetraps, the average life of a premodern Japanese theatre having been estimated at about ten years. As the next chapter clearly demonstrates, there are many old theatres dotting the countryside, particularly in farming and fishing villages, some with histories older even than the Kanamaru-za's. Nevertheless, they are considered unworthy contenders for the honor of Japan's oldest *kabuki* theatre because they are either open air theatres established on shrine grounds for amateur performances at religious festivals by local farmers or fisherfolk, or have been so extensively renovated that they no longer bear anything like their original appearance. The Kanamaru-za was established as a first-class theatre for professional actors, and as such is unique in retaining something like its pristine form. There are several comparable theatres in Japan,[7] the most prominent being the Yachiyo-za in Yamaga, Kumamoto prefecture, and the Kōraku-kan, in Kosaka City, Akita prefecture. Both, built in the early twentieth century, are discussed in the following chapter.

Kotohira was an entertainment center from the time of the Genroku period (1688-1704), being particularly active during the town's three annual festivals, in the third month, the sixth month, and the tenth month (according to the old lunar calendar). The town, which now has a permanent population of 11,983, was home to 2,781 in 1840, although its numbers were (and are) regularly swelled by the constant influx of pilgrims and tourists. A screen painting from the early eighteenth century depicts a wide assortment of side shows and more formal entertainments, including an outdoors *nō* play being performed at about where the Kanamaru-za was eventually built. Sumo wrestling was an especially popular crowd pleaser, but following a riot during a match in the 1750s, sumo was forbidden and came increasingly to be replaced by theatre and acrobatics.

Largely because of its popularity as a religious mecca, Kotohira enjoyed many privileges rare outside of the major cities. Among such privileges were the establishment of a brothel district and, from 1825, the institution of a lottery, both of which the officials chose to ignore, although not granting them official licenses. The site of the Kanamaru-za was used not only by *nō* actors, but was also the frequent location for the construction of temporary *kabuki* and puppet theatres, built as needed. In fact, by 1825 the town was considered the nation's chief theatre venue following Edo,

Osaka, and Kyoto. The future Kanamaru-za location was also used for a kind of lottery called *tomigushi* that contributed considerably to the already prosperous town's wealth. When the Kanamaru-za was built, it was with the express purpose of serving as a lottery hall when not in use for theatrical productions. The relationship between the municipal government and theatrical art was thus quite strong in Kotohira, unlike the more adversarial situation then prevailing in the major theatre cities.

In addition to the recent restorations, which incorporated as many of the original elements as possible, the Kanamaru-za underwent minor renovations over the years, perhaps the most extensive being the replacement of its hip gabled roof in 1890. And for much of the present century, its old-fashioned straw mat floor seating was abandoned in favor of Western-style chairs and its "secondary" or *kari hanamichi*[8] runway was removed.

After receiving permission from the shrine and temple officials serving the area's powerful Takamatsu clan, a local carpenter built the Kanamaru-za as a replication of one of the three major Osaka theatres, the Ōnishi Shibai (later called the Chikugo-za and the Naniwa-za),[9] whose plans he obtained on a trip to Osaka. Construction of the theatre, first called Konpira Ōshibai,[10] cost about 1,000 *ryō*. Funds for the project were raised by the local geisha, who accumulated money by clipping the incense sticks by whose burning (a stick an hour, more or less) they calculated the time they spent entertaining their clients. Thus they were able to serve more clients in a shorter period of time. This method of raising funds was also sometimes used to collect enough to pay visiting companies to remain a full month. Such money was called *hanekin* ("clipped money") or *fujōkin* ("dirty money"). The theatre built by these means was appreciated by traveling actors as the only one of its class to the west of the Kyoto-Osaka region (known as Kamigata).

On visiting the town, a troupe of actors would be welcomed with considerable fanfare according to the Kamigata custom of *norikomi* ("boarding and entering"). The theatre's personnel would turn out in full dress to greet them as they came along the highway from Tadotsu, after which the actors—much like barnstormers who toured to European towns at the same time—would march through the town in a parade called the *machi mawari* ("around the town") to make their presence known, until they at last entered the theatre, where a ritualistic, rhythmic handclapping ceremony (*teuchi shiki*) would be held to greet them. This old practice continued until as late as the twentieth century's twenties.

The theatre was under the control of a local temple, the Kanemitsu-in, until the Meiji period. When the hereditary abbot of the temple, a man of surpassing respectability, chose to attend the theatre, he did so privately, when no ordinary spectators were present. It was normally forbidden for priests from his temple to venture outside its precincts. In the company of a select group of distinguished samurai, he watched the play from a place in the second floor galleries (*sajiki*) located on what is designated the "western" (*nishi*) side of the house, where his presence was masked by a bamboo blind. Such visits were termed *oshinobi* ("incognito").

In 1877, the playhouse passed into the hands of a man named Kyōhō, known as an *otokodate*, the Edo era term for swaggering commoners who protected their class from overbearing samurai. He was head of a local gang called the Ippō Gumi ("One Way Gang"), and was also the founder of the town's fire brigade. When he became the theatre's proprietor, he set up a fire alarm in front of it and hired men dressed in *haori* jackets to keep the place safe from conflagrations. He also changed the theatre's name to the Inari-za (Inari—widely depicted as a white fox—is an important agricultural deity worshipped throughout Japan, especially by actors). During these years, plays were usually given in full-length, all-day (*tōshi*) performances, rather than the growing practice elsewhere of staging only favorite scenes (a practice called *midori*), and productions began at 10 A.M., closing at 9 P.M. The place's name was altered to Chitose-za (Thousand Years Theatre) when it was bought in 1897 by Kawazoe Sadaji, who revised the frontage's appearance to reflect that of Osaka's Kado-za.[11] Business was poor so the theatre passed over in 1900 to Kanamaru Genjirō, who paid 4,500 yen for it and gave it its final name.

From the top of the steps leading to the theatre's plateau is a lovely view of the lower reaches of Kotohira (figure 158), and the mountains beyond. Nearby is a booth selling tickets to visitors wishing to examine the building. In August 1995, the price was 300 yen (around $3.00) for an adult. All that was available at the theatre for reference purposes was a recent program, a postcard-ticket combination, and an illustrated flyer, printed on two sides, but containing some useful, if compactly presented information. Despite the dozens of souvenir shops that proliferate all over town, none sold any sort of books or pamphlets about the theatre. There is, moreover, no museum attached to the theatre,[12] where information would easily be available. At any rate, apart from a handful of tourists, visible in some of the photographs, the theatre was practically deserted.

Figure 158. View from theatre's plateau.

The facade of the theatre contains much of interest, although I visited during the off season when no performances are in progress. During the *kabuki* presentations—an annual event since 1985—the theatre is vividly adorned with banners and lanterns (as in the past) and the drum tower (*yagura*) over the entrance is draped in a curtain bearing the familiar crane crest of Shōchiku, the monolithic entertainment company that now controls most *kabuki*. As figure 159 makes clear, the *yagura* was undraped on the day I attended. The Edo-period tradition was to drape the tower—whose presence was the public sign of a theatre's offical license to produce—only when a company was in residence, and to take down the curtain on closing day. In the old days, a large drum would have been placed in this enclosure

to announce by its beating the commencement of performances.

Figure 159. Exterior of the Kanamaru-za.

The theatre's frontage measures 13 *ken*, 2 *shaku* (about 80 feet).[13] The vertical sign-boards (*kanban*) hanging from beneath the eaves list the names of actors who recently appeared on the stage, and the (artificial) bales of rice piled up at the front represent gifts from corporate sponsors or groups of fans. At the left is a vertical banner bearing the name of the actor Nakamura Baigyoku IV. It is not clear from the picture, but there are three entrances (*kido*) into the theatre, left, center, and right, under the eaves. Those to the left (the *ōkido*, "large entrance") and right (*goyō kido*, "honorable use entrance") are of normal height, but that in the center is very low, forcing theatregoers to bend over in order to enter (figure 160). This is the *nezumi kido* ("mouse entrance"), so named because of its supposed resemblance to a mouse hole. It was standard in all Edo-period theatres as an effective means of crowd control, so that only one person at a time could enter, making it difficult to get in without a ticket. I did not avoid banging my head upon entering. In the nineteenth century, my head might also have been bashed—had I started a fight or tried to gate-crash—by a stick-bearing guard hired to keep order here. At first this was the job of a local gang leader, but from 1858 it belonged to an infantryman recruited from the samurai barracks at the Kurayashiki battle camp in Bizen.

In the big cities, theatregoers could enter either via the *kido* or via the adjoining teahouses (*shibai jaya*) at either side, where reservations could be made. There was no such arrangement in Kotohira, so the front entrances were used by all classes of people. Important persons used the *ōkido*, persons associated with the Kanemitsu-in used the *goyō kido*, and the average playgoer used the *nezumi kido*. Edo-period theatregoers were sold a ticket in the form of a flat, oblong, wooden board called a *fuda* (or *torifuda*). It was 7 *sun* (about 10 inches) in length, and 2 *sun*, 1 *bun* (about 3 1/2 inches) in width. The Kanamaru-za's *fuda*-selling place used to be located to the right of the *nezumi kido*. The price depended on the seat desired.

Figure 160. *Nezumi kido* ("mouse entrance"). Bales of rice are piled at the right.

On entering the theatre, the visitor steps into a wide but shallow lobby area, the first part of which is for removing one's shoes. Slippers are available for those who wish them. One then moves onto a hardwood floor to the left of which (figure 161) is a staircase leading to the second floor. The doorway, back-lit by the sun in the picture, leads to the left side (or eastern, *higashi*, side) of the auditorium. To its right is a curtained room (the *toya* or *agemaku*) from which actors make their entrance onto the "main" or *hon hanamichi*.

Figure 161. Left-side lobby staircase to second floor.

To the right of the lobby (figure 162) is another staircase to the second floor. The sliding doors along the lobby wall lead to an audience area at the rear of the auditorium. At the far end of the wall, just before the stairs, can be seen the curtained entranceway to the right side of the auditorium.

Figure 162: Right-side
lobby staircase.

Once through
the entranceway to the
left (figure 163), the
visitor has access to
the *tatami* seating
along that side of the
house. This is the
sajiki seating, which
runs along the east
and west sides of the
theatre on both floors. Visible is the *tatami* seating that juts out several feet
into the auditorium from beneath the overhead gallery. To its immediate
right is another *tatami*-mat area for smaller groups, each section separated
from the next by a wooden board. Just to the right of the latter area is the
hanamichi—8 *ken*, 3 *shaku* long (about 50 feet)—at the far end of which is
the stage, with its musicians' room (*geza* or *hayashibeya*) at stage right. Because of its proximity to the *hanamichi*, which allowed its occupants to
view the actors' backs so closely, the area to the left of the runway is called
the *geiura* ("behind the acting"). These seats were originally lower in price
than those in the pit (*hiradoma* or *hiraba*). The most expensive seats, as
they still are even in the major cities, were in the *sajiki*. Electric lights that
simulate shielded old-time candles can be seen burning in front of the stage,
which is dressed with the nonlocalized pine tree back-ground used for those
kabuki works, like *Kanjinchō*, that derive from the *nō* theatre and are called
matsubame mono ("pine tree board plays").

Figure 163. Entry to first-floor, left-side
seating.

In the *toya* (figure 164), a full-
length mirror awaits the actors for
last-minute adjustments before they
make their entrance into the
auditorium, which can be seen
through the door at the left. The
signboard leaning against the wall simply says "*toya*" and is for the benefit
of visitors.

Viewing the auditorium from the *toya* with the *agemaku* pulled to the
side, the visitor—like an actor about to enter—sees the *hanamichi* stretch-

ing before him to the stage and a *tatami*-floored pit to the right (figure 165). The pit, originally the *doma* ("earth place"), was often later called the *hiraba* ("level place") or *hiradoma* ("level earth place") to distinguish it from the "raised" doma (*takadoma*) seating introduced in nineteenth-century theatres along the sides in front of the lower *sajiki*. It is divided into small seating areas called *masu*, after the name for a type of Japanese rice measure. Unlike the visitors in the picture, who are seated on the wooden partitions,[14] theatregoers sat on the floor (with or without cushions), eating and drinking and capable of turning easily in any direction to follow the action on one or the other *hanamichi*. Sitting in a chair in a contemporary *kabuki* theatre does not permit such freedom of movement. (The *hiraba* is in fact gently raked to permit better visibility.)

Figure 164. Inside *toya*.

The photos also show a large TV set on stage. This is used to show visitors a continually repeated videotape of a documentary about the theatre. The tape has generous portions devoted to recent productions showing the theatre in action with a full house. The four metal columns supporting the roof are not from the 1835 building but were installed during the renovation of 1890, when the original roof beam was removed.

Figure 165. View of *hanamichi* and auditorium from *toya*.

Having entered the *hiraba* and turned momentarily from the stage to the *toya* (figure 166), the spectator sees the

(top) Figure 166. *Toya* entranceway onto *hanamichi*. Note railed-in *takaba* area.

Figure 167. Auditorium seen from stage left. At rear are *aoda* and *ōmukō*.

(bottom) Figure 168. Side view of *ōmukō* seating.

opening from which the actors enter. Closer inspection reveals the railing for the stairs that lead up to the *toya* from the area beneath the stage (*naraku*). Apparent as well is the little enclosed space directly in front of the entrance where a theatre functionary used to sit and oversee the auditorium. The diamond shaped plaques along the side of the *hanamichi* indicate the row numbers. A similar system of plaques runs across the front of the stage, using characters from the Japanese syllabary, to further help spectators find their places. Woodblock prints of the nineteenth century also show such seat markers, although not necessarily using the system seen at the Kanamaru-za. The system of using a combination of syllabary characters and numbers was sometimes replaced in other theatres by indicating rows with terms such as *take* ("bamboo") or *matsu* ("pine").

We can now move closer to the stage and survey the auditorium from the stage left side (figure 167). At the rear is the other side of the wall of sliding doors seen on entering the lobby. Before it is an undifferentiated area for audience members. This is the *aoda* ("green fields"), a space formerly set aside for nonpaying spectators. The term derives from a farmer's phrase, "the green fields have produced a poor harvest" (*aoda ni miirinashi*). To its left is a small platform from which another functionary helped keep order. Above it is a balcony area, the *ōmukō* ("great beyond"), a place which came to be known in all *kabuki* theatres as the seating area preferred by connoisseurs (*tsu*), presumably because it was less expensive, allowing for repeated visits. A closer view of the *ōmukō* (figure 168) shows it to be on three levels, each with *tatami* flooring. Figure 169 reveals the area over

the *ōmukō*, with its post and beam architecture.

(top) Figure 169. Area over *ōmukō*.

Figure 170. Paper lanterns over auditorium.

(bottom) Figure 171. Auditorium from stage right. *Karaido* is at junction of stage and *hanamichi*.

Paper lanterns (lit today by electricity) decorate the theatre's ceiling (figure 170) and interior, the latter seen from the stage in figure 171. The auditorium is further dressed up with cherry blossoms and the like during actual performances. Figure 171 also reveals a feature no longer found in *kabuki* theatres, the *karaido* ("empty well"), a square opening (closed over when not in use) located at the junction of the *hanamichi* and the stage. Actors can appear from it via steps leading from the basement. Because the actor using it is moving under his own volition, it allows him to time his entrance more precisely than when he rises on the slow-moving elevator trap (*suppon*) on the *hanamichi*. The *karaido* was also used to represent a muddy pond or rice paddy in scenes set near such locales, and the well would be filled with a mud-like concoction that would cling to the actors realistically when they fell into or emerged from this spot. When filled with mud it was known as the *dorobune* ("mud boat"). The Kanamaru-za is the only theatre that still retains the *karaido*.

(top) Figure 172. View of *hanamichi* and *suppon* from *sajiki*.

Figure 173. Close-up of *suppon*.

(bottom) Figure 174. View of *hanamichi* in *suppon* area as viewed from *masu*.

The *suppon* can be seen in figure 172 at a position between the metal column at the center and the flat dividing board in the *geiura* seating at the bottom right. (This board is also visible in the plan shown in figure 176 and may have been used to provide easy access to the *hanamichi* for audience members on special occasions.) The *suppon* is operated manually, as of old, from beneath the stage. Figure 173 provides a closer view of this device from the perspective of an actor moving toward the stage. Figure 174 shows that the *suppon*, situated at the *hanamichi* position called *shichisan*, is precisely in line with the fifth row, vertically, of *masu*. The angle at which a theatregoer seated on the floor in *masu* row five views the *hanamichi* is shown in figure 175. Used mainly for the entrances of mystical characters, the *suppon* creates a magical effect when they appear and disappear within an auditorium that is considerably more intimate than the huge theatres in

which *kabuki* is generally produced today. The effect is enormously enhanced when the theatre is darkened and the face of the strange figure slowly emerging on the elevator is illuminated by the *sashidashi*—a long, slender, black pole with a candle at its end, held by a black-robed stage assistant (*kurogo*).

Figure 175. Same view as in figure 174, but from seated perspective.

Figure 176. This plan of the first story is based on one provided with the theatre's ticket brochure. Key: (A) *nezumi kido*, (B) lobby area (*uchi kido*), (C) patrons' footwear storage (*gesokuba*), (D) west lavatory, (E) east lavatory, (F) west (*nishi*) *sajiki* and east (*higashi*) *sajiki*, (G) *hiraba*, (H) *aoda*, (I) *toya*, (J) *geiura* (the brochure says *hi no shusseki*, or "eastern seats"), (K) main (*hon*) *hanamichi*, (L) secondary (*kari*) *hanamichi*, (M) *karaido*, (N) *demago*, (O) *geza*, (P) *mawari butai*, (Q) *seri*, (R) *suppon*, (S) *gakuya*, (T) *furo* (bath), (U) *kodōgu beya* (prop room), (V) connecting board. Terms are both those on the brochure itself and those provided by the author.

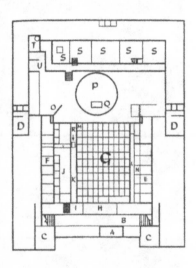

The theatre holds from 1,000 to 1,200 persons, whereas Tokyo's Kabuki-za seats 2,600. A good sense of the theatre's intimacy relative to modern *kabuki* venues can be gleaned from figure 177, which does not include the seating areas to the sides of the two *hanamichi*.[15] Figure 178, though, takes in the *kari hanamichi* and the raised *tatami* seating to its side. In Edo, the latter would have been called the *takadoma*, but in the Kanamaru-za they are called by the strange name of *demago* ("thrust-grandchild").[16] To their right is the first floor "west" *sajiki*, beyond which runs a veranda on the outside of the theatre. The rain shutters along the wall have been opened to allow light to stream in.

Figure 177. View of stage from rear of house.

Whereas the *hon hanamichi* is about five feet wide, the *kari hanamichi* is about half of that. When necessary for certain plays, such as the "Numazu" scene from *Igagoe Dōchū Sugoroku*, a plank is set up across the rear of the pit so that the actors may leave the stage by the *hon hanamichi*, traverse the pit (with spectators to their front and rear), and move back to the stage via the *kari hanamichi*. The relationship between the height of the slightly raised runways to the

Figure 178: View down *kari hanamichi* on right side of house.

position of the floor-seated spectators creates a truly exciting dynamic between audience and actor, completely unlike the effect of actors walking down the aisles of a Western-style theatre. As might be expected, all sense of intimacy with the performance on the *hanamichi* is lost as one gets increasingly further away from it in balcony seats at theatres like Tokyo's Kabuki-za, where there are many seats from which the *hanamichi* is only partially visible or even completely invisible. This distancing effect does

not occur at the Kanamaru-za, as one sees from figure 179, taken from the
ōmukō balcony overlooking the runway. However, those not seated near the
front railings of the upper *sajiki*, as in figure 180, will clearly have trouble

seeing the *hon hana-*
michi, so sightline
problems do occa-
sionally arise. The
depth of the *sajiki*
can be seen even
more clearly in fig-
ure 181.

Figure 179. View
of stage from
sajiki.

Figure 180. Inside left-
side *sajiki*.

Figure   182,
taken from roughly
the same position,
expresses much of
the theatre's atmo-
sphere. It shows the
west side upper and
lower   *sajiki*,   the
closed *shōji* screens
behind the second
story *sajiki*, and the
shōji (backed by rain shutters) at the upper-most level of the west wall. On
the wall of the corridor outside the *sajiki* is a row of additional rain shutters,
as seen in figure 183. Such shutters are called *madobuta* ("window lids") or
akari mado ("lighting windows"). Outside them is platforming for stagehands. These outer shutters do not slide, but lift up from the bottom and are
held in place by wooden poles. Shown again in figure 184, where they are
fronted by *shōji*, these shutters were the principal means of illuminating and
darkening the house during the pre-electricity years, when candles were
used very sparingly because of their danger. Plays at the Kanamaru-za are
now staged using the old technique of having the stage hands outside the
shutters open and close them on cue, creating relatively quick—if noisy—
lighting changes, which are especially effective in gloomy ghost plays.

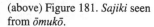

(above) Figure 181. *Sajiki* seen from *ōmukō*.

(left) Figure 182. View of right side of house from *ōmukō*.

(below left) Figure 183. Corridor outside upper *sajiki*, with rain shutters on left.

(bottom) Figure 184. View of *madobuta*.

Kabuki theatres always have an orchestra present, but unlike Western theatres, which usually place their musicians in a designated place between the auditorium and the stage, where only the conductor is prominent, *kabuki* prefers to have its musicians perform from an onstage position. Sometimes, especially in dance plays, they are visible in formal costuming; most often, usually in dramas, they are invisible as they play in the offstage music room called *geza* ("lower seat") or *hayashibeya* ("musicians' room"), built with a latticed screen that allows them to see the stage action while remaining hidden. The musicians, who in Edo were at first on stage left, then upstage, and finally, by the nineteenth century, on stage right, where they still are, remained on stage left in Kamigata. The Kanamaru-za, however, elected to have such a musicians' room on either side of the stage, an idiosyncratic convention that was useful when two different schools of music were used in the same piece (a convention called *kakeai*), each school occupying a different music room. As now constituted, the stage left room is gone, replaced by a low, railed-in area,[17] over which remains a second-story, screened-in room (the *yuka*) employed by the chanter (*tayū*) and shamisen player combination (called *chobo*) in works influenced by or adapted from the puppet theatre. The bamboo screen or blind (*sudare*) can be rolled up to reveal the performers. A similar room is in this position in most theatres, and can be seen at the center of figure 185. Directly in front of it hangs the vertically striped traveler curtain (*hikimaku*)—green, persimmon, and black—that has come to be associated with *kabuki*. (In the past, however, these colors were not ubiquitous and each theatre had its own distinctive scheme.) The curtain has been tied back to hang here in full view of the audience, as it used to do (although most old prints show it on the other side of the stage), but in modern theatres it is pulled into the wings when not in use. Old *kabuki* theatres lacked the proscenium (introduced during the Meiji period) that would have allowed the hiding of the curtain.

Figure 185. Stage-left curtain position and *chobo yuka*.

The stage opening, measured between the two supporting pillars (*daijin bashira*) at either side, is 8 *ken* (about 48 feet). When one compares this with the almost 90-foot-wide opening of the Kabuki-za, it becomes clear how much has been lost as modern *kabuki* theatres moved increasingly toward gigantism and away from the most effective means for expressing theatrical art. In this regard, an easy comparison can be made between *kabuki* history and the process of enlarging—and artistically weakening—the great London theatres, Drury Lane and Covent Garden, during the eighteenth and nineteenth centuries.

(descending order)

Figure 186. Revolving stage.

Figure 187. Steps to *naraku*.

Figure 188. Passage under *naraku*.

Figure 189. *Suppon* framing and mechanism.

Over the stage is a gridwork of bamboo poles that in Edo was called *sunoko* ("drainboard"), but in the Kanamaru-za is known by the Kamigata term of *budōdana* ("grape shelf"). Although, traditionally, *kabuki* sets make only sparing use of flown-in scenic elements (such as clouds), a grid is necessary not only for scenes requiring flying but, more importantly, as a place from which to drop the thousands of tiny, triangular pieces of paper that stand for snow, the pink ones for cherry blossoms, or the silver ones used for rain. If one of the stagehands in the flies were to accidentally drop a sandal along with the snow, it was sufficient incentive for playgoers in the *ōmukō* to throw their seat cushions at the stage. A fly gallery with a pulley system (*rokuro*) and numerous ropes is situated on the stage left wall in the wings.

The Kanamaru-za, as a *kabuki* theatre worthy of the name, includes a manually operated revolving stage (*mawari butai*), whose outline can be seen in figure 183. To examine its mechanism, one must descend into the *naraku* ("hell") area beneath the stage. Until the theatre's modern renovation, its *naraku*, whose height is a bit over six feet, was considered truly hellish, being damp, dirty, and decrepit, and supposedly haunted by the ghosts of actors rumored to have been buried there after dying in stage fights fought with real swords to settle personal grudges. One of the purposes of the *naraku* is to provide a quick and easy means of connection under the *hanamichi* between the *toya* and the backstage dressing rooms (*gakuya*). This is especially useful for quick-change effects. However, actors came to find the Kanamaru-za's *naraku* so distasteful that they chose to run along the veranda (*nure'en*) outside the lower *sajiki* to get from one place to the other. Figure 184 exposes the steps leading from the *toya* to the now presentable *naraku*, whose floor has been covered with boards. The path through the *naraku* to the dressing rooms is seen in figure 185, which also shows the wooden structure supporting the *hanamichi*. Stopping for a moment along this path allows for a view (figure 186) of the *suppon's* elevator trap arrangement.

(left) Figure 190. Support structure for revolve. Vertical beam fixed in position with rope is used to push revolve.

Figure 191. Ladder to dressing rooms from beneath the stage.

Beneath the stage itself are the wooden beams and platforming used to power the revolving stage and the trap (*seri*) set into it. There is only one trap on the stage proper, unlike the three found on such large stages as the Kabuki-za's. Its frame is visible amidst the beams supporting the revolve. Figure 190 displays the thick central axle on which the revolve swivels, the hanging beams (there are three)—tied in place with ropes when not in use—against which stagehands place their shoulders to move the disk, and the framed structure surrounding the main elevator trap. On the floor are stones set into the earth (now a layer of concrete) as foot grips. Nearby is a small ladder leading to the *karaido* entrance that will allow the actor to suddenly emerge practically in the laps of the audience. Another ladder unit (figure 191), at the far end of the path under the *hanamichi*, leads to the backstage and dressing room (*gakuya*) areas.

Backstage, on the stage left side, is another set of ladder-like stairs leading to the room from which the *chobo* performers accompany certain plays. (See figure 185 for the audience view of this room.) The veranda outside the first floor west *sajiki* can be seen at the rear. The dressing room area—where graffiti from actors of yore, scratched in the wood, can still be seen—is located on two floors, as it was in Kyoto and Osaka, unlike Edo, where it was on three floors.[18] According to Kusanagi (1955, 8), the theatre was built with eight small dressing rooms, in addition to a large, communal one (the *ōbeya*, or "big room"). There were three individual rooms to the west of the *ōbeya*, and two to its east. That at the extreme west was reserved for the actor-manager (*zagashira*). The renovations appear to have kept the number of individual dressing rooms, but they have been redistributed: there are now five on the first floor and three on the second, in addition to the *ōbeya*. Two are to the west of the *ōbeya* and one to the east. These are visible in the floor plans (figures 175 and 189). Among these small rooms, intended for the leading actors, is that in figure 195, designated for *onnagata*, and that in figure 194, for the musicians. Figure 193 depicts the *ōbeya*, used by the lower-ranking actors who figure in crowd and fight scenes. This room was also used for rehearsals. The lower-ranking actors are themselves called *ōbeya*, among other terms. To get to this room, located on the upper floor, one must climb yet another steep ladder, the opening for which can just be seen at the left of the picture. Outside the *ōbeya* is a corridor that runs over and across the backstage area (figure 196). From it can be seen the rear of the flats used for the stage setting.

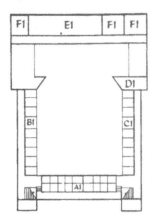

Also backstage, visible in the plan for the first floor at the extreme left of the rear wall, is a small room with a bath (*furo*). The equally small space in front of it is now designated as a prop room (*kodōgu beya*).

Figure 192. Plan for second story. Key: (A1) *ōmukō*, (B1) second-story (*nikai*) east *sajiki*, (C1) second-story west *sajiki*, (D1) *yuka* room for *chobo*, (E1) *ōbeya*, (F1) *gakuya*.

During the twentieth century, the Kanamaru-za was mainly used as a movie theatre. It did not reemerge as a regular center for *kabuki* until after its major renovation. What has now become a brief, annual festival began when Nakamura Kichiemon II (b. 1944), Sawamura Sōjūrō IX (b. 1933), and others produced the play *Saikai Zakura Misome no Kiyomizu* and the dance *Niwaka Jishi*, for three days from June 27, 1985, shortly after they had staged the program at Osaka's Naka-za. Kichiemon I was very impressed with the theatre, which,

with its two *hanamichi* and old-time lighting, he found more appealing than the Naka-za. This led to his returning not long after to produce television productions of two more works, designed to exploit the theatre's resources to the fullest. Eventually, all of *kabuki's* greatest contemporary stars trekked to Kotohira to offer their services in an annual *kabuki* festival at the end of every April. The festival came to be called Kotohira *Kabuki*. In 1995, seats for this limited engagement ranged from $70 to $120.

(top) Figure 193. *Ōbeya*. Stairs lead up to it at extreme left.

(above left) Figure 194. Musicians' dressing room.

(left) Figure 195. *Onnagata's* dressing room.

(bottom) Figure 196. Corridor outside dressing rooms.

For those interested in comparative studies, one of the most remarkable things about *kabuki* is the unusual number of ways in which—without documented influence—it paralleled European theatre history, especially England's, during the seventeenth through nineteenth centuries. Company organization, relations with government authority, commercial business practices, role typing, increasing realism and spectacle, stage technology, acting traditions, the star system,

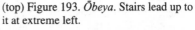

and many other facets of *kabuki* reflect practices that, while being innately Japanese, nevertheless are strikingly similar to what was happening in the West.[19] When, therefore, Westerners acquainted, even modestly, with theatre history, but not with Japanese theatre, enter the Kanamaru-za, they will not feel as if they have crossed the border into some exotic theatrical environment (like a *nō* theatre, for example), where architectural features—for all their beauty—may feel somehow alien because of their relative oddness. They are more likely to feel, for all the obvious differences, rather comfortably at home. Of course, they might note with some initial confusion the twin *hanamichi* where there should be aisles, and the partitioned, empty *masu* where fixed seating ordinarily would be. But they will quickly observe a stage that, like a conventional one in the West, fills up one end of a familiar-looking auditorium and, despite its lack of an obvious proscenium arch does, after all, contain wings, a revolve,[20] and an elevator trap.[21] They will notice that the more-or-less square auditorium—like the oblong playhouses of seventeenth-century France, and the opera houses that soon proliferated all over the continent—allows people at the sides to look across the pit to those on the other side. They might then realize that, even more importantly, the Kanamaru-za's shape enhances the sightlines for the important acting that occurs on the culturally specific *hanamichi*. Moreover, awareness would dawn that, like many contemporary Western theatres and opera houses, the Kanamaru-za contains a rear balcony and *sajiki* seating containing boxes that reach all the way along the walls to the stage itself. Fire laws prevented Japanese theatres from having more than two levels of such seating (as did Drury Lane during the Restoration period), although eighteenth- and nineteenth-century European playhouses, like fancy wedding cakes, tended to add additional layers. Further striking a note of familiarity would be the angled musicians' rooms, downstage right and left, which recall the similarly placed doorways (for entrances and exits) found on English stages of the late seventeenth through mid-nineteenth centuries. All in all, Westerners in the Kanamaru-za would not have to strain their imagination to feel as if they were in a box-pit-and- gallery structure, albeit one designed in wood by a Japanese architect.[22]

Despite the existence of *kabuki* theatres in more accessible places, none provides anything approximating the flavor of an Edo-period playhouse as closely as does the Kanamaru-za. Visiting it in the off-season allows unhurried theatre lovers the pleasure of investigating its every nook and cranny with no one looking over their shoulder. Visiting it when *kabuki* is being produced, however, will undoubtedly conjure potent images of a time far removed that until now could be revisited only in old theatrical woodblock prints. No matter when one visits, though, it will be an experience to savor.[23]

NOTES

This is a slightly revised version of an essay that first appeared in *Asian Theatre Journal* 14:1 (Spring 1997).

1. The film's attempt to recreate an old-time audience is effective but, either for artistic or technical reasons, not always accurate. For example, while trying to show the appearance of an onstage audience, it packs a group of spectators together at stage right, but does not employ the upstage right bleachers called *rakandai* and *yoshino*, where such audiences would normally have sat, watching the actors from the rear. (There were once such seating areas at the Kanamaru-za.) For further information on terms, theatres, and actors mentioned in this report, see Leiter (1997). My research in Japan was made possible by a grant from the Professional Staff Congress of the City University of New York, and acceptance as a Visiting Scholar at Waseda University, Tokyo, for which I thank Professor Torigoe Bunzō. A number of helpful facts about the Kanamaru-za were supplied in a letter from the Kotohira Board of Education, to whom I hereby express my gratitude.

2. A still-performed Konpira play is *Kuwanaya Tokuzō Irifune Monogatari*, first staged in 1770.

3. This is another name for the theatre, Kyū Konpira Ōshibai.

4. Literally, "thousand *ryō* actor," to designate the actor's high salary in gold pieces (*ryō*).

5. An untranslated line at the bottom of the sign asks people not to throw their cigarettes here.

6. I am grateful to Professor Eloise Pearson Hamatani and Hamatani Hiroshi (formerly stage manager of the Kokuritsu Gekijō [National Theatre]) for providing me with a copy of a small volume (Kusanagi 1955) about the theatre. Professor Barbara Thornbury supplied me with helpful information on Kotohira. Justin Leiter created the graphics of the Kanamaru-za's groundplans.

7. Professor Laurence Kominz provided me with information on these theatres. (See also Peyotoru 1992: 8-9, and the following chapter in the present volume, "Gimme that Old-Time *Kabuki*.")

8. The *kari hanamichi* is often called the "temporary" *hanamichi* in English—as opposed to the "regular" or *hon hanamichi*—because it is used only occasionally in major *kabuki* theatres, and is removed when not required. I prefer to call it the "secondary" *hanamichi* because the *kari hanamichi* at the Kanamaru-za is permanent, like its predecessors from the time when such runways were called by such terms as *higashi no ayumi* ("eastern walkway"). As this term suggests, the use of "eastern" and "western" differs in Kotohira from the practice in the major cities, where audience left is west and audience right is east.

9. The Ōnishi got its name ("Great Western Theatre") from its location. Its more successful rivals were the Naka-za (Central Theatre) or Naka no Shibai

and the Kado-za (Corner Theatre) or Kado no Shibai. All were located in the still flourishing Dōtonbori entertainment district. The Naka-za, although in a twentieth-century building, was recently demolished and its functions taken over by the nearby, thoroughly renovated Shōchiku-za.

10. *Ōshibai* refers to first-class theatres with official licenses from the shogunate to perform, designated by the drum tower outside the front of the building over the entrance. In opposition were the *koshibai* (small theatres) or *miyaji shibai* (temple or shrine theatres) that were licensed by religious offices, and were restricted in the number of days they could perform. Like the "illegitimate" theatres of European cities, such as London and Paris, the smaller theatres were often a serious thorn in the flesh of the majors, and frequently ignored restrictions imposed upon them. Such theatres do not seem to have competed with the Kanamaru-za, which was apparently the only game in town. Despite the town's small size, its prospective theatregoing population would have swelled tremendously given the place's popularity as a mecca for pilgrims.

11. Tokyo's Meiji-za, still in operation although in a later building, opened in 1885 under the name Chitose-za.

12. The aforementioned Yachiyo-za, however, has its own museum and shop. It is discussed in the next chapter.

13. One *ken*=1.987 yards. One *shaku*=0.995 feet.

14. Spectators viewing the annual productions still sit on the floor, despite the discomfort such a position now holds for most Japanese, who have become accustomed to chairs. In the past, one could rent a small cushion (*hanjō*) for additional comfort. Like the Western custom of bombarding actors with tomatoes, Japanese audiences often threw their cushions at ineffective actors.

15. These photos were taken with an instamatic type camera, sans wide angle or—beyond the most primitive—zoom possibilities.

16. The wider, but equivalent, seating on the east side of the house is not designated by this unusual term.

17. The old double *geza* arrangement was removed during the 1970 renovations, to allow more room for the actors.

18. Fire regulations prohibited three-story construction in theatres, but the managements got around the proscription by calling the second floor a mezzanine (*chūnikai*).

19. Many of these issues are taken up in this volume's concluding essay.

20. Although revolving stages were known to certain court designers of the Renaissance, and some even have claimed that the Greek *ekkyklema* may have operated as a partial revolve, they were not introduced into conventional Western theatres until 1896, when Karl Lautenschlaeger installed one at the Munich Residenztheater, possibly because of Japanese influence. The first Japanese revolving stage is said to have been invented during the Shōtoku and Kyōhō eras (1711-35), when the Edo playwright Nakamura Denshichi devised a primitive mechanism called the *bun mawashi*. A more advanced version was created by playwright Namiki Shōzō I for a play of his at Osaka's Kado-za in the twelfth month of 1758. This is the type that was installed at the Kanamaru-

za, although Edo began using somewhat different technology for its revolves from 1793. In 1847, an Edo production first used a revolve within a revolve, each capable of moving in a different direction, but this was not used at the Kanamaru-za.

21. Traps were known to European theatre since the medieval period, and even ancient Greece is said to have had a trap-like device in its "Charon's stairs," but its existence is unclear. Japan did not have a stage trap until Higuchi Hanemon invented a mechanism for the puppet theatre during the Hōei period (1704-10). It was the creation of Namiki Shōzō I, however, that came to be used in *kabuki* after being introduced in a 1753 play he wrote for Osaka's Ōnishi Shibai, the theatre on whose architecture the Kanamaru-za was based.

22. For comparative purposes, see Leacroft (1984).

23. The theatre's office may be reached at (0877) 73-3846. It is open every day but Tuesday, from 9 A.M. to 5 P.M.

REFERENCES

Fujiya Hotel. 1950. *We Japanese.* Yokohama: Yamagata Press.

Kusanagi Kinshirō. 1955. *Genzai Saiko no Gekijō Kanamaru-za.* Kotohira: Kagawa-ken Tosho Kabushiki Kaisha.

Leacroft, Richard, and Helen Leacroft. 1984. *Theatre and Playhouse: An Illustrated Survey of Theatre Building from Ancient Greece to the Present Day.* London: Methuen.

Leiter, Samuel L. 1997. *New Kabuki Encyclopedia: A Revised Adaptation of Kabuki Jiten.* Westport, Ct.: Greenwood Press.

Peyotoru Kubō, ed. 1992. *Kabuki wa Tomodachi.* Tokyo: Peyotoru Kubō.

Gimme that Old-Time *Kabuki*:
Japan's Rural Theatre Landscape

For most Japanese and foreign theatregoers in Japan, a visit to *kabuki* means going to a large, urban playhouse in Tokyo, Osaka, Kyoto, or Nagoya. These modern theatres represent a blend of twentieth-century Western theatre architecture and technology with elements from *kabuki's* premodern past. They may house traditional *kabuki* performances with the finest contemporary actors, but it is undeniable that—in the interests of creature comforts and modernity—they lack the intimacy and atmosphere afforded by theatres of the Edo period. As pointed out by the preceding chapter, "The Kanamaru-za: Japan's Oldest *Kabuki* Theatre," however, the nation possesses a considerable number of old-style playhouses, most of them primarily used for the activities of local amateur performers. The Kanamaru-za is only the best known of the small-town and village theatres in which something of that "old-time *kabuki*" feeling can still be savored. These regional theatres and the groups that perform in them are usually called *ji kabuki* or *ji shibai* (some areas use the term *jige* instead of *ji*); *ji* can mean "ground" or "rural," although it can also suggest local, farmers', or fishermen's *kabuki*.[1]

This chapter surveys what intrepid travelers are likely to find as they journey to one or more of Japan's over 100 important *ji kabuki* sites—some older than the Kanamaru-za—in hopes of recapturing a theatrical experience no longer available in the major cities; such an experience can otherwise only be imagined by viewing an old *ukiyo-e* print showing an Edo-period theatre in action. In a number of these theatres twenty-first-century theatre lovers can relive something of what it was like when transfixed audiences sat on an indoor theatre's floor or an outdoor theatre's ground, eating box lunches and drinking sake, as brilliantly garbed actors with mask-like faces came and went on *hanamichi* located at either side, or sets changed before their eyes on manually operated revolving stages, everything dimly lit by sunbeams streaming through ceiling level windows or brilliantly illuminated by the sun itself. And because there has been a revival of interest in precisely such an experience, audiences in Japan are once more doing just this.

Although several recent Japanese books have attempted to review the subject, barely any prior discussion of these theatres exists in English. In order to bring some focus to so much information in a limited space, I have organized the material in a way that mentions all principle examples while touching on points of commonality and difference. The chapter closes with a somewhat more detailed examination of one of the best-known examples, the Yachiyo-za in Yamaga, Kumamoto prefecture, on Kyūshū, Japan's southernmost large island.[2]

Roofed, Indoor Theatres

There are basically three kinds of old-time *kabuki* theatres, that is, theatres designed primarily for the performance of *kabuki* or *kabuki*-type plays. One kind is akin to the Kanamaru-za, that is, roofed theatres (*shibai goya* [*koya*]); another is the small, outdoor structures found mainly on or adjacent to shrine grounds; third are theatres built on movable wagons. Each will be described in turn. In addition, it should be mentioned that there are numerous towns and villages which, despite a history of either roofed or unroofed playhouses, now are forced to play in elementary or junior high school gyms or auditoriums, civic and cultural centers, city halls, or even senior citizen centers. This is true, for example, of Fukuura, on the Shimonokita Peninsula, Aomori prefecture; Handa, near Shibukawa, Gunma prefecture; Shibukawa itself; Katanoo, Ryōtsu, Sado Island; Kushihara Village, Aichi prefecture; Higashi Shirakawa Village, Gifu prefecture; Takao, Gifu; Kosai, Shizuoka prefecture; Obara, Aichi; Tsukude Village, Aichi; Toyohashi, Aichi; Hosshōji, Seihaku, Tottori prefecture; Yokosen, Okayama prefecture; Abason, Okayama; Kiriyama, Yamaguchi prefecture; and Ōhito, Miyazaki prefecture, Kyūshū. Some groups play in both shrine theatres and public buildings, according to the circumstances.

The mostly wooden, two-story interiors of the roofed theatres instantly evoke Edo-period nostalgia in their architectural layout of *doma* or *hiradoma* (pit), *masu* (separated floor areas for seating), and two-story *sajiki* (galleries). These theatres are invariably equipped with all the standard technical features associated with *kabuki*: *hanamichi* (most have two), *suppon* (*hanamichi* trap), *seri* (elevator stage traps), *mawari butai* (revolving stage), *chobo yuka* or *tayūza* (chanter/shamisen dais), *geza* (offstage musicians' room), and the somewhat less ubiquitous *budōdana* (over-the-stage bamboo grid). Some are provided with a *naraku* (below-stage area), which allows access to the cellar mechanisms and may also contain a passageway by which actors, after exiting on stage, can move beneath the *hanamichi* on their way to making a surprise entrance in a changed costume from that runway's rear room. These theatres resemble the general features described for the Kanamaru-za, although each has something unique about it. No two are exactly alike. Like the Kanamaru-za, big city theatres inspired a number of them. The Kyōraku-kan, built in 1931 in Hitachi, Ibaraki prefecture, for instance, used Tokyo's Kabuki-za for its source; the Ebisu-za, in Hirukawa Village, Gifu prefecture, based its design on Nagoya's Misono-za; and the Okina-za, erected in 1923 in Jōge, Hiroshima prefecture, was inspired by Kyoto's Minami-za.[3]

Apart from the Kanamaru-za, all such roofed theatres were built after the end of the Edo period. Several have been moved from their original locations, one example being Japan's second oldest indoor *kabuki* theatre (after the Kanamaru-za), the Kureha-za, in Inuyama, Aichi prefecture, constructed in 1874. Its inside and out conform to classical requirements, even to the relatively rare existence of a drum tower (*yagura*) over its front entrance. A lobby area like that at the Kanamaru-za is separated by a wooden wall from the pit, which seats only 200 (the other parts of the house are not used). The lobby is memorable for the framed photographs hanging there of famous persons of the late Meiji and early Shōwa (1926-1989) eras, including such actors as Kawakami Sadayakko and Kawakami Otojirō; this reflects the theatre's onetime fondness for producing not only *kabuki* and *shinpa* but the kind of politically oriented, late-nineteenth-century drama called *sōshi shibai* that evolved into *shinpa*. The Kureha-za was originally situated near Ebisu Shrine in Ikeda, part of Osaka prefecture, and was first known as the Ebisu-za (not to be confused with an identically named theatre mentioned below); it was moved in 1892 to Nichimoto-chō (today's Nishinoguchi), Ikeda, where it acquired its present name, possibly because of a connection with a nearby Kureha Shrine. It was moved yet again, in 1970, to Meiji Village in Inuyama, where it formed part of a reconstructed Meiji-period village designed for historical and cultural appreciation. It now houses a variety of presentations, with several days of *kabuki* provided by visiting professionals in June and October.

Another interesting example of a theatre that moved is the Hirose-za, Japan's third oldest theatre. Built in 1887 in Yamakawa, Fukushima, Kyūshū, it had a horrible experience after the national government decided in 1986 to widen the Hirose River, on whose bank it sat, because flooding had damaged the theatre's interior. The project led to the theatre's sinking into the river, so community activists banded together to salvage the structure and move it to Fukushima, Nagasaki prefecture, which is also on Kyūshū, where it was reopened in 1994. This 800-seat playhouse retains all of its old-style interior features and technical appurtenances. When first built it was situated on an amusement street facing the river and was considered the town's symbol. Unfortunately, it no longer houses *kabuki* and serves as a museum.

The most unusual case of a theatre's moving concerns the combining, in 1976, of two old theatres into one on a site nowhere near those of the originals. The result of the combination is the Aioi-za in Mizunami, Gifu, located in the unexpected environment of the Hie Highland golf course. It was created by combining the auditorium section from an earlier Aioi-za in Gero with the stage from the old Tokiwa-za (not to be confused with other theatres of that name) in Akechi. Both Gero and Akechi are nearby towns. The new Aioi-za inspired star actor Ichikawa Ennosuke III (b. 1939) to dedicate its opening performance to an old-time, candlelit production in which a water-filled trough was built in front of the stage so that he could hold a "carp-wrestling" (*koitsukami*) scene there. This was nine years before the renovated Kanamaru-za, also devoted to recreating the conventions of Edo-era *kabuki*, began its highly publicized operations.

One of the finest roofed theatres is the Kōraku-kan in Kosaka, Akita prefecture, in northeastern Japan. Its 1911 birthdate makes it the fourth oldest of its kind. The interior possesses all the desired classical attributes. The fifth oldest theatre, the 650-700-seat Uchiko-za (whose traditional pit is sometimes filled with chairs) was built in 1916 in Uchiko, Ehime prefecture, on the island of Shikoku. Its most uncommon feature hangs on its walls: pale-blue signboards on which Chinese characters advertise the names of local businesses active when the theatre opened. Old as these signboards are, some of the firms they mention are still operating. Over the stage is a large signboard reminding the audience that "there's fun in art" or to "enjoy art" (*gei ni asobu*). Reminiscent of these signs but located in an odder place are those that form the ceiling panels directly over the audience at the above-mentioned Yachiyo-za, which also has them on the theatre's front and side walls directly below the ceiling and above the heads of those seated in the upper galleries.

Like these signboards, something individualistic can be discovered inside each *shibai goya*. Turning again to the Kōraku-kan, for instance, we might notice that the Western-style ceiling is constructed with elaborate octagonal-shaped planking surrounding a chandelier with tulip-shaped fixtures. Also idiosyncratic are the wide grooves set into the railings along this theatre's second-floor gallery for the placement there of the spectators' small packages. Another playhouse proud of a chandelier with tulip-shaped fixtures is the Uchiko-za, which sometimes forgoes electric lighting in favor of performances lit by both daylight and candles. Moreover, while most old theatres equipped with revolving stages continue to move them by manual power, the Uchiko-za's revolve is electricity powered. Old-fashioned Western-style lighting fixtures are surely part of these mildly hybrid theatres' charm; nevertheless, another traditional playhouse, the intimate,

500-seat Tokiwa-za, in Fukuoka, Gifu, changed its unpleasant fluorescent fixtures in 1996 for lighting designed in a traditional Japanese manner.

One of the notable features at the Azuma-za in Shirakawa, Gifu, is the large signboard (*kanban*), with the theatre's name carved into it, hung above the front curtain. These curtains, too, can be unique, as witness the one used at Kashimo Village's Meiji-za, Gifu, where the bright blue fabric's design consists of dyed-on labels giving the personal and "shop names" (*yagō*) of numerous village girls who resided there when the place was built in 1894, right in the midst of the Sino-Japanese War. Records at this old-time theatre—the best documented of all *shibai goya*—show that 800 people used to be able to squeeze into it; presumably because of modern dietary changes only 600 can get in now. The theatre's frontage is 19.6 meters and its depth is 25.71 meters, with a stage (including wings) measuring 19.6 meters wide and 7.85 meters deep. The revolve is 5.5 meters in diameter. Impressive as the theatre is, the town it stands in once had seven such theatres. Of the two that were active until the end of the war, one was torn down in 1963, leaving only the Meiji-za.

Eight hundred and forty can fill the Hōō-za in Gero, situated on its present site since 1827, when moved there from the local Hie Shrine. Somewhat smaller than the Meiji-za, its frontage measures 18.3 meters, and its depth is 24.5 meters. The area once had ten similar playhouses. The present auditorium structure dates from 1883, but the stage is fairly recent, having been erected in 1953; otherwise, this would count as the nation's third oldest theatre.[4] A number of distinguished *kabuki* actors both before and shortly after the war played here. Unlike most of its indoor peers, it has no revolve, the original one having been eliminated and the space beneath the stage filled with stones during the 1953 reconstruction. Its rival theatre, however, the Hakuun-za, also in Gero, has both *hanamichi*; somewhat more special is its possession of a rare kind of old-fashioned revolve called *komamawashi*—found in a small number of other old theatres—in which the disk sits atop the stage rather than being cut into it. Its width is 16.38 meters, its depth 20.02 meters, and it seats from between 3 and 400. It is believed to have been constructed in 1890.

As can be seen from some of the above, the seating capacity of these theatres varies. Some theatres have room for only a few hundred, others for considerably more. One of the largest theatres is the Kaho Gekijō, in Iizuka, Fukuoka, Kyūshū, where up to 1,500 can be seated. The theatre makes 1,300 cushions (*zabuton*) available for those who wish them. Among other memorable things at this two-story theatre are the beautifully carved wooden finials fitted onto the corner posts of the *sajiki* sections. In addition, lovely Meiji-period-style lamps decorate the front of the upper *sajiki* overlooking the auditorium. This theatre is the successor to an earlier one, the even larger Naka-za, built in 1922 in the style of Osaka's famous theatre of the same name. The present structure went up in 1931 after the first theatre was destroyed by fire in 1928, and its replacement was lost in a typhoon only fourteen months later; typhoons, by the way, were responsible for the loss of several other theatres as well. The 1931 version of the Kaho Gekijō is somewhat smaller than its ill-fated predecessors. It is the only remaining playhouse along the Onga River, where once there were more than forty. Another rarity is that it is the only regional theatre of its kind operated by a single person—a woman whose father built the original structure—and not a civic group. But its operations—which involve about fifty to sixty performances a year (down from over 200 in the early 1960s) of various genres—are assumed by local volunteers, with no governmental assistance, some of which is provided to all of Japan's older theatres. The owner's family not only performs in the plays but, along with the volunteers, takes immaculate care of the theatre, which permits no footwear of any type, not even slippers. Because of its size and well-kept beauty, the theatre is home to the annual Zenkoku Zachō Taikai (All-Japan Theatre Conference), a gathering of performing groups from Kyūshū and everywhere else in Japan. Spectators from the country's most distant places arrive to watch the shows, which are usually of the *kabuki*-influenced popular theatre called *taishū engeki*.

Figure 197. Western-style exterior of the Kōraku-kan. (Photo: from *Zenkoku Shibai Goya Meguri*.)

Just as distinguishing as old signboards, tulip-shaped lighting fixtures, and carved finials are these theatres' exteriors, which, although sometimes similar to one another, do not conform to a uniform type. For example, the Kōraku-kan presents the visitor with the surprising image of a turn-of-the-twentieth-century American Gothic look, which is why its early patrons dubbed it "The Lady of Meiji" (*Meiji no ifujin*). The Hirose-za also has a striking wooden exterior, but it is in a more traditional Japanese style, including a gabled roof and a surface of unadorned cryptomeria wood. Several theatres with traditional exteriors, including the Kyōraku-kan, Uchiko-za, and Yachiyo-za, display a decorative tile ornament (*onigara* or *shishiguchi*) beneath the gabled roof's ridgepole. These ridgepoles are sometimes in the ornate *hako mune* (box-shaped ridgepole) style. Carved on the *onigara* can be the *mon* (crest) of the theatre, that of the group originally responsible for the theatre (like the miners in a mining town), or that of the local municipality that controls the theatre.

Figure 198. Exterior of the Uchiko-za, with its elaborate tower construction and, just below it, its *onigara* ridgepole decoration. The tiny statue of a fox can be seen sitting beneath the peaked *kirizuma* roof. (Photo: from *Zenkoku Shibai Goya Meguri*.)

Figure 199. The gabled entrance to the Nagame Yokyōjō. (Photo: from *Zenkoku Shibai Goya Meguri*.)

Japanese writers describing exterior theatre architecture often mention the traditional roof style called *kirizuma*, which has a simple mountain-like appearance, each sloping side rising toward a highly decorated ridgepole running from front to rear along the top. The Kureha-za, Uchiko-za, Meiji-za, and Yachiyo-za are among theatres with this familiar roof. Another is the Tokiwa-za, in Fukuoka, Gifu, which, like the Kasuga-za in Okayama prefecture, looked at below, also has the kind of white plastered outside walls once seen on many old theatres, including the Kanamaru-za.

Among the features dressing up the appearance of the Uchiko-za is a gorgeously decorated tower-like appendage at the peak of the roof, overlooking the entranceway. A small statue of a fox, the theatre's protective spirit, sits on the eaves just below the main roof. These features contribute to an overall architectural appearance that local people describe—in calligraphic terms—as of a "square character" (*kaisho*) as opposed to the more famous Yachiyo-za's "cursive character" (*sōsho*).

The Nagame Yokyōjō, a theatre built in 1937 in Ōmama, Gunma prefecture, is known for another feature. Audiences entering this theatre—located in Nagame Kōen, a park near the Tonase River famed for its scenic beauty—pass through a beautifully carved gabled archway redolent of Edo-period architecture. Such an entrance is not found in any other rural theatre in Japan.

There are many reasons behind the erection of these old-time theatres, but most were put up because of some local theatre-loving group's activism and desire to bring a touch of traditional culture to their backwater community. Some of these towns and villages, of course, took pride in other cultural accomplishments, in some natural scenic beauty, in a local product, or in some important historical connection. But the presence of a theatre made a special contribution because such places allowed groups of people to spend their leisure time—either as spectators or participants—in an enjoyably traditional experience shared with friends and neighbors. *Kabuki* (generally referred to by the popular term *shibai*) was known throughout the land as the national theatre and was appreciated as the embodiment of the people's history and culture. This was as true for those who had never seen a professional performance as for those who had. These people may not have been able to travel to the big cities to see *kabuki* in person, but they could at least participate in their own version of it, often under the guidance of some local citizen who had studied Japanese dance or acting. The joy that *kabuki* brings to these communities is tangible when performances are under way, not only in audience delight, but in the colorful advertisements, banners, lanterns, and the like that dress up the theatre's frontage, and the related activities that are sometimes presented. For example, when the amateur actors perform at Jōge's Okina-za, a colorful rickshaw procession goes around the town carrying actors, musicians, and banners, announcing the imminent performances. This recalls the *machi mawari* (around the town) processions that barnstormers of the Edo period engaged in on arriving at a new town.

In at least two cases, the entertainment needs of a mining community sparked the creation of a theatre. Kosaka's Kōraku-kan, one of the most elaborate of the small-town roofed theatres, was designed for the pleasure of the local theatre-loving miners, who boasted of their town's advanced technology and culture. A theatre was a necessary adjunct of such status. Local miners also received a respite from their labors at the largest provincial *kabuki* theatre, the 1,800-seat Kyōraku-kan, in Hitachi, considered a sister city of Kosaka.

In general, shows in these roofed theatres—like those in the unroofed ones described below—are offered on a sporadic basis; when they do present it is normally in connection with a nearby shrine festival. Frequently, during the long periods between *kabuki* productions, the otherwise dormant place will host one of a number of community functions, house visiting productions from one or more non-*kabuki* groups, or be used as a cinema. The Kōraku-kan, for example, has hosted performances by *shingeki, shinpa,* dance companies, and other forms, and has been used for movies, lectures, and other cultural purposes. The Tokiwa-za, which gives one *kabuki* performance a year, fills its stage on selected occasions with concerts and other public events.

An interesting example of a theatre intended to have a mixed personality, but which chose to move in another direction, is Hirukawa's Ebisu-za. It was built in a town with an amateur *kabuki* tradition that began in the nineteenth century, when two groups were united as one and built themselves a fine, new theatre. Known at first by an anglicized name, the Ebisu Club, it gave so many performances that it acquired the more formal theatrical name of Ebisu-za. After falling into disrepair, however, the building was demolished. In 1949, the Occupation army's call for Japan's democratization led to the town's construction of what was intended as a multipurpose building in which socially important community events— especially youth-oriented ones—could be held. However, the town's governing council was made up of *kabuki* lovers nostalgic for their prewar theatrical memories. Ignoring its name of Kōminkan (Community Center), they decided to use the place primarily for *kabuki*. Local youth groups, influenced by democratization, were upset by this reactionary behavior and formed an opposition movement, ultimately succeeding in turning at least part of the premises over to nontheatrical uses.

In many cases, theatres—roofed and unroofed—that remained solvent or, at any rate, active, for long periods, even those used for multiple purposes, fell increasingly into financial straits in the postwar years. Some theatres had histories of one or more centuries of annual performances until the war caused them to cease. When the war ended, however, most theatres were unable to pick up where they left off, although many tried, but too many factors militated against continuation. For example, postwar economic conditions caused local interest to slacken so that people were forced to turn their energies and attention elsewhere. The arrival of television is another oft-cited cause for a diminished interest in traditional theatre. Often, a town's population would begin to thin out as people left for better prospects in the big cities. All these factors played a role, for instance, in the decline of the Kōraku-kan, which stopped presenting in 1970, although it became active again in the late 1980s.

A major diversion from the original purpose of a good number of theatres was their use as movie houses; as already intimated, they still may occasionally show films or serve nonperformative purposes even when—after near-death experiences—they have been restored to use for plays. The Uchiko-za's story is typical. It went out of use after the war, became office space for the chamber of commerce, and gradually became so leak-ridden that its demolition was considered. Saved from this cruel fate by the citizenry—who had been inspired by the recent "Save the Yachiyo-za" movement in Kumamoto—it was restored in 1988, including being provided with the still not universal convenience of flush toilets; two years later, it returned to theatrical production, but also became a low-cost multipurpose center for town use. One such function was the provision of *kabuki* instruction to high school students. Perhaps eighty or ninety days a year see its occupancy for one purpose or another.

The Nagame Yokyōjō has a similar story. It saw its last play produced, by a touring company, in 1965, after which it reverted to a movie house, its traditional *sajiki tatami* seating replaced by chairs. This continued to 1987 when it closed down. Three years later a local group saw to its restoration and it reopened as a venue for jazz, storytelling, movies, as well as the occasional touring production. Among other theatres with somewhat related experiences are the Hirose-za and Kyōraku-kan. In fact, the latter is now also known as the Budō-kan (Martial Arts Center) because of its use as a martial arts training school. Even Iizuka's Kaho Gekijō was on the verge of closing down on several occasions, but when the owner was unable to find a buyer because the space was too large for any practical use, even for a supermarket, the owner and her family chose to keep it alive.

A couple of indoor theatres are still on their way back from the dead. One, the Okina-za, saw its live performances replaced by films in 1947, followed by the closure of the theatre once TV became popular in the 1950s. Following a movement for revival by local youth in the late 1980s, it reopened in 1995 with a locally produced variety show mixing live and filmed action, and drew full houses. It could not operate regularly, though, because of the ongoing need to raise additional funds to complete the restoration.

While theatres like those described see plays performed very infrequently, there is an exception in the Azuma-za, which was used for both films and plays through 1965 and then, as was common, fell a victim to TV's popularity. It deteriorated badly over the next two decades but was restored in 1991. After that it began housing local *kabuki* over 100 times a year, with community meetings and other town hall-like purposes filling its other dates. Its springtime productions, called Kurokawa *Kabuki* after the local region of Kurokawa, are presented by a highly organized amateur group of fifty actors and ten technical specialists. There are about sixty titles in its repertoire. Spectators receive a program and, in return for depositing their footgear before entering, a wooden tag on which the title of the day's play is printed. These tags have become collectors' items. The Azuma-za, like the Kaho Gekijō, is one of the only privately owned playhouses, although it is run by a steering committee. Most other theatres are civic operations.

The Azuma-za's story, like so many others, demonstrates how, despite the onetime decline of most of these venues, they have over the past several decades seen a remarkable turnaround sparked by local citizens, both individuals and groups, who wished to restore their local playhouses to something of their former glory. Although there are even earlier examples of theatres coming back to life, the 1986 restoration of the Kanamaru-za was an especially strong incentive for many rural towns to do likewise, especially for theatres like the Nagame Yokyōjō, which were seriously threatened with demolition or reconfiguration as something else. Some of them were in terrible physical shape and in need of extensive restoration funding. In the case of the Yokyōjō, 600 townspeople banded together under the name Nagame Kurogo no Kai (Nagame Association of Stage Assistants) to get the town to buy and restore the place; they also took over its management and publicity functions.

Such local activism on behalf of theatres that, even when in good shape, produce only a few days a year is a marvelous tribute to people who, despite their residing in the nooks and crannies of the national landscape, take great pride in both their local customs and in the traditions and arts they share as part of their regional and national culture. Representative of the many theatres that have benefited from this surge of local activism is the Kōraku-kan, which was physically restored after becoming the property of the town of Kosaka in 1986. This led to its being designated as a "Prefectural Important Cultural Property." Similar landmark status terms, such as "National Important Tangible Cultural Treasure," bestowed by municipal, prefectural, or national bodies, were granted to numerous other theatres, roofed and open air. In fact, a theatre's official recognition is often precisely the spark needed to ignite local interest in reviving moribund performance traditions.

As Ennosuke III's appearance at the opening of the Aioi-za demonstrates, professional actors often have blessed new or renovated provincial theatres with their presence at their openings. The visitor may be a superstar like Ennosuke or Nakamura Kankurō V (b. 1955), who opened the renovated Azuma-za, or someone lower on the scale, such as when Osaka actor Onoe Matsuzuru and his company participated in the Kōraku-kan's ritual opening ceremonies (*kokera otoshi*) during the Meiji period. The Ebisu-za in Hirukawa Village also opened with a traditional *kokera otoshi* ceremony, highlighted by a troupe starring the respected Bandō Jūzaburō IV (1886-1954).

Subverting much of what I've said about old-style theatres is one that until recently produced in a big city, Nagoya. This place, the Ōsuen Gekijō, was formerly used mainly for *rakugo* storytellers and *manzai* comedians. In the late 1970s it began to house a professional company twice a year for the performance of traditional *kabuki* plays with rock music accompaniment. Following the failed attempt of wealthy real estate operator Adachi Hideo to run a variety theatre (*yose*) on the site, his director friend, Iwada Nobuichi—who had been active on the 1960s avant-garde rock scene and who had grown up seeing lots of rural *kabuki* performances—convinced Adachi to transform the place into a physically conventional, old-style *kabuki* house with artistically unconventional productions that ignored the classical stage business (*kata*) associated with mainstream *kabuki*, although conventional wigs, costumes, and makeup were worn. A trial performance in 1977 demonstrated the idea's viability and the result was Super Ichiza Rock Kabuki, whose success was great enough to result in European tours. When *kabuki* was offered, seats in the gallery-less auditorium were removed and twin *hanamichi* set up.

Outdoor, Unroofed Theatres

Figure 200. Bundled-up spectators watching an outdoor performance of Kuromori *Kabuki*. (Photo: from *Zenkoku Shibai Goya Meguri*.)

Spectators at roofed theatres like the Ōsuen are made comfortable in cold weather either by the use of central heating or space heaters. Those who attend the infrequent winter performances at outdoor *kabuki* theatres, most of them associated with Shinto shrines, must bring their own heating equipment, from thick, insulated clothing and blankets, to hand and foot warmers, to bottles of heated sake. The best example of such a winter scene, with old and young bundled in colorful fabrics that make the spectators—seated on straw matting placed over the earthen floor—resemble a patchwork quilt is at the Hie Shrine theatre in Sakata, Yamagata prefecture. The amateur performances given here at the shrine festival every February in the bitter cold—and even during heavy snowfalls—are called Kuromori *Kabuki* (after the name of the local area). This agricultural community has a tradition of amateur *kabuki* going back to the early eighteenth century. Seeing plays under such circumstances is considered a special delight for the 300-400 hardy fans who attend (there used to be more than 1,000)—much as some people take pride in jumping into the ocean in arctic temperatures. Often they spread their blankets and pillows on thick piles of snows. There are a small number of other cold weather outdoor theatres, like the large one in Ogano, Saitama prefecture, where the audience gathers round a big bonfire in the pit.

Figure 201. The Hitoyama Rigū Hachiman Shrine theatre, with its *yosemune zukuri* roof, and the audience seated on earthen risers under a protective vinyl awning. (Photo: from *Zenkoku Shibai Goya Meguri*.)

Nevertheless, most people prefer their outdoor theatre in warmer climates. There is even a saying: "Winter in Kuromori, summer in Hinoemata." This alludes to the shrine theatre at Hinoemata Village, Fukushima, which, together with the theatre in Kuromori, is known as one the two finest *kabuki* shrine theatres in Tōhoku, the northern region of Honshū, Japan's main island. The theatre—dubbed the Chiba no Ie Hanakoma-za (Hanakoma-za for short)—is a tiny one, built during the Meiji period, and equipped with a gabled, thatched roof.

Such roofs are a feature one often finds on shrine theatre structures, although each roof has its own distinctive look; these can be thatched or tiled (ceramic or wood). One significant style, for instance, is the *yosemune zukuri*, which consists of a central ridgepole running from side to side along the width of the sloped roof. A joint is formed at each end from which, respectively, two additional ridgepoles descend to the corners of the eaves. This divides the roof into four sections, the two at either end forming a mountain shape or triangle. Such a roof, with the upper portion thatched and the lower tiled, is visible on the well-equipped theatre at the Kasuga Shrine in Nakayama, Shōdo Island, in the Inland Sea, Kagawa prefecture, Shikoku, which is changed every twenty years, and also on the nearby stage at the Rigū Hachiman Shrine, Hitoyama, Tonoshō, where performances have been dated to 1683. Some theatres that formerly used thatch later switched to tiles, and a few theatres make do with tin roofs.

What one sees on visiting these sites when no performance is being given is generally a plain, small, freestanding wooden structure with a raised stage hidden from view by wooden shutters. Such theatres, which resemble other shrine structures, are not at first sight especially noticeable as places for performing plays, although some can seat over 1,000 spectators. In most cases, the space before the stage takes the form of a large clearing. In some cases—such as the one at the Tatekoto Shrine in Tōbu, Nagano prefecture, the shrine stage at Ikeda on Shōdo Island, the same island's Rigū Hachiman Shrine, or the Akasaki Shrine theatre, built into a hillside in Yamaguchi prefecture—a more or less fan- or horseshoe-shaped earthen seating area rises away from the stage, even to the extent of having stone or earthen risers surrounding the open "pit" for seating that creates an outdoor version of an indoor theatre's *sajiki*. The feeling provoked by the Akasaki space, some say, is similar to that experienced at a classical Greek theatre although no plays are produced here any more. The Hitoyama audience sits on twelve graded levels, each two designated for one of the six districts into which Hitoyama is divided, with the designation altered annually so that people sit closer to the stage one year, further the next. The seats themselves are distributed according to a drawing. A feature found only here is the roofed *sajiki* seating at stage right for the area's ancestral families. The Tatekoto theatre, by the way, is one of two separated from one another by only a few hundred yards; it is known as the "Eastern Town" (Higashi-machi) stage, while its neighbor—at another shrine—is the "Western Shrine" (Nishino-miya) stage.

Figure 202. Scene outside the Murakuni-za, whose open doors allow people in the street to watch the show inside without entering. (Photo: from *Zenkoku Shibai Goya Meguri*.)

Almost all shrine theatres are of the open-air type just described. There are several exceptions, however, such as the Murakuni-za, at the Murakuni Shrine, Kakamigahara, Gifu, a town that had seen farmer's *kabuki* from the mid-Edo period. This fully equipped indoor shrine theatre, built in 1877 but not formally opened until 1882, was long used by strolling players as well as by local villagers, although the former eventually stopped coming. Essentially similar to other indoor theatres, it has a curious arrangement whereby the musicians' room is on stage left, behind the *chobo yuka* platform. Once a common practice, this is rarely seen today, when the musicians are typically situated stage right. Also, the rear of its pit, where other theatres have seats facing the stage, is equipped instead with a barn-door-like opening, where those unable to find space to sit on the floor stand as the daylight floods in around them. Because of the free access in and out afforded by this arrangement, many more people visit the performance than the 6-800 who are crowded in at any one time. Another roofed shrine theatre, the Kasuga-za, is situated on land adjacent to the 1,000-year-old Kasuga Shrine in the Awai region, Sakutō, Okayama prefecture, where the preferred term for such theatres is *jige kabuki*. Its predecessor, however, was an open-air theatre built in 1868, but closed in 1992 after it fell into a dangerous state of disrepair. The roofed version opened nearby a year later. Its intimate, 300-seat, *sajiki*-less interior has most of the traditional features, but the atmosphere is decidedly less rich than that of its outdoor ancestor. From the outside, though, it looks like a smaller version of the Kanamaru-za, which, in fact, was its inspiration.

Perhaps because of their weathered wooden exteriors, many open-air theatres generally appear cruder than the roofed ones, but most of them are surprisingly well equipped. They usually have revolving stages, traps, *naraku* spaces, *budōdana* grids, and *chobo yuka* at stage left. The "Western Shrine" stage, built in 1816, bears one of the rare *komamawashi* revolves mentioned above. It is reputed to be the oldest extant revolving stage in Japan, three years older than the conventional revolve on the stage at Kamimihara, Gunma. There is an identical device at the Higashi (1817).

The *naraku* space in some theatres is deep enough for dressing rooms to be situated there. (The woodwork of many dressing rooms, in roofed theatres as well, still bears the scratched-in graffiti of actors going back to the Edo period; such scrawls often provide valuable information to historians.) On the other hand, the Ichijō Shrine stage in Ōshika Village, Nagano, is in a two-story structure with its dressing rooms on the second floor.

Elevator traps are other important devices often found at these theatres, some having as many as three traps of differing sizes. The *hanamichi*, however, is generally set up for production only, and may not be visible when the theatre is in recess.

Some theatres possess special features that mark them off from others, like the highly decorated *chobo yuka* platform for the chanter and shamisen player team used at the theatre in Kozuo, Tochigi prefecture, rebuilt in 1991. This unit, which has its own roof, was taken from a nearby city's festival float. It perfectly sets off the theatre's unusual practice of having three chanters and two shamisen players, when most theatres use only one of each.

Draw curtains (*hikimaku*) are also very much in evidence, opening from stage right to left, as in mainstream theatres, although Gifu is known for theatres whose curtains open in the opposite direction; these include the Ebisu-za in Hirukawa Village, and the Murakuni-za. Some theatres have multiple curtains for use on special occasions.

While most theatres are permanent structures, there are at least two significant exceptions. One is erected in Shidara for the hamlet of Damine, Aichi, where every February sees *kabuki* performed in a tent—the Tanika-za—on the grounds of the local Kannon Temple. Once inside the visitor sees a dome-like ceiling supported by 120 arching, bow-like bamboo poles connected at either side to wooden pillars. The shape thus created has been likened to a North European drawbridge. Local bamboo farmers contribute the poles for this tent theatre, which takes eight men a single day to erect. Within this environment are traditional *kabuki* architectural features.

The other fit-up venue exists in the Tokyo suburb of Akigawa, where at the Masakatsu Shrine in the section called Akiruno, Sugao-chō, the theatre is set up for each festival and then torn down. The construction is precisely according to the old standards—it is held together with mortise joints and rope instead of nails—and materials—cypress and cryptomeria wood—used when the first theatre here was built in 1899. The anomalous stage is built to narrow as it recedes upstage, thereby enhancing the scenery's sense of perspective.

The theatre at Akigawa is also exceptional in its location near Tokyo, being only ninety minutes from midtown. There were once many more *ji kabuki* near Tokyo but this is the only one remaining. Founded by a family of performers specializing in *kagura*, the kind of folk performances associated with shrines, it flourished in the old days with two rival companies that offered as many as 250 performances a year, but it deteriorated during World War II and afterwards. The Kurizawa Ichi-za troupe—led by the Kurizawa family—is still active and includes "children's *kabuki*" as one of its distinctive features. Children's *kabuki* is usually called *kodomo kabuki* or *kodomo shibai*, but some locales say *chigo kabuki* or *chinkon kabuki*.

Kodomo kabuki may, indeed, be found at many *ji kabuki* theatres. There is a long tradition of children's *kabuki*, both amateur and professional. During the Edo period children's *kabuki* was a flourishing professional enterprise, especially in Osaka. Some Meiji- and Taishō-period companies also starred children, but—apart from occasional presentations by the offspring of famous stars in all-children productions at the major theatres—children's *kabuki* is today found only among the amateurs of the *ji kabuki* world. One of the best-known children's companies is that at the Murakuni-za, where the kids—many of whose parents acted here in their own youth—do not only *kabuki* but newly choreographed, traditional-style dances (*shin buyō*). Earlier performers here were mainly young men, but they gradually disappeared during the boom economy days of the 1950s, when they moved to the big cities. The theatre ceased operations in 1959 but, after reopening in 1973, the plays were cast with fifth- and sixth-grade boys and girls. As the need for more child actors grew, younger children, even those in first grade, began to appear, and the tradition has taken root to such an extent that almost every local child performs at least once. Other examples of children's *kabuki* are described below.

As noted, numerous *ji kabuki* theatres and troupes perform during festivals at local shrines, whether located on the shrine grounds or not. Despite being a secular theatre, *kabuki* has always had religious associations. These go back to the time of *kabuki's* founder, Okuni, reputed to have been a renegade shrine dancer whose performances of a kind of popularized prayer dance called *nenbutsu odori* were a major source of what evolved into *kabuki* dance and theatre. Every important *kabuki* theatre has its own miniature shrine—guarded by stone foxes—to a pantheon of gods called Inari, and actors and management pray here for good fortune. Thus the location of theatres on shrine grounds should come as no surprise. In fact, during the Edo period there were numerous theatres granted temporary licenses and permitted to give commercial performances on important shrine grounds, where they were supervised by the neighborhood's shrine official, unlike the licensed theatres, which were overseen by a civil official. No theatre is ever opened in Japan without a Shinto ceremony—the *kokera otoshi* mentioned earlier—and a performance of a ceremonial play. And religious ceremonies are still often conducted in connection with festival performances. At the Tokiwa Shrine in Fukuoka, Gifu, for example, which has a long *kabuki* tradition, there is a custom that men born in years considered inauspicious should perform here in auspicious plays as an exorcistic act designed to drive out bad fortune. Another religious connection is evident from the many illustrated votive plaques (*ema*) donated as offerings to shrines located near theatres. Such *ema* normally picture religious symbols, like horses, but theatrical ones usually show pictures of actors in character. There are many other connections between *kabuki* and religion—both Shintoism and Buddhism—that can be drawn, so it is only natural that the amateur performances given on rural shrine stages partake of rituals designed both to please the shrine's tutelary god and to bring good fortune to both the community and the performers. For this reason, shrine ground *kabuki*, by and large, is seen during festivals, some attracting visitors from all over Japan and even the occasional foreigner. Such festivals were originally created, in most cases, as opportunities to express thanks to the deities for a successful harvest. The performance of *kabuki* was deemed a special gift for the deities.

Local superstitions and folk customs are often intimately connected to a town's theatre practices as well. For example, at Yokosen, where it was common for all local men to perform before they were twenty, it was said that those who failed to do so would never find a bride. And at Yokoo, there used to be a custom whereby any local boy who failed to take part in *kabuki* would be scalded in his bath.

From a financial point of view, there are two kinds of performances one may encounter at such theatres. One is designed to raise money for the shrine, and can thus be considered a form of religious benefit. A rarer kind, although often at the same shrine but given at another time, is to raise money for the continuance of performances; such performances are mainly concerned with the theatre's function as a provider of entertainment, not its potential as a religious offering. The money raised often comes in the form of contributions rather than admission fees. Such contributions are called *hana* (gifts) and the theatres that collect such gifts are known as *hana shibai*. In many cases, the contributions are noted on handwritten sheets of paper (*abare noshi*) that are hung around the auditorium, listing the names of the contributors and the nature of their contribution, which may be in the form of cash or goods (such as sake or cakes). Monetary contributions at some theatres range from several thousand yen to multiples of ten thousand yen. The white paper sheets, on which the Chinese characters are boldly written in black against the background of an auspicious symbol in red—like a prawn (*ebi*)—create a wonderful atmosphere of community involvement. The Hanakoma-za in Hinoemata is one such theatre, the only one remaining of what were once many similar places in Tōhoku. Another is located at Hitoyama, in Tonoshō, on Shōdo Island, where performances go on even in the rain, with blue vinyl awnings strung over the audience. (This theatre is famous in Japan because of its appearance in a movie titled *Nijūyon no Hitomi.*) Even indoor theatres may be bedecked with these announcements, as at the Murakuni-za, which not only hangs them from the galleries but also strings them across the auditorium over the audience's heads, where their appearance, like drying laundry, adds a special homegrown aura to the place.

Another way to contribute to the theatre is to toss small, colorfully wrapped packages—resembling large candy "kisses"—containing one or more coins (and sometimes cakes), onto the stage. These gifts—which pour like snowflakes in front of the actors during the performance, and whose pattering sound as they descend adds a certain piquancy to the show—are called *ohineri*, and are one of the widely practiced traditional customs at many shrine theatres, and even at several roofed theatres, like the Azuma-za.

Figure 203. *Abare noshi* hang from the rafters and elsewhere inside the Murakuni-za during a performance. (Photo: from *Zenkoku Shibai Goya Meguri.*)

Because of their link to festivals, only a limited number of annual perfor- mances are given at shrine theatres, and two or three days of performances in a year is not unusual, although some places offer a bit more and a few groups—like that at Abason—can only manage performances every few years or so. Some shrines perform at only one annual festival, some at two, and a small number at three. The "Eastern" and "Western" theatres at Tōbu, however, see action only once every seven years, an arrangement also found at a few other old theatres. The dates are established by tradition and interested sightseers can learn these by contacting local chambers of commerce. Occasionally, important *ji kabuki* theatres host "summits" or "conferences," during which a number of invited *kabuki* groups from elsewhere convene to provide a showcase of their work. The highly respected Ōshika *Kabuki* tours to other towns several times a year and has even gone abroad.

Rural shrine performances of *kabuki* go back in a small number of cases to the seventeenth century, thus constituting over three hundred years of tradition, but the oldest extant theatres are somewhat younger. Although the stages in Tōbu were built in 1816 and 1817, for some reason, credit for being the oldest shrine playhouse is typically given to the one in Akashiro Village, Kamimihara, Gunma, built in 1819. Perhaps some later reconstruction of the earlier theatres disqualifies them from consideration. Other *ji kabuki* playhouses are of relatively recent construction, some being replacements for structures that were destroyed by natural disasters—such as the typhoons mentioned earlier—or by fire. For example, a postwar fire brought down the Edo-period theatre at the Hachiman Shrine in Yamamoto, Akita, a theatre built in the form of a log structure surrounded by blinds. Its interesting origins involve a wandering mountain ascetic priest (*yamabushi*) who fell ill there and who, on recovering, paid the villagers back by teaching them *kabuki*. The present structure was built as recently as 1965.

Performances in honor of the tutelary deity continue here once a year in what is known as Moritake *Kabuki*.

A priest's being responsible for founding a *kabuki* tradition is unusual. A bit more common is the inspiration of local *kabuki* brought by traveling actors, which is what happened when an actor from Hiroshima visited the town of Sada, Shimane prefecture. Sada's Murakumo-za, by the way, is the only rural *kabuki* theatre in Shimane, despite that prefecture's being where Izumo, hometown of *kabuki's* founder, Okuni, is located. Murakumo-za *kabuki* goes back only as far as the Taishō era, however. Far older is the tradition in Gujō Hachiman, Gifu, which also began under the influence of traveling actors, and which goes back to at least 1776. The people were so taken by *kabuki* that they even created their own costumes out of heavy-duty paper. Other actor-inspired traditions may be found in the tiny fishing village of Fukuura, where strolling players, who settled nearby in the Meiji era, taught the locals how to perform. Also in Meiji, a strolling player was responsible for bringing *kabuki* to the fishing-farming village of Ryōtsu, located on the eastern side of Sado Island in the Japan Sea. (For another theatre inspired by an actor, see Ogano *Kabuki*, described below.)

Other vivid tales about local theatres include the claim by participants in Hineoemata's theatre that it was founded by villagers who stopped in Edo and viewed *kabuki* on their way back from pilgrimages to the Ise Shrine. Each year's pilgrims would not only watch the plays but buy scripts of the plays in their puppet versions and then stage them when they got home. Then there is the case of Tsukude Village, which, after the decline of local *kabuki* in the postwar years, saw a group of middle-aged townswomen band together in 1985 to form an all-women's theatre group called the Wakaba Kai, which initiated a yearly *kabuki* festival. The Damine tent theatre cited earlier also has an interesting story. During the Edo period the town was struggling to survive so the villagers cut down trees from the protected mountain forest and sold it. The authorities found out, though, and threatened to behead the perpetrators. The townspeople prayed to the Goddess Kannon and snow fell in August, hiding the evidence of the bamboo stumps and the sentenced men were saved. So happy were the people that they vowed to produce *kabuki* every year as an offering to Kannon. In Kiriyama, Yamaguchi, there is a legend that local *kabuki* was inspired by a Hōreki-period (1751-64) man who, having served in Edo, was on his way home through Osaka, where he visited the playhouses. Later, he had a dream in which a formally dressed old man told him to present *kabuki* as an offering at the Hachiman Shrine. Thereupon he sent his son to Osaka to study *kabuki*. When the son returned he began to produce plays, thereby initiating a still-extant tradition. Some believe this story was a strategy created by the townspeople to justify the hedonism of theatre by associating it with the gods.

There are also interesting stories regarding the restrictions placed on various theatres by the authorities, especially during the late Meiji and Taishō periods, when thought control was becoming increasingly common. Even out-of-the-way locations Fujimi Village, Gunma, or Kashimo Village had to produce plays sub rosa during those years because of censorship fears. Moreover, both professional and amateur actors had to be licensed to perform. Such restrictions put a crimp in the production schedules of a number of theatres. Such pressures became even more severe during the militaristic prewar Shōwa period.

Productions at the outdoor shrine ground theatres are generally—but not necessarily—more makeshift than those in the large indoor venues. The quality of costumes used in these old wooden structures ranges from the more-or-less well preserved and artistically faithful to those scrounged together from the wardrobes of local citizens. For example, because of a lack of funds many of those used in Moritake *Kabuki* are donated bridal kimono, supplemented by much-worn robes that in some cases are over a century old. Shibukawa's theatre must borrow its costumes from others. The Hanakoma-za proudly maintains costumes, wigs, and sets dating to the Edo era, but it performs with repaired or newly made versions, preserving the older materials as historical artifacts. Most of Kuromori *Kabuki's* old costumes were destroyed in a fire, but some still remain from the early nineteenth century. The group owns about 600 old wigs, but many are unusable. They also own costumes donated by the Shōchiku production company, including one for Matsuō in *Terakoya* worn by Ichikawa Danjūrō XI (1909-65) at Tokyo's Kabuki-za and worth a small fortune. Such authentic costumes are not worn during performances in the rain, and are substituted for by those made locally. Another well-supplied group is Yokoo *Kabuki*, in Yokoo, Shizuoka, who perform at the Kaimei-za with a collection of over 200 costumes and 300 wigs, many over a century old. And the *kabuki* group that holds sway in the tiny village of Ōhito, Kyūshū, whose performances date back to the seventeenth century, are said to possess over 1,000 costumes and 130 male and female wigs.

The repertory of these rural shrine theatres typically contain the *kabuki* classics known throughout the country, albeit with local variations that sometimes preserve stage business (*kata*) no longer seen in mainstream theatres. A few groups, like that at Fukuura, take pride in creating their own *kata* exclusive of the traditional ones. There is a strong inclination toward such classic history dramas from the *maruhon* repertory (plays adapted from the puppet theatre), such as *Ōshū Adachigahara, Ehon Taikōki, Terakoya, Kumagai Jinya, Chūshingura, Yaguchi no Watashi, Benkei Jōshi,* and *Kamakura Sandaiki*. Domestic dramas, which are less flamboyant, are not as common, although *Benten Kozō* is very popular. Children's performances of its "Seizoroi" scene are very common. *Kotobuki Sanbasō* is often staged as a celebratory ritualistic dance offering, while *kabuki's* old bravura play *Soga no Taimen* is frequently encountered.

Local groups can often boast of having extensive repertories, some boasting of up to fifty plays, and many having at least twenty, with new ones added yearly. Several groups are able to offer only four or five plays. Some places, like Hitoyama, also take pride in having plays indigenous to their community, dealing with famous people and events associated with the area. Ōshika's troupe, which has thirty standards in its repertoire, also performs the nearly two-hour long "Shigetada Yashiki" scene from a play called *Rokusen Ryō Gojitsu no Bunshō*, about Japan's ancient Heike-Genji conflict, and centered on the Heike hero Kagekiyo. This play, never seen elsewhere any more, is believed by some to have been originally created by the great actor Ichikawa Danjūrō I (1660-1704), and to have been introduced here by Danjūrō IV (1712-78), who appears to have had a close relationship with the village. Hinoemata Village does *Minamiyama Gimin no Ishibumi*, a play written in 1933 and very similar in plot to the more famous *Sakura Sōgo*, about a local peasant who was severely punished for going to Edo on behalf of his fellow townsmen to complain to the officials about unfair taxation. And Kashimo Village presents a play called *Bunkaku Shōnin Yukari Ōsugi*, which honors a holy man who had a connection to a certain large cryptomeria tree in the town.

Despite the ongoing efforts of local communities to keep their *kabuki* traditions alive, one group after another worries about the continuation of performances. The chief reason does not lie in the dearth of actors or audiences, however, but in the need for specialists in performing the narrative accompaniment (*gidayū*) required by many plays adapted from the puppet theatre; over the last two decades, there has been an increasingly short supply of both chanters and shamisen players in small communities, although many people in large cities continue to practice these old performing arts. The use of multiple shamisen players and chanters at the theatre in Kozue is considered an anomaly among groups that go begging for such artists. Interestingly, lack of local teachers inspired Kozue's shamisen players to learn the art on their own. Aware of the community's desperate need for classical musicians, several young guitar-playing musicians began to study shamisen music with audiotapes, slowly transposing the sounds to their guitars, and then moving on to the use of shamisen. Their first effort was with *Ehon Taikōki*. They found that, having gotten through this trial by fire, learning additional plays became increasingly easier. Perhaps other communities might try similarly innovative ways to increase their supply of shamisen players. As it is, electronic means, especially videotapes, are becoming more common as training tools for all aspects of performance, despite their obvious limitations.

As with many amateur arts, practitioners—whether performing in open-air or roofed theatres— take their work with extreme seriousness and dedication. Although the quality of performance varies from place to place, even those at the least physically impressive venues sometimes demonstrate truly first-rate work. This is usually most evident in older theatres with long, continuous traditions, and when there is available some highly trained artistic director familiar not only with local traditions but with all the classical techniques and training methods needed to produce outstanding revivals. (Several such experts provide their services to more than one area theatre.) Often, the participants are the descendants of earlier ones, and—like professional *kabuki* actors and practitioners of other traditional arts—take great pride in their belonging to an artistic tradition in which their parents, grandparents, and great-grandparents were involved. Some amateur groups even consider themselves heir to secret artistic traditions known only to them. This is particularly evident in the group that runs the Hanakoma-za, who trace their traditions back as far as the late seventeenth century. The company has actors whose local theatrical descendants go back at least six generations, and can even point to *kata* used in plays by Chikamatsu Monzaemon that are no longer known to professional actors and cannot be found anywhere else. In several places, like Fukuura, actors inherit roles from their predecessors, while elsewhere, as at Damine, in Shidara, Aichi, the traditions are so entrenched that actors—with permission—have assumed the names of star families, such as Ichikawa, Nakamura, and Onoe. On the other hand, the group that performs at the Aioi-za, the golf course theatre mentioned earlier, is made up entirely of the course's employees, whose high-quality productions require the actors to rehearse until late at night despite their need to be at work at seven in the morning, and then to use their two-hour midday break for more rehearsal. They, too, pride themselves on using *kata* no longer seen in mainstream *kabuki*, taught them by the specialist who directs their work. The actors here double as crew members, an uncommon arrangement. However, there are several problems in such an employees-only concept: one is the requirement that actors leave when they reach the fixed retirement age; another is the lack of children, as all the workers are adults. Thus the loss of veteran actors creates a vacuum that is hard to fill with younger employees, who lack the years of training necessary to sustain the now expected level of acting artistry.

When theatres exist in close proximity to one another, there is always the possibility of intense rivalries evolving, which is precisely the case in Gero, Gifu, where the troupes associated with the Hōō-za in the part of town called Mimayano and the Hakuun-za, which faces the Hakusan Shrine in Kadowasa (and also is known as the Kadowasa no Butai or Kadowasa

Stage), annually try to outdo one another in displaying a higher level of skill. Each company has a respected choreographer on staff to help with the staging, and rehearsals are long and arduous. Since 1984, they have presented cooperative productions that allow their work to be compared. On these occasions, the companies forgo the use of their landmark playhouses and appear instead on the large stage of a contemporary public hall, the Kankō Kaikan. The atmosphere when these companies perform is of the greatest seriousness. No eating during the performance is allowed, nor are *ohineri* gifts tossed on stage—even during the children's *kabuki* that makes up one act of the Hakuun-za's shows—and the audience watches in rapt silence broken only by stylized audience shouts of encouragement (*kakegoe*).

Just as with the indoor theatres, the roughhewn outdoor theatres are supported by community activists who drum up interest in the survival of local *kabuki*. Often, these activists come from unexpected sources, such as youth groups, who—in modern, technologically advanced Japan—might otherwise not be considered fertile ground for the maintenance of traditional arts. But, as in industrial societies elsewhere, small-town life moves at a pace far slower than in the big cities, and people in such environments often may be found continuing traditions that big cities have abandoned. Some northern communities—like that of Hinoemata—are covered in snow for half the year, and one way to get through these periods when little else is going on is to rehearse with the town's *kabuki* group. *Kabuki* clubs in small-town elementary, junior high, and high schools are another component in the theatre life of these communities. At any rate, young people are often responsible for the establishment of the many "preservation societies" (*hozon kai*) that have sprouted in rural towns and villages all over Japan, while the theatres they support frequently boast octogenarians who have been performing locally for almost all their lives.

These preservation societies are run according to different principles, of course, but one of the best organized is that in Ōshika, where every village resident is a proud member. Founded in 1986, this society is divided into three units, one for general members, one for those financial supporters, and one for production team members.

In some cases, local *kabuki* is known not so much by a specific playhouse but by a company that plays at various nearby shrine venues. A prime instance is in Ogano, Chichibu, Saitama, home to Ogano *Kabuki*, which offers about eight performances a year at several different festivals. Ogano *Kabuki* was founded by Bandō Hikogorō, a little-known nineteenth-century *kabuki* actor, on his return to his hometown. He taught *kabuki* to the local youngsters and his students spread the practice to many nearby towns. Ogano *Kabuki* normally plays on one of the six standard shrine stages available to it, but also performs—at December's Hachiman Shrine Teppō

Festival—on one of the elaborate wagon stages described below. The company contains about 150 actors, ranging from aged veterans to enthusiastic grade school students, and they offer performances of "young male *kabuki*" (*wakashu kabuki*), "girls' *kabuki*" (*onna kabuki*), and children's *kabuki*. This well-organized institution—anxious to preserve Ogano *Kabuki*—even offers training classes for backstage personnel. The organization contains five subsections, each located in a different community, and their members form the core of festival presentations given in the group's locale.

Some areas of the country are especially blessed with *kabuki* shrine theatres, even today, when many older examples have disappeared. There is, for example, the Aizu region of Fukushima, where village *kabuki* long has flourished, both in the form of local amateur performances given for the sheer enjoyment of the experience and in that of visiting commercial troupes. Theatres—some designated as landmarks—dot the local countryside, although many are fated to vanish because they are disintegrating and are no longer used. Another group of such theatres can be found around Ogano, most of them near the left bank of the Ara River, where their stages were the sites for performances by regional farmers. Until the late 1960s it was rare that these shrine stages—several dating back to the nineteenth century—were not performing *kabuki* during festival seasons. Despite their relative proximity, each theatre is physically unique and not easily confused with any of the others. Yet another place known for its accumulation of old stages is the village of Ōshika. The deep affection for *kabuki* of this mountain village of 1,800, whose theatre traditions date back to 1767, is signified by its preservation of four stages, two of them still regularly used, one at the Ichijō Shrine (built in 1851, rebuilt in 1972), the other at the Taiseki Shrine.

Yokosen, a place in northeast Okayama at the foothills of the Nagi mountain range, is also fairly well stocked with shrine theatres, there having been at least ten such structures operating locally during the 1930s. The area is believed to have been visited by Okuni in the very earliest days of *kabuki*, and has long preserved an interest in the art among local residents who used to flock to annual spring and fall visits by strolling players. These, in turn, influenced the development of a strong amateur tradition. The best known of the region's still active shrine theatres is the Nakajima Higashi no Butai (Nakajima Eastern Stage) on the grounds of the Matsukami Shrine, Nakajima, where an annual October performance called Yokosen *Kabuki* is given by actors whose polished performances result from at least fifty rehearsals. One sign of the region's interest in *kabuki* is a competition for new plays based on legendary local figures, although the traditional repertory remains the mainstay of production.

The already mentioned islet of Shōdo has a 300-year history of doing *kabuki* and is known for its residents' extreme fondness for performing. Despite its minuscule size it once was home to over thirty stages, with 6-700 people taking part. Even today, half the population—100 participants from approximately 200 families—is involved, and they use two of the remaining six stages for their work. In fact, the sparseness of local populations is often not related to either the existence or endurance of *kabuki* performance. Time and again one comes across villages of little more than a few hundred people continuing their traditions, although, of course, audiences may be drawn from larger surrounding areas. The previously cited Ryōtsu on Sado Island, for example, manages to preserve *kabuki* performances in a place inhabited by a mere seventy families totaling around 300 people.

No region, however, has the abundance of still active old-time *ji kabuki* as does Gifu, which—as can be seen from this essay's coverage of roofed theatres—also continues to have a larger number of those than anywhere else. In Shirakawa alone, there were still twenty-one local theatres in the 1930s, although only one is still standing—the roofed Azuma-za, whose stage was built in 1889 and whose seating area was added in 1900. Gifu, which possessed 273 theatres during the Hōreki period (1751-64), today is home to twenty-seven of them, the greatest concentration in Japan. Most are in the eastern part of the prefecture and it is possible to visit all of them in a single day's automobile excursion. A prefectural preservation society has been charged with overseeing all these old theatres, although the local communities have their own preservation groups as well. Among the prefecture's most prominent shrine theatres is that at Tokiwa Shrine in Fukuoka, founded in 1891, where performances—some by children—are called Fukuoka-machi *Kabuki*, and whose stage was restored in 1995 after having been turned into a munitions factory in 1944.

Wagon Stages

The third kind of *kabuki* stage found in rural Japan—mainly in the prefectures of central Honshū—is, as mentioned above, found on movable stages, quite similar to the pageant wagons we read about in medieval England and elsewhere in Europe. Depending on regional practices, these wagon stages, or floats, are called by any one of an array of names, including *dashi, yatai, sasahoko, yamahoko, danjiri, hikiyama, taikodai,* and *yama.* They are unusually ornate—especially their gabled roofs—somewhat like the famous nontheatrical examples that move through the streets of Kyoto at each summer's Gion Festival. The floats are said to symbolize mountains (*yama*), considered very holy places where gods reside. Thus the gods are believed to descend to these gorgeous floats during the festival. Floats of one sort or another appear at more than a thousand annual *hikiyama matsuri* (wagon stage festivals), but only a very small number contain practical stages. Among them are those seen at an annual December festival in Chichibu, where they move through the streets to the loud beating of big drums, and then line up on the main avenue to present *kabuki* plays on their cramped and narrow stages. Four local towns are represented, each float belonging to a separate group whose members, wearing matching kimono, parade through town with their float. Most of the floats—each of which is associated with a specific shrine—are quite old, some of them dating as far back as the late eighteenth century, but they are exceptionally well preserved, their cinnabar paint and gold and silver leaf seeming freshly applied. Several have unique features, like the one with separate side stages (*haridashi*) flanking a central acting area. Their general appearance suggests houseboats and, in fact, their lower area is swathed in bright blue and white cloths on which wave patterns have been dyed.

When the *hikiyama matsuri* were first instituted in 1766, the floats were rather simple, it is said, but during the early nineteenth century they grew increasingly gorgeous as local silk merchants vied to demonstrate their wealth by paying for more and more spectacular stages. Seen at night, under lantern-light, the floats provide an especially memorable sight. Crowds of close to 300,000 that clog Chichibu at festival time attest to the continuing popularity of the festivals.

There are two famous *hikiyama matsuri* in Komatsu, Ishikawa prefecture. The Nagahama Festival, held over four days in April, involves twelve wagon stages used by four companies each year on a rotating basis, so that only four wagons are used at any one time. Each company gets to perform once every three years. The actors—in line with a local tradition going back to the late eighteenth century—are all five- to twelve-year-old boys, making this an example of children's or *kodomo kabuki*. In fact, *kodomo kabuki* is typically the featured performance type at these festivals. The children are excellently drilled and give highly touted performances. Komatsu's other *hikiyama matsuri*, the "traveling" or Otabi Festival, also features children; it was begun in 1766 and is seen every May. Of its ten floats built in the late eighteenth century, two were burned in 1926, leaving eight. It originated in a festival during which villagers carried a portable shrine (*omikoshi*) from home to home, and was originally called the "going around" or Owatari Festival, but the name was eventually changed to its present one. Here, the children perform for four days and nights, giving as many as thirteen separate performances. What is most notable about these children is that they are all girls. This is a change from the festival's former practice of using only boys. Apparently, study of *kabuki* performance had been a part of the elementary school curriculum for boys up until the Russo-

Japanese war, but was then removed from the curriculum as inappropriate, leading to a lack of child actors. To keep the performances going, girls studying traditional performing arts in nearby Kanazawa, a much larger city, were recruited for the festival; they were replaced after World War II by girls from Komatsu itself.

Figure 204. Children performing on a float at a festival in Tonami, Toyama. (Photo: from *Zenkoku Shibai Goya Meguri.*)

Children—boys only before World War II, an equal allotment of girls and boys after it—also star at the *hikiyama matsuri* at Shinmei Shrine in Tonami, Toyama prefecture, where, in a tradition two centuries old (one float goes back to 1789), floats operated by each major area within Tonami give eight shows one day and five the next on two days every April, the final performance not ending until near 9:30 PM. A recent festival saw one cast perform the first half of *Ōshū Adachigahara* on one float, with the second half being shown on a following float after the first group finished and moved on. One of the singular features of this festival is the required presence of the boys and girls at a ritual cleansing ceremony (*oharai*) in the shrine prior to the performance, and their subsequently being carried from the shrine to their stages by the adults who act as stage assistants; the children, once spiritually cleansed, are not permitted to touch their feet to the ground before they reach their floats. Some of the older children are rather heavy and carrying them can be a burden. Apart from the desire to keep their costumes from being soiled or torn, it is not clear precisely why this custom of forbidding the children to walk to their stages persists. Area children—not only those who perform—grow up being quite familiar with *kabuki*, which not only forms a part of their school curricula but is considered something they must regularly observe at the annual festivals.

In Ibigawa, Gifu, only boys perform. They appear on five floats, one for each of five districts, and they perform at various intersections and in the middle of certain streets as they progress through the town. On the final day, the children parade through the streets in costume with their parents alongside.

Although the use of ceremonial floats—prior to their use for plays—is said to have been introduced in Nagahama in the sixteenth century during the time of Hideyoshi, even older is tradition belonging to Tarui, Gifu, where, in the fourteenth century, three floats were presented in a ceremony to entertain the retired emperor Gokoson. In the 1770s stages were added to them for the performance of *nō* and *kyōgen* plays during years of bounteous harvests, and these were gradually replaced by *kabuki* plays performed by adults. In the 1820s the stages were reconstructed and children's performances commenced. Three floats are now used, one for each of the town's three sections.

The Yachiyo-za

Mentioned in several places above is the Yachiyo-za, one of the most important of all *shibai goya*. Its experiences may be considered paradigmatic of those encountered by other theatres of its ilk, and its physical appearance is representative of the surprising things that may still be found in unexpected corners of Japan.[5]

Figure 205. Exterior view of the Yachiyo-za, Yamaga. (Photo: courtesy of Hidehiko Nagaishi.)

Ask the average Japanese in Tokyo if they have ever heard of Yamaga and they will likely come up blank. Actually, it has a long history, its name first appearing during the ancient Nara period, when it gained a reputation for its hot springs, which were its chief claim to fame for eight hundred years. It also came to be known because of its proximity to many old mound-tombs (*kofun*) in the vicinity dating from 4-600 BC. During the Edo period it was a post-town for daimyo coming and going on their triennial trips to and from Edo, and it was also known as a place for cultural and commercial interchange. It became best known, however, during the Meiji period, when it built a reputation as a crossroads for the transfer and distribution of goods, for its silk industry, its lantern and umbrella making, its tea and sake manufacture, and for the continued excellence of its spas. Yamaga was only the second city in Kumamoto prefecture to have telephone service, which it acquired in 1899, with limited electrical power arriving in 1914. The presence of phone service even prior to the general availability of electric lighting helped the town's businesses to prosper. Although a Meiji-era railway connected the city to Ueki, and thus to the rest of Japan, it is no longer possible to get there by train, which is unusual in a nation that seems so linked by rail service.

To reach this out-of-the-way, physically bland, and geographically sprawling provincial tank town of about 30,000, you must first travel to the city of Kumamoto, an important railway stop in Kyūshū, and then board a bus at the railway station for Yamaga, which is about an hour away. The driver will let you off at a bus stop on the main street in the heart of a faceless middle-class suburban environment devoid of noticeably tall buildings or eye-catching architecture. You walk up the slight incline of the nearest street to the right, passing various traditional shops, notice an interesting lantern museum on the left, and then turn right down a narrow street. As you do you notice that, in contrast to the street's narrowness, there stands to the left the imposing edifice of the Yachiyo-za. This theatre is not situated, like Tokyo's Kabuki-za or Kyoto's Minami-za, on a site facing a broad boulevard, nor is it on an entertainment promenade, like the theatres in Osaka's Dōtonbori, but is something entirely unexpected, sitting in serene majesty on what is practically a back lane. When performances are in session, the street outside the theatre is jammed with spectators who have to walk there, no space being available for the passage (much less the parking) of cars or buses.

The theatre was built during the city's commercial heyday in the late Meiji period when it filled a need for a cultural center that could reflect local pride and self-confidence in the area's prosperity. Money for its construction, which came to 20,957 yen, was raised by a stock offering of 500 shares at 30 yen a share, with 63 people buying shares, and the largest stockholder holding 50 shares. All of Yamaga celebrated its New Year's season opening on January 11, 1911, with a traditional *kokera otoshi* ceremony and a performance by the Matsushima company of the auspicious *kabuki* dance, *Kotobuki Shiki Sanbasō*, followed by the such standards as *Kiichibō, Sesshū Gappō ga Tsuji*, and others. The twenty-day run took in a substantial 1,400 yen. Soon after, the Yachiyo-za played host to visiting troupes, movies, new plays, and so on, taking in 2,556 yen and thereby earning an eighth of its cost in three months. It continued to flourish, welcoming such stars as Matsui Sumako (1886-1919) in 1917, when she was touring in Tolstoy's *Resurrection*. In 1933, the great beauty Okada

Yoshiko (1902-92) set young men's hearts dancing in the play *Tōjin Okichi*. However, after a brief period of success lasting into the early Shōwa years, the Yachiyo-za declined in fortune. During the war it was used for many patriotic events, including fund-raisers to collect money for war victims, which temporarily gave it a new lease on life. It was visited by such *kabuki* stars as Matsumoto Kōshirō VII (1870-1949), Ichikawa Danjūrō XI (1909-1965), and Ichikawa Ennosuke II (later Ichikawa Eno, 1886-1963), while the postwar period witnessed performances by Kataoka Nizaemon XIII (1903-94), Nakamura Kan'emon III (1901-82), the great actress Mizutani Yaeko (1905-79), and others, including an array of comedy actors and popular singers in varying genres new and old, who performed there into the 1950s.

Its postwar years saw the Yachiyo-za's conversion to an independent business venture, but its physical condition grew worse and by the early 1950s it was in serious need of repair. Nevertheless, despite its economic woes, it continued to draw people, even though they could pay only low prices for the sake of whatever entertainment was available during financially strapped times. However, television soon appeared, and in Japan's now booming economy, every family bought one and stayed home while theatres languished. As elsewhere in Japan, the new electronic diversion seriously damaged the theatre's position. By 1973, even its function as an assembly hall for the town's elders came to an end and the Yachiyo-za was closed down. This only hastened its shameful physical deterioration.

Figure 206. The Yachiyo-za in 1911, at the time of its opening. (Photo: Yume Kogura.)

A 1974 newspaper article titled "The Yachiyo-za is Still Alive" spurred renewed local interest in its fate and a campaign to rescue it from possible demolition got underway. The city council even approved a 600,000-yen allocation for research into the situation, and the engineering department at Kumamoto University undertook to investigate the feasibility of restoration. As interest in the project slowly began to spread, Yamaga received the theatre as a donation from its owner and it became city property. This did not stop its continued degeneration, though, as city money for repairs remained in short supply. Officials and everyday citizens pondered whether to tear it down, take it apart and rebuild it elsewhere, restore it to its pristine form, or rebuild what some thought a hopelessly out-of-date white elephant. Time, however, seemed to be running out for the nearly octogenarian playhouse.

A big step in generating interest was taken in 1984, when the Yamaga municipal government held a thirtieth-anniversary symposium whose chief subject was the Yachiyo-za's future. Soon after, meetings among local social and business groups helped spark a "Save the Yachiyo-za" movement, and young people's groups, the Bunkazai o Mamori Kai (Protective Association for Cultural Properties) and the Yamaga Hyakuninshū (Yamaga Hundred), were founded, with a fund-raising drive following. Regional newspapers threw in their support, two separate film directors used the theatre's stage as a location, and various expressions of outside interest quickly appeared. The recent success of a similar movement at the Kanamaru-za helped motivate Yamaga's people, just as Yamaga's activity did the same for those working to save Aichi's Uchiko-za.

An unexpected natural disaster only served to make people redouble their efforts. As discussions and panels on the theatre's future went on a violent storm erupted, blowing away the blue vinyl sheathing that had been put up to protect the theatre while repairs were underway. The rain poured in and did even more damage. Until now, young people had been among the prime movers in the campaign to save the theatre. The rain damage, however, sparked the town's 4,000-member senior citizen association (*rōjin kai*) to collect from each member 2,000 yen (around fifteen dollars at the time), the cost of a single tile; thus began a "one man-one tile" campaign. Within four months, from October 1984 through January 1985, 6,000,000 yen was collected by this means. The movement gained momentum, and the city government designated the theatre a "Municipal Cultural Property." The following year the city council appropriated 25 million yen for the theatre's revival, leading to the creation of an association dedicated to carrying out the project. In 1987, townspeople young and old got on their bicycles and rode around the city gathering donations, raising an additional 400,000 yen. Repairs gradually began on the roof, the pit, and other endangered sections. In the following year, 1988, Japan's Ministry of

Culture (Bunkachō) named the Yachiyo-za a "National Important Cultural Property." The Yachiyo-za thus joined the Kanamaru-za and Kureha-za as one of only three *kabuki* theatres so designated, but it also meant that renovations had to protect the architectural integrity of the place. In other words, nothing new could be added that might alter the theatre's looks. At this point, the theatre still was forty percent away from completing its renovation.

Figure 207. View of the Yachiyo-za auditorium from the stage. (Photo: courtesy of Hidehiko Nagaishi.)

Perhaps the local citizen most obsessed with restoring the theatre was a photographer named Koga Naoko, who was so enamored of seeing the place returned to its erstwhile use that she created a mock photo to show what it would look like if *kabuki's* most popular player of female roles, Bandō Tamasaburō V (b. 1950), were to appear on the stage. She pursued the subject with friends until she finally sent Tamasaburō photos and other materials about the place and wondered if he might not wish to give a dance concert there. She never thought she would get a reply but the great star gave her the surprise of her life by having his manager contact her to express the actor's interest. She and a representative of the young men's association went to Tokyo to see the star perform in his native habitat, the Kabuki-za, but the experience depressed them because of the grandiosity of the place and the beauty of Tamasaburō's presence on its stage. They thought he would never really come to their little town, and that they would never be able to accommodate his genius at the Yachiyo-za. The star confounded all expectations, though, and, in 1990, Tamasaburō made the first of what became annual Yachiyo-za dance recitals. Meanwhile, the renovations continued, progress being made year after year.

This is a classic premodern-style wooden theatre, equipped with drum tower, revolving stage, trap (built into the revolve), *naraku* running beneath the main *hanamichi*, *kari hanamichi*, *suppon*, two-story *sajiki* fronted by bright red handrails, and *masu* seating in the *tatami*-covered pit, which is built on three increasingly higher levels, from front to rear. The revolve, *suppon*, and trap are all manually operated. A footnote concerning this revolve would reveal that the circular track set into the *naraku* floor on which it runs was manufactured by Germany's Krupp Steelworks firm, and that this famous company's name is also embossed on the twenty-three steel wheels that move the revolve. As in other *naraku* with revolves, stage assistants lean against horizontal beams extending from the central axle to rotate the heavy disk overhead. Stage features are much like those in other full-scale *kabuki* theatres, with a musicians' room at stage right placed on an oblique angle to the front of the stage, and a two-level *chobo yuka* structure at the left. Their uppermost pillars are called, as is traditional, *daijin bashira* (minister's pillar).

In the auditorium, four people can sit in each of the 81 *masu*, which are arranged 9 lengthwise and 9 widthwise. The *sajiki* on the second floor facing the stage, generally known elsewhere as the *ōmukō*, is divided into three sections called the "front boat" (*maebune*), "middle boat" (*nakabune*), and "rear boat" (*atobune*). The first-floor audience right *sajiki* differs from those on the other side of the theatre in being divided into two rows of *masu*; that on audience left is undifferentiated. Moreover, the *sajiki* on either side are on three levels, which is not seen anywhere else, although visibility from the third level is considered poor. At the rear of the third level is a passageway.

On entering the theatre, one encounters a wooden-floored lobby (*genkan*) where one removes one's shoes and deposits them at counters to the right and left, as in the Kanamaru-za. As in that theatre, a wooden wall separates the lobby from the auditorium. Overhead hang six wooden signboards announcing the show's highlights.

Backstage there are two levels of dressing rooms, including a large one (*ōbeya*) in the center of the first floor grouping, which contains seven small rooms measured at 4.5 *jō* (1 *jō*=1 *tatami* mat). The second floor's nine rooms are 6 *jō* each. There is a hairdresser's room in upstage left and a prop room upstage right. Flats are stored nearby on both upstage left and right. Only one bathroom remains backstage, upstage right, but there once was one on the other side as well.

When the theatre was built, in 1911, *kabuki* theatres elsewhere were gradually adding features designed to add to the comfort of their spectators. Premodern audiences normally had access to adjacent teahouses for their physical needs, from food to bathrooms, but theatre teahouses disappeared during the Meiji period and were gradually replaced by such amenities as gardens, promenades, rest rooms, restaurants, and shops. Some of these—including a garden—were included in the Yachiyo-za as well. Promenade spaces are located in corridors outside the upper *sajiki*.

The theatre is of substantial size, being about 32 yards wide and 38 yards deep, with an original seating capacity of 1,274, although now restricted to 700. Its stage is almost 19 yards wide and 11.5 yards deep, with a 9.3-yard diameter revolve.

Figure 208. The Yachiyo-za exterior as it looked during reconstruction in May 2000. (Photo: Samuel L. Leiter)

The main roof is in *kirizuma* style, but this is combined with the kind of hip-gabled roof extensions called *irimoya*. An elaborate *hako mune* ridgepole runs along the top of the main roof. Flat tiles with circular holes in them were attached to its side. The space behind the holes was closed up with zinc or plaster, except for every fourth one, to allow for ventilation. A similar arrangement is often seen on temple roofs. The ridgepole's front and rear are capped by a decorative *onigara* end-tile on which the theatre's crest (see below) is engraved. All roof sections are covered in pale blue ceramic tiles that make a distinct contrast with the white-plastered exterior walls. There are around 56,000 tiles on the roofs. These are all new tiles added in 1987 when leaks began appearing in the original roof. The new tiles are common house tiles, but about 1,500 of the fancier old tiles can still be seen on the roof extension over the front entrance.

There is neither central heating nor air conditioning here, and the interior is known as a refrigerator in winter and a furnace in summer. Wintertime theatregoers used to rent small braziers for three *sen*, with extra charcoal for two *sen*, and, with padded clothing, could endure the icebox temperatures. But they could not as easily take the sweltering summer heat, when a large overhead fan's rotation barely stirred the air, and the auditorium was constantly aflutter with the waving of personal fans.

Kimura Kametarō, an amateur architect also known as a talented lantern maker and painter/illustrator, built the theatre. A major historical feature of the place is the still extant advertisements he painted on rectangular panels set into framed areas on the ceiling and around the upper perimeter of the auditorium. To prepare for his theatre's design, he traveled to Tokyo, Osaka, Shimoseki, Nagasaki, Kumamoto, and elsewhere to survey the theatres there; he even went overseas to study foreign playhouses. The theatre he chose as his main model was the now vanished Yamato-za, in Kumamoto. However, he used Western-style trusses to support the roof and galleries. This also allowed for improved sightlines in the auditorium, as there are no pillars there creating obstructed views of the stage.

Figure 209. Four of the ads designed to be seen over the Yachiyo-za's auditorium or around its perimeter. (From *Yamaga Yachiyo-za*.)

During the Taishō period, several years after the theatre had begun operations, two extensions to the front of the theatre at either side were added to create smoking rooms for patrons. The one on the theatre's left when facing it is visible in figure 200. The absence of these extensions is notable in figure 201, taken when the theatre was new. The extensions give the theatre one of its most idiosyncratic features. Also seen from outside the theatre are the two ticket windows, located in the wooden wall forming the theatre's facade.

The theatre's crest, decorating various parts of the theatre structure, as well as its lanterns, tickets, cushions, and curtains, is a clever rebus design composed of a circle formed by eight Chinese characters for the syllable "chi" (meaning "one thousand"). This reflects the meaning of "yachi," or "eight thousand." Inside the circle is the syllabic character for the sound "yo," thus completing the word "Yachiyo." No one is quite sure why the name Yachiyo itself, which means 8,000 generations, was given to the place, but the name is not uncommon, there having been three such theatres in Kyūshū when this one was built, with others known to have existed elsewhere, including in Osaka. The name suggests a desire for continued prosperity, as in the names Sakae (to flourish) and Chitose (1000 years), also common among theatres.

Across the street from the Yachiyo-za is the Yume Kogura, an intimate museum devoted to artifacts from this theatre's past. For a small fee one can peruse the theatre's old posters, advertisements, costumes used in famous productions, props, armor, playhouse models, and even the theatre's one-time movie projector.

Figure 210. A showcase with *kabuki* props on display at the Yume Kogura. (Photo: Samuel L. Leiter)

Conclusion

This survey should make abundantly clear that, with a little effort, theatregoers can still find a *kabuki* experience that comes close to replicating the look and sound of premodern times. Theatres are scattered widely, in small cities, and farming and fishing villages, where local citizens avidly prepare to perform on stage themselves or to turn out in force for brief visits from touring companies, some of them headed by the greatest artists in the land. But also apparent is the enormous hunger in many communities not only for the thrill of being on stage but of being able to point with pride to a local playhouse that goes back in appearance, and often in time, to a period when giants walked the stage.

NOTES

1. Other names include *mura shibai* (village theatre), *noson kabuki* (farming village *kabuki*), *ji kyōgen* (local plays), *gyōmin kabuki* (fisherman's *kabuki*), etc. There are also several purely local usages, like *shibaiya* (something like "theatre company").

2. I am especially indebted to Akashi (1995) and Ōzaki (1995). Each of these slim volumes provides brief essays on various important theatres, supplementing them with useful photos. Neither, however, correlates the descriptions or provides a broad overview.

3. Many of these towns have additional terms, like "shi," "machi," "chō," or "mura," each of which suggests a town or village, attached to them. Thus Jōge is technically known as "Jōge-chō." I have omitted most of these terms except for places using the suffix "mura" (village), as in Hirukawa Village. I have employed the English term "prefecture" for *ken*, using it only the first time a specific prefecture is named. To find most of these towns and villages I recommend *Japan: A Bilingual Atlas* (1991). Those searching for these places should be cautioned that several bear names that are found in more than one location in Japan.

4. Because this theatre is a shrine theatre, and was not intended for professional purposes, it is not generally counted as the nation's third oldest roofed theatre, although its age should put it ahead of the Hirose-za.

5. The following account is based on various documents provided by the Yachiyo-za's museum, the Yume Kogura (Dream Museum), and *Yamaga Yachiyo-za* (1993), a collection of numerous photographs accompanied by brief essays by various writers. The author visited the theatre in May 2000 when it was undergoing major renovations that went beyond those described below to prepare it for a grand reopening in 2001.

REFERENCES

Akashi Kazumi. 1995. *Zenkoku Shibai Goya Meguri*. Tokyo: Shōgakukan.
Japan: A Bilingual Atlas. 1993. Tokyo: Kodansha.
Ōzaki Norio. 1995. *Noson Kabuki*. Tokyo: Asahi Bunsha.
Yamaga Yachiyo-za. 1993. Tokyo: NTT Publishing.

IV

HISTORY

From the London Patents to the Edo *Sanza*: A Partial Comparison of the British Stage and *Kabuki*, ca. 1650-1800

It is a source of never-ending wonder to discover that widely disparate cultures often have created remarkably similar artifacts and institutions. In the realm of theatre history we are especially fascinated by comparative studies that examine the resemblances and differences between the West and the East, as, for example, between Aristotle and Bharata, Aeschylus and Zeami, and Shakespeare and Chikamatsu, or between such forms as *nō* and Greek theatre, *kabuki* and Elizabethan theatre, and so forth. Does not a large part of this fascination stem from the thrill of realizing that there are certain threads that constitute what it is to be human, and that these threads often tie us together with peoples to whom we might not otherwise have felt thus connected? If so, how much more exciting must it be when cultures thought profoundly dissimilar prove, under their external differences, to have remarkable kinship.

A prime example of this phenomenon is the premodern Japanese and English theatre. Most previous comparisons of these national theatres have focused on the work of playwrights Shakespeare and Chikamatsu, or on the staging methods of the *kabuki* and Elizabethan theatres, or on similarities between *nō* and the medieval stage (see, for example, Pronko 1967, Fujita and Pronko 1996, and Tsubouchi 1960). Little attention has been paid, though, to the even more striking correspondences between *kabuki* and the English theatre from roughly 1650 to 1800. This seems a far more fertile ground for investigation not only because of their chronological coexistence but also because the period offers a compelling picture of two similar and tantalizingly comparable theatrical cultures, coexisting on islands at opposite ends of the world, with only the slightest knowledge of one another.

What were some of these shared features? In both countries, theatrical business was highly commercialized and expensive, controlled to a great extent by manager-actors and their business representatives. They were devoted to annual seasons of nonreligious performances, new and revived, and made use of print media to advertise their wares. Audiences were composed primarily of an urban mercantile class mixed with aristocrats, and many spectators sat on the stage itself. At the beginning of the period, the theatre was allowed to resume performances after having been closed down by the authorities, and it continued to operate under an ever-censorious government's eye. The government strictly limited the number of licensed, competing playhouses, which had to fight for audiences not only with one another but also with various unofficial minor theatres. The profession promoted the skills of highly paid stars, many of whom established a company system of actor-management, and the public lionized actors while considering them socially inferior. Actors closely modeled their interpretations on those of their predecessors, and roles were distributed according to specializations. Among some actors' specialties was the ability to play roles of the opposite sex. Performances were held in box, pit, and gallery theatres using a stage employing a front curtain, apron, and technically advanced mechanical devices for scene shifting and special effects. The changeable scenery was sometimes fantastical and sometimes relatively realistic and was composed of platforms and flats that could be instantly transformed before the audience's eyes. Dramas often incorporated musical accompaniment and dancing. A flourishing tradition of strolling players brought theatre to the countryside. Moreover, the period saw theatre criticism experience its birth pangs

This list—covering the seven broad groupings of management, government regulation, actors, audiences, architecture/stage machinery, repertory, and criticism—provides a sturdy platform from which to compare the English and Japanese theatres of the mid-seventeenth through eighteenth centuries.[1] Of course, several of these characteristics could be found in a few other Asian countries but certainly not in aggregate and not during the period being discussed here.[2] I will confine myself here to five of these areas: government regulation, actors, the combined area of theatre architecture and scenography (including special effects and lighting), audiences, and repertory.[3] Although I will discuss the world of actors, I will have to eliminate comparative discussion of the potentially rich topic of acting methods. What remains will still reveal not only distinct patterns but, just as important, significant differences that allow us to gain an even clearer picture of the theatres of these widely separated nations during the period in question.

The dates covered are not, of course, precisely symmetrical but are close enough to be of interest. The English side begins with the Restoration (generally given as 1660-1700), the Japanese with the Jōō era (1652-55), although the period that most closely parallels the Restoration is Genroku (technically 1688-1704 [sometimes given as 1688-1703] but usually widened to include the period from 1670 to the 1730s).

England and Japan share certain historical and cultural resemblances beyond their approaches to theatre. Their existence as culturally advanced island nations offshore from enormously vital and tremendously influential mainland societies—from which they nevertheless managed to maintain a powerful sense of difference—surely might be plumbed, if only teasingly, for answers to the riddle of why so many similarities arose. Within the fifty-to-seventy-five-year period preceding that covered here, each nation had experienced a shift from an agrarian to a highly commercialized, consumer-oriented urban society, with the consequent growth of a sophisticated townsman culture. On the other hand, England, having defeated the Spaniards, was feeling its expansionist oats, whereas Japan, having established the Tokugawa shogunate, isolated itself from the world; each position led to remarkable cultural developments. As Yamazaki Masakazu has explained recently (1994), the premodern Japanese were actually more humanistically individualistic than has been previously thought, and they shared many cultural affinities with the West. Searching for answers to the riddle in such events and affinities will always remain pure speculation, giving off heat if not much light. Ultimately, the causes for such parallelism can never be ascertained, and the role of pure coincidence must definitely be allowed in the majority of correspondences cited. Yet the very existence of correspondences is intriguing to ponder if only because it offers a means to understanding what may, at first, seem too much "the other" for ready comprehension. Likewise, and perhaps ironically, seeing the eighteenth-century English theatre held up to its Asian mirror may allow us to view it in a new and illuminating light.

Government Regulations

Managers in both England and Japan had to endure the frequent interference of governmental authorities, usually expressed in repressive edicts. Japan was subject to so many that Donald Shively asks rhetorically, "Why did they not abolish *kabuki* outright?" His answer: "The attitude of the *bakufu* [military government] seems to have been that *kabuki* was, like prostitution, a necessary evil. These were the two wheels of the vehicle of pleasure, useful to assuage the people and divert them from more serious mischief" (Shively 1955, 336).

Shively notes that antitheatrical laws passed in Edo were of three principal types: (1) those that segregated theatre people from ordinary society, (2) sumptuary edicts that maintained limits on the extravagance of lifestyles and stage productions in a society that could not condone actors showing greater luxury than what was appropriate to their low social class, and (3) regulations restricting dramatic themes to what would not threaten the political or social status quo. The latter included plays of too much sexual suggestiveness, although homosexual as well as heterosexual frankness still managed to figure in many plays. Shively reflects on but does not list restrictions on architectural arrangements, the use of candles, and building materials—most of which stemmed from fear of fire. (See "The Development of the Physical Theatre" in Ernst 1974.)

Plays in both countries were canceled for allegedly subversive material but not in great numbers. This normally occurred in Japan after a play opened, there being no office comparable to the Lord Chamberlain's until 1875 to exercise prior restraint. *Kabuki* did not seek to criticize government so much as it sought to avoid crippling restrictions on the use of certain kinds of material. The theatre could not openly subvert official restrictions, but it managed to devise methods that—despite occasionally intense efforts at surveillance—allowed it to deal with restricted material with a limited degree of freedom. For instance, in 1644 the government issued the first of repeated edicts against the dramatization of events relating to the contemporary samurai class. This was emphatically reinforced in 1703 after the theatre began to introduce scenes inspired by the recent Asano family vendetta, in which forty-seven samurai faithfully avenged their lord, a story best known from its 1748 dramatization as *Chūshingura*. *Kabuki* soon created a coded system in which certain times, places, and individuals from the past were substituted for individuals of present or recent times. The camouflage was usually so thin that the government had to have known that its rules were being violated, but as long as it recognized an effort being made to conform to its proscriptions, it was content to look the other way. There is widespread belief that the heroes of several tremendously popular, never repressed, and, in fact, practically worshipped, plays like *Sukeroku* or *Shibaraku* were subversive figures whose dynamic victories over evil samurai represented wish fulfillment for townsmen oppressed by the warrior class.

In contrast to the three main grounds for Japanese censorship, Calhoun Winton presents five for the English theatre of the time. He lists (1) criticism of the government, (2) critical depictions of foreign allies, their rulers, or people, (3) "comment on religious controversy," (4) blasphemous or profane language, and (5) satirical attacks on important persons (1980, 294). All these items could conceivably be conflated into Shively's third category (that is, politically or socially offensive subject matter). Despite these restrictions, such transgressions were not absent from English drama. A number of plays, mainly the comedies, made fair game of actual political figures or of social groups—such as the anti-Charles I merchants or "cits" negatively portrayed in Restoration plays—who represented particular ideologies. As in Japan it was necessary, when skewering important figures, to disguise their actual personages. To defer legal action, periods and locales might also be altered, as in *Venice Preserved* (1682), but not always: John Gay's *The Beggar's Opera* (1728), which satirizes Robert Walpole, and *The Critic* (1779), which attacks Lord North, were set in contemporary England. The existence in England of opposing political parties allowed for more freedom of thought in that country; in Japan there was one dictatorial "party," so opportunities were notably rarer. Regardless of the existence of an official English censorship, the office seems to have acted repressively only at certain times, most vividly for several years after Walpole passed the Licensing Act of 1737 and in the closing years of the century, following the outbreak of the French Revolution. In both Japan and England, audiences, being largely conservative, were not seriously disturbed by overt censorship. Fear of being shut down was strong enough in both countries to prevent noticeable rule breaking, and theatre labored under the burden of a rigorous self-censorship, which many will agree is the worst kind.

One of the most oppressive restrictions in both England and Japan had to do with the number of theatres legally allowed to operate. In the early seventeenth century, although regulations existed, the right to run a theatre in Japan and England was relatively easy to obtain. There were far more theatres operating in London before the Commonwealth (1642) and in Edo-Osaka-Kyoto before the 1650s than afterward. With the coming of the Restoration London was forced to get by with two royally approved theatres, the patent houses. For a time in the late seventeenth century, only one was operating. By the 1730s, after the rise and fall of several other venues, Londoners had ready access to four theatres: Goodman's Fields and the Little Theatre in the Hay were giving regular performances in addition to the licensed houses, the new Covent Garden (1732) and the old Drury Lane (1663). This number was halved again by the Licensing Act of 1737, allowing only Covent Garden and Drury Lane to produce plays, although they continually had to battle infringement by nonpatents (the "minors"), many of which continued to appear, finding one way or the other to circumvent the licensing laws. From then into the nineteenth century the patents held fast to their monopoly as the only legitimate, nonoperatic theatres allowed to produce both spoken drama and all sorts of musical and pantomimic genres, sharing their rights only with the Little Theatre in the Hay, which was granted a patent in the summer months from 1766. From 1766, then, London had three officially licensed theatres for (primarily) straight drama, although there were many "illegitimate" venues producing entertainments, some suppressed by the law and others protected by various ruses.

Each of Japan's theatre cities was also limited to a small number of officially licensed playhouses. From the mid-1650s, following a brief period in which *kabuki* was banned (see below), there were four major theatres (*za*) in Edo: the Yamamura-za, founded in 1642; the Nakamura-za, founded in 1624; the Ichimura-za, founded in 1660; and the Morita-za, founded in

1663. In 1714, following the discovery that a lady-in-waiting at the shogun's court had been dallying at the Yamamura-za with a handsome star, the parties to the affair were exiled and the theatre was liquidated, leaving only three licensed theatres, the so-called Edo *sanza* (Edo's "three theatres"), one or the other of which was occasionally replaced by an "alternate theatre" (*hikae yagura* or *kari yagura*)[4] when business was bad. The *sanza* restrictions were not lifted by official action until the early 1870s, whereas the equivalent English event occurred in 1843.

Japan had a host of minor playhouses (*koshibai* and *miyaji shibai*) in addition to the majors (*ōshibai*). These were low-price theatres granted temporary permission to produce plays on the grounds of shrines and temples (and elsewhere) during special, festival-related occasions, They were not unlike the profusion of lesser, often short-lived theatres (especially the fairground variety) that existed in London as a perpetual pain to the patents and whose numbers no one knows for sure. One recent estimate suggests that there may have been an average of about twenty theatres, major and minor, giving productions in each of the major Japanese cities of the period (see Torigoe 1997). The duration of permission was typically one hundred days of good weather, but ways were found to circumvent this rule. The majors were strictly confined to specific neighborhoods, but the minors could be anywhere in the city. Whereas their English equivalents were deprived of certain rights in their repertory, the Japanese minors were denied physical features, such as a draw curtain, that would have given them equal dignity with the majors. Still, they provided significant competition and on rare occasions produced actors who became stars at the majors, just as did Goodman's Fields when it gave David Garrick his first claim to fame. However, once a *kabuki* actor left the majors to play in the minors, he could not return. English actors had no such restrictions. Over and over the minors in England and Japan came back to life after being repressed by the authorities. The theatre workers of both countries were clever at getting around authority.

Actors

One of the first things one learns about *kabuki* is that it is, and always has been, dominated by its actors. For all their dramaturgic qualities, *kabuki* plays were conceived as vehicles for great stars, who freely adapted and revised the repertory to suit their personal tastes. Playwrights did not gain substantial authority until the nineteenth century and then only rarely. Likewise, as Marion Jones notes, London's theatre was emphatically nonliterary: "We should bear in mind that for the whole of this period the theatre in England was an actors' theatre. . . . Their [the actors'] professional objective was the display of each actor's person and techniques to the best advantage within the context of a given play's demands" (1976, 131-32).

In response to the outbreak of civil war in 1642, the Puritans in Parliament closed London's theatres. As Simon Trussler suggests, this was probably intended as a temporary move, but it led to what was—despite momentary flare-ups of activity—the cessation of theatre in London throughout the eighteen-year Commonwealth period (1994, 115). Ten years later, in 1652, the Tokugawa shogunate banned *kabuki* because of brawls inspired by rivalries over the performers in the homosexual boys' *kabuki* (*wakashu kabuki*). In this case the ban lasted less than a year. When *kabuki* was reinstituted, however, it was with certain legal pressures, including a proscription against the word *kabuki* and a prohibition against the boys unless they abandoned their fashionable forelocks and shaved their heads in the less attractive adult male style. Official sanctions against using the stage as a marketplace for bedroom favors led to rapid developments in the art of acting as women, and roles for females became increasingly important and complex.

When Charles II was restored to the British throne in 1660, the London theatre was reestablished, but the pre-1642 practice of boys playing females was discarded. Thus just around the time that the art of female impersonation was being seriously advanced in Japan, the art of the actress was coming into its own in England. As has often been the case, governmental proscriptions were responsible for artistic revolutions.

Women, having been officially outlawed in Japanese theatre since 1629 (despite occasional reappearances into the 1640s), could not continue on stage, so it fell to men to play their roles. In England women had never been legally barred but were prevented by convention from performing. The convention changed when the needs of the new, foreign-influenced drama and theatre were instituted under Charles II. Actresses appeared as a natural outgrowth of artistic developments in London, just as did the female impersonators of Japan. In each case there could have been no other step.

Cross-dressing had been a convention of *kabuki* from its early days for both sexes until the actresses were banned, but in post-Restoration England, for all its frequency, the practice was mainly restricted to women playing men in the popular "breeches" roles that allowed them to show off attractive figures normally hidden by ample dresses. An excuse could always be found: circumstances might force the character to disguise herself, which allowed for the inevitable "disguise penetrated" shock, or she might choose to do so as an expression of her free will, in one of the popular "roaring girl" roles. Occasionally, an actress actually played a male role, Peg Woffington as Sir Harry Wildair (originally written for a man) being a famous example. Nevertheless, apart from its earliest years, when pre-Restoration female impersonators like Edward Kynaston returned to the stage, the post-Restoration English theatre never exploited cross-dressing on a level anywhere near its Japanese counterpart.

The number of women in a typical British company was always about half the number of men. The *onnagata* were even more greatly outnumbered by actors of male roles. Whereas a Restoration company typically had twenty-five to thirty actors, an average figure for an English playhouse of the 1729-1747 period was seventy-four (Scouten 1968, cxxv). Two Edo theatres in 1769 had sixty-one actors, and the third had forty-nine (Hattori 1993, 83). Eight actors were strictly *onnagata* at one, five at another, and three at the third, so male role actors were obviously required to play female roles on frequent occasions. In the same year, an Edo company, including actors, resident dramatists, musicians, backstage and front-of-house personnel, came to 346 at one house, 323 at another, and 211 at the third (Hattori 1993, 85). On the other hand, "The two patent theatres . . . supported about three hundred actors, actresses, dancers, singers, musicians, house servants and itinerant troupers" (Stone 1968, lxxxvii). *Kabuki* thus had a smaller acting company but a much larger group of nonperforming employees. English actors were hired by specific theatres for varying periods—brief during the Restoration, but later three years became common. Japanese players were contracted for only one season at a time and, except for emergencies (as when their theatre burned down), could not act for another company until their term was up.

Great versatility was expected of actors in both England and Japan. Specialization was also prevalent among actors of both traditions. As a consequence, many roles were specifically written with particular Japanese or English players in mind. Sometimes such roles became associated with an actor for life. English actors had far more roles in their standard repertory than did Japanese thespians because their bills changed more frequently. Drury Lane produced seventy plays during the 1721-1722 season; John Mills played fifty roles that season (Avery and Scouten 1968, cxxviii)! A more standard figure was about fifteen roles a season. This was closer to what most leading Japanese actors could expect to play annually, as they appeared in only five or six plays, which, lasting from dawn to dusk, often saw them handling two or three roles in what English actors called "doubling." Many *kabuki* roles, in fact, were written to reveal widely contrasting qualities, as Jekyll and Hyde-like characters often waited in disguise to reveal their true natures. A single role, then, was often the equivalent of two, and to it an actor might add other roles as well. Doubling was not uncommon in England, but it fell out of favor as the companies expanded.

The social position of actors in both nations was very low, despite their fame and, in some cases, wealth. In Japan they were "riverbed beggars" (*kawara kojiki*), among other slurs, and in England they were legally tagged as "rogues, vagabonds, sturdy beggars, and vagrants." Gradually, the dignified reputations of various actors began to elevate the profession.

Some English actors were able to join exclusive clubs, and some *kabuki* stars became recognized participants in respected social and literary circles. In both cultures the profession of acting was open to anyone with the talent and will. *Kabuki* had so many families in the early seventeenth century that no actor of worth was likely to be turned away, but as the years passed it became increasingly difficult to break in without a strong family connection, even if by adoption. English actors, too, could find the path to success strewn with hardship, as Philip H. Highfill, Jr., writes: "There were only a few ways for aspirants to gain the boards of the London patent theatres. A youth of talent could be born into a family connected to a London theatre and obtain preferential treatment and early training" (1980, 153). The next-best thing was to obtain an important actor or manager as a patron, which is not terribly different from the custom of being adopted or taken in as an apprentice by the equivalent person in Japan. Some English actors were able to gain attention at provincial or minor London theatres (Garrick did both), and Nakamura Utaemon I (1714-91), son of a rural physician, became a big star in the city only after gaining valuable experience as a strolling player (Nomura 1988, 204).

The highly conventionalized nature of *kabuki* acting meant that young actors had to learn—as they still do—in a strict master-apprenticeship system instituted early in *kabuki's* history. Ichikawa Danjūrō V (1741-1806) went beyond the system by establishing actor-training workshops and allowing even nondisciples to participate. No comparable training workshops evolved for contemporary British actors, and sporadic attempts to found schools or "nurseries" were abortive. Actors did learn the standard roles via a method like that of the Japanese, at least until the mid-eighteenth century. As Jones writes: "In practice the best way to be sure of pleasing in any established role was to play it as exactly like its acknowledged master as possible" (1976, 142). Despite the power of convention in the acting of famous parts actors occasionally offered revolutionary interpretations, such as Charles Macklin's Shylock in 1741 and Nakamura Nakazō I's (1736-90) radical version of Sadakurō that startled audiences in the 1766 revival of *Chūshingura*.

In London not only were aristocrats allowed in the playhouses, but many enjoyed interacting with the players. Some noblemen even had pretensions to acting talent, and instances are known where they might rent a theatre to display their skills. In Japan, the samurai class was legally barred from going to *kabuki*. Nevertheless, many of them were so inordinately fond of theatricals that they attended in disguise. Records prove that, from the mid-eighteenth century, this fondness extended to avid studying of *kabuki* vocal and musical skills and giving amateur performances of *kabuki* dramas in their homes, a practice deemed so inappropriate to their station that it was officially banned during the Kansei reforms of the 1790s (Kominz 1993, 67).

There were few restrictions on romantic or marital relations between English players and the upper classes, but, as the previously cited scandal concerning the court lady and *kabuki* star attests, such freedom was not allowed in Japan. There was, though, considerable dalliance—homosexual as well as heterosexual—between actors and the townsman class.

Acting dynasties were known in eighteenth-century England, as witness such names as Kemble and Hallam. Their numbers and artistic significance, however, were dwarfed by the theatre families of Japan, where the Ichikawas, Nakamuras, Onoes, and others continue to thrive.

Actors of eighteenth-century England and Japan were increasingly subject to the kind of public fascination with their offstage lives we find today in our tabloids and TV shows. Publication of biographical and autobiographical writings and of anecdotal commentaries revealed their private lives to their fans. Gossip about actors was devoured ravenously by English and Japanese fans. Serious writings on acting also appeared. Japan, for example, produced such famous actor commentaries (*geidan*) as the *Yakusha Rongo* (see Torigoe and Dunn 1969); and Nakamura Nakazō I's two-volume autobiography reminds one of such memoirs as those of Anne Oldfield and David Garrick. The annual actors' critiques (*yakusha hyōbanki*) were another source of personal as well as artistic commentary (see "Yakusha Hyōbanki" in Leiter 1997). In addition, each actor was given a precise ranking, something no English actor of the day had to tolerate.

A popular top-ranked *kabuki* actor could earn a fortune. Ichikawa Danjūrō II received the highest annual salary of the century, estimated at what today might equal half a million dollars. Although the leading English actors made comfortable livings, not even the best paid of them could command anything like this sum. On the other hand, those few who, like Garrick, combined successful managerial careers with acting could retire in considerable comfort. In England actors were paid only for those days on which they performed, but *kabuki* actors seem not to have faced this problem. Actors in both nations are known to have supplemented their incomes with outside businesses, and *kabuki* actors were also able to earn handsome sums by endorsing commercial products.

Each country had an active provincial touring system, with clearly defined "circuits," during the eighteenth century, and the actors experienced similarly harsh conditions. The provinces were deemed a good training ground for future success in the big cities. Major stars sometimes earned substantial amounts by playing with touring companies during the summer seasons. The English actors were hired according to their specialties or "lines of business," a loose equivalent to the Japanese players' system of "role types" (*yakugara*). After gaining official approval to perform, the actors would announce their arrival in a new Japanese or English town by marching through the streets, accompanied by a drummer. Actors in both cultures had to put up not only with rascally managers but with rowdy audiences who would talk back to the dramatic characters and sometimes even mistake stage events for the real thing. (See Nishiyama 1997 for details on Japan's strolling actors, and Rosenfeld 1970 for background on British strollers.)

Theatrical Architecture, Scenic Methods, and Lighting

When the Restoration began, the only remaining unroofed London theatre was the soon-to-be-disused Red Bull. *Kabuki* theatres, however, remained either completely or partially unroofed until 1723 (Shively 1978, 15). English and Japanese theatres had more than roofs in common. Both were equipped with elevator traps, for example. England's traps evolved much earlier than Japan's, going back to the Middle Ages, and they apparently were included in early Restoration theatres. According to Gunji, inconclusive evidence suggests that there may have been pre-elevator *kabuki* traps in 1683, 1694, and 1699, with the first elevator version possibly appearing in 1700 (Gunji 1970, 11-12). Most other sources, though, suggest later dates. Elevator traps capable of moving "People, properties, machines, and scenes" (Visser 1980, 94) were common in eighteenth-century London and operated on principles akin to *kabuki's*. The *kabuki* elevator allowed supernatural figures to appear on its smaller trap, but, with one or two exceptions, reserved use of its *hanamichi* trap (*suppon*) for magical figures or spirits. On the London stage, which had no *hanamichi*, traps were traditionally the province of "ghosts, demons, allegorical figures, or gods" (Visser 1980, 96). Thunder or lightning effects hid the sound of the elevator in England, whereas in Edo—where conventionalized musical passages usually stood in for more literal sound effects—eerie drumbeats suggesting thunder or wind did the same. English and Japanese traps could also serve for any space that had to be lower than the stage locale, such as cellars, wells, bodies of water, and the like. Elaborate devices rose from underneath in both countries, and, although *kabuki* is renowned for its ability to raise entire multistory sets by these means, the eighteenth-century English stage could perform wonders of its own.

Playhouse architecture in Japan and England shared many similarities. Theatres of the 1730s in both countries were essentially rectangular spaces, although the corners of the English rectangles were rounded. Interiors were somewhat differently arranged and *kabuki* had the unique feature of one, and later, two *hanamichi*. But English and Japanese theatres were fundamentally similar in being laid out in a box, pit, and gallery plan (see "The Kanamaru-za" in this volume for pictures and diagrams of an extant Edo-period theatre). Of course, Japanese audiences sat on the floor and English spectators used chairs. The auditorium floors in both were raked. Moreover, the *hanamichi* was only occasionally a part of *kabuki* playhouses of the day and was not permanently installed until the 1740s (see "Suwa Haruo's 'The Birth of the *Hanamichi*'" in this volume). In addition, British and Japanese theatres did not differ greatly in size during the first half of the eighteenth century, when capacity was around one thousand. England's theatres eventually expanded in much greater increments, especially after the 1790s renovations to Drury Lane and Covent Garden, which made them gargantuan in comparison not only to their earlier forms but to contemporary *kabuki* theatres as well. The largest *kabuki* houses appear to have held about fifteen hundred by the century's end, when London's held over three thousand. Raz reminds us that *kabuki* theatres could pack as many people in for a hit as possible and that one record speaks of the incredible sum of five or six thousand crammed into a theatre in Nara, while another one thousand milled around outside, unable to enter (1983, 173).

Actor-audience intimacy in *kabuki* and English theatre was further intensified by the important adjunct of an apron allowing those in the pit to surround downstage action on three sides. This extension, the *tsuke butai*, was added in the late seventeenth century and lasted in most theatres into the nineteenth. The British forestage was whittled away sooner, but its side doors lasted until the 1820s. A slight difference between English and Japanese forestages is that the latter allowed small areas of pit space on either of its sides, between the stage and the side boxes, whereas the English forestage ran smack into the side boxes.

During the eighteenth century the proscenium arch was one prominent architectural feature found in the English theatre and not in the Japanese. Nevertheless, a singular Japanese element served to frame much of the action upstage of the apron until theatres began to remove it in 1796. This was the stage roof supported by onstage pillars, derived from the *nō* theatre. When it was removed a framing arrangement similar to the proscenium was effected by the overhead cloth border (*ichimonji*) but the general impression was similar to that of a contemporary endstage. English stages were masked overhead by a more elaborate system of borders, usually designed to match the side scenes and shutters and confined in most cases to sky, tree, and architectural features. *Kabuki* employed a variety of decorative borders at the front, either of colorful curtains or of hanging branches (*tsuri eda*) dressed with seasonal flora.

England and Japan were both preoccupied with the development of ever more illusionistic scenery and special effects. Scene shifting that allowed sets to be transformed from one reality to another before the spectators' eyes was a goal of *kabuki* and English theatres, both of which painted much of their scenery on flats. *Kabuki* had devices for rapid shifts that would not have been out of place at Drury Lane or Covent Garden. In fact, a British scenic transformation device called the "Falling Flaps" is the same as *kabuki's aorigaeshi* (or *uchigaeshi*). Noting that the Western device goes back to at least 1743, Richard Southern quotes an 1803 account that describes "those double flat scenes, which are also used to produce instantaneous changes. The whole scene being covered with pieces of canvas, framed and moving upon hinges, one side [of each of these hinged flaps] is painted to represent a certain scene, and the other to represent one totally different" (Southern 1957, 800). The flaps were raised and showed their obverse sides to the spectators; when a catch was removed, gravity caused them to fall, revealing their reverse side and creating an altogether different picture. The comparable *kabuki* method was invented by playwright Kana Sanshō (1731-97). A version known as *dengakugaeshi* is pictured in figure 53 in this volume's chapter, "'What Really Happens Backstage." I have described *aorigaeshi* elsewhere in these words: "a painted flat . . . is built with a separate section attached to its center by hinges. When the extra section is moved from one side to the other, like a page in a book, a new painted surface is revealed" (Leiter 1997, 16).

Flying, too, was known in both England and Japan. Eighteenth-century English flying was usually by means of "machines" that allowed individuals or groups to descend to the stage or rise to the flies, with the possibility of up-and-down or horizontal movement. *Kabuki,* which introduced flying (*chūnori*) in the late seventeenth century, preferred to fly individual actors across the stage or over the heads of the spectators on a wire or rope. Numerous other such effects were shared by England and Japan, including the use of onstage water tanks, small models for *trompe l'oeil* perspective, and pyrotechnics. (See "*Keren*," in this volume.)

Although both Japan and England depended for many years on stock scenic units, scenery became increasingly local and play-specific as time passed. Scene painting techniques were highly sophisticated in both traditions. Some *kabuki* scenery, like the river flowing toward the audience in *Imoseyama*, even employed perspective effects (see "'What Really Happens Backstage'"), although *kabuki* had no raked stage. Western perspective was being imported at the time by Japanese print artists, so the only surprise here is that the stage did not make even more use of it. There is also an extraordinary resemblance between the two nations' means of producing the flowing water effect, that is, contiguous large rollers painted with waves and with handles at either end rotated by stagehands.

The chief source of *kabuki* lighting from the 1720 or 1730s was actually from removable sliding windows (*madobuta* or *akari mado*) high up over the left and right galleries (*sajiki*), where theatre workers manipulated the amount of daylight streaming in (see this volume's "The Kanamaru-za"). Early Restoration performances, staged during the daytime, also employed natural light available from playhouse windows or from the cupola. Decorative paper lanterns (*bazuri chōchin*) adorned with actors' names were introduced in the 1760s. Illuminated by candles (oil was considered too dangerous), they hung from the ceiling and side galleries but offered minimal illumination, certainly nothing like what was provided by the chandeliers over the English pit. But *kabuki* did have a novel way of lighting an actor's face when necessary. In scenes requiring a feeling of mystery, the overhead shutters would be closed, darkening the house, and stage assistants would hold long, flexible bamboo poles (*sashidashi*), with upright candles fitted to their ends, before the actor's face, thereby spotlighting him. By the late eighteenth century, however, England was making far more rapid technological progress in lighting than was Japan.

The eighteenth-century English theatre used footlights (either candles or oil) from the time of the Restoration. *Kabuki's* candle footlights (*izaribi* or *sashikomi*) first came into use toward the end of the eighteenth century. The candles were attached to squared-off poles that sat in holders affixed to the front of the stage, their flames commencing a foot and a half to two feet higher than the stage floor. These holders are invariably seen in woodblock prints of theatre interiors from the late eighteenth century on. Because of frequent proscriptions against open flames, small metal hand lanterns (*kantera*) came into use in the 1780s for local illumination. Theatres in Japan constantly burned down, their average life being ten years, whereas only two major conflagrations consumed London theatres during our period.

It is instructive to compare the sizes of London's theatres with Edo's, although some of the figures given are conjectural. From 1732 to 1782—when it held 1,400—Covent Garden's exterior dimensions were a width of 62' by a depth of 117', and Drury Lane's exterior proportions from 1674 to 1775—when it at first held from 500 to 1,000, and then from 1,800 to 2,300—were 58' or 59' by 114'. The Nakamura-za in the 1690s was 71' by 97.5'. Thus *kabuki* theatres, or this typical one at any rate, were originally wider but less deep than the major English examples. However, late-eighteenth-century renovations saw the English playhouses grow considerably larger. Covent Garden after 1792 was approximately 62' by 180' and seated 3,000, and Drury Lane after 1794 was 86' by 204' and held 3,611. The Nakamura-za never was larger than in 1809, when it measured 80' by 138.5' and held about twelve hundred. (English figures cited here are from Langhans 1980, 61~62; Japanese figures are from Shively 1978, 14.) Apart from the great depth of the 1794 Drury Lane, the principal London and Edo playhouses were not very different in exterior proportions, but the interior arrangements of the English playhouse included several tiers of boxes whereas only two tiers were permitted in Japan. Thus far more audience members could attend a London playhouse than one in Edo.

The curtain first became a major feature of the London stage in the early Restoration, just about the time that it was introduced into *kabuki*. Curtains are a relative rarity in Asian theatre, but *kabuki* practically makes a fetish of them. At first sight the use of the curtains in Japan and England looks similar, but there are significant differences. London's curtain long remained a green "French valance," which rose in festoons, whereas the standard *kabuki* curtain was (and remains) a traveler, usually in vertical stripes, the most familiar colors being the now ubiquitous green, persimmon, and black. This curtain was (and is) run on and off by a stage assistant, whose timing contributes significantly to the opening or closing mood. Apart from occasional exceptions, the English curtain rose after the prologue and descended at the end of the play, so, with most scene changes done in full view, and with established conventions to indicate the ends of scenes and acts—such as actors exiting after reciting a couplet—its presence was not necessarily a factor in dramatic structure. In Japan, however, the *kabuki* curtain was invented in 1664, at the same time as—and possibly because of—the advent of multiact dramas, and became very useful as a way to mark the passage of time or shifts in locale. The presence of the curtain surely helped *kabuki* develop changeable scenery, which, like the advent of the *onnagata's* art, made the theatre more realistic. (For a summary of English curtain usage see Visser 1980, 61-62; for *kabuki* curtains see "Maku" in Leiter 1997, 384-85.) In fact, eighteenth-century critic John Dennis's remark that the Restoration's patentees "alterd all at once the whole Face of the stage by introducing scenes and Women, which added probability to the Dramatick Actions and made evry thing look more naturally" (quoted in Southern 1976, 120-21) could be—with *onnagata* substituted for "Women"—equally descriptive of *kabuki* in the 1660s. The English stage enjoyed the advantage of wing and groove shifting, which could look magical when well done. This occurred before *kabuki* created its methods of shifting sets by sliding and revolving stages; it therefore needed to hide the changes. The technological advances of wagons and disks, so crucial to eighteenth-century *kabuki* history, would remain absent from England until the twentieth century

Audiences

Kabuki was a theatre of the common people; and samurai (whose official theatre was the austere *nō*) were proscribed from attending, although they often did, incognito.[5] There were no such prohibitions against the nobility attending the London theatre, which in fact frequently counted court circles (apart from the early eighteenth-century, prior to the accession of King George I in 1714) among its strongest supporters. Seating at an eighteenth-century London theatre was divided by classes. Both before and after 1750, writes Michael R. Booth, "The upper classes still sat in the front and side boxes; the 'critics' and professional men, civil servants, tradesmen and a general cross-section of the middle class in the pit and lower gallery; the working class, including servants, journeymen, apprentices, sailors and their womenfolk in the upper gallery" (1975, 4). *Kabuki* did not isolate its men and women so, and the class distribution varied a bit from London's. The wealthy merchants and their families occupied the expensive gallery boxes; the average worker, shop assistant, maid and servant, and others from the lower economic strata sat in the pit. Connoisseurs who made repeated visits to the theatre sat in the special gallery (*ōmukō* or "great beyond") at the rear of the house, which provided relatively cheap seating, although there were even cheaper seats on the stage itself, occupied by the poorest theatregoers, who had to save up for even so humble a place. As in London, audiences entered a theatre by separate passageways according to the quality of their seating. The hoi polloi at a *kabuki* playhouse entered by bending down to pass through the low doorway called the "mouse entrance" (*nezumi kido*), designed for crowd control (see "The Kanamaru-za," figure 155). Those able to afford gallery box seating entered from the adjoining teahouses, preventing them from directly mingling with their social inferiors.

Langhans uses a painting of Drury Lane's interior in 1795 to remark that the huge interiors of the late eighteenth century encouraged the audience to be more aware of itself: "The play and the audience, the stage and the auditorium are all part of a theatrical event, a performance by all concerned, a social occasion at which the play was not necessarily the thing"(1980, 52). Much the same could be said of a *kabuki* audience of that day, for whom the theatregoing experience was an unusually memorable one, including the bringing along by women spectators of multiple changes of clothes, turning theatregoing into a fashion show with which the actors, not unwillingly, had to compete. As Raz reveals, in words that echo Langhans's: "Theatre-going meant enjoying the auditorium scene as well. Theatrical experience included being an audience. . . . [T]here was no question of separation of distinction between the stage and the audience" (1983, 173-84).[6]

Among those enjoying themselves, in more ways than one, in London playhouses, were prostitutes (known early in the period as vizard masks), who, despite efforts to be rid of them, freely practiced their trade in theatre boxes. Prostitution, of course, was closely associated with *kabuki*, whose plays are filled with action set in the pleasure quarters, located in a segregated area not far from the theatres. The ladies of the pleasure quarters were as idolized by the public as were the actors. Those most likely to have been prostituting themselves in *kabuki's* boxes, however, were most likely not the licensed courtesans, whose movement outside the pleasure quarters was strictly regulated (although they could, apparently, visit the theatre on certain occasions), but the actors themselves, particularly handsome youths, whose favors were avidly sought by patrons of all persuasions. Despite numerous proscriptions (and accompanying punishments) against sexual intimacy with spectators, the practice lingered.

Old-time *kabuki* audiences were known for their boisterousness and informality, which was especially true of the actors' fan clubs (*hiiki renchū*), whose drunken members often got into fights.[7] English audiences were prone to get rowdy, too. Stone notes how often havoc was wreaked in "situations . . . prompted by quarrels among spectators . . . ; quarrels among actors spilling out onstage; quarrels between political factions; trampled personal loyalties and tensions; management errors; premeditated damnation; and spontaneous eruption" (1980, 190). When they were not tearing theatres apart, angry English audiences—all social classes were included—tossed fruit (sold by a concessionaire), or hissed and catcalled. Disgruntled *kabuki* audiences threw their rented cushions (*hanjō*), or shouted out nasty epithets (*akutai*), such as *daikon* (a large, white radish), or *hikkome* ("Get lost!"). Unlike the applause of the English stage, however, the Japanese audience had recourse to an elaborate vocabulary of perfectly timed shouts of praise (*kakegoe*) meant to encourage their favorites, among them "Just like your father," or "I've been waiting for that."

The phenomenon of *kabuki* fan clubs, which played an enormous role in supporting the theatre, is well described by Raz (1983, 190-92). Nothing like them existed in England, the closest thing being organized groups of a nontheatrical nature, like the Freemasons, which sometimes made it their business to condemn or support a production. Political partisanship, with groups on one or the other side of an issue represented in a play, could also lead to success or failure. However, the benefit performances of England offer a curious parallel to the Japanese fans' support of their favorites. What Allardyce Nicoll describes as the "family party atmosphere" (1980, 93)—an expression redolent of *kabuki* theatregoing—promoted by the intimacy between eighteenth-century English actors and their audiences, was especially evident on these occasions. Stipulated in the actors' contracts, they were a considerable boost to their annual incomes, as were many of the elaborate gifts—not excluding cash—given to *kabuki* actors by their patrons during breaks in the dramatic action. English actors at the non-patents often had to swallow their pride and drum up their own support, but the *kabuki* clubs did this on the actor's behalf.

As mentioned, cheap seats at *kabuki* were available onstage. There was a regular two-level seating area near upstage right, positioned so that it faced directly into the audience.[8] In England, onstage seating, placed before the side boxes (see Nicoll 1980, frontispiece and plate 67) or on bleachers arranged at the sides and upstage of the action, was expensive although, as in Japan, the actors were viewed from a disadvantageous viewpoint. In both countries, the stage mob could be distracting and boisterous. When a *kabuki* play was a hit, managements were not averse to crowding the stage with additional spectators until the actors had barely any room in which to maneuver.[9] A Japanese comic poem, alluding to crowding at such a performance, ran: "A big hit—the action is performed in a six-foot square" (Shively 1978, 19).

Onstage seating in London was deemed a privilege of English gentlemen, who felt free to wander backstage as well, and their presence was tolerated but not appreciated by English managements. The strongest advantage they and their lady friends provided was additional income at benefits, to which they were primarily restricted. There sometimes were two hundred onstage spectators, precipitating a situation like that in the Japanese poem, as John Jackson—recalling an Edinburgh benefit in which he entered as Hotspur to duel the Prince of Wales—wrote: "we had not room enough to stand at sword's length" (quoted in Nicoll 1980, 93).[10] After fruitless attempts dating to the 1740s, Garrick, desirous of improving the visual beauty of his productions, rid Drury Lane of onstage seating in 1762, but only by increasing auditorium seating to make up for the lost stage income. The custom seems to have persisted at Covent Garden for two more decades; in Japan it lasted at some theatres until the end of the Edo era.

Before and after the show, London audiences enjoyed the services of nearby coffeehouses and restaurants. Well-off *kabuki* theatregoers frequented the numerous teahouses the kabuki theatres. *Kabuki's* teahouses (*shibai jaya*) did not really serve the same functions as the coffeehouses, and they shared a much more intimate relationship with the theatres they served, but, on the whole, their purpose in providing food and drink for theatregoers was similar to their English analogues. However, since *kabuki* theatregoing was an all day affair, those in the private galleries had direct access to the adjoining teahouses (which also arranged their ticket purchases), and were served throughout the day without having to leave their places. This was also true of those in the pit, and many prints show audiences enjoying a wide assortment of edibles as the show goes on and vendors ply their wares (see Ernst 1974, figure 10).

Repertory

The subject of repertory undoubtedly requires a far broader forum than it can be given here. Dramaturgy, of course, followed quite different principles in England and Japan, but that does not obviate the fact that many Japanese dramas of the Edo period have a narrative strength, character development, and interestingly realistic dialogue that is rare in non-Western theatres. The plays may often be loosely strung together and highly episodic, employing a familiar set of formulaic elements, but their individual segments are frequently well-constructed, suspenseful, self-contained dramas[11] that are the dramaturgic equivalents of many good English plays. Although there were a number of other entertainment forms available for Japanese eighteenth-century urban audiences, including the puppet theatre and various storytelling arts, *kabuki* comprised within itself multiple genres and dramatic types. The Japanese commoner did not have access to the extremely wide-ranging diversity of specialized commercial genres found in London, where spectators could find straight drama, burletta, comic opera, pantomime, melodrama, ballet, burlesque, opera, and the like. Most Japanese equivalents in the non-puppet theatre were covered by *kabuki's* umbrella, where lyrical, mainly atmospheric dance plays with few words spoken by the dancers shared the stage with dramatic dance plays provided with abundant dialogue and plot, and where history plays were part of the same lengthy, all-day works that comprised domestic dramas. The century's *kabuki* plays are occasionally quite realistic (although—as in England—this aspect would be more fully developed in the coming century), just as there are scenes of utter fantasy[12] that bring to mind the extravagances of John Rich's pantomimes or Davenant's operatic version of *The Tempest.* Comedy, although available, is in fairly scarce supply in eighteenth-century *kabuki,* usually being used as relief to more serious concerns. Melodrama flourishes in abundance.

The characters and situations in *kabuki* may require understanding of the social contexts that instigate and restrict behavior and attitudes, but, with few exceptions—the characters are quite human, the protagonists seeking to work their way out of conflicts and problems in a manner best befitting their sense of dignity and honor. Conflicts between duty (*giri*) and personal feeling (*ninjō*), in fact, are not too far distant from those found in much Western drama of the period. They are recognizable despite their, at first sight, unusual movements, language, makeup, and costumes.

In connection with the repertory, it should not be forgotten that in neither England nor Japan was the text a sacred object. Shakespeare was cut and revised in notorious ways, as were all lesser writers, a practice that was just as widespread for Japanese authors, be they the great Chikamatsu or not. Always the actors' preferences came first. Often, the brilliance of a performance is impossible to discern from the reading version of a play revised for the talents of a genius actor, as when Garrick played Don John in Fletcher's *The Chances* or when Nakamura Nakazō I played Sadakurō in *Chūshingura.* Certain subjects dramatized for *kabuki* plays became so popular that they fostered entire genres of plays with the same characters, often transmuting them into new environments and backgrounds. This was a practice known in England as well, where *Romeo and Juliet* could become Otway's *Caius Marius,* or *Antony and Cleopatra* Dryden's *All for Love.*

New twists on familiar stories were likely to be found in both theatres, so that Nahum Tate could give *King Lear* a happy ending, or the commoner hero of *Sukeroku* could turn out to be the famous, much-dramatized historical samurai Soga Gorō in disguise. When George Winchester Stone, Jr., writes that "changes in text were . . . often substantive and the audiences loved the resulting plays" (1980, 187), he could as easily be writing about *kabuki* as about the London stage. Such adaptations often went hand in hand, in both theatres, with an advance in acting styles.

Conclusion

Many more comparisons could be made between the English and Japanese stages of the years considered here, and everything that has been addressed is open to further discussion. Clearly, it would be difficult if not impossible to find outside of the West so many features in any one form that resemble, as do *kabuki's,* those of the English stage of the same time. I believe that seeing *kabuki* in the light of contemporary Western practices helps not only to illuminate this theatre form itself but to shed light on the non-Japanese theatre as well.

NOTES

This is an expanded version of an essay that appeared in *Theatre Symposium* 6 (1998). I wish to thank Dr. James R. Brandon for his helpful comments on the earlier draft. (See n. 3, below, for comments on material added to the present version.)

1. I know of one previous attempt at a similar comparison: Waterhouse (1981). However, the essay, which Waterhouse admits is "hasty, rambling, and incomplete," is so riddled with problems of substance and fact that I believe a fresh look is warranted. Richard Southern makes some brief but interesting comparisons between scenic developments of the classical Japanese (*nō* and *kabuki*) and English theatres of roughly the same periods (1976, 117-18).

2. I am grateful to Dr. Kathy Foley for verifying the validity of this statement with regard to theatrical cultures of Southeast Asia and South Asia.

3. When originally published, this essay compared only the first three of these. I have added the sections on audiences and repertory. An early draft also compared managerial methods. It touched on the similarities and differences in the managerial hierarchies that ran the theatres on a day-by-day basis; the relative profitability of London's theatre business contrasted with the frequent bankruptcies of Japanese producers; the use of an alternative management system (*hikae yagura*) for troubled *kabuki* theatres; the shared dependence on box-office income supplemented by outside investors; resemblances and divergences in the average annual season (for example, London theatres performed

210 nights over eight months; Japanese theatres operated 220 days over eleven months); the position of long runs (more prevalent in Japan than in England, whose long-standing record of a 62-performance run of *The Beggar's Opera* [1728] was overshadowed by such examples as the 280 showings of *Okama Akinai Soga* [1721]); and each country's methods of advertising, as in posters, programs, onstage announcements, billboards, etc. For background on Japanese methods, see the following entries in Leiter (1997): "Banzuke," "Chōmoto," "Hikae Yagura," "Kanban," "Kōgyō," "Nadai," "Yagura," "Zagashira," and "Zamoto." For British methods, see Milhous (1980).

4. *Yagura* refers to the drum tower at the front of the theatre. It served as public acknowledgment of the theatre's licensed status.

5. *Sajiki* seating with privacy provided by bamboo blinds was provided for the samurai class, beginning in Edo in 1646, leading to a series of repeated edicts over the years against such blinds or other devices. During the late seventeenth century, the managements, anxious to sell these expensive seats, contrived various means to foil the authorities. The upper-ranking samurai, fearing punishment, eventually abstained from regular attendance, but the lower ranks frequently attended. (See Shively 1955, 343.) That the upper ranks did not entirely cease attending is demonstrated by the diary of Lord Yanagizawa Nobutoki (1742-1792), who retired in 1773 and spent his remaining years writing poetry and visiting the theatre, which he did on 119 occasions over the next thirteen years. His being in retirement seems to have given him the freedom to attend with such frequency that his starstruck obsession was even lampooned in a comic illustrated novel. (See Clark and Ueda 1994, 28-30.)

6. Raz (1983) is especially good on old-time kabuki audiences, as is Shively 1955, 23-29. For a lively discussion in Japanese, see Hattori 1993, 38-72.

7. For an Edo period spectator's remembrance of the reasons for fights at the kabuki, see Raz (1983, 178).

8. The area itself was called *rakandai* because it resembled a platform (*dai*) on which a host of Buddhist avatars (*rakan*) were crowded. The upper level was the *yoshino*, because those in it had a good view of the stage border of cherry blossoms, for which Mount Yoshino was famous.

9. An idea of this can be gained from a print dated around 1796 and reproduced in Jenkins (1993, 235). A crowd of people can be seen watching not only from the upstage right area, but from upstage left as well. Ernst (1974, figure 9) reproduces an 1802 picture with an even denser onstage mob.

10. Another account describes onstage spectators—including "apprentices"—sitting downstage several rows deep, and facing upstage to view the action (Nicoll 1980, 93).

11. This is particularly true of plays adapted from puppet theatre originals, such as *Shunkan* (1719) or *Terakoya* (1746).

12. For realism (heightened, of course, by exquisite acting conventions), Act VI in *Chūshingura* (1748), during which Kanpei commits a gruesome suicide by disembowelment, is one example, while *Natsu Matsuri* (1721) presents

a horrific murder scene, played amidst blood and mud. For fantasy, see, for example, the scene in Act IV of *Yoshitsune Senbon Zakura* (1747), where a samurai reveals that he is really a magical fox in disguise, and flies away after assuming his true form. These examples are from plays originally written for the puppet theatre.

REFERENCES

Avery, Emmet L., and Arthur Scouten. 1968. *The London Stage, 1660-1700: A Critical Introduction.* Carbondale: Southern Illinois University Press.

Booth, Michael. 1975. "The Social and Literary Context." In *The Revels History of Drama in English.* Vol. 6. *1750-1800*, eds. Clifford Leech and T. W. Craik. London: Methuen.

Brandon, James R., ed. 1982. *Chūshingura: Studies in the Puppet Theatre* Honolulu: University of Hawaii Press.

_____, William P. Malm, and Donald Shively, eds. 1978. *Studies in Kabuki: Its Acting, Music, and Historical Context.* Honolulu: University of Hawaii Press.

Clark, Timothy, and Osamu Ueda, with Donald Jenkins. 1994. *The Actor's Image: Print Makers of the Katsukawa School.* Art Institute of Chicago in association with Princeton University Press: Chicago.

Dunn, Charles J., and Torigoe Bunzō, eds. and trans. 1969. *The Actors' Analects.* Tokyo: Tokyo University Press.

Ernst, Earle. 1974. *The Kabuki Theatre.* 2d ed. rev. Honolulu: University of Hawaii Press. Originally published 1956.

Fujita Minoru, and Leonard Pronko, eds. 1996. *Shakespeare East and West.* New York: St. Martin's Press.

Gunji, Masakatsu, with Chiaki Yoshida. 1969. Kabuki, trans. John Bester. Tokyo and Palo Alto, Ca.: Kodansha.

_____. 1970. *Kabuki Bukuro.* Tokyo: Seiabō.

Hattori Yukio. 1993. *Edo Kabuki.* Tokyo: Iwanami Shoten.

Highfill, Philip H., Jr. 1980. "Performers and Performing." In *The London Theatre World: 1660-1800*, ed. Robert D. Hume. Carbondale: Southern Illinois University Press.

Hume, Robert D., ed. 1980. *The London Theatre World: 1660-1800.* Carbondale: Southern Illinois University Press.

Ihara Seiseien [Toshirō], ed. 1956-63. *Kabuki Nenpyō.* 8 vols. Tokyo: Iwanami Shoten.

Jenkins, Donald, ed., 1993. *The Floating World Revisited.* Honolulu: University of Hawaii Press.

Jones, Marion. 1976. "Actors and Repertory." In *The Revels History of Drama in English.* Vol. 5. *1660-1750*, ed. John Loftis, Richard Southern, Marion Jones, and A H. Scouten. London: Methuen.

Kanasawa Yasutaka. 1972. *Ichikawa Danjūrō.* Tokyo: Seibō.

Keene, Donald. 1971. *Chūshingura; The Treasury of Loyal Retainers.* New York: Columbia University Press.

Kominz, Laurence R. 1993. "Ichikawa Danjūrō V and *Kabuki's* Golden Age." In *The Floating World Revisited,* ed. Donald Jenkins. Honolulu: Portland Museum and University of Hawaii Press.

Langhans, Edward. 1980. "The Theatres." In *The London Theatre World: 1660-1800,* ed. Robert D. Hume. Carbondale: Southern Illinois University Press.

Leiter, Samuel L. 1997. *New Kabuki Encyclopedia: A Revised Adaptation of Kabuki Jiten.* Westport, Ct.: Greenwood Press.

London Stage, The: A Critical Introduction. 1968. 5 vols. Carbondale: Southern Illinois University Press.

Milhous, Judith. 1980. "Company Management." In *The London Theatre World: 1660-1800,* ed. Robert D. Hume. Carbondale: Southern Illinois University Press.

Nicoll, Allardyce. 1980. *The Garrick Stage: Theatres and Audiences in the Eighteenth Century.* Manchester: Manchester University Press.

Nishiyama Matsunosuke. 1997. *Edo Culture: Daily Life and Diversions in Urban Japan, 1600-1868,* trans. and ed. Gerald Groemer. Honolulu: University of Hawaii Press.

Nomura Jusaburō. 1988. *Kabuki Jinmei Jiten.* Tokyo: Nichigai.

Pronko, Leonard. 1967. "*Kabuki* and the Elizabethan Theatre." *Educational Theatre Journal* 19 (March).

————. 1994. "Creating *Kabuki* for the West." In *Japanese Theatre for the West,* ed. Akemi Horie-Webber. Special issue of *Contemporary Theatre Review* 1 (part 2).

Raz, Jacob. 1983. *Audiences and Actors: A Study of Their Interaction in Traditional Japanese Theatre.* Leiden, The Netherlands: Brill.

Rosenfeld, Sybil. 1970. *Strolling Players and Drama in the Provinces.* Cambridge, Eng.: Cambridge University Press. Originally published in 1939.

Scouten, Arthur H. 1968. *The London Stage, 1729-1747: A Critical Introduction.* Carbondale: Southern Illinois University Press.

Shively, Donald. 1955. "*Bakufu* versus *Kabuki.*" *Harvard Journal of Asiatic Studies* 18 (December). Reprinted in Samuel L. Leiter, ed. *A Kabuki Reader: History, Performance.* 2001. Armonk, N.Y.: M.E. Sharpe.

————. 1978. "The Social Environment of Tokugawa *Kabuki.*" In *Studies in Kabuki: Its Acting, Music, and Historical Context,* ed. James R. Brandon, William P, Malm, and Donald Shively. Honolulu: University of Hawaii Press.

Southern, Richard. 1957. "Trickwork on the English Stage." In *Oxford Companion to the Theatre,* ed. Phyllis Hartnoll. 2d ed. London: Oxford University Press.

————. 1976. "Theatres and Scenery." In *The Revels History of Drama in English.* Vol. 5, *1660-1750,* eds. John Loftis, Richard Southern, Marion Jones, and A.H Scouten. London: Methuen.

Stone, George Winchester, Jr. 1980. "The Making of the Repertory." In *The London Theatre World: 1660-1800,* ed. Robert D. Hume. Carbondale: Southern Illinois University Press.

Suwa Haruo. 1991. *Kabuki no Hōhō.* Tokyo: Benseisha.

Torigoe Bunzō. 1997. "*Kabuki:* The Actors' Theatre," trans. and adap. James R. Brandon. In *Japanese Theatre in the World,* ed. Samuel L. Leiter. New York: Japan Society.

Trussler, Simon. 1994. *The Cambridge Illustrated History of the British Theatre.* Cambridge, Eng.: Cambridge University Press.

Tsubouchi, Shōyō. 1960. "Chikamatsu's Resemblance to Shakespeare." In Tsubouchi Shōyō and Yamamoto Jirō, *History and Characteristics of* Kabuki, trans. and ed. Ryōzō Matsumoto. Yokohama: Yamagata Heiji.

Visser, John. 1980. "Scenery and Technical Design." In *The London Theatre World: 1660-1800,* ed. Robert D. Hume. Carbondale: Southern Illinois University Press.

Waterhouse, David. 1981. "Actors, Artists and the Stage in Eighteenth-Century England." In *Theatre in the Eighteenth Century,* ed. J. R. Browning. New York and London; Garland.

Winton, Calhoun. 1980. "Dramatic Censorship." In *The London Theatre World: 1660-1800,* ed. Robert D. Hume. Carbondale: Southern Illinois University Press.

Yamazaki Masakazu. 1994. *Individualism and the Japanese: An Alternative Approach to Cultural Comparison,* trans. Barbara Sugihara. Tokyo: Japan Echo.

GLOSSARY

Only brief descriptions are provided. Fuller explanations for many terms may be found in Samuel L. Leiter, *New Kabuki Encyclopedia* (see bibliography). Cross-referenced words in entries are in bold italics.

abare noshi, strips of paper hung in certain rural theatres to note donors' contributions.

agemaku, draw curtain at the end of the *hanamichi*.

akari mado, overhead windows used for illuminating old-time theatres.

akuba, character type of "evil woman."

akutai, formalized type of insult speech.

aoda, "green fields," seating area at rear of Kanamaru-za.

aorigaeshi, method of changing scenic flats by flipping them over from side to side, as in a book.

aragoto, flamboyant style of masculine acting.

atobune, rear seating area at Yachiyo-za.

ayumi, old term for *hanamichi*-like walkway.

batabata, rapid beating of the *tsuke* clappers.

bazuri chōchin, decorative lanterns in old-time theatres.

budōdana, grid-like structure over old-time stages.

bukkaeri, type of partial quick-change technique.

bunraku, classical Japanese puppet theatre.

bunshichi, stage fighting convention whereby weapons are thrust to either side of the hero.

butsudan gaeshi, trick stage device in *Yotsuya Kaidan* that allows ghost to appear through a Buddhist altar.

chidori, stage fighting convention whereby a group of attackers move by the hero in turn, one by one.

chigo kabuki, one of several terms for children's *kabuki*.

chinkon kabuki, see previous entry.

chobo, shamisen player-narrator/chanter combination that accompanies many plays derived from the puppet theatre.

chōchin nuke, trick effect in *Yotsuya Kaidan* that allows ghost to appear through a lantern.

chūnori, technique of flying through the air in *kabuki*.

daijin bashira, "minister's pillar," part of *kabuki* stage structure borrowed from *nō*.

danjiri, one of several names for festival wagon stages.

dashi, see previous entry.

demago, seating area at the Kanamaru-za, equivalent to *takadoma*.

dengaku, type of folk performance; also a kind of scene change whereby a flat revolves on a skewer-like axis attached at either side to a standing frame.

dengakugaeshi, see previous entry.

dōgu nagashi, scene in which rollers are used to give the effect of a river flowing toward the audience.

dokegata, comic character type.

dokufu, character type of "evil woman."

doma, pit area in old-time theatres.

dorobune, "mud boat," small space at junction of stage and *hanamichi*, used for unusual entrances and exits and for scenes acted in mud or water.

dorodoro, ominous offstage drumbeats.

dote, canal embankment, part of many *kabuki* sets.

ebigaeri (no mie), backbend pose resembling shape of a prawn.

ebizori (no mie), see previous entry.

Edo *sanza*, the three licensed theatres of Edo after 1714: Nakamura-za, Ichimura-za, Morita-za.

ema, votive plaques, sometimes with theatrical images, left at shrines.

emen mie, a kind of final tableau.

enkiri, theatrical convention of contrived lovers' divorce or breakup.

ennen, kind of ritual shrine dance.

fuda, wooden tags used as theatre tickets.

Fudō mie, pose modeled on god Fudō.

fujōkin, "dirty money," funds raised by geisha for building of the Kanamaru-za.

fukigae, actor's double.

furikomi, method of whirling one's stick while attacking with it.

furo, bath.

gakuya, dressing rooms or "backstage."

gandogaeshi, spectacular scene change in which roof of a large building flips upwards as building beneath rises on trap.

geidan, artists' written commentaries on their art.

geidō, an artistic "way."

geiura, seating area to the left of the *hanamichi* at the Kanamaru-za.

gekijō, a theatre.

genkan, lobby or foyer.

genroku mie, exaggerated pose performed by *aragoto* superheroes.

Genzō modori, section in *Terakoya* when Genzō returns.

geta, clog-shaped mechanism for old-time actor's flying device.

geza, offstage room for musicians.

gidayū, narrative musical style originated in the puppet theatre.

giri, sense of obligation, in contrast to *ninjō*.

goshiki no iki, "multicolored breath," a section of *Terakoya*.

goyō kido,entrance to Kanamaru-za.

gunbei, a soldier.

gyōmin kabuki, farmer's *kabuki*.

hakama, culotte-like trousers worn with formal garments.

hako mune, box-shaped ridgepole style used on old-time theatres.

hana, the "flower" of art; also, gifts given to actors by patrons.

hana matsuri, "flower festivals."

hanamichi, stage right runway through *kabuki* theatre.

hana no mai, flower dance.

hana no yakusha, "flower actor," or beautiful star actor.

hana shibai, rural theatres that accept gifts (*hana*).

hana yoten, "flower warrior," a kind of group fighter who attacks the hero.

hanekin, money raised by geisha for construction of the Kanamaru-za.

hanetsurube, "well sweep," mechanism used to manipulate ghosts.

hanjō, small sitting mats rented to Edo-period spectators and often thrown at unpopular actors.

haradatashiku omoiire, "irritated expression," a stage direction.

haragei, internalized kind of acting founded by Ichikawa Danjūrō IX.

harakiri, suicide by disembowelment.

haridashi, side stages used on certain festival floats.

harimono, a scenic flat.

hashibako, effect that allows ghost to appear through lantern by lying in a contraption resembling a chopstick box.

hashigakari, *nō* runway; the predecessor of the *hanamichi*.

hashiramaki no mie, pose in which actor wraps arms and a leg around a pillar.

hayagawari, quick-change techniques.

hayashibeya, offstage musicians' room.

heimagaeri, technique whereby Senō does a forward somersault from a sitting position when he is decapitated in *Sanemori Monogatari*.

henge buyō, dances in which star plays a sequence of sharply contrasting roles.

hengemono, see previous entry.

hiiki renchū, Edo-period fan clubs.

hikae yagura, alternate managements that operated when one or the other of the **Edo** *sanza* had to cease operations.

hikimaku, *kabuki's* draw curtain, usually with vertical stripes of green, persimmon, and black.

hikinuki, quick-change costume device by which threads are pulled from kimono so that it can be yanked free quickly, revealing another one beneath.

hikiyama, one of several names for festival wagon stages.

hikiyama matsuri, festivals in which plays are performed on wagon stages.

hippari no mie, final tableau in which leading stars hold positions in opposition to one another.

hiraba, pit in an old-time theatre.

hiradoma, see previous entry.

hirayama mie, a pose during the *monogatari* in "Kumagai Jinya."

hon butai, the main stage.

hon hanamichi, the main *hanamichi*, as opposed to the **kari hanamichi**.

honmizu, real water.

hozon kai, preservation societies, responsible for preserving rural *kabuki*.

ichimonji, black border over *kabuki* stage.

ie no gei, family art or specialty of an acting family.

irimoya, hip-gabled roof extensions on old-style theatres.

iroha okuri, funeral ceremony sequence in *Terakoya*.

ishinage no mie, pose in which character seems to be throwing a stone.

izaribi, candle footlights in Edo-period theatres.

ji kabuki, local or provincial *kabuki*.

ji kyōgen, see previous entry.

ji shibai, see previous entries.

jidaimono, history plays.

jige kabuki, rural *kabuki*.

jigei, realistic acting.

jitsuaku, type of villain.

jitte, truncheon carried by *kabuki* policemen.

junshi, killing oneself to follow one's master in death.

jutsunaki omoire, "free expression," stage direction giving the actor freedom to play a moment as he wishes.

kagura, general name for a variety of shrine performances.
kaidanmono, ghost plays.
kaishaku, "second" at a ritual suicide.
kajō no chigo, boys who carried flower staffs in certain festivals.
kakeai, use of two or more musical styles in the same piece.
kakegoe, audience shouts during a performance.
kakesuji, a kind of track device used to help actors "fly."
kanban, any one of a number of different billboard types.
kantera, small Edo-period lighting device.
kaomise, annual eleventh month "face showing" performances during which a company revealed its new lineup of actors.
karaido, square space at junction of stage and *hanamichi* used for special entrances and exits.
karami, a kind of fighter in stage battles.
kari hanamichi, secondary *hanamichi*.
kari yagura, alternate management for one or the other of the **Edo** *sanza* during the Edo period.
kasha kubi, nineteenth-century trick for making it seem that an actor's head is going in circles while in flames.
kata, formalized stage business or other theatrical conventions.
kataginu, vest-like overgarment worn with formal clothing.
katakiyaku, villain character.
katsureki, "living history" plays, which adhere to historical accuracy.
keisei, high-class courtesans.
keren, general term for special effects and acrobatic acting.
keren gei, the art of *keren* performance.
keren mono, plays in which *keren* are a crucial component.
kerenshi, actors who specialize in *keren*.
ki, two oak sticks struck together for special auditory effects and as a signal for a number of conventions.
kido, gateway.
kimari, formalized pose associated with female characters.
kimochi, actors' feelings during performance.
kinpira jōruri, seventeenth-century puppet theatre known for its hero, Kinpira, and for violent effects.
kinshi yoten, soldiers' costumes sewn with gold threads.
kiriana, opening in stage floor.
kirizuma, traditional kind of roof seen on old-style theatres.
kitsune roppō, bounding *hanamichi* exit in a manner suggesting a fox.
kiyomoto, major form of musical accompaniment.
kodōgu, small props.
kodōgu beya, storage room for small props.

kodomo kabuki, children's *kabuki*.

kodomo shibai, see previous entry.

koitsukami, scenes in which hero battles with a giant carp.

kojōruri, general term for seventeenth-century puppet theatre before the advent of Chikamatsu Monzaemon and Takemoto Gidayū.

kōken, formally dressed stage assistant.

kokera otoshi, ritual ceremony to celebrate opening of new theatre.

kokyū, Chinese fiddle.

komamawashi, unique kind of "top-like" revolving stage found in certain old-time theatres.

koroshiba, murder scenes.

koshibai, small theatres of Edo period, in contrast to *ōshibai*.

kubi jikken, scenes of head inspection.

kubinage, fight scene convention of throwing one's opponent by grabbing his head first.

kudoki, scenes of lamentation.

kumadori, wide variety of stylized makeups.

kuro yoten, stage fighters dressed in black.

kurogo, black-garbed stage assistants.

kuromisu, offstage musicians' room.

kuyashiki omoiire, stage direction meaning "mortified expression."

kyōgen, classical form of comic theatre; also, a generic word for "play."

ma, the moment of pause in acting; also, timing in general.

machi mawari, ceremony of a troupe's marching around town and beating a drum to announce its presence.

madobuta, overhead windows used for illuminating old-time theatres.

maebune, forward seating area in pit at Yachiyo-za.

makusoto no hikkomi, *hanamichi* exits made outside the closed curtain.

manzai, a kind of comic entertainment.

masu, boxed-in seating compartments in the pit of old-time theatres.

masukata, another name for the *nanoridai*.

matsubame mono, plays performed in a manner resembling their *nō* play origins.

mawari butai, the revolving stage.

miarawashi, "revelation" of a character's true nature through a formalized pose.

michiyuki, conventionalized "travel scene," usually showing lovers going to commit double suicide but sometimes showing characters journeying through the countryside.

midori, programs madeup of popular scenes and dances rather than complete plays.

mie, wide variety of formalized poses.

migawari, scenes in which one character substitutes for another.

minzoku geinō, folk performing arts.

misemono, side show acts.

miyaji shibai, shrine ground theatres.

mizubune, water basin used in an old theatrical water trick.

mizugei, acting using water effects.

mizugo, water-colored camouflage worn by stage assistant.

mizumono, plays in which water effects play an important role.

modori, scenes of "return," in which a supposedly guilty character reveals his true motives.

mon, family crests.

monogatari, narrative sequences in which hero accentuates his tale with movements of a fan.

mukō sajiki, gallery area facing stage at rear of auditorium.

mura shibai, village theatre

nagabakama, long, trailing *hakama*.

nagauta, major style of musical accompaniment.

nakabune, middle portion of pit seating at Yachiyo-za.

namigo, wave-colored camouflage worn by stage assistant.

nanoridai, platform once attached to *hanamichi* and on which characters announced their presence.

naraku, "hell"-like cellar area beneath stage and *hanamichi*.

nenbutsu odori, group dance to Buddha that was important in development of early *kabuki*.

nezumi kido, low "mouse entrance" through which spectators entered Edo-period theatres.

nihon buyō, classical Japanese dance, as seen in *kabuki*.

nijiyori, fight sequence where opponents advance toward each other using shuffling foot movements.

nimaime, romantic young leading male characters and the actors who play them.

ninjô, character's feelings, in contrast to his or her *giri*.

nō, austere classical theatre that predates *kabuki*.

norikomi, ceremonial entrance by boat into Osaka by visiting or returning actor.

noson kabuki, farmer's *kabuki*.

ōbeya, large dressing room for secondary actors.

ōdaiko, large offstage drum.

ōdōgu, large set pieces.

oharai, ritual cleansing ceremony.

ohineri, wrapped gifts of coins or cake thrown onto stage in rural theatres.

ōkido, large entranceway at Kanamaru-za.

omikoshi, portable shrine.

omoire, "expression," a common stage direction.

ōmukō, gallery area facing stage.

onigara, decorative roof ornament on old-time theatres.

onna kabuki, girls' or women's *kabuki*.

onnagata, female-role specialists.

ōshibai, large, licensed theatres of the Edo period, in contrast to unlicensed *koshibai*.

oshidashi, actor's charisma or stage personality.

oshimodoshi, demon-quelling supermen characters.

oshinobi, incognito theatre visits by samurai.

otokodate, chivalrous townsmen who protected citizens against overbearing samurai.

oyajigata, roles of old men.

patangaeshi, method of changing flats by having them flip forward on a hinge, revealing the one behind.

rakandai, onstage seating area, upstage right, in Edo-period theatres.

rakugo, traditional storytelling art.

renribiki, convention whereby ghost draws fleeing character back as if pulling invisible strings.

rikisha, strongman or wrestler.

rokuro, pulley system for flying an actor.

roppō, bounding exit on the **hanamichi** of which there are several types.

sajiki, galleries at either side of a traditional theatre.

sakaomodoka, Soga Gorō's armor.

sakigane, metal pole with hook on its end that attached to nineteenth-century actor's sash for help in making him fly.

sasahoko, one of several names for festival wagon stages.

sashidashi, flexible bamboo pole manipulated by stage assistant, with flame burning at one end.

sashigane, flexible bamboo pole manipulated by stage assistant, with small animals or props attached to one end with wires.

sashikomi, candle footlights in Edo-period theatres.

sasumata, one of several names for festival wagon stages.

seinen kabuki, "junior" *kabuki*, performances with young, up-and-coming actors.

seisatsu kabuki, "signboard *mie*" in "Kumagai Jinya."

semeba, torture scenes.

senkai, circular head movement seen in *mie*.

sen ryō yakusha, "1,000 *ryō* actor," a great star.

seppuku, suicide by disembowelment.

seri, stage traps.

seriage, rising trap platform.

serifu, dialogue and speech.

serisage, descending trap platform.

sewamono, domestic drama.

shamoji, device on which actor stands to glide in and out in supernatural scenes.

shibai goya, generic term for old-time roofed theatres.

shibai jaya, theatre teahouses.

shibaiya, rural term for theatre troupe or playhouse.

shichigochō, seven-five meter.

shichisan, position on *hanamichi* seven-tenths from rear of theatre.

shienkai, young acting company that bands together to try its hand at plays and roles otherwise unavailable to it.

shimai, *nō* dance sequence performed without traditional costume.

shin buyō, new dances.

shin kabuki, modernized *kabuki* plays written during the twentieth century.

shingeki, European-influenced modern drama.

shinjū, double suicide.

shinobi, secondary spy-like character added to certain plays for dramatic interest.

shinpa, late nineteenth-century theatrical form that lies midway between *kabuki* and modern drama.

shinuki, stage fighting convention whereby several characters step out of the way to do battle in individual ways.

shishiguchi, decorative roof ornament on old-time theatres.

shōchū, chemical mixture that produces phosphorescent flames for use in supernatural scenes.

shōne, a character's true nature.

shosagoto, dance play.

shudō, homosexuality.

shūmei hiro, onstage assumption of a name by an actor.

sokotsu-shi, expiatory *seppuku* in which someone kills himself to right a wrong he has committed.

soku mie, pose in which the actor stands with his feet close together.

sōshi shibai, political drama related to origins of *shinpa*.

su odori, dance performed without theatrical costume.

sunoko, overhead gridwork in old-time theatres.

suppon, elevator trap on *hanamichi*.

tabi, bifurcated Japanese socks.

tachimawari, choreographed fight scenes.

tachiyaku, actors of male roles.

taikodai, one of several names for festival wagon stages.

taishū engeki, form of popular theatre influenced by *kabuki*.

takadoma, raised seating at the sides of the pit in traditional theatres.

takemoto, narrative musical accompaniment borrowed from the puppet theatre.

takiguruma, "waterfalls wheel" used in *dōgu nagashi* technique to make it look as though a river is flowing toward the audience in *Imoseyama*.

tashinami, proper behavior or "etiquette" observed by old-style *onnagata* in their private lives.

tate, choreographed fight movements.

tateshi, fight choreographer.

tenchi, "heaven and earth," pose in which one character stands and another kneels at his or her side.

tenchijin no mie, three-person pose with each one on a different level.

tennōdai, scarlet-covered platform on which hero stands during certain fight scenes.

tenugui, hand towel, a ubiquitous prop.

teoi no jukkai, acting convention associated with wounded, dying character who makes some sort of last-minute confession.

teoigoto, the art of acting seriously wounded characters.

terako aratame, sequence in *Terakoya* where the schoolchildren are inspected.

tesuri, low railing dividing the space laterally on puppet theatre stage.

teuchi shiki, fans' hand clapping ceremony.

tobi kubi, technique that makes it seem as if a head is flying around.

tobi roppō, bounding *hanamichi* exit suggesting that the character is flying off.

toitagaeshi, trick effect in *Yotsuya Kaidan* during which the same actor plays two corpses lashed to a raindoor that has been thrown in the canal and that floats on stage and stops at an embankment.

toitawatashi, see previous entry.

tokiwazu, important style of musical accompaniment.

tomigushi, Edo-period type of lottery.

tonbo, somersault.

torifuda, wooden tag used as ticket in Edo-period theatres.

torite, *kabuki* policemen.

tōshi, production of a full-length play to fill a program, in contrast to the *midori* system.

toya, small room at the end of the *hanamichi*.

tsuke, wooden clappers struck against a wooden plate at stage left and used to accentuate various stage business.

tsuke butai, forestage in old theatres.

tsuke hashikakari, old name for a kind of forestage.

tsukeuchi, the man who beats the *tsuke*.

tsukidai, sliding seat used in nineteenth-century *tobi kubi* trick.

tsukitoi, elevator platform used in nineteenth-century *tobi kubi* trick.

tsukuri butai, one of several seventeenth-century terms for a forestage.

tsurane, speech in which character announces him or herself.

tsuri eda, decorative branches of flowers or leaves hanging over the stage.

tsuzumi, hand drum.

tsuzura nuke, special effect by which character emerges from a wicker basket as it flies over the auditorium.

uchigaeshi, method of changing scenery by flipping a scenic unit over to reveal a hidden face.

utai, *nō* singing.

wagoto, gentle style of acting associated with delicate young men.

wakashu kabuki, boy's *kabuki*, outlawed in 1652.

watari zerifu, rhetorical convention of "passed-along dialogue."

yagō, actor's nickname by which fans often refer to him.

yagura, drum tower outside Edo-period theatres that signified their licensed status.

yakugara, role types.

yakusha hyōbanki, annual actor critiques of the Edo period.

yama, one of several names for festival wagon stages.

yamahoko, see previous entry.

yanagi, fight scene convention of parrying a sword blow.

yarō kabuki, mature male *kabuki*, which succeeded *wakashu kabuki*.

yatai, scenic unit of house or attached room.

yatai tsubushi, effect of making a stage house collapse.

yose, variety theatre.

yosemune zukuri, kind of roof used in traditional theatres.

yoshikibi, beauty of form.

yoshino, upstage right seating area in Edo-period theatres.

yoten, a kind of stage fighter and his costume.

yuka, platform on which *chobo* sits.

yukizeme, scene of torturing a beautiful woman in the snow.

zagashira, acting company star and leader.

zangirimono, cropped-hair plays in which Meiji manners are reflected.

zankoku no bi, aesthetic of cruelty.

zōri uchi, scenes in which the ultimate insult of one character striking another with a sandal is enacted.

Selected Bibliography

This bibliography is restricted to works cited in the text.

Akashi Kazumii. 1995. *Zenkoku Shibai Goya Meguri*. Tokyo: Shōgakukan.

Aoe Shunjirō. 1971. "Hanamichi Shiko." In *Nihon Geinō no Genryū*. Tokyo: Iwasaki Bijutsha.

Avery, Emmet L., and Arthur Scouten. 1968. *The London Stage, 1660-1700: A Critical Introduction*. Carbondale: Southern Illinois University Press.

Bach, Faith. 1989. "New Directions in *Kabuki*." *Asian Theatre Journal* 6: 1 (Spring).

Bandō Mitsugorō VIII. 1974. "Koroshi no Gei." In *Kabuki-Bunraku-Nō Zankoku no Bi*, ed. Hattori Yukio. Tokyo: Hōka Shobō.

Barrett, Laurence. 1969. *Edwin Forrest*. New York: Benjamin Blom.

Benedict, Ruth. 1946. *The Chrysanthemum and the Sword: Patterns of Japanese Culture*. Tokyo and Rutland, Vt.: Tuttle, 1954. Originally published 1946.

Booth, Michael. 1975. "The Social and Literary Context." In *The Revels History of Drama in English*. Vol. VI. 1750-1800, eds. Clifford Leech and T. W. Craik. London: Methuen.

Bowers, Faubion. 1974. *Japanese Theatre*. Tokyo and Rutland, Vt.: Charles E. Tuttle. Originally published 1952.

Brandon, James R., William P. Malm, and Donald Shively, eds. 1978. *Studies in Kabuki: Its Acting, Music, and Historical Context*. Honolulu: University of Hawaii Press.

Brandon, James R. 1978. "Form in *Kabuki* Acting." In James R. Brandon, William P. Malm, and Donald H. Shively, eds. *Studies in Kabuki: Its Acting, Music, and Historical Context*. Honolulu: University of Hawaii Press.

_____, ed. 1982. *Chūshingura: Studies in the Puppet Theatre* Honolulu: University of Hawaii Press.

_____, trans. 1992. "Kumagai's Battle Camp." In Kabuki: *Five Classic Plays*. Honolulu: University of Hawaii Press. Originally published 1975.

_____. 2000. "Performance and Text in Kabuki." In *Japanese Theatre and the International Stage*, ed. Stanca Scholz-Cionca and Samuel L. Leiter. Leiden, The Netherlands: Brill.

Cavaye, Ronald. 1993. *Kabuki: A Pocket Guide*. Tokyo and Rutland, Vt.: Charles E. Tuttle.

Clark, Timothy, and Osamu Ueda, with Donald Jenkins. 1994. *The Actor's Image: Print Makers of the Katsukawa School*. Art Institute of Chicago in association with Princeton University Press: Chicago.

Coquelin, Constant. 1958. "Actors and Acting." In *Papers on Acting*, ed. Brander Mathews. New York: Hill and Wang.

Cummings, Alan, trans. 2002. "The Revenge at Tengajaya." In Kabuki *Plays On Stage: Villainy and Vengeance, 1773-1799*, eds. James R. Brandon and Samuel L. Leiter. Honolulu: University of Hawaii Press.

Cummings. 2002. "Gorozō the Gallant." In Kabuki *Plays On Stage: Darkness and Desire, 1804-1864*, eds. James R. Brandon and Samuel L. Leiter. Honolulu: University of Hawaii Press.

Darbyshire, Alfred. 1969. *The Art of the Victorian Stage: Notes and Recollections*. New York: Benjamin Blom.

Diderot, Denis, and William Archer. 1957. *The Paradox of Acting* and *Masks or Faces*. New York: Hill and Wang.

_____. 1970. "The Paradox of Acting." In *Actors on Acting*, ed. Toby Cole and Helen Krich Chinoy. New York: Crown.

Dunn, Charles J., and Bunzo Torigoe, eds. and trans. 1969. *The Actors' Analects*. Tokyo: University of Tokyo Press.

Engekikai. 1955, 1957, 1959, 1960, 1962, 1965, 1966, 1968, 1970, 1975, 1991. Miscellaneous issues.

_____. 1962. Special commemorative Ichikawa Danjūrō XI issue. 20: 4 (April).

_____. 1966. Special commemorative Ichikawa Danjūrō XI issue. 24: 2 (February).

Ernst, Earle. 1974. *The* Kabuki *Theatre*, 2d ed. rev. Honolulu: University of Hawaii Press. Originally published 1956.

Fischer-Lichte, Erika. 1997. *The Show and the Gaze of Theatre: A European Perspective*. Iowa City: University of Iowa Press.

Fujii Yasuo. 1978. "*Ichinotani Futaba Gunki*." *Engekikai* 36 (April).

Fujino Yoshio, ed. 1961. *Maruhon Kabuki: Gikyoku to Butai*. Tokyo: Sekigaku Shobō.

Fujita Minoru, and Leonard Pronko, eds. 1996. *Shakespeare East and West*. New York: St. Martin's Press.

Fujiya Hotel. 1950. *We Japanese*. Yokohama: Yamagata Press.

Genshoku Ukiyo-e Daihyakka Jiten Daikkan. Vol. 2. Tokyo: Daishūkan.

Gotō Keiji. 1925. *Nihon Gekijō Shi*. Tokyo: Iwanami Shoten.

Gunji Masakatsu, with Chiaki Yoshida. 1969. Kabuki, trans. John Bester. Tokyo and Palo Alto, Ca.: Kodansha.

_____. 1970. *Kabuki Bukuro*. Tokyo: Seiabō.

_____. 1971. *Kabuki Karā Konpakutu.* Tokyo: Zayūtama Kankōkai.

_____. 1972. "Zankoku no Bi." In *Kabuki no Bigaku.* Tokyo: Engeki Shuppansha.

Hamamura Yonezō. 1921. *Kabuki no Mikata.* Tokyo: Hagino Yasha.

Hattori Yukio, ed. 1967. *Okyōgen Gakuya no Honsetsu, Kabuki no Bunken.* Vol. 2. Tokyo: Kokuritsu Gekijō.

_____, ed. 1969. "Natsu Kyōgen Han—Shin Okyōgen Gakuya Honsetsu." *Kabuki* 5.

_____. 1980. "Hanamichi Kō." In *Edo Kabuki Ron.* Tokyo: Hōsei Daigaku Shuppan Kyoku.

_____. 1993. *Edo Kabuki.* Tokyo: Iwanami Shoten.

Hayashiya Tatsusaburō. 1931. "Kabuki no Gekijō Kōzō no Shinka." In *Kabuki Gashō.* Tokyo: Tōkyōdō.

Highfill, Philip H., Jr. 1980. "Performers and Performing." In *The London Theatre World: 1660-1800,* ed. Robert D. Hume. Carbondale: Southern Illinois University Press.

Hirose Chisako. 1978. "Onnagata no Geidan." *Engekikai* 36 (June).

Honma Hisao. 1960. *Kabuki.* Tokyo: Shohakusha.

Hume, Robert D., ed. 1980. *The London Theatre World: 1660-1800.* Carbondale: Southern Illinois University Press.

Hyland, Peter. 1987. "'A Kind of Woman': The Elizabethan Boy-Actor and the *Kabuki Onnagata.*" *Theatre Research International* 12:1.

Ichikawa Ebizō Butai Shashin Shū. 1954. Tokyo: Wakei Shoten.

Ichikawa Ennosuke. 1984. *Ennosuke no Kabuki Kōza.* Tokyo: Shinchōsha.

Ihara Seiseien [Toshirō], ed. 1956-63. *Kabuki Nenpyō.* 8 vols. Tokyo: Iwanami Shoten.

Ikeda Yasaburō. 1956. "Gekijō (Kankyaku, Seki, Sajiki, Butai, Hanamichi) Sono Geinō Shiteki Kōsatsu." In *Kabuki Zensho Daiichi Ikkan.* Tokyo: Tōkyō Sōgensha. Reprinted in *Nihon Rekishi Shinsho: Edo Jidai no Geinō,* 1960. Tokyo: Shibundō.

Imao Tetsuya. 1979. *Kabuki o Miru Hito no Tame ni.* Tokyo: Tamagawa Daigaku Shuppanbu.

Inoura, Yoshinobu, and Toshio Kawatake. 1981. *The Traditional Theater of Japan.* New York and Tokyo: Weatherhill.

Irving, Henry. 1969. *The Drama: Addresses.* New York: Benjamin Blom.

Irving, Laurence. 1952. *Henry Irving, The Man and His World.* New York: Macmillan.

Japan: A Bilingual Atlas. 1993. Tokyo: Kodansha.

Jenkins, Donald, ed., *The Floating World Revisited.* Honolulu: University of Hawaii Press.

Jones, Marion. 1976. "Actors and Repertory." In *The Revels History of Drama in English.* Vol. 5. *1660-1750,* ed. John Loftis, Richard Southern, Marion Jones, and A H. Scouten. London: Methuen.

Jūgosei Ichimura Uzaemon Butai Shashin Shū. 1951. Tokyo: Wakei Shoten.

Kabuki Daichō Shūsei Daiikkan. 1983. Tokyo: Benseisha.

Kagayama Naozō. 1957. *Kabuki no Kata*. Tokyo: Tōkyō Sōgensha.
_____. 1965. "Enshutsu to Engi." *Engekikai* 14 (August).
_____. 1968. *Kabuki*. Tokyo: Yazankaku.
Kanasawa Yasutaka. 1972. *Ichikawa Danjūrō*. Tokyo: Seibō.
Katsuo Shin'ichi, ed. 1970. "*Keren*." *Kabuki* 11.
Kawatake Shigetoshi. 1955. *Nakamura Kichiemon*. Tokyo: Toyamabō.
_____. 1956. *Nihon Engeki Zuroku*. Tokyo: Asahi Shinbunsha-kan.
Kawatake Toshio. 1971. *Kabuki Meibutai*. Tokyo: Zenkoku Jūshō Shinshin Shogaiji (sha) o Mamoru Kai.
_____. 1972. "Onnagata no Kiseki." *Kabuki* 19.
_____. ed. 1982. *Genshoku Kabuki Shōsai*. Tokyo: Gurafusha.
Keene, Donald. 1964. "Realism and Unreality in Japanese Drama." *Drama Survey* 3 (Winter).
_____, trans. 1971. *Chūshingura; The Treasury of Loyal Retainers*. New York: Columbia University Press.
Kominz, Laurence R. 1993. "Ichikawa Danjūrō V and *Kabuki's* Golden Age." In *The Floating World Revisited*, ed. Donald Jenkins. Honolulu: Portland Museum and University of Hawaii Press.
Komiya, Toyotaka, comp. and ed. 1956. *Japanese Music and Drama in the Meiji Era*, trans. and adap. Edward G. Seidensticker and Donald Keene. Tokyo: Ōbunsha.
Kusanagi Kinshirō. 1955. *Genzai Saiko no Gekijō Kanamaru-za*. Kotohira: Kagawa-ken Tosho Kabushiki Kaisha.
Laderierre, Mette. 1989. "The Early Years of Female Impersonation in *Kabuki*." *Maske und Kothurne* 35.
Lane, Richard. 1978. *Images of the Floating World: The Japanese Print*. New York: Konecky and Konecky.
Langhans, Edward. 1980. "The Theatres." In *The London Theatre World: 1660-1800*, ed. Robert D. Hume. Carbondale: Southern Illinois University Press.
Leacroft, Richard, and Helen Leacroft. 1984. *Theatre and Playhouse: An Illustrated Survey of Theatre Building from Ancient Greece to the Present Day*. London: Methuen.
Leiter, Samuel L. 1997. *New Kabuki Encyclopedia: A Revised Adaptation of Kabuki Jiten*. Westport, Ct.: Greenwood Press.
_____, trans, and ed. 2000. *The Art of Kabuki: Five Famous Plays*. Rev. ed. Mineola, N.Y.: Dover. Originally published 1979.
_____. 2001. "From Gay to *Gei*: The *Onnagata* and the Creation of *Kabuki's* Female Characters." Originally published in *Comparative Drama* (Winter/Spring 2000). Reprinted in Samuel L. Leiter, ed., *A Kabuki Reader: History and Performance*. 2001. Armonk, N.Y.: M.E. Sharpe.
_____, and Kei Hibino, trans. 2002. "The Picture Book of the Taikō." In *Kabuki Plays On Stage: Villainy and Vengeance, 1773-1799*, eds. James R. Brandon and Samuel L. Leiter. Honolulu: University of Hawaii Press.

London Stage, The: A Critical Introduction. 1968. 5 vols. Carbondale: Southern Illinois University Press.

Longstreet, Stephen, and Ethel. 1970. *Yoshiwara: City of the Senses.* New York: McKay.

MacKaye, Percy. 1927. *Epoch, The Life of Steele MacKaye, Genius of the Theatre, in Relation to His Times and Contemporaries.* Vol. 1. New York: Boni and Livewright.

Milhous, Judith. 1980. "Company Management." In *The London Theatre World: 1660-1800,* ed. Robert D. Hume. Carbondale: Southern Illinois University Press.

Mitford, A.B. 1966. "An Account of the Hara-Kiri." In *Tales of Old Japan.* Tokyo and Rutland, Vt.: Tuttle. Originally published 1871.

Miyake Saburō. 1956. *Kabuki o Mirume.* Tokyo: Shinjusha.

Mokuami, Kawatake. 1966. *The Love of Izayoi and Seishin,* trans. Frank T. Motofuji. Tokyo and Rutland, Vt.: Tuttle.

"Nanoridai." 1962. In Tsubouchi Memorial Theatre Museum, ed. *Engeki Hyakka Daijiten.* Tokyo: Heibonsha.

Narasaki Muneshige. 1989. "Saruwaka Kanzaburō Shijō Gawara Shibai Kōgyō Zukan." *Kokka* 1127 (October).

Nicoll, Allardyce. 1980. *The Garrick Stage: Theatres and Audiences in the Eighteenth Century.* Manchester: Manchester University Press.

Ningyō Butai Shi Kōhen: Daini Bunsatsu: Kaisetsu no Bu. 1980. Tokyo: Kokuritsu Gekijō.

Nishiyama Matsunosuke. 1969. *Hana—Bi e no Kōdō to Nihon Bunka.* Tokyo: Nihon Hōsō Shuppan Kyōkai. Reprinted in *Nishiyama Matsunosuke Chosakushū Daihakkan.* 1985. Tokyo: Yoshikawa Hiroshi Bunkan.

Nishiyama Matsunosuke. 1997. *Edo Culture: Daily Life and Diversions in Urban Japan, 1600-1868,* trans. and ed. Gerald Groemer. Honolulu: University of Hawaii Press.

Noguchi Tatsuji. 1965. *Kabuki.* Tokyo: Bungei Shunka Shinja.

Nomura Jusaburō. 1988. *Kabuki Jinmei Jiten.* Tokyo: Nichigai.

Numa Kusaame. 1973. "Shinro Sen no Kabuki." *Engekikai* 31 (February).

Okamoto, Shiro. 2001. *The Man Who Saved Kabuki: Faubion Bowers and Theatre Censorship in Occupied Japan,* trans. and adap., Samuel L. Leiter. Honolulu: University of Hawaii Press.

Onnagata Shashin Chō. 2000. Tokyo: Engeki Shuppansha.

Onoe Kikugorō VI. 1947. *Gei.* Tokyo: Kaizōsha.

Origuchi Shinobu. 1976. "Muromachi Jidai no Bungaku." In *Chū Kobun Gura: Origuchi Shinobu Zenshū Daijūnnikan.* Tokyo: np.

Ōzaki Norio. 1995. *Noson Kabuki.* Tokyo: Asahi Bunsha.

Peyotoru Kubō, ed. 1992. *Kabuki wa Tomodachi.* Tokyo: Peyotoru Kubō.

Pronko, Leonard. 1967. "*Kabuki* and the Elizabethan Theatre." *Educational Theatre Journal* 19 (March).

_____. 1994. "Creating *Kabuki* for the West." In *Japanese Theatre for the West*, ed. Akemi Horie-Webber. Special issue of *Contemporary Theatre Review* 1 (part 2).

Raz, Jacob. 1983. *Audiences and Actors: A Study of Their Interaction in Traditional Japanese Theatre*. Leiden, The Netherlands: Brill.

Richardson, Gary A. 1998. "Plays and Playwrights: 1800-1865." In *The Cambridge History of American Theatre*, ed. Don B. Wilmeth and Christopher Bigsby. Vol. 1. Cambridge, Mass.: Cambridge University Press.

Richie, Donald, and Miyoko Watanabe, trans. 1963. *Six* Kabuki *Plays*. Tokyo: Hokuseido.

Rosenfeld, Sybil. 1970. *Strolling Players and Drama in the Provinces*. Cambridge, Eng.: Cambridge University Press. Originally published in 1939.

Saintsbury, H.A., and Cecil Palmer, ed. 1969. *We Saw Him Act: A Symposium on the Art of Sir Henry Irving*. New York: Benjamin Blom.

Salter, Denis. 1992. "Henry Irving, The 'Dr. Freud' of Melodrama." In *Melodrama, Themes in Drama*, ed. James Redmond. Vol. 14. Cambridge, Eng.: Cambridge University Press.

Saltzman-Li, Katherine, trans. 2002. "The Sanemori Story." In Kabuki *Plays On Stage: Brilliance and Bravado, 1697-1766*, eds. James R. Brandon and Samuel L. Leiter. Honolulu: University of Hawaii Press.

Scott, A.C. 1999. *The* Kabuki *Theatre of Japan*. Mineola, N.Y.: Dover. Originally published 1956.

Scouten, Arthur H. 1968. *The London Stage, 1729-1747: A Critical Introduction*. Carbondale: Southern Illinois University Press.

Seward, Jack. 1968. *Hara-Kiri: Japanese Ritual Suicide*. Tokyo and Rutland, Vt.: Tuttle.

Shaver, Ruth. 1966. Kabuki *Costume*. Tokyo and Rutland, Vt.: Tuttle.

Shively, Donald. 1955. "*Bakufu* versus *Kabuki*." *Harvard Journal of Asiatic Studies* 18 (December). Reprinted in Samuel L. Leiter, ed. *A Kabuki Reader: History and Performance*. 2001. Armonk, N.Y.: M.E. Sharpe.

Shively, Donald. 1978. "The Social Environment of Tokugawa *Kabuki*." In *Studies in* Kabuki: *Its Acting, Music, and Historical Context*, ed. James R. Brandon, William P. Malm, and Donald Shively. Honolulu: University of Hawaii Press.

Shuzui Kenji, ed. 1928. *Nihon Meicho Zenshū; Kabuki Kyakuhonshū*. Tokyo: Nihon Meicho Zenshū Kankōkai, 1928.

_____, and Akiba Hami, eds. 1931. *Kabuki Zusetsu*. Tokyo: Manyōkaku. Reprinted in *Shuzui Kenji Chosakushū Bekkan*. 1977. Tokyo: Kasama Shoin.

Southern, Richard. 1957. "Trickwork on the English Stage." In *Oxford Companion to the Theatre*, ed. Phyllis Hartnoll. 2d ed. London: Oxford University Press.

_____. 1976. "Theatres and Scenery." In *The Revels History of Drama in English*. Vol. 5, *1660-1750*, ed. John Loftis, Richard Southern, Marion Jones, and A.H. Scouten. London: Methuen.

Stone, George Winchester, Jr. 1980. "The Making of the Repertory." In *The London Theatre World: 1660-1800*, ed. Robert D. Hume. Carbondale: Southern Illinois University Press.

Suda Atsuo. 1949. *Nihon Engeki Shi no Kenkyū*. Tokyo: Sagami Shoten.

Suwa Haruo. 1970. *Kabuki Kaika*. Tokyo: Kadokawa Shoten.

_____. 1979. *Kabuki no Denshō*. Tokyo: Senninsha.

_____. 1991. *Kabuki no Hōhō*. Tokyo: Benseisha.

Suzuki Shunba. 1927. *Kabuki no Kata*. Tokyo: Kabuki Shuppanbu.

Tahara, Mildred, trans. 1969. "*Kumagai Jinya*." In souvenir program of touring *kabuki* troupe. New York: Program Publishing Company.

Terry, Ellen. 1969. *Ellen Terry's Memoirs: Being a New Edition of The Story of My Life, with a Preface, Notes, and Additional Biographical Chapters by Edith Craig and Christopher St. John*. New York: Benjamin Blom.

Tobe Ginsaku. 1971. "Onnagata no Gihō to Seishin." *Kabuki* 12.

Tobe Ginsaku. 1973. *Kabuki no Mikata: Gihō to Miryoku*. Tokyo: Daiichi Hōki.

Toita Yasuji. 1945. *Waga Kabuki*. Tokyo: Wakei Shoten.

_____. 1948. *Tsuzuki Waga Kabuki*. Tokyo: Wakei Shoten.

_____. 1981. "Hōru Hirayama no Mie." *Engekikai* 39 (April).

"Tsuke Butai." 1962. In Tsubouchi Memorial Theatre Museum, ed., *Engeki Hyakka Daijiten*. Tokyo: Heibonsha.

Tomita Tetsunosuke. 1970. "Yoshitsune Senbon Zakura Saiken." *Kabuki* 9.

Tsubouchi, Shōyō, and Jirō Yamamoto, 1960. *History and Characteristics of Kabuki, The Japanese Classical Drama*, ed. and trans. Ryōzō Matsumoto. Yokohama: Heiji Yamagata.

Vakhtangov, Eugene. 1947. "Preparing for the Role: From the Diary of E. Vakhtangov." In *Acting, A Handbook of the Stanislavski Method*, comp. Toby Cole. New York: Crown.

Yakusha Gan Hodoki. 1716. Kyoto: np.

Yamaga Yachiyo-za. 1993. Tokyo: NTT Publishing.

Yamamoto Jirō, Kikuchi Akira, and Hayashi Kyōhei, eds. 1971. *Kabuki Jiten*. Tokyo: Jitsugyō no Nihonsha.

Young, Margaret Hershey. 1953. *Japanese Kabuki Drama; The History and Meaning of its Theatre Art Form*. Ph.D. diss., Indiana University.

INDEX

CORNELL EAST ASIA SERIES

80 Mark Peterson, *Korean Adoption and Inheritance: Case Studies in the Creation of a Classic Confucian Society*
81 Yenna Wu, tr., *The Lioness Roars: Shrew Stories from Late Imperial China*
82 Thomas Lyons, *The Economic Geography of Fujian: A Sourcebook*, Vol. 1
83 Pak Wan-so, *The Naked Tree*, tr. Yu Young-nan
84 C.T. Hsia, *The Classic Chinese Novel: A Critical Introduction*
85 Cho Chong-Rae, *Playing With Fire*, tr. Chun Kyung-Ja (1997)
86 Hayashi Fumiko, *I Saw a Pale Horse and Selections from Diary of a Vagabond*, tr. Janice Brown
87 Motoori Norinaga, *Kojiki-den, Book 1*, tr. Ann Wehmeyer
88 *Sending the Ship Out to the Stars: Poems of Park Je-chun*, tr. Chang Soo Ko
89 Thomas Lyons, *The Economic Geography of Fujian: A Sourcebook*, Vol. 2
90 Brother Anthony of Taizé, tr., *Midang: Early Lyrics of So Chong-Ju*
91 Chifumi Shimazaki, *Battle Noh: Parallel Translations with Running Commentary*
92 Janice Matsumura, *More Than a Momentary Nightmare: The Yokohama Incident and Wartime Japan*
93 Kim Jong-Gil, tr., *The Snow Falling on Chagall's Village: Selected Poems of Kim Ch'un-Su*
94 Wolhee Choe & Peter Fusco, trs., *Day-Shine: Poetry by Hyon-jong Chong*
95 Chifumi Shimazaki, *Troubled Souls from Japanese Noh Plays of the Fourth Group*
96 Hagiwara Sakutarō, *Principles of Poetry* (Shi no Genri), tr. Chester Wang
97 Mae Smethurst, *Dramatic Representations of Filial Piety: Five Noh in Translation*
98 Ross King, ed., *Description and Explanation in Korean Linguistics*
99 William Wilson, Hōgen Monogatari: *Tale of the Disorder in Hōgen*
100 Yasushi Yamanouchi, J. Victor Koschmann and Ryūichi Narita, eds., *Total War and 'Modernization'*
101 Yi Ch'ŏng-jun, *The Prophet and Other Stories*, tr. Julie Pickering
102 S.A. Thornton, *Charisma and Community Formation in Medieval Japan: The Case of the Yugyō-ha (1300-1700)*
103 Sherman Cochran, ed., *Inventing Nanjing Road: Commercial Culture in Shanghai, 1900-1945*
104 Harold M. Tanner, *Strike Hard! Anti-Crime Campaigns and Chinese Criminal Justice, 1979-1985*
105 Brother Anthony of Taizé & Young-Moo Kim, trs., *Farmers' Dance: Poems by Shin Kyong-nim*
106 Susan Orpett Long, ed., *Lives in Motion: Composing Circles of Self and Community in Japan*
107 Peter J. Katzenstein et al, *Asian Regionalism*
108 Kenneth Alan Grossberg, *Japan's Renaissance: the Politics of the Muromachi Bakufu*
109 John W. Hall & Toyoda Takeshi, eds., *Japan in the Muromachi Age*

110 Kim Su-Young, Shin Kyong-Nim, Lee Si-Young; *Variations: Three Korean Poets*; Brother Anthony of Taizé & Young-Moo Kim, trs.

111 Samuel Leiter, *Frozen Moments: Writings on Kabuki, 1966-2001*

112 Pilwun Wang & Sarah Wang, *Early One Spring: A Learning Guide to Accompany the Film Video* February

113 Thomas Conlan, *In Little Need of Divine Intervention: Scrolls of the Mongol Invasions of Japan*

114 Jane Kate Leonard & Robert Antony, eds., *Dragons, Tigers, and Dogs: Qing Crisis Management and the Boundaries of State Power in Late Imperial China*

115 Shu-ning Sciban & Fred Edwards, eds., *Dragonflies: Women in Twentieth-century Chinese Fiction*

116 David Goodman, ed., *The Return of the Gods: Japanese Drama and Culture in the 1960s*

FORTHCOMING

Yanghi Choe-Wall, *Vision of a Phoenix: The Poems of Hŏ Nansŏrhŏn*

S. Yumiko Hulvey, *Ben no Naishi Nikki: A Poetic Record of Female Courtiers' Sacred Duties at the Kamakura-Period Court*

Mae J. Smethurst, ed., *The Noh Ominameshi: A Flower Viewed from Many Directions*

Brett de Bary, ed., *Deconstructing Nationality*

Charlotte von Verschuer, *Japanese Foreign Trade from Antiquity to the Sixteenth Century*, tr. Kristen Hunter

Michael D. Shin, ed., *Landlords, Peasants, and Intellectuals in Modern Korea*

Fan Pen Chen, *Visions for the Masses: Chinese Shadow Plays*

Joseph Murphy, *The Metaphorical Circuit: Negotiations Between Literature and Science in Twentieth-Century Japan*

Ann Lee, *Yi Kwang-su, Mujŏng, and Modern Korean Literature*

Joan Piggott, ed., *Court and Countryside in Japan, 300-1185: Japanese Research Interpreted by American Scholars*

Cornell East Asia Series, East Asia Program, Cornell University, 140 Uris Hall, Ithaca, NY 14853-7601, USA; phone (607) 255-6222, fax (607) 255-1388, ceas@cornell.edu, www.einaudi.cornell.edu/eastasia/CEASbooks

SB/11-02/.7M pb